The Conquest of Mexico

The Conquest of Mexico

*The Incorporation of Indian Societies
into the Western World,
16th–18th Centuries*

Serge Gruzinski

Translated by Eileen Corrigan

Polity Press

English translation © Polity Press 1993
First published in France as *La colonisation de l'imaginaire*
© Editions Gallimard 1988.
This translation first published 1993 by Polity Press
in association with Blackwell Publishers.

Published with the assistance of the French Ministry of Culture.

Editorial office:
Polity Press
65 Bridge Street
Cambridge CB2 1UR, UK

Marketing and production:
Blackwell Publishers
108 Cowley Road
Oxford OX4 1JF, UK

238 Main Street
Cambridge, MA 02142, USA

ISBN 0 7456 0873 6
ISBN 0 7456 1226 1 (pb)

British Library Cataloguing-in-Publication Data
A CIP catalogue record for this book is available from the British Library.

Typeset in 10 on 12 pt Sabon
by Best-set Typesetter Ltd., Hong Kong
Printed in Great Britain by Biddles Ltd, Guildford

This book is printed on acid-free paper.

Contents

Abbreviations

AGI	Archivo General de Indias (Sevilla)
AGN	Archivo General de la Nación (Mexico City)
AHPM	Archivo Histórico de la Provincia Mexicana de la Compañía de Jesús
AMNAH	Archivo del Museo Nacional de Antropología e Historia (Mexico City)
ARSI	Archivum Romanum Societatis Jesu (Rome)
BN	Biblioteca Nacional (Mexico City)
exp.	*expediente*: file
FCE	Fondo de Cultura Económica (Mexico City)
HMAI	*Handbook of Middle American Indians*
INAH	Instituto Nacional de Antropología e Historia (Mexico City)
leg.	*legajo*: bundle
PNE	Papeles de Nueva España
RGM	*Relaciones geográficas de Michoacán* (José Corona Nuñez ed., 1958)
SEP	Secretaría de Educación Pública (Mexico City)
UNAM	Universidad Nacional Autónoma de México (Mexico City)

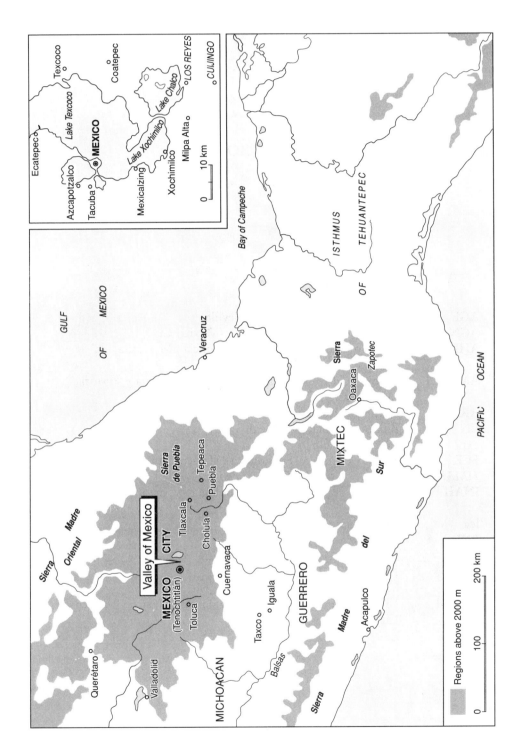

Introduction

How does a culture come to life, change and decline? How is a credible environment generated and reproduced in the midst of apparently unparalleled political and social upheavals, disparities in modes of living and thinking and demographic crises? How, in more general terms, do individuals and groups contrive and experience their relations with the real[1] in a society disrupted by an absolutely unprecedented external domination? Travelling through the prodigiously interesting territory that made up the Mexico conquered and ruled by the Spanish from the sixteenth to the nineteenth century, one inevitably asks questions such as these, not to satisfy a craving for the exotic and the archaic – which has nothing in common with history and anthropology – but to understand better what the impact of sixteenth-century western Europe might have meant for America. It was a completely new experience, all the more remarkable since America was the only continent to have had just fleeting contacts with the rest of the world for tens of thousands of years. It was an experience notable also for the wealth of accounts that can shed light on it, and the many questions it still raises about the Indians, and even more about ourselves.

Elsewhere, I have tried to follow the history of the body, of marriage and the introduction of western European sexuality as well as the fate of the representations and practices of power in the indigenous world (Gruzinski, 1982; 1989a). These first steps helped me to discover and to reexamine the instruments of the conversion of Mexico to Christianity and what was at stake; to highlight the multiplicity of cultural levels among the Indian peoples; to analyse the forms of a practically uninterrupted creativity.[2] In this study, I have preferred to investigate other fields and to work on other subjects, seeking as much to discover the modification in forms and in what was at issue as to describe the substance. The revolution in the modes of expression and communication, the disruption of memories, the transformations of the *imaginaire*, the role of the individual and of social groups in the genesis of syncretic expressions, are inescapable for the historian of colonial Mexico. Following these lines has made it possible to exploit the already considerable knowledge of demographic, economic and social history, while reaching beyond the flat, reductive and distant vision often established by apparently exhaustive statistics and the rigidity of superimposed patterns.

Actually, many of these topics were still to be explored. With certain brilliant exceptions,[3] anthropologists have systematically missed out the period of the Spanish domination that transformed Mexico, dismissing in a few pages processes of the greatest complexity. In the same way, prehispanic archaeology and history have often forgotten that most accounts of the period before Cortés were conceived and written in the drastically changed context of the nascent New Spain, and that they offer above all a reflection of this period.

Most historians and anthropologists have disregarded the revolution in modes of expression – the passage from pictograph to alphabetic writing in sixteenth-century Mexico – although it was probably one of the major side-effects of the Spanish domination: in a few decades the Indian nobility not only discovered writing but also often combined it with the traditional forms of expression, based on the image, that they continued to cultivate. The twofold nature of the indigenous sources of the sixteenth century (painted and manuscript) leads one to study what writing implied in restructuring and altering the Indian view of things, and prompts an assessment of the control that Indian circles continued (or not) to exercise on communication, or at least some of its forms. The use of writing changed the manner of fixing the past. How, then, could one fail to inquire into the evolution of the organization of the indigenous memory and the transformations undergone by its contents, or the distances assumed in relation to ancient societies and the degree of assimilation of new ways of life? The more so since until now this question too has had little attention. But the modifications in the Indian relationship to time and space suggest a further line of inquiry, more global and more difficult to undertake: to what extent could the Indian peoples' perception of the real and the imaginary have changed, in what way, and under what influence? It is true that the relative scarcity of sources hardly permits a reconstruction of an 'ethnic' or 'cultural unconscious', still less an understanding of its metamorphoses. One must settle for a few modest reports, pointing the way, and follow a handful of personalities in their attempts to construct syntheses and fashion compromises between these worlds – which recalls that cultural creation is as much the task of individuals as of groups. Styles and techniques of expression, memory, perceptions of time and space, the *imaginaire*, thus provide material for exploring the confusion of borrowings, the assimilation of European characteristics and their distortion, the dialectics of misunderstanding, appropriation and alienation. At the same time, one must not lose sight of the political and social stakes involved, which meant that a reinterpreted feature, a concept, a practice, could strengthen a threatened identity while in the long term it was likely to bring about a slow dissolution or a complete reorganization of the group that welcomed it. That is how I envisage coming to grips with the dynamics of the cultural entities that the Indians of New Spain ceaselessly reworked.

Of course all these fields of research come together in a quest, not so much to penetrate indigenous worlds in order to unearth an 'authenticity' miraculously preserved or irrevocably lost, as to take stock over three centuries of a process of westernization, in the sense of Europeanization, in its least spectacular but perhaps most insidious manifestations: a last resort that admittedly responds as much to constraints inherent in the sources as to the deliberate orientation of our inquiry.

A good deal of documentation, scattered in Mexico, Spain, Italy, France and the United States, makes it possible to study the Indians of New Spain, or more precisely to apprehend what they represented for the Spanish authorities: a population of tributaries, of pagans to convert to Christianity, of neophytes to watch and catch out, of *pueblos* to set up, shift, concentrate, and set apart from those of the Spanish. The colonial view was a measuring up of bodies, goods and souls, in which one reads constantly of the encounter, the collision between an unlimited will to ascendancy and groups that willingly or not accepted submission to it. Moreover, this material has inspired an institutional, demographic, economic and social history of the Indians of the colony, successfully illustrated by the works of Charles Gibson, Sherburne F. Cook, Woodrow Borah or Delfina López Sarrelangue.[4] To reinforce this colonial view, we have the exceptional work of the ecclesiastical chroniclers of the sixteenth century, Toribio de Benavente, known as Motolinía, Bernardino de Sahagún, Diego Durán, Gerónimo de Mendieta and many others concerned to put an end to idolatry, to describe the indigenous societies before their contact with western Europe, but preoccupied also with safeguarding what they perceived to be best in them. This was a remarkable approach for its time, prefiguring the ethnographic process, but its richness and apparent comprehensiveness might well often conceal subtle or obvious preconceptions imprinted on the indigenous reality. It is hardly surprising that these authors explored the Amerindian world using European grids and vocabularies.[5] In fact, it often happens that the exotic quality that we experience in reading their accounts actually emanates more from sixteenth-century Spain than from the indigenous cultures. It is none the less true that these sources sketch in the incomparable outlines of an overall grasp of the indigenous worlds at the time of the conquest and, we would add, throughout the sixteenth century. It is regrettable that these texts – copiously exploited by archaeologists and historians to describe religions, societies and ancient economies – have less often served to shed light on their own world, which was already converted to Christianity and acculturated when they took shape.

There remain the indigenous sources. However paradoxical or surprising it might be, the Indians of colonial Mexico have left an impressive quantity of written testimony. They expressed a passion for writing often tied to the will to survive, to keep safe the memory of the lineage or the community, to preserve goods and identities. That is the case of the Indian historians and priests whom the works of Angel M. Garibay have helped to make better known but about whom much remains to be said. It is also true of a rich literature from the Indian communities – the Annals, the 'Primordial Titles' – which is less known, usually anonymous, and reveals in many regions the precocious existence of the practice of writing and an altogether original concern with expression. To which one must add the vast collection made up by the Indian *escribanos* and towns, wills, deeds of sale and purchase, gifts, proceedings, accounts – all more stereotyped and more subject to the constraints of Spanish law – written in the indigenous language and which James Lockhart and others have drawn to the attention of scholars. It is true that only the nobles and notables wrote. It is no less true that one must part with the cliché of 'peoples without writing'. In many *pueblos* of Mexico the quill was handled as often as and perhaps better than in the villages of Castile or Europe in the same period. Finally, not a few Indians had to give an oral account of behaviour or beliefs that the Church condemned. Every trial, each interrogatory yields its share of data, provided that one knows how to evaluate what the filter of writing, the aims of the investigator, the questioning of the judge, the intervention of the notary and the *escribano* or the chances of preservation have been able to add to (or subtract from) the original account.

This cluster of sources cannot then be dissociated from European modes of expression or colonial situations. Only archaeology and an analysis of the pictographs afford the theoretical possibility of breaking through the western European filter – theoretical, since the absence of the filter paradoxically does not resolve very much. The Indians who painted the codices, aligning their multicoloured pictographs on *amate*, have hardly left a guide to reading them (Plate 1). The key, the meaning of this mode of expression – without equivalent in our world – still largely escapes us, however innovative the work carried out in recent years, the more so since many of the 'prehispanic' pieces were in fact painted after the conquest and might lead us to take for an indigenous feature a subtle assimilation, a first, hardly discernible reinterpretation. Once more we face the close or distant spectre of the Europeanization that shadows every step of the historian.

The unavoidable filter of writing, whatever the source, and the resulting impossibility of getting in touch with the original oral culture, the inevitable relations with western Europe in the form of the parish priest, the judge, the tribunals, the administrators, the tax collector, indicate and clarify the limits of this exploration of indigenous worlds. But let us not conclude that we are condemned, for want of a better possibility, to decode the discourse on the Indians. Let us simply admit that we apprehend only reflections of the indigenous world mixed unmistakably and with greater or lesser confusion with our own. To claim to pass through the looking glass, to grasp the Indians apart from the western European influence, is a perilous and often impracticable and illusory exercise; unless one accepts losing oneself in a maze of hypotheses that must ceaselessly be challenged. There remains, however, a still considerable field: indigenous reactions to models of behaviour and thought introduced by the Europeans; analysis of their perception of the new world established by the colonial domination in violence and often chaos. Let us now pick up and interpret these reflections, which by their very survival provide exceptional accounts, with scarcely an equivalent on the European side of the Atlantic.

This book was written between 1982–1985 and is a considerably abridged version of my doctoral thesis presented in January 1986.

1
Painting and Writing

It is difficult to imagine the extraordinary complexity, the population density and the cultural diversity of Mexico on the eve of the Spanish conquest. Before beginning to explore the more noteworthy characteristics of this universe, it is vital to make a detour by way of certain essential landmarks; otherwise there is too great a risk of getting lost. Central Mexico – from Michoacán and the Bajío, from the Chichimec border in the north to the region of Oaxaca in the south – is known to have accommodated a sizeable population at that time, dispersed among numerous communities and several large agglomerations. It is calculated that between 10 and 25 million souls inhabited these lands in 1519 (Cook and Borah, 1971–9), together making up a singularly dense linguistic and cultural political map. Nahuatl-speaking peoples dominated in the centre, in the valleys of Mexico, Toluca and Puebla, in the semi-tropical Morelos and part of Guerrero. The Purepecha occupied Michoacán, while in the southeast, Zapotec and Mixtec shared the mountains of Oaxaca. So much for the most powerful groups. Less numerous or less influential, other peoples had a personality, a history, that set them apart from the foregoing. Consider the Mazahua and especially the Otomí of the north of the valley of Mexico, from Sierra de Puebla and Tlaxcala; the Chontal of Guerrero; the Mixe, Trique, Chatino, and many others, of the region of Oaxaca. It is impossible to do justice to each of these groups and cultures. At the very most, one can keep in mind their diversity, their interweaving, their belonging to quite different linguistic families: Uto-Aztec for Nahuatl; Maya for Mixe, Zoque, Totonac; Macro-Otomanguean for Mazahua, Otomí and Matlaltzinca, Mixtec, Zapotec, while the Tarasc (or Purepecha) of Michoacán made up still another group. Certain languages dominated in this mosaic: Mixtec, Zapotec, Tarascan, and above all the Nahuatl of the central valleys, which served as *lingua franca* in the other regions.

South of the Bajío, inhabited by the nomad Chichimec hunters and gatherers, peasant societies were generally to be found, maintaining by their tribute the artisans, priests, warriors and shopkeepers in the framework of political units that the Nahua called *tlatocayotl*, the Spaniards translated as *dominios* and the Anglo-Saxons city states – although they were in fact neither cities in the Greek sense nor states in the modern sense of the term. A so-called city state was rather a vague entity made up of a political, administrative, urban centre (more or less developed, according to the ethnic group), and of a series of villages and hamlets, and even scattered farms. Among the Nahua peoples, these villages and hamlets corresponded to *calpulli*; in other words, to territorial units based on kinship, a relative hierarchy of lineages, a tendency to endogamy, communal ownership of land, material and military solidarity, and the cult of a tutelary god, the *calpulteotl*, whose force resided in an image or a sacred bundle. At least that is what one can deduce from sources that are at the same time copious, contradictory and incomplete (López Austin, 1980, I, pp. 75–80).

Embedded among the domains and the free or enforced alliances, the confederations made up more or less extensive, more or less ephemeral, more or less centralized political units after the fashion of those constructed by the Mixtec of Tilantongo, the Nahua of Tlaxcala and particularly those of México-Tenochtitlán, Texcoco and Tlacopan in the valley of Mexico. Alliances were made and unmade in tandem with the invasions and movements of people. So it was that during the three centuries that preceded the Spanish conquest, the Nahuatl-speaking tribes of the north penetrated into the valley of Mexico and mixed with local populations in successive waves. 'Cities' such as Culhuacán, Azcapotzalco and Coatlinchan prospered, then declined. In the fifteenth century, about 1428, Texcoco and Tlacopan, under the leadersip of the Mexica of Tenochtitlán, set up a confederation or league, the Triple Alliance, which drained tribute from the valley and from far more distant lands. Built in the middle of the lake of Texcoco, Tenochtitlán, with its network of canals, became the largest agglomeration of the American world at that time, with more than 150,000, and possibly more than 200,000 residents. However, we must be wary of seeing it as the head of a modern empire or a centralized bureaucracy, or the heart of an irresistible dominion. The ascendancy of the Triple Alliance basically took the form of the levying of tribute, the possible installation of garrisons, the imposition – or rather the superimposition – of its gods on the local pantheons, and above all the setting-up of extremely dense networks of marriages and bonds of kinship. The Triple Alliance was new and as politically fragile as earlier hegemonies, possibly because of the lack of a system of writing that measured up to its ambitions. It covered basically the centre of Mexico, that is, a territory of about 200,000 km sq. (Calnek, 1982). It did not however include Tarascan Michoacán, the domain of Tlaxcala (likewise Nahua), which alongside its allies of Huejotzingo and Cholula stood up to the Mexica and the Triple Alliance.

Finally, in the course of their migrations or their periods of settling down, all these peoples underwent a continual process of acculturation. This was recalled by some when they compared the Olmec and Toltec of old, bearers of the refinements of civilization, to the Chichimec hunters and gatherers, and even when they mentioned the Toltec-Chichimec groups that resulted from their encounter. Ancient and autochthonous peoples coexisted with the new arrivals, who assimilated the local traditions at the same time as they lent their services. We must bear in mind that these historical acculturations, these progressive passages from a nomadic to a sedentary life, formed the background of indigenous memories. We must equally beware of considering these cultures and societies as homogeneous wholes: it is established in the case of Tenochtitlán (and is doubtless true of other cities as well) that deep differences separated the urban communities, devoted to business and arts and crafts, from rural settlements. If the variables introduced by the diversity of social groups, if not of social classes, are added to these many economic, ethnic and historical levels, one gets a kaleidoscopic picture that rules out categorizing the Indian worlds as stable entities, monolithic and immobile societies, totaritarian before the term had been invented, or miraculously anchored outside history. It is equally untenable to confuse them with the farming communities or exploited marginals that they have become in our time (Calnek, 1974).

Let us stay for a while with the indigenous nobility, for it was in their midst that appeared one of the most remarkable features of these societies. Of all the groups that dominated the peoples of central Mexico – Tarasc *achaecha*, Mixtec *tay toho*, Otomí or Zapotec lords – it is the *pipiltin*, the Nahua nobles, who are probably best known to us (Carrasco, Broda, et al., 1976; López Sarrelangue, 1965; Spores, 1967; Olivera, 1978; Monjarás-Ruiz, 1980). The *pipiltin* legitimized their powers and conceived the world in which they lived by relying on the learning that they held dear. This learning recorded ways of life, traditions to be preserved, inheritance to be transmitted, all that can be designated in a general way by the Nahuatl term *tlapializtli* (Léon-Portilla, 1980, pp. 15–35). To the cosmos, this learning was supposed to impart a rule, a moderation, a stability. To society it provided an order, a direction, a meaning. At least so claimed the four elders who invented 'the account of fates, annals and the account of years, the book of dreams'. An ancient patrimony, meticulously preserved, implemented and transmitted from people to people, this learning was the origin of a singularly developed system of education. Temple-schools reserved for sons of the *pipiltin* prepared the future rulers. Within these *calmecac*, wise men – 'those called the owners of the books of paintings', 'the knowers of hidden things', 'the keepers of tradition' – dispensed to the young nobles an education as austere as it was sophisticated, which associated knowledge with modes of speaking and ways of being. Among other things, they learned 'verses of songs so as to be able to sing what they called divine hymns that were written in characters on painted books' (ibid., pp. 190–204). It was this education that from birth set the nobles apart from the plebeians, the *macehuales*, by making them intellectually and morally superior beings, these 'sons of the people', these 'hairs' and these 'nails of the people', who were all dedicated to the functions of ruling (López Austin, 1980, I, pp. 443–67).

But what is undoubtedly the main thing is that all the learning that expressed and synthesized the image that these cultures – or more precisely these ruling circles – cherished of the world, flowed into two modes of expression that seem predominant and at home in the Mesoamerican world: oral transmission and pictography. So it was for the ancient Nahua, the Mixtec and the Zapotec of the Oaxaca region and also, perhaps to a lesser degree, for the Otomí. The Tarasc of Michoacán, on the other hand, seem not to have known pictographic expression, since they have left us nothing comparable to the annals or the calendars.

The cultures of central Mexico were in the first place oral cultures. They took great pains to cultivate oral traditions and to codify, verify and transmit them. In their highly variegated expressions, the Nahua sources of the colonial period have preserved a sense of this creativity. I shall give just a brief survey the better to suggest the range that it covered. The Nahua distinguished at least two major bodies of work composed of numerous and contrasting genres: *cuicatl* and *tlahtolli*. *Cuicatl* designated warriors' songs and songs of 'friendship, love and death', hymns to gods, and poems combining intellectual and metaphysical speculation. *Tlahtolli*, on the other hand, were concerned with relations, narration, discourse and oratory. Also classed as *tlahtolli* were 'the divine words' (*teotlahtolli*), which told of deeds of the gods, the origins, cosmogony, cults and rituals; 'stories about ancient things' with a historical flavour; fables, *zazanilli*, and the famous *huehuehtlahtolli* or 'ancient words', those elegant speeches about the most varied subjects: power, the domestic circle, education or the gods.

Taught in the schools of the nobility, the *calmecac*, some of these pieces were recited or sung at the great festivals where the *pipiltin* gathered. If the *huehuehtlahtolli* tended to be the prerogative of the nobles and the lords, the hymns and songs of a ritual character were disseminated among the whole of the population and especially in their schools. The priest who undertook to transmit them saw to it that they were reproduced faithfully – he was given the title of *tlapizcatzin*, 'he who preserves' – while another priest was engaged in examining the newly composed songs, demonstrating that a society without writing can be quite familiar with both the true copy and censorship. It is possible that the narrator of *tlahtolli* was able to speak more freely if he was a pleasing and skilled reciter; but we have every reason to believe that the 'tales of ancient things', or the 'divine' narrative were also supposed to be subject to checking and censorship. Strictly controlled by institutions, tied to circumstances and contexts, oral productions were also subservient to a complex and subtle interplay of internal constraints. The transmission, learning and memorizing of this patrimony put the most varied resources to work. So it is, for example, that the *cuicatl* have their own rhythm, metre, style and structure. They were composed of a sequence more or less studded with expressive units – the equivalent of our verses and strophes – which were linked in groups of two. Parallelism (constructions of symmetrical phrases) and diphrasism (the juxtaposition of two metaphors to call to mind a concept, such as water and fire to designate war) were used constantly. Inserted syllables probably marked the metre, while others, of the type *tiqui, toco, toco, tiquiti*, perhaps indicated the rhythm and the pitch of the musical accompaniment. In general, the *cuicatl* cannot be dissociated from its accompanying means of expression, even if we have lost almost every trace of it. That is true of the music and dancing that occupied a significant place in public celebrations. Doubtless less varied but just as established, analogous stylistic processes structured the *tlahtolli*, among them parallelism, diphrasism, the piling up of predicates about the same subject, conceived to organize a temporal sequence or to make something explicit by convergent and complementary terms. Compositional techniques such as these often give these texts a disconcerting, repetitive and cumulative pace. They also undoubtedly made learning and memorizing the texts simpler, in the absence of written versions, while providing guidelines for improvisation and creation.[1]

The sophistication of the compositions entrusted to oral transmission, the range of genres, the considerable significance given to teaching, eloquence and the word, must not induce us to forget that these societies also had a graphic mode of expression. If they knew no form of alphabetical writing before the Spanish conquest, they none the less expressed themselves in various media – paper of *amate* and agave, deerskin – which could take the form of either elongated and narrow leaves that were rolled or folded in accordion pleats, or else large surfaces that were spread out on walls to be viewed. On these surfaces the Indians painted glyphs. Pictographic expression has a long and complicated, not to say obscure, history in Mesoamerica, which cannot be summarized here (Plate 1) (Robertson, 1959; Dibble, 1971; Glass, 1975a; Glass and Robertson, 1975; Galarza, 1972). It will suffice to sketch what we know of the practices in effect in central Mexico among the Nahua peoples. They had three types of signs of unequal importance, which we cover by the term 'glyphs'. *Pictograms* proper are stylized representations of objects and actions: animals, plants, birds, buildings, mountains, scenes of dance or procession, sacrifice, battle, gods and priests, etc. *Ideograms* call to mind qualities, attributes or concepts associated with the object depicted: an eye signifies vision; footprints designate a trip, dance, or movement in space; the headband of a noble indicates the chief (*tecuhtli*); shields and arrows stand for war, etc. Let us say that in general the pictogram denotes, the ideogram connotes. Finally *phonetic signs*, few in number, are close to the glyphic expression of western alphabets. Exclusively for transcribing syllables, these signs relate to toponymy, anthroponymy and chronology. Examples are the Nahua locative suffixes (*-tlan, -tzin, -pan*) that in various forms come into the composition of toponymic glyphs. This embryonic phoneticism, which the Maya and the Mixtec also knew, is like a rebus to the extent that it uses easily deciphered and identified homonyms that give a sound close to or reminiscent of the one to be indicated.

Nahua pictography on the eve of the Spanish conquest was a mixed system, whose nascent phonetization was possibly tied to the military and economic expansion of the Triple Alliance dominated by the Mexica. Repeated contacts with other ethnic groups, enemies or subjects, may have made it increasingly necessary to paint place names and the names of exotic characters, and this practice would have posed the problem of the phonetic transcription of isolated words. It cannot be excluded either that the morphological characteristics of Nahuatl lent themselves to this evolution to the extent that it was an agglutinative language, which could easily be broken into syllables. It is none the less true that there was no large-scale coupling of the written form with the word, as in our alphabets.

The pictographic, ideographic and phonetic signs were scattered no more haphazardly on the leaves of *amate* or agave than words are strung along the lines that are so familiar to us. The glyphs were organized and articulated according to criteria that are still not well understood. The page make-up, the scale of the signs, their relative position, their orientation, their association and grouping, the graphic links between them, are all elements constituting the meaning of the 'painting' and, more simply, the meaning of the reading. The colour that fills the spaces defined by the thick, regular line drawn by the painter, the *tlacuilo*, adds the significance of chromatic modulations, even if the Spanish saw it as a decorative element, leading them to refer to the glyphic productions by the misleading term, usual in the sixteenth century, of 'paintings'.

Moreover, pictographic expression compressed in the same space planes that the European eye usually distinguishes for purposes of analysis, but that were probably without relevance for the Indian 'reader'. So it was that reports that we would characterize as economic, religious or political could be grafted on a framework composed of topographical elements. Routes for the collection of tribute, prehispanic sanctuaries, a group's signs of hegemony, were merged, composing a work imprinted with a strong thematic and stylistic unity. Even though it permits us to grasp the contents by having recourse to modern grids, our exegetical reading of the 'paintings' often condemns us to miss the specificity of a grasp of reality and its representation. One might add that this formal specificity is quite unlike an artifice of presentation.

Whatever its apparent depths, the pictographic field of expression is astonishingly vast. It covers fields as varied as chronicles of war, catalogues of wonders and climatic accidents, the gods, cartography, business, finance, the transfer of goods. It appears, however, that divinatory works were the most numerous: 'books of years and times', 'of days and feasts', 'of dreams and omens', 'of baptism and the names of children', 'of rites of ceremonies and of omens to observe in weddings'.[2] The predominance of divinatory works can be read in the pictographic representation of a *tlacuilo*, where the painter is represented in the guise of an Indian holding a brush 'above the glyph of the day'. It is true that consulting divinatory books regularly punctuated the existence of individuals and the group. One might believe that the apparently rudimentary character of the technique of expression implies an undeveloped organization of information, like that which prevailed in the ancient near east before the conquest of alphabets. And it is true that lists or inventories order the data contained in the 'paintings', such as lists of conquered provinces, borders, merchandise delivered as tribute, lists of years or rulers. But it would unduly restrict the significance of these documents to reduce them to inventories, primarily because the combination of things signified in the design of an ideogram enabled the Indians to express highly complex concepts and to handle the most abstract notions and the most imaginary constructions. That is true for example of the joined pictograms of water and fire used to designate the Nahua notion of sacred war; the sign *ollin*, to render the movement of the cosmos; the compositions arranged to depict the different 'avatars' of the gods. But if the 'paintings' are more than lists, it is because they also have a visual dimension that has sometimes been underestimated. The 'paintings' are *images* as much as texts, and demand to be treated as images. That is to say, they should be seen as perceptual as much as conceptual, which poses a problem: while we perceive this dimension intuitively, it is difficult to verbalize and thus to transcribe. Let us say that this dimension corresponds to the combinations of forms and colours, to the organization of space, the relations between figures and ground, contrasts of light and shade, geometrical laws received and employed, the activity of reading, the varying complexity of the representations.

Nevertheless, the mechanisms of 'reading' and, *a fortiori*, of the preparation of pictographic documents, remain barely understood. The accounts are usually those of European observers, complete strangers to these practices. It is known that the glyphs were 'read' by being checked off with a rod, that mnemonic texts guided the deciphering of the 'paintings', bringing to bear enlightenment, complementary information, or even both at the same time. The Indian 'reader', taught in one of the *calmecac*, had the habit of saying: 'Like the parrot in bloom, I make the leaves in the house of paintings speak (León-Portilla, 1983a, p. 64). 'To make speak' consisted in drawing from carefully memorized sources the elements of a verbalization that incorporated explanation and interpretation in the standardized form of a parallel and complementary discourse. It is tempting to confuse this exercise with the medieval gloss, but this would probably represent the sin of ethnocentrism. The 'painting' was linked to discourse by a two-way street: if it is true that one 'made the books speak', the 'paintings' also served to support oral expression: 'the students in the *calmecac* were taught hymns, the ones called divine hymns, by following the paintings'. It would no doubt be just as wrong to make the 'paintings' simple auxiliary mnemonic devices, as the missionaries of the sixteenth century were inclined to do. It seems more likely that the transmission of information implied a simultaneous and not redundant recourse to verbal memory and to painted ground, in accordance with an inextricable combination of the image and the word.

Only a minority of individuals was able to reconcile this learning, these techniques and these sophisticated imperatives: the nobles who attended the *calmecac* and sometimes dedicated themselves to the service of the gods – without it being necessary to distinguish too precisely between the laity and the 'clergy' – or the *tlacuilo*, who painted the glyphs, also products of the same circles. But if it is true that, as tradition held, 'those who mastered black and red ink and what is painted lead us, guide us, tell us the way' (Léon-Portilla, 1959, p. 76), pictography and discourse were far more than the expression of a class or an instrument of power. As with the laws of discourse and song, the canons of painting were not just the reflection of a superior world or an invisible order. Beyond the contents of the teachings dispensed, they participated systematically in the organization of a reality that intimately associated human experience and the world of the gods. They extracted from it the most salient characteristics, designated the most significant elements, setting aside the accidental, the arbitrary and the individual. In this way they stressed re-presentation, revelation, more than communication. They contributed actively to forming a perception of things, a relation to reality and to existence, that the Spanish conquest must have challenged fundamentally.

The torn net

The campaigns of evangelization that the Franciscans conducted after their arrival in 1523, by provoking disturbances for many years, contributed to scattering and sometimes destroying a large part of this oral or painted patrimony. We know, for example, that in 1521 the Indian allies of Cortés set fire to the archives of Texcoco, one of the three capitals of the Triple Alliance. But it was in 1525 that the systematic demolition of the temples in the valley of Mexico and at Tlaxcala began, after the Franciscans had forbidden any form of public cult. The incessant persecutions to which the Indian clergy were subjected from then on enable us to date to these years the dismantling of educational institutions and the definitive closing of the *calmecac*. At the same time the first missionaries decided to take in hand the education of the children of the nobility. If the destruction of the temples and the idols was the primary objective of the 1520s and 1530s, the Franciscans, followed by the other mendicant orders, also confiscated all the 'paintings' that appeared to them to go against the faith, 'burning all that related to the ceremonies and that was suspicious'. It is true that they tried in principle to separate the wheat from the chaff, tolerating the works that seemed to them to be of a historical nature, but without displaying excessive naivety. The difficulty of determining where the 'error and deception of the devil' began, the distrust that overshadowed all of these products, weighed heavily in the fate of the 'paintings'. They were often destroyed without any distinction, as the chroniclers deplored in not a few sources: 'the ignorant had them burned, believing that they were idols, although they were chronicles worthy of being saved'.[3]

The years 1525 to 1540 were the age of violent and spectacular persecutions: 15 years, in the course of which whole aspects of indigenous culture sank into clandestinity, to acquire in the light of the Christianity of the conquerors the cursed and demonic status of 'idolatry'. In a few years Indian lords had to proceed to a complete reordering of their ancestral practices. They had to abandon the sanctuaries in the cities, to choose remote spots, the secrecy of caves and mountains, the deserted banks of lakes, the protection of night. They had drastically to restrict the practice of human sacrifice, to form a network of informers and hiding places capable of thwarting the vigilance of the Spanish and the spying of the neophytes, obtained by blackmail and the threat of collaboration or at least the silence of the populace.[4]

Progressively cut off from their material and social base, isolated by the missionaries and the conquerors from the groups to which they belonged to become 'religions' and 'idolatry', whole or partial manifestations of Indian culture underwent a redefinition incomparably more shattering than the passage to clandestinity. At the very moment when the conquest forced them into a space entirely invented by western Europe, imposed by the Spanish and labelled with superimposed terms and concepts – 'superstitions, beliefs, cults, sacrifices, adoration, gods, idols, ceremonies,' etc. – these cultural manifestations were indicted as errors and false. All at once the Indians learned that they 'adored gods' and that these 'gods were false'. What had been the meaning and interpretation of the world became a 'rite', a 'ceremony', pursued, marginalized, discredited, a false 'belief', an 'error' to be rejected, to renounce, a 'sin' to confess before ecclesiastical judges. What had corresponded to an indisputable and tacit apprehension of reality, what had been the subject of an implicit, immemorial consensus and had rendered an account of a totality had from then on to confront an exotic system obeying other principles, based on other premises, fabricated from quite different categories and, let us not forget, completely rejecting any compromise. And yet, whatever we might think of it, 'book censorship' was not an innovation introduced by the conquerors. Already in the fifteenth century, under the Mexica ruler Itzcóatl, 'paintings' had been destroyed to eradicate memories or to throttle particularism; but now it was a question of annihilating a whole and not of expurgating parts. We understand that Indians then experienced a loss of coherence, an erosion of meaning, the ancestral patrimony being nothing more, in their words, than *una red de agujeros*, a 'net full of holes'.[5] Another option was to reject the non-sense of the Other, as did the Indians of Tlaxcala, who in 1523 decided that the first missionaries were 'madmen'. Or they could make the friars monstrous creatures come to destroy mankind, or the living-dead, baleful sorcerers.

Others took refuge in traditional learning, the 'prophecies of their parents', confident of finding nothing there that announced the 'Christian doctrine'. Following the example of the *cacique* of Texcoco don Carlos Ometochtzin, they deduced the hollowness of Christianity: 'Christian doctrine? It is nothing at all, and there is nothing sound in what the Brothers say'.[6]

Many Indians in these first years more or less openly, more or less deliberately, preferred to Christianity the world expressed in the songs, the 'ancient texts' and the 'paintings'. For the painted 'books', like the idols, were hidden. The stakes were just as high, since the celebration of feasts or the reading of fates was dependent on the decipherment of ancient computations. The specialists – the 'counters of the sun and the feasts of the demons' – were secretly asked to seek the dates of the feasts in the paintings, to 'look at' the particulars of the rites and the names of the divinities to be honoured. It is doubtless worth while to focus on the learning laid down in the ancient calendars, to evaluate better what their loss or destruction could have meant. The divinatory calendar, the *tonalpohualli*, was based on a conception of time, the cosmos and the person that cannot be restricted to the narrow sphere of ritual, or even to the more ample but more problematic sphere of religion. For the ancient Nahua mythical time – the time of the successive creations that had seen the appearance of the precursors of men and then men themselves – exercised a determining influence on human time to the extent that the encounter, the coincidence of a moment of human time with one of the ever-present moments of mythical time, determined the substance of the experienced moment. These meetings, these correspondences, obeyed complex cycles of variable scale, whose combination and articulation structured the human moment. The conjunction of these cycles in effect governed the order of route and the arrival on the terrestrial plane of good or harmful forces that acted on the individual, caught up from birth in chains of events whose movement hung over him, without for all that completely crushing him. The same combinations of forces regulated in a more general way the dynamics of the cosmos: they produced change and movement at the same time as they shaped time. In these conditions we can imagine how the knowledge of cycles, the calculations to which they gave rise and the physical medium that alone made these operations possible took on crucial importance for the individual and society. To master the divine forces, to take advantage of or counteract them, it was necessary to see through their appearance and to know how to put to work an arsenal of practices intended to ensure the survival of all. That was the role of the 'counters of the sun', the *tonalpouhque*, whose learning and 'paintings' oriented all human activity, war, business, crafts, work in the fields, the rites of passage and marriage: 'everything had its computation, its reason, and the day that corresponded to it'. Knowledge was also power. People could influence their destiny with the help, obviously, of the *tonalpouhque*. Thanks to them it was possible, when a child was born under an unlucky sign, to choose a more favourable day to give him a name. It was also they who examined the compatibility of the signs of future spouses and, if necessary, advised against marriage (López Austin, 1980, I, pp. 68–75).

Several indications suggest that the calendars, as well as many other works, often escaped destruction: near Mexico, the *cacique* of Texcoco don Carlos Ometochtzin hid at his house a *tonalamatl*, the 'painting or account of feasts of the demon that the Indians had the custom of celebrating, following their law'; in the far more distant land of the Totonac, the *cacique* of Matlatlán had at least two 'pieces of cloth bearing attributes of idols and ancient paintings' that he appears to have had from Indians from Azcapotzalco, northwest of Mexico. Some Indians even managed to paint on the gate of the Franciscan convent of Cuauhtinchan a calendar 'with these characters or these signs, full of superstitions'.[7] Even though we have little information about it, there is reason to believe that the circulation – we saw an example above – and the production of 'paintings' were not interrupted by the Spanish conquest, despite the risks and persecutions. Painters from the valley of Mexico, from the region of Tlaxcala, from the region of Oaxaca, continued to handle the 'red ink, black ink'. In those troubled times, they painted most of the pieces preserved today, which figure among the most beautiful expressions that the native cultures have left us. Under the Spanish rule were produced the *Codex Borbonicus* (Mexico) and the *Tonalamatl Aubin* (Tlaxcala), which contain the computation of the cycles and the feasts. If we turn to the Mixtec of Oaxaca, the *terminus ad quem* of the *Codex Selden*, uncontested masterpiece of the traditional style, can be dated 1556. The existence of these 'paintings' demonstrates the continuation over a good 50 years of a pictographic production in the genres forbidden by the Church. Their form is sometimes so 'classic' that we might hesitate over the prehispanic or colonial date of certain works. These documents confirm, as other sources also indicate, that ancient learning and techniques continued to be transmitted.

It was far simpler to preserve the oral traditions, since learning and reciting the songs or texts left hardly any compromising traces, unless the 'ears' acquired by the friars took it upon themselves to inform against what was going on. In the 1570s the Dominican chronicler Diego Durán noted not without dread that the old men continued to teach the young lords 'the life and customs of their fathers, their grandfathers and their ancestors'. In the same period, the songs that commemorated the past grandeur of the princes still accompanied the public dances in which the indigenous nobility took part. At the same time the calendars and the oral teachings that went with them survived: 'Few are the places where they are not preserved, where they are not much read, and where they are not taught to those born today so that they shall always be remembered'.[8] The custom that was kept up of choosing the indigenous name as a function of the day of birth, the skill with which the Indians put forward or postponed the celebrations of the new patron saints so that they would coincide with the forbidden feasts, the observance of the agrarian calendars secretly set by the elders corroborate the preservation in the last decades of the sixteenth century of an oral and pictographic transmission condemned by the Church. In 1585, the Third Mexican Council once again had to forbid the Indians to sing 'the songs of their ancient history or their false religion'. That of course did not exclude the considerable evolution of the genre under the influence of European canons.

These scattered signs suggest the diffusion of an attitude impervious – or very nearly – to the upheavals that were rocking indigenous societies. Some sectors of the Indian population appear to have succeeded, not without risk, in preserving the traditional core. However, what we can infer about this period presents a far from static and reductive vision. It would undoubtedly be useful to distinguish an initial stage covering the first 20 years after the conquest, from about 1520 to 1540. Despite the material and intellectual implications of a clandestinity that had become the norm and of a constant and inevitable confrontation with Christianity, it was still possible to keep up many practices. During this period, everywhere but where the Spanish were established in force – essentially at México-Tenochtitlán, Tlaxcala and their environs – the temples still standing continued to be attended by Indian priests, who discreetly saw to the service of the gods and collected the revenues of the lands attached to the shrines. Among the Otomí Indians, children spared baptism were initiated to the priesthood. Among the Nahua, 15- or 16-year-old adolescents were set apart from the others to become *achcautin* – that is, high priests – or to carry out other functions such as the preservation of sacred objects or propitiatory fasts.

Things changed quite a bit after 1540. Under the direction of the bishop of Mexico, the episcopal Inquisition achieved spectacular successes in getting rid of certain active and dangerous opponents: it arrested a priest of the god Camaxtli, Martín Ocelotl, who was plotting with the aristocracy and predicting the end of the world; it seized an Indian who travelled through the Sierra de Puebla to stir it up by claiming to be a god. Already in 1539, it had struck a decisive blow by condemning don

Carlos Ometochtzin, the *cacique* of Texcoco, whom it turned over to the secular arm. The death on the pyre of this important figure of the aristocracy of the valley of Mexico seems to have had a profound impact. Many panic-stricken Indians decided at that point to destroy their 'paintings', or to give up these compromising objects (Gruzinski, 1989a, pp. 33–5). It was also in 1539 that the *Junta eclesiástica* met and reinforced the Church's control over the subject populations. More priests, deeper penetration, helped by a better knowledge of the land, the repression practised by the monastic, then episcopal Inquisition under the leadership of the bishop of Mexico, Juan de Zumárraga, irreversibly altered the relations of power. But other perhaps more decisive factors influenced the attitude of the Indian nobles. These circles had lost their political and cultural cohesion since many had chosen to join the conquerors and Christianity.

To these divisions, in which opportunism and calculation were probably more important than conversion, were added other divisions that the friars themselves had instigated in setting Christianized children against their 'idolatrous' parents. From 1540 on, the new generations, who had participated with a sometimes murderous zeal in the campaigns of incrimination and eradication, came to power in ever greater numbers. The recruitment of pagan priests suffered from this, while the stones of the old sanctuaries served regularly to construct churches and convents. More decisive still, the ravages of the first waves of epidemics weakened and frayed the fabric of indigenous societies. Confronted with these difficulties and not without clearsightedness, the nobles resigned themselves to accept Christianity and the colonial domination. More or less sincerely converted, they chose the way of accommodation, and were at pains to preserve the signs of their origins, the 'paintings' of history and genealogy that legitimized their power. It was undoubtedly in these circumstances that the *Mapa de Sigüenza* and the *Tira de la Peregrinación* (*c.*1540) were composed, which illustrate the origin and migrations of the Aztec on their departure from Aztlán, and, between 1542 and 1548, the *Mapa Quinatzin*, which recorded Chichimec history, and the *Codex Xolotl* were painted. Before 1550 genealogy inspired the *Mapa Tlotzin* of Texcoco and in the region of Oaxaca the *Lienzo de Guevea* (1540) or the *Codex Selden* (1556).[9] Among the Nahua, the Mixtec or the Zapotec, the line that separated clandestine production from history painting was obviously as thin and arbitrary as the Christian and European criteria that distinguished the memory of Indian 'false religions' from a strictly historical tradition. When in 1539 a painter from Culhuacán, near Mexico, painted the genealogy of his family, he represented 'a kind of cave where his forefathers and *also certain gods* were born'.[10] The painter don Andrés belonged to a family of priests close to the old Mexica king. Openly Christian in 1539, he nevertheless had an extensive and puzzling learning: puzzling because it was ambiguous, since his genealogy intermingled allusions that were far from being mythological embellishments. He was nevertheless devoid of that European insistence on opposing idolatry to history or myth to authenticity.

However it was done, whether by the secret byways of clandestinity or the authorized roads of history, some of the ancient techniques and learning survived the disaster. It was the same with manifestations of the oral inheritance, whose ethical scope attracted the friars, who sought to take advantage of it in their best interests. It was also true of the enthronement speeches, which were probably kept up as long as the old allegiances survived. In other words, despite persecutions, epidemics and turmoil, the defeated nobilities confronted the colonial reality that progressively took shape before their eyes with a baggage that was no doubt censored and reduced but was still considerable.

A new look

Nevertheless, it is difficult to follow the paths that led from resistance to accommodation, that expressed a progressive separation from the old cultures – albeit a separation that would never become irreversible abandonment. Although analysing the colonial 'paintings', and to a lesser degree the evolution of oral traditions during the sixteenth century, does not resolve this question, it provides valuable and often unforeseen indications. For instance, the precocity with which the Indians painted the society in formation around and among them cannot be other than disconcerting because, on the one hand, it rules out considering colonial pictographic expression as a fixed art, an inert survival, a cumbersome archaism; and, on the other hand, it bears witness to the unflagging curiosity shown towards an unusual and hostile world. As early as 1545, Indian nobles at a secret meeting prided themselves on having learned all that they wanted to know from the Spanish, 'all the technique of the Spanish, their way of fighting, their strengths, their horsemanship and all the rest that we were ignorant of and did not know'.[11] This will to know and to discover, even at the price of a trip to Spain, likewise incited the Indians to reconstruct or rather to construct new relations to beings and things, thus gradually filling the voids, the 'holes in the net', left by the Spanish conquest.

From the first contacts, the indigenous painters contrived to render the irruption of these beings, who were at first taken for gods. By this means Moctezuma learned, well before Cortés, of the arrival of the fleet of Narváez, and the Indians of Chalco and Tlalmanalco transmitted strategic information to Cortés by painting on *henequén* canvases the Mexica troops threatening them.[12] Thus from the beginning the 'paintings' recorded recent history, while a few years later, among both the defeated Indians and the indigenous allies of the invaders, songs told of the extent of the Mexica disaster and the desolation of the ruins.

After the first two decades the political landscape changed. New generations arose and left important productions, for example that which, more than 30 years after the conquest, illustrated and exalted the Tlaxcaltec collaboration in the Spanish invasion. The *Lienzo of Tlaxcala* (Plate 2) was probably painted to order for the viceroy don Luis de Velasco between 1550 and 1564. It is thus a commissioned work, 7 by 2.5 metres, which reconstructs the Tlaxcaltec version of events in 87 pictures. For these Indians it was also a political manifesto that did not hesitate to disguise events when they might refute the indestructible attachment of the Indians of Tlaxcala to the cause of the conquistadores.[13] Until the arrival of the Spanish, the Nahua of Tlaxcala had been able to withstand the advances of the Mexica and the Triple Alliance. Tlaxcala was a powerful State, located between the warm lands of the gulf of Mexico and the valley of Mexico, and, after having fought it, resolved in the end to support Cortés's expedition. It was beyond a doubt thanks to this ally that the Spanish overcame the Mexica hegemony, and they showed their gratitude by giving the Tlaxcaltec relative autonomy within New Spain. In the course of the three centuries that the Spanish rule endured, the Tlaxcaltec did not fail to take pride in the support they had provided or to attribute their privileges to it. It was most certainly in this spirit that the prudent authors of the *Lienzo* already preferred to keep quiet about the clashes at the very beginning, when they had opposed the Spaniards (Gibson, 1952, pp. 247–53, 229–34).

Although colonial in content, the *Lienzo* still in many respects belongs to the native tradition. Names of places and protagonists and dates were indicated according to custom by glyphs. The Indians were represented in profile with the attributes of their functions, the signs of their power – the *icpalli* seat – the clothes of their rank, the hairdos of their tribe. Many objects – baskets full of *tortillas*, turkeys, birds in cages, canoes, shields and standards – were inspired by the native figurative tradition. The presentation of bouquets to Cortés as a sign of welcome also belongs to the indigenous repertory of gestures. The representation of water, fire and rivers likewise remains in keeping with traditional canons, as does the architecture of palaces, pyramids and temple *patios*: no perspective, no 'realistic' proportion but, on the contrary, an advanced stylization which integrates the toponymic glyph with the building it is supposed to designate. Still, western European features are visually present in the *Lienzo* when, for example, the old style interpreted the universe that the Indians were discovering, as in the caravans and war machines constructed by Cortés, stylized by the painters and reduced to two wooden uprights covered by a roof. The show of novelty even led to enriching the pictographic repertory when marks of horseshoes, after the fashion of the traditional footprints, signal the movements of the Spanish horsemen, or when a sun in the European manner serves as a glyph designating the conquistador Alvarado whom the Indians assimilated to the sun, *Tonatiuh*. But sometimes the western European tradition invaded the space of the *Lienzo* to the point of imposing its own language and perception of things; for example, in the realism of gestures and poses: here the horses graze on grass, there the Spanish rest, dozing after their exhausting flight from Mexico. But it is also present in the 'realism' of the frontal or three-quarters view portraits, the expressiveness of the faces, the drawing of the eyes, the fall and folds of fabrics. It is visible too in the beginning of three-dimensionality, when groups stand out against the background of lances which suggest others, further away. It is not without significance that objects of European origin were frequently represented according to European canons, as in the Virgin with Child or the crucifixion. The representation of the conquistadores was also drawn from European iconography, the source of the dynamic motif of the charging horseman, holding a lance. Finally, the Nahuatl legends that summarize the subject of a painting in a succinct sentence set up a relationship to the image that breaks completely with the native tradition.

Can we speak of the juxtaposition, the coexistence, of two styles? We cannot avoid it for many pictures: at Atliuetzyan (Tehuitzila), for example, where the group of conquistadores appears above the glyph for water. At other times the whole composition is inspired by European models: whether the 'Reception of Cortés at Tlaxcala' or the 'Baptism of the Tlaxcaltec lords', the succession of planes, the gestures of the Christian priests, the faces of the assistants, enliven a scene of almost European workmanship, to the point that one would be inclined to attribute them to a more acculturated painter if other features did not link these paintings closely to the rest of the work. On the other hand and even more often, the traditional organization of the picture plane seems to prevail. For the battles that took place in Mexico, the buildings and cities are the subject of a pronounced stylization that defines the conventional framework where the protagonists of the drama are disposed. Everything takes place as if each time the authors had to represent a vast open space – a temple, a city, roads crossing a country – they had recourse to the autochthonous system of representation. That system permitted the inclusion in the same composition of simultaneous or successive scenes. Thus in the painting dedicated to the 'Surrender of Cuauhtémoc' several scenes can be distinguished: Cuauhtémoc confronted with Cortés, the capture of the Mexica dignitaries, the arrival of the Mexica women, their reception by Cortés. It is true, on the other hand, that certain subgroups are European in conception: for example, the scene of Cortés welcoming the Mexica women. But the overall disposition is governed by a distinctively native staging, even if it evokes the decor of the great tapestries of Arras and Brussels. We must refrain from attributing to the Spanish a conception of space too strictly modelled on the Italian quattrocento.

What can be deduced from these first observations? That in the middle of the sixteenth century the Tlaxcaltec *tlacuilo* practised a mixed art. That they were already quite capable of representing an exotic element such as the crucifix, or even a given scene such as baptism, by exploiting the canon of western European art, but that as soon as it was a question of taking on more, they reverted to the native style, ordering planes according to principles that obeyed neither the laws of perspective nor the constraints of a given scale. The undeniable kinship of the *Lienzo* with high-class tapestry was perhaps not displeasing to the Spanish who gazed at it, setting up a familiarity as immediate as it was misleading – an unforeseen conjunction, like other examples that we shall see, which probably favoured the preservation, or rather the reconversion, of ancient models.

Finally, let us pause before the large fresco crowning the work. At the same time as it proclaims the insertion of Tlaxcaltec lords into colonial society and the new hierarchies, this fresco achieves the felicitous fusion of western European and indigenous symbolism. European heraldry – another encounter – imperial arms, Christian emblems (the cross, the instruments of the Passion, the image of the Virgin) combine with the glyphs of the four lords of Tlaxcala. At the heart of the composition, overwhelming it, the arms of Charles V overhang the cross that the conquistadores are setting up, while on each side, symmetrically disposed, are aligned the houses of the Tlaxcaltec lords. By associating the two-headed eagle of the Hapsburgs with the heron of Mazihcatzin, lord of Ocotelulco, the *Lienzo* shows in a spectacular manner the meeting of two symbolisms of power, without failing to mark the submission of the Indians to the victors: a juxtaposition of two visions and a striking record of an unmistakable relation of forces.

Other 'paintings' seek to represent the new political scene or, more precisely, to locate native power in relation to the State apparatus put in place by the Spanish Crown as a way of redressing the balance and redefining the situation within the shredded rules of the game.[14] This was notably the case with the *Codex of Tlatelolco* (Plate 3).[15] Supplanted and subjected by Mexico in 1473, Tlatelolco nonetheless remained until the conquest an important commercial pillar of the Mexica 'empire'. Its market tapped the commodities of the whole *altiplano* and even further afield. Taken over by the conquistadores, shortly after the conquest Tlatelolco became one of the great homes of Franciscan evangelization and from 1536 was the site of the school that educated the Indian elite of the sixteenth century. Located just a few kilometres north of México-Tenochtitlán, the city was the preferred site for the religious and intellectual acculturation of the Indian nobilities. In this context, highly sensitive to the influence of western Europe, the *Codex of Tlatelolco* was painted towards 1565. Therein are described the history of the city in the years 1554–64, the expedition of Mixtón narrated by the *cacique* don Diego de Mendoza Huitznahuatlailotlac, the beginnings of the construction of the new cathedral of Mexico, the raising of tribute, the abdication of Charles V, the accession of Philip II (1557) up to the death of the viceroy Luis de Velasco (1564). Tlatelolco was not only taking the centre of the colonial stage – by its active participation in the crushing of the rebellious Indians of Mixtón – but was also relating itself to the dynastic history of the Hapsburgs. One can see this series of representations as an act of allegiance to the Spanish Crown, a recognition of the colonial domination. And it is. But it expresses much more: it illustrates the abandonment of a defeated status in favour of collaboration with the Spanish authorities, incarnated in the painting by the viceroy Luis de Velasco and the archbishop Montufar. The collaboration was quite unlike humiliating subjection, to judge from the gigantic stature of the *cacique* of Tlatelolco before the members of the *Audiencia* to whom he is speaking, or by the Spanish horsemen of the Mixtón expedition, who are dwarfs in relation to the *caciques* who accompany them. This interplay of scales expresses not only an awareness of the political and military role played by Tlatelolco in the first decades of colonization, but probably just as much the exaltation of a local grandeur now liberated from the domination of the Mexica sovereign. Other texts written in Latin characters render still more explicitly this unexpected fallout of the Spanish conquest, examples of which could be multiplied: the crushing of the Triple Alliance gave their heads to a crowd of local autonomous entities within the limits, it goes without saying, of the new order. It seems that throughout the 'painting' the task of the *tlacuilo* was guided by identical considerations and that he strove formally to assert a native and local specificity, while at the same time seeking connections with the culture and world of the conquerors. The medium was traditional: a band or *tira* of *amate* paper, 40 cm by 3.25 m. Traditional too were the organization of space, the use and distribution of toponymic glyphs, the representation of *caciques* (seated, represented in profile and flanked by their glyphs). Traditional remained the graphic links (the usual footprints to mark movement), the representation of speech (a volute emerging from the mouth of the speaker) and of time, which followed the indigenous calendar. Tradition ruled, although the painter never stopped gathering borrowings as if it were a question of multiplying the bridges, the connections, between the indigenous lordship and the new forms of legitimacy: whence, as at Tlaxcala, the presence of the emblematic European – the banners of the viceroy, heraldry, the seal I.H.S.; whence also the profusion of objects denoting Spanish hegemony under the most diverse guises – gallows, seats of authority, bells, chalice, tabernacle, and even that clock that marked the introduction of another way of measuring time. The *caciques* flaunt on their persons the choice pieces of a sartorial acculturation that made them the equal of the Spanish notables without depriving them of their indigenous finery: shoes, socks, white breeches, swords were thus added to the diadem and cape of old. Objects, insignia and emblems were borrowed, as well as a style, that of European engraving, which inspired the line of fabrics and armour, guided the drawing of architectural and decorative elements and all that derived from western European models. The catafalque of the viceroy, the skeleton of death, or the representation of the martyr-dom of St Sebastian reproduced Renaissance prototypes so minutely that their association with native canons produces the strangest effect. The encounter was still more subtle when the *tlacuilo* disguised an indigenous chronological indicator in the representation of the martyr-dom of St Sebastian, or when he crowned a Christian tabernacle with *quetzal* feathers.

It is a measure of the stylistic and expressive mastery attained by the Indian painter that he learned even to shade the surfaces to suggest relief. None the less, recourse to a European stylistic and iconographic code concerned only isolated subgroups, figurative and decorative elements that served in the end to enrich a group composition whose conception remained traditional. If it is undeniable that the *tlacuilo* was familiar with European forms to the point of making use of a double coding, it is still more obvious that he continued to locate himself within a native mode of expression, as if the overall organization of the pictorial field escaped the influence of Europe, as if the painter placed himself on the frontiers of his own culture, on borders open to all borrowings, without the original matrix ever being open to question. I prefer to see in the *Codex*, rather than an inability to duplicate the European manner, a desire to satisfy the taste and demand of the local nobility and, beyond that, the pictorial expression of a cultural and political strategy. As at Tlaxcala, local ambitions sought to stake out a space of their own by opening themselves to the Spanish world without denying their roots. The creativity and receptivity of the *tlacuilo* enabled the dynamism of a twofold depiction of reality to emerge, where Indian representations cheerfully integrated certain elements of European perception. In painting colonial society 40 years after the conquest, the *Lienzo of Tlaxcala* and the *Codex of Tlatelolco* reveal some of the facets of an identity in gestation, which the *Codex* developed in a remarkable image, when it made the eagle-knights and the jaguar-knights dance at the feet of the viceroy and the archbishop. There we see an evocation of the nobility, by reference to the finery and the dances that expressed its power and gallantry, but also an act of allegiance to a new political order whose twofold nature, temporal and spiritual, the Indians had learned to distinguish.

As well as telling of the recent past and the colonial regime, the 'paintings' served to perform more practical tasks. Though it is true that, since before the conquest, the Indians had used this medium to draw up the registers of tributes, note the quantities due and the terms to be observed, the 'paintings' executed under the colonial domination were used quite early on to record the economic, commercial and financial transformations introduced by the invaders. From the 1530s, for example, the merchants of Tlatelolco kept pictographic inventories, where cotton cloaks and the gold coins of the conquerors appeared side by side. One of the most telling examples of this opening-up is undeniably provided by the *Códice Sierra*.[16] Unlike the preceding examples, this document did not emerge from the studio of one of the capitals of the Nahua world. It came from a small lordship, Tejupan, located in one of the rare valleys of the Mixtec highlands. In this region of mountains, which extend as far as the valley of Oaxaca, dwelled cultures whose apogee occurred in the fourteenth century. These cultures left striking works in gold and evidence of a pictographic tradition whose exceptional importance is recognized. In the fifteenth century, the Mixtec had to defend themselves against Mexica advances, sometimes without success. Moreover in these circumstances Tejupan passed under Mexica control and had to pay tribute to them. A contemporary of the *Codex of Tlatelolco*, painted between 1550 and 1564, the *Códice Sierra* is a book of accounts; it describes the expenditures made by the *pueblo* of Tejupan (Plate 4). It used old notations: Mixtec glyphs indicated the year and its rank, 7 Tecpatl (1552), 8 Calli (1553), 9 Tochtli (1554); others served to mark place names (Mexico, Tejupan,

Ocotepec) or quantities (the banner *pantli* for 20). Objects of native or local origin received their usual depictions – the *icpalli* seat, the mat, the *quetzal* feathers; and graphic links and symbolism in current use were also used – footprints for a trip, or volutes for speech. But the pictographic expression was open to an extended range of 'exotic' objects, as were the *Lienzo of Tlaxcala* or the *Codex of Tlatelolco*, although here the process was systematic. The most varied fields were tackled: daily life, the raising of the silkworm and the cultivation of the vine, the raising of sheep, food (wine, cheese), cutlery and table linen (knives, spoons, plates, tablecloths, napkins), furniture (chair, writing desk). One also notes the irruption of the European technique, used for so many new glyphs. The page is covered with objects hitherto unknown, now almost familiar: nails, locks, chains, hinges, bolts for ironmongery, spindles for silk, hoes, sieves, pickaxes, soap, horse saddles, gold chalices and liturgical ornaments, to which can be added the writings, deeds, orders and *cédulas* of the Spanish administration. The heterogeneous enumeration renders a precise image of what the penetration in the mid-sixteenth century of the European west into a remote Mixtec village could produce and signify: doors that closed, uaccustomed table manners, objects of iron – a new metal under these skies – domestic animals, horses, medicines from Castile and . . . writing. The frequent references to the purchase of silkworm larvae and, from 1561, the sale of silk recall the international importance that the Mixtec highlands acquired in this field under the impetus of the Spanish. Of all that the pictographs leave us many precious glimpses. But they show themselves to be just as capable of rendering new, much more abstract, references; for example, Christian dates to which correspond particular glyphs created for the purpose: a cog wheel for St Catherine, a porch for Christmas, a key and a sword for St Peter and St Paul, a banner topped with a cross for St James. However, it may be the fact that the document is a set of accounts that holds our attention. The *Códice Sierra* associates three distinct forms of numbering: glyphs expressing the indigenous vigesimal system, Arabic numbers and Roman letters. Spanish coins are represented in forms that further enlarge the pictographic repertory: discs decorated with an 8, and others with a Maltese cross, reproduce the peso of 8 *reales*. The coins are aligned side by side up to the count of 20, when the *tlacuilo* draws a single coin surmounted by the banner *pantli*, sign of the number 20 in the native numbering system. One could not better signify the irruption of the monetary economy into a universe that had never before known anything but cacao beans and cotton cloaks as units of counting.

But one further characteristic should be pointed out. The *Códice Sierra* is not exclusively pictographic. It also includes texts in the

Nahuatl language, until the seventeenth century the *lingua franca* of New Spain, and thus in alphabetic characters, which make explicit the contents of the glyphs and confer on the whole document a mixed structure: each page is divided into horizontal bands containing pictographs, lines in Nahuatl and amounts in pesos and Arabic numbers, side by side. The result has the appearance of a European accounts book which gathers up scattered fragments of traditional 'painting'. The invasion of writing and its relation to the pictographs undeniably constitute a remarkable innovation which was much less perceptible in the *Lienzo of Tlaxcala* or the *Codex of Tlatelolco*. Pictographic expression could be integrated in a European-style book of accounts and provide all the material and monetary data required by such an instrument to complete satisfaction. Nothing can better convey this malleability than a little scene painted by the author of the *Códice Sierra*. There we see the annual audit of the accounts of Tejupan: three Spaniards seated behind a table covered with a green carpet; in the centre, one of them piles up coins so as to count them; to his right the interpreter translates; to his left the writer notes the figures on a sheet of paper. There we have an Indian painter's view of other accounting techniques, other modes of expression (writing) and other modes of payment (coins). It is a view whose richness we are far from having exhausted, and which showed that it was quite capable of responding to the conditions of a disrupted environment and the demands of new masters, at the price of certain accommodations (alphabetical writing and coins), to make itself understood. Throughout New Spain painters tried to take up the same challenge. Let us mention only the painter of the *Codex Chavero* who, at a later date (1579–80), represented beside the measures full of grains the sums of money that the Indians of the region of Huejotzingo had each year to pay to the Crown. In exercising a fiscal policy that took over the raising of tribute, the Spanish authorities had no doubt encouraged the painters to continue the old registers while adapting them to the necessities of the time, the spread of coinage, and the new calendar.

It may be that 'paintings' had been produced before tribunals or the equivalent institutions since the prehispanic period. No trace remains. It is, however, indisputable that they proved useful to the Indians who had recourse to the new judicial proceedings set up by the Spanish. Very early on, from the 1530s, the Indians worked out the mechanisms of the civil or ecclesiastical proceedings and were sometimes able to take advantage of them. In 1545, the Indians translated into Nahuatl the laws of the Crown that protected them, while others, ever more numerous, nobles, communities or individuals, appealed to the justice of the king.[17] The 'paintings' probably continued to play the role that they had before the conquest, when 'very able painters noted with their characters the people who pleaded'. The scenario was generally as follows: the plaintiff presented to the Spanish authorities – to the *corregidor*, for example – a painting that set out the subject of the litigation, and it was on the basis of this document that witnesses were heard and interrogatories took place. Additional examples could be adduced. The documents presented in 1549 by the Indians of the Cuernavaca region against the Marquis del Valle[18] – none other than the son of Hernán Cortés – whom they accused of having appropriated their lands, were of traditional workmanship: glyphs were used to express measurements and the shape of the fields, place names, the type of tree or plant cultivated, the duration of the misappropriation, the roads, the names of the plaintiffs. All the necessary information was recorded in each 'painting' with a remarkable economy of means. Other documents throughout New Spain were progressively covered with new glyphs to note the innovations introduced by the Spanish, as at Tlatelolco or Tejupan. In 1552, in a 'painting' from the region of Tepotzotlán attributable to Indians who complained of having been ill treated, appeared coins, pigs, and a Spanish armchair on which was seated an Indian judge. A lawsuit at Cuautitlán on 8 April 1558 indicated the dispute which set Indian carpenters against the *alcalde mayor* concerning payment for a bench: this piece of furniture of Spanish workmanship is painted frontally without perspective, thus in the traditional manner, while the chain symbolizing the unjust incarceration of the plaintiffs evinces too 'realistic' a treatment to be untouched by European influences. To express Sunday – a white circle topped by a cross – and the Christian names of certain protagonists, the painter drew widely upon a pictographic register already appreciably reshaped, after the fashion of the author of the *Códice Sierra*. In other words, the 'paintings' remained effective in the defence of indigenous interests to the extent that they very ably delineated the new situations that continually confronted the Indians. That was so until the seventeenth century, as may be seen from the *Codex Teteutzinco*, which catalogued the complaints of an Indian community from the Taxco region in 1622.[19] It would be useful to study many other works – the *Humboldt VI Fragment*, the *Codex Kingsborough* or the *Mémorial of the Indians of Tepetlaoztoc*, the *Codex Osuna*, the *Codex Acasuchitlán* – but they would simply corroborate the continued efficacy of the 'paintings' in such a crucial field.

None of the 'paintings' that have been mentioned fail to call to mind in one way or another the imprint of the preaching. The *Tlaxcala Lienzo* incorporated whole scenes, such as the baptism of the Tlaxcaltec lords. In the *Codex of Tlatelolco* were painted representatives of the

Catholic clergy: the Franciscans, the archbishop; hagiographic themes: the martyrdom of St Sebastian. Objects used in the cult were also depicted: bells, which marked the memorable dates in the local history of Christianity. The *Códice Sierra* drew up even more precise inventories and, like the *Codex Cuautitlán*, took care to note the dates of the Christian calendar and to attribute glyphs to the saints of the conquerors. Christianity spread its images throughout the large cities of the *altiplano* and into the mountains of the Mixtec highlands. But could the 'paintings' offer a more immediate and active support to the undertaking of evangelization?

They did, but this time by the intermediary and under the impetus of the missionaries, who discovered in the image a convenient means, particularly at the beginning, of compensating for their ignorance of indigenous languages. The experiment of the Franciscan Jacobo de Testera is known: when he arrived in 1529, he used a canvas on which the mysteries of the faith were painted, to be explained to the neophytes by an Indian interpreter. Other more sophisticated techniques were developed: one, in the manner of a rebus, consisted in finding images of objects whose pronunciation was close to that of the words in Christian prayers. Thus the signs of the banner *pantli* and of the prickly pear *nochtli* would correspond to the first syllables of the *Pater noster* (*Pan...Noch*). *Amen* was rendered by adding to the sign for water *atl* that for agave *metl*. This process continued to the point that the Dominican Las Casas could write towards 1555 that he had seen 'a good part of the Christian doctrine written with their figures and their images, which they [the Indians] read thanks to them like I read what is written in our characters on a sheet'.[20] It is undeniable that, although the Spanish turned it to their account, the process required the constant collaboration of Indians familiar with the repertory of glyphs, able to provide signs and to paint them to the order of the missionaries. The process also involved a corruption, or perhaps rather a utilization, of pictographic expression that stressed phoneticism, possibly precipitating an evolution towards syllabic notation. We shall return to this point. Nor can we neglect the catechisms erroneously called 'Testerian', which organized rapidly sketched Christian pictures (God the father, the Virgin, the Trinity) in accordance with a reading direction that generally followed a horizontal alignment, covering the recto and verso of a sheet. This time, recourse to visual memory carried the day, as did European iconography, mixed occasionally with glyphs of prehispanic inspiration – the flower, the sky – or colonial creations. We know little about its origins but it appears that, even if the process was invented by the missionaries, the Indians had a large part in its development. This explains the tribute that the Jesuit José de Acosta did not fail to render to the 'lively spirits of these Indians'. Moreover, there were also indigenous initiatives on the fringe of these guided experiences. For example, those that the Franciscan chronicler Motolinía dated to the 1530s: the Indians drew their sins before confessing them and showed the priest this graphic account, not being able to communicate orally in Spanish or Nahuatl. There too the ingenuity and the limits of the undertaking are manifest: these Indians had to know how to 'paint' in the traditional meaning of the term, and to give to the signs that they shaped the meaning that their confessors believed they detected in them. As with the rebus, misunderstanding, approximation and confusion proliferated. None the less, once again the 'paintings' endeavoured to record the categories, beings and things that the newcomers imposed on them. They penetrated piecemeal into a Christian universe apparently unyielding to their own, possibly even before describing the strange society, institutions, powers, political and economic relations that the colonization invented and put in place (Glass, 1975b, pp. 281–96; León-Portilla, 1979). Some stretched the boundaries of orthodoxy, mixing with the images of the ancient gods a drawing of the Crucified and a representation of Mass.[21]

This opening up to the colonial world should be put into perspective by recalling the extent to which these various processes simply followed prehispanic paths, whether by converting or adjusting them. From the chronicle of the conquest to the Testerian catechism, all had to a greater or lesser degree a native equivalent or precedent. It was also a field where, under the impetus of the friars, Indian- painters were induced radically to alter their point of view, that of sociological and ethnographic introspection. It is known that Franciscans such as Motolinía, Olmos and Sahagún and Dominicans such as Durán under-took systematic investigations of the prehispanic world that enabled them to produce exceptional works. Thus they compelled their in-formants to embark on a profound reflection about the group of cul-tures to which they belonged and to extract from them as exhaustive and synthetic an image as possible. This unprecedented work of select-ing and organizing data was accompanied by a process of double distancing, since the cultures painted were in principle those of before the conquest and some of the characteristics depicted from then on were taken to be demoniacal. We shall return below to the impact of different periods and the modalities of this irremediable condemnation. The chronicles of the mendicants or the writings of Alonso de Zorita were not alone in gathering the fruit of this effort. The 'paintings' bore the mark of it, such as the third part of the *Codex Mendoza*, for which we know of no precolumbian precedent (Robertson, 1959, pp. 95–107; Glass and Robertson, 1975, pp. 160–1). Painted under the direction of the *maestro de pintores* Francisco Gualpuyoguálcal and at the request of the viceroy Antonio de Mendoza in the years 1541–2, the *Codex Mendoza* unfolds a film of daily life in the Nahua world. Birth, marriage, education, war, justice, prevention of crime, drunkenness, adultery, theft, were all in turn conjured up in pictures. The lower classes and daily life made a notable apparition: the peasant with his stick (*coa*) and his basket (*huacal*), the artisan, the carpenter, the stonecutter; even deviants of all kinds, the thief, the hobo, the inveterate gambler. It is as if there suddenly emerged in to pictorial existence layers of the population and types to which *tlacuilo* of other periods seem to have paid little heed, being more inclined to work on the imposing images of gods and the powerful than on the delineation of the lowly. The extension of the field of observation seems moreover to be coupled with a small iconographic revolution: the decontextualization of the image. Pictographic expression once related to contextualized elements: it called to mind the marriage of a prince and not the institution of marriage; it described the punishment of a noble and not repression *per se*. In the *Codex Mendoza*, on the other hand, the compositions are removed from all anecdotal colour, from every particular historical or ethical reference. They become exemplary snapshots, prototypes, anonymous genre scenes able to satisfy the scrutiny of missionaries and viceroys. So it is with the images dealing with birth or the education of children. The third part of the *Codex Mendoza* attests to the fact that pictographic expression could *also* offer a comprehensive, encyclopaedic view of the world and the society from which it emerged, by recording what it would once have judged too ordinary or too obvious to be painted. But this self-examination, and often examination of a bygone self, was not innocent since it constructed and imposed, at the same time as it recorded, the stereotyped image that we must keep or recover of these dead societies. We generally forget that the vast majority of the accounts of the prehispanic world that we have were produced in the exceptional post-conquest circumstances and reflect them as much as the societies that had disappeared. Finally, the distancing that this process implied was not limited to the narrow circles of painters and informants. It was just the intellectual crowning of the process at work throughout indigenous societies, all confronted with Christian models of behaviour, new family, matrimonial, ritual and other practices, all forced to focus on, define and challenge behaviour that had until then been self-evident (Gruzinski, 1982). That is to say, even before destroying a feature or modifying it, acculturation can intervene more insidiously by forcing it to be grasped in a different perspective, lit by a different light. The demolition of the temples and the 'ethnographic' investigation were in fact just two ways of marking and increasing the distance between the world of the defeated, which was receding, and the new society emerging from the ruins.

The transformations of pictographic expression

If Indian painters managed to render the colonial reality that they discovered and to respond to the demands of the Spanish while remaining faithful to their art, it was because they were able to modify their instrument and to develop its potential. Fostered by the interest of the conquerors in the pictographic mode of expression, the product of a constant interaction between tradition and exotic contributions, between free choice and the imperative, this malleability in the field of expression reveals some of the processes that marked in a general way the emergence of a mixed culture in the middle of the sixteenth century.

As we have said, the glyph was not a fixed sign. We have seen how the Nahua were at times constrained to transcribe foreign words – for instance about the conquests – that took them to the area of the Mixtec and the Zapotec in the region of Oaxaca. This requirement made it possible to embark on the beginnings of a phoneticism that the Spanish conquest precipitated. How otherwise to render the galaxy of unknown terms introduced by the invaders? Recent studies[22] have drawn attention to the problem posed by the pictographic expression of saints' names and Christian feast days. These terms early on became essential indicators, since all the Indians had to observe the Christian calendar – even if in secret they kept other reckonings – and had received at baptism a name that they were obliged to use in their dealings with the Church or the colonial administration. We have already seen some hints in the *Códice Sierra* of the solutions which were found. Thus the painters chose to break the exotic term into its phonetic components, while using isolated elements from Nahua words with a pictographic equivalent: for example, the sign that represented a 'brick wall', a parapet, served to paint the word saint (*san* or *santo* in Spanish) because it had the phonetic value of *xan* and *xante*. Another process involved enriching the traditional repertory by proceeding to a reduction and a graphic stylization of Christian attributes and symbols. The key designated St Peter, the grill St Lawrence, the sword St Paul, etc. Far from being an innovation, the selection of a feature to indicate the whole took up the age-old custom of representing indigenous gods by reference to a costume or ornament. A sign could also be the result of original creation, such as the corpse ready for cremation and surmounted by a candle, which was supposed to mark the feast of the dead on 2 November. The two phonetic and metonymic steps were in no way mutually exclusive. For St Francis, for example, a phonetic solution was sometimes preferred to the drawing of the cowl or the cord with three knots that characterized the saint. A third possibility could be envisaged: the painter could exploit the phonetic and symbolic value of a traditional glyph. Finally, it was possible to make up a composite glyph that articulated a symbol and a phonetic sign; for example, to render the name Miguel by adding angel wings to the sign *miquetl* (cadaver).

The diversity of combinations cannot conceal the limits of these processes, which were quickly reached. Transcriptions of Christian names were often partial, as were the accepted phonetic equivalences. Thus *Cilco* was supposed to render Francisco, while *Xo* (from *xochitl*, flower) was meant to refer to José. It was up to the Indian reader to guess and to complete this mnemonic kernel. Moreover, Christian symbolism was not always clearly understood. To represent St John the painters depicted a cup from which emerged a dragon, which sometimes took on the appearance of a swan or an eagle! It was not terribly easy to represent the fantastic bestiary of western Europe. Far from being uniform, the transcriptions show many and various initiatives. There were at least two possible phonetic transcriptions for Estebán (Stephen), and thus two completely different glyphs. Finally, a new glyph could be drawn in several ways in the same document: the convent of San Agustín de las Cuebas in the *Códice Aubin* is represented by a burning heart pierced by an arrow, whose drawing at times obeyed European canons and at others native traditions. Beyond these choices, beyond the hesitations and approximations of a mode of expression in search of itself, impinged the concerns of indigenous groups directly confronted with colonial institutions and novel political and cultural demands: it was necessary to be able to transcribe a baptismal name on a 'painting' for it to be acceptable to the Spanish tribunals; it was necessary to find the means to paint the Christian calendar to assimilate the periodicity of the Catholic feast days and to familiarize oneself with the time of the conquerors. Moreover, we find not just an enforced and opportunistic adaptation of the ancient to the new world. Among the Indians of the second generation, there was doubtless also a considerable effort to find a lost order, as if to invent and establish new landmarks with the help of a detailed knowledge of the Christian iconography with which they were visibly imbued. It is true, however, that only the Indians equipped with this knowledge were able to decipher the inventions of the Christian *tlacuilo* and to put them into circulation.

This attempt is understandable only in societies where pictographic expression remained predominant and imposed the requirements of communicating essential information in a form that was, in spite of everything, quite traditional. However, one can already detect the presence of a rival destined to carry the day. Recourse to Christian symbolism by the painter and his 'readers' did not depend exclusively on contemplation of the statues and frescos decorating the churches and convents, mostly in the course of construction. The impact of the European book can also be recognized: it alone could provide a detailed and abundant repertory of images, while its text even helped to identify the drawings and to find the Latin words – *Visitatio, Expectatio*, etc. – that the new glyphs sought to render. The influence of the book was perhaps still more profound and, attracted by the completely phonetic system of notation that they had before their eyes, the Indian painters might have tried to work this vein in their own sphere. The practice of reading might even have stimulated the invention of more sophisticated pictographic processes. We know, among other things, that to render the plural *santos* (saints) the painters came to use the Nahuatl plural ending (-*me*), expressed phonetically by the glyph for agave, *metl*. Does that mean that pictographic expression was moving towards a slow but inexorable phoneticization? The evolution seems clearly to have begun by about the middle of the sixteenth century. It is attested before 1550 in the *Codex Mendoza*. In the *Codex Kingsborough* (towards 1555) the elements making up the glyph multiplied (up to five instead of one or two), taking on a phonetic value and being ordered according to the succession of syllables.[23] A shift from the syllable to the letter can even be glimpsed, for the vowel *a*, for example, without an alphabet ever having been constituted. This is how the matter would stand. Did the Indian painters end up by succumbing to the convenience of the Latin alphabet? Did they judge it superfluous to pursue the creation of an alphabetic and syllabic notation? Or did European writing, profiting from the strengthening and stabilizing colonial presence, acquire a decisive supremacy in the second half of the sixteenth century resulting in the drying up, and progressive abandonment of the pictographic system? Let us leave these questions up in the air, contenting ourselves with recalling that it is perhaps excessive, if not wrong, to force the attribution of a syllabic or even an alphabetic destiny on to a mode of expression that was much more than an embryonic form of writing. The consummate art of the *tlacuilo* of the *Codex Mexicanus 23–24* (1570), who painted a pictographic version of the Christian calendar, or that of the author of the *Codex Santa Anita Zacatlalmanco* (1600–1604), who at the very beginning of the seventeenth century still mingled phonetic signs, Christian glyphs and traditional glyphs, induces us to look still further into the details of this language and its conventions.

Attention focused on the sign, on the originality of its creation, might well cause us to lose sight of the whole to which it belonged. Isolated from the framework where it was linked with other signs in relations of meaning, form and colour, the glyph was no longer quite what it had been. Very early on, this overall structure underwent a certain number of modifications. Once again the influence of the western European book was not unfelt, providing the example of a format whose borrowing imposed on the painters an insidious reorganization of pictorial space: reduction of size in the case of the *lienzos* led to more modest proportions, or redistribution by pages in the case of the old screenfolds. So it was that in the *tonalamatl* painted in the *Codex Ríos* and the *Codex Telleriano-Remensis* (1562–3), a panel came to occupy two pages in such a way that the disposition of the glyphs of days and protective gods found itself perceptibly altered. But there were still more profound transformations. The system of lines, of frames, that once – and still in the *Codex Borbonicus* – served as framework, as skeletal structure for the group of representations, collapsed. One has the impression of passing from a space saturated with precisely distributed forms – the scattered-attribute space – to an empty sheet of figures floating without support: what Robertson designated a 'landscape without space', figures without a ground that seem to call up a third dimension, a horizon line, a kind of background (Robertson, 1959, pp. 60–2, 111–13). Another *tonalamatl*, that of Sahagún in the *Florentine Codex*, illustrates the outcome of this transformation: a landscape was sketched, the third dimension was established, but already the pictographic image was changing into the illustration of a text written in Latin characters. The rabbit, designating a day of the calendar, was from now on painted in this *tonalamatl* under the traits familiar to us of a small animal frolicking in a landscape.

We have until now mentioned only Nahua examples and trajectories. But we can easily trace a similar evolution among the Mixtec: while the *Lienzo of Zacatepec I* (1540–60) bore only signs of places and figures, the *Lienzo of Zacatepec II*, conceived about 1580–1600, one or two generations later, was inhabited by a profusion of animals and plants whose presence was probably more decorative than significant. Painted in 1579, the map of Tejupan that accompanied the 'geographical report' of this *pueblo* also testifies to the irruption of the ornamental landscape.[24]

We can thus, with Robertson, reconstruct in a few words the major phases of this evolution: the shift from a continuous flux of images to a European composition of pages, to a more constricted cut-out, followed by the destructuring of two-dimensional space in favour of three-dimensionality. It goes without saying that we are rendering schematically a far more complex evolution whose detailed analysis can be found elsewhere. It must suffice to emphasize that the transformation of glyphs on the formal and phonetic level was contemporary with and inseparable from a complete reorganization of painted space. Other elements make it possible to appreciate the changes in the old mode of expression; for example, the line. The traditional line, thick, precise and continuous, traced the outlines of the forms represented in a way that isolated them from daily space. After the conquest, the line lost its consistency, its thickness varied without our understanding if this evolution corresponded to a loss of the ancient mastery or to a will to render the expressiveness of the European contour line by imitating its visual effects and plastic force. However, this time the change was no longer attributable to the Spanish book, but to engraving.

The drawing of the human figure represents a particular but no less instructive example of this sort of evolution. In one generation, from the 1540s to the 1560s, painters forsook a representational convention that respected traditional proportions in favour of a cursive, more expressive line that substituted faces with finer outlines for massive heads, by drawing shorter heads and longer bodies like those found on the 'Plan of agave paper'. It seems that Mixtec paintings broke more gradually with a representation of the body made up of an assembly, a collage, of separate pieces, in favour of a homogenous silhouette, conceived as a whole. However that may be, it is a similar tendency. We can wonder about the meaning of this last pictorial evolution and see it as just the aesthetic influence of western European models. However, I would put forward another hypothesis. Could there be any link between the transformation of representations of the body and the human being and the introduction, by means of evangelization, of quite a different conception of man? The ancient Nahua thought of man as the conjunction of three autonomous vital entities located in the head, the heart and the liver. These entities each corresponded closely to three superimposed levels of the world, and could in some circumstances desert the part of the body that served as receptacle. On the other hand, not only did the Christian dichotomy of soul and body challenge the unity of the person, but it belonged to a train of thought that favoured the uniqueness and autonomy of every being confronted with the divinity. Should we believe that when the colonial *tlacuilo* sketched less stereotyped characters, detached from the old hieratic manner, the line conveyed a different relation to the body and the person, influenced by the preaching of the missionaries and the new iconography?

On another level, let us finally mention, without dwelling on it, the evolution of the narrative line. Mixtec paintings offer a specific illustration: still traditional in the *Lienzo of Zacatepec I* (painted between 1540 and 1560), in the form of the meander pattern, followed in the *Map of Teozacoalco* (1580) by a movement from bottom to top along columns as if tending to follow the European model, and thus writing.

Whatever the local variants, in the second half of the sixteenth century, from the valley of Mexico to the Mixtec regions, we witness the birth of a different approach to the pictorial field and to form. Not only was the glyph transformed, the framework also changed and suffered, it appears, more decisive upheavals. One cannot speak of alterations, but rather of an accumulation of inflections from which certain major trends emerge: the development of phoneticization, a more or less extensive adoption of the third dimension, the influence of western Europe on the human figure and feature. These innovations belonged to the indigenous generations educated after the conquest, who became adults after 1550. As a result, they were able to separate themselves from traditional canons to adopt and establish modes of expression closer to those of the Spanish, for which we find manifestations until the eighteenth century in regions as diverse as Oaxaca, Guerrero or the valley of Puebla.

Pictographic expression survived not only in the 'paintings'. It succeeded in maintaining its position where it had always been seen, on monumental architecture, even if it was the architecture of the invaders. Concerned to mark their presence spectacularly and to replace the destroyed temples by still more imposing buildings, Franciscans, Dominicans and Augustinians launched construction campaigns throughout the country. The friars were the masters of the works but they relied on the constant and indispensable collaboration of the local people. Glyphs quickly flourished on the great stone constructions put up by the friars, on the convent walls, church façades, open chapels and portals that covered New Spain in the course of the sixteenth century. Some came from the ancient sanctuaries, like much of the re-used material, while others were sculpted to order. Place glyphs at Tultitlán and Tlalnepantla; date glyphs at Cuilapan, in the open chapel of Tlalmanalco, at Huaquechula, etc. Some signs are nevertheless disconcerting, recalling the ancient cosmogony: the eagle, or *chalchihuitl* – a precious green stone – and the Fifth Sun *Nahui Ollin* decorate numerous Christian sanctuaries. These glyphs taken together offer a sort of abridged version of the Nahua cosmogony. Was it not necessary, to delay the death of the fifth and last Sun, to feed it with the precious water (*chalchiuhatl*), water that was none other than the blood of the prisoners of the sacred war (*atl-tlachinolli*), whose glyph (which intertwines water and fire) also crept on to church façades?

The insertion of these glyphs lends itself to contradictory interpretations. Could it be a discreet sign of the pagan appropriation of a Christian building, of the assertion of a surreptitious continuity where the missionaries would tolerate nothing but a break? It might be admissible for the first decades of evangelization to see it as the silent revenge of those whose 'paintings' were being burned. Could it be rather an indigenous interpretation or transcription of Christian themes? This was undoubtedly the case when the glyph for precious water was associated on Franciscan coats of arms with the blood of Christ rather than with the blood of sacrificial victims. Or should we see it as a simple decorative invention, when at Apasco, for example, the two-headed eagle of the Hapsburgs was combined with that of the Indians, or when only the geometric and stylized aspect of the glyphs was retained, ready to blend into the great decorative compositions? Depending on the case and the sculptor, continuity could be symbolic or simply ornamental. The manner of insertion also varied: it could take the form of a recessed fitting, in a font or a wall; or a juxtaposition, a glyph at the feet of the statue of a saint; or a decorative exploitation, reducing the glyph and alternating it with motifs of European inspiration in the fashion of, for example, that stone rose of San Miguel Chapultepec, made up of the four circles of the sign of solar radiance repeated eleven times (Reyes Valerio, 1978, pp. 288, 286, 278, 272, 246–66, 276, 265, 262). Colonial, Christian sculpture and architecture thus unexpectedly provided a base for certain ancient glyphs during the sixteenth century. They enabled Indian artisans to keep visible to all signs that were officially banned, without the friars perceiving what they might conceal that was incompatible with the new faith. But the misunderstanding that these glyphs took advantage of could turn against them: tolerated as decoration, thus without symbolic content, extracted from their traditional contexts, dissociated from the steles and reliefs of old, they appeared in predominantly European compositions that treated them as ornamental motifs. Unlike the glyphs in pictographic manuscripts, they became part of a whole that was no longer Indian. One must therefore ask to what extent this systematic subjection to the western European iconographic code diverted the glyphs from their original meaning and use, corrupting and in the medium term drying up the inspiration of the sculptors. The question also arises for indigenous colonial painting, when ancient glyphs were lost in European compositions. The association could produce striking effects, like the frescos of the Augustinian church of Ixmiquilpan where, in the midst of a profusion of grotesques and acanthus leaves, Greek centaurs confront the jaguar-knights of the precolumbian armies. But generally the presence of pictographs was much more discreet, as in the frescos of the Apocalypse of Tecamachalco, entirely attributable to the hand of an Indian painter, Juan Gerson. The purely ornamental path followed by pictographic expression joins the transformations and trends on my list. It corroborates the vitality and ubiquity of this indigenous language; it also announces the crisis and stagnation that it now remains to explore.

But this is not easy, because of the dispersion, the small number and the contextual and chronological uncertainty surrounding most of the accounts that have reached us. Studying the decline – that is to say, the moment the object was modified to the point that it lost its substance and its reason for being – would thus be a delusion if it were not for an exceptionally rich source designated by the convenient term of pictographic maps. Cartography as practised by the ancient Nahua was far removed from the map-making familiar to us. It appears to have been based principally on a representation of space that distributed place names in a regular, geometric manner, a bit like our underground maps. These consist of diagrams governed by the shape of the sheet that they occupy rather than by topography. It goes without saying that this approach favoured the order of succession of the toponyms at the expense of the real distances that separated them. Apart from this 'underground' type (of which the *Map of Cuauhtinchan* in the valley of Puebla, Plate 5, would be an example), there appears to have existed quite a different prototype, which appeared in the region of Texcoco. This second type seems to have taken account of certain topographic characteristics and of their respective position. In other words, several approaches would have guided the painters before the conquest:

a stylized and conventionalized representation, at the extreme limit of the first type;

a rendering, however approximate, of the orientation and the distances between places (the Texcocan type);

a mixed type, combining the two preceding modes, in which the centre was devoted to observations of topographical distribution, while the margins were occupied by collections of information organized according to far more conventional criteria;

finally, urban cartography (Robertson, 1959, pp. 179–80; Yoneda, 1981).

This typology remains highly hypothetical; if the 'underground' style is incontestably prehispanic, we have every reason to ask if the 'Texcocan prototype' does not represent a projection into the past before Cortés of an already acculturated layout. The same is true of the city maps whose existence can be induced exclusively from colonial documents. At any rate, depending on the hypotheses maintained or dismissed, whether one accepts or rejects the existence of a Texcocan prototype with a more sustained geographical 'realism', the innovations introduced under Spanish influence stand out as quite different. Moreover, like the earlier 'paintings', the maps underwent spectacular transformations, from the *Codex Xolotl* to the *Mapa de Santa Cruz*, the more so as they played an essential role in a colonial society that made private ownership of the land a major issue, and in which Indians and Spanish were forced to define their powers and their territory. It appears that, lacking enough cartographers, the Spanish administration was not unaware of indigenous skilfulness and knowledge in this field, and indeed of the system of sophisticated conventions offered by the glyphs. It thus commonly had recourse to Indian painters, particularly in the decades that corresponded to investigations for the geographical reports, to the policy of the concentration of Indian populations, or to the massive granting of lands to the Spanish, that is, from 1570 to 1600 approximately.[25]

The indigenous colonial map, like the historical or economic paintings, was able to open itself to new experiences. Alongside the traditional symbolism, used for signifying running water, springs, mountains, roads, or settlements, it made room for the new signs become indispensable with the colonial penetration: the church with its square and bell, the chequerboard plan of the *pueblo*, the *estancia* and the *hacienda*, the *corral*, water mills, and covered wagons drawn by cattle (Plates 6, 7). Although new, these signs observed the canons of indigenous iconography. The *estancia* (usually a cattle farm) was a development of the 'house' glyph, to which was added a gabled roof; while a church was rendered in a stylized, two-dimensional manner, reviving native decorative elements as required.[26]

Nevertheless, the enrichment of the repertory cannot conceal the slow deterioration of forms. If at the end of the sixteenth century one still finds glyphs that are classic in line and painted with confidence, more often the line was distorted. In the last two decades of the century the 'running water' glyph was reduced to two wavy lines, a roughly sketched spiral, or even a simple line (Plate 10); the 'mountain' sign became a protuberance with imprecise outlines, deprived of its stylized basis; summarily drawn, the footprints, indicating the lines of communication, became unrecognizable spots. The 'house' glyph was often no more than a barely identifiable graffito. Even the most common signs ended by losing their identity. The renunciation of colour was contemporary with the deterioration of the glyphs. When the chromatic range can still be observed, it can bring together nearly 10 different tonalities. Maps of the 1570s alternated blue-green or blue-grey for running water and springs, yellow ochre for hills and fallow lands, mauve, brown and pink for dwellings and churches, green for Spanish *estancias*, brown for roads (Plate 8). We know that indigenous chromatic expression constituted an essential element of pictographic expression, even if its meaning and function often escape us. It is probable that it indicated the quality or purpose of the lands represented, but also that it located each space on a perceptible and sacred scale, by marking the contrasts, transitions or continuities, noting presences completely imperceptible to the Spanish eye. For example, the colour and drawing of water were also – indeed, above all – the symbol and attribute of Chalchiuhtlicue, the aquatic goddess, the Lady of running waters. Despite that, chromaticism continued to lose ground. Completely painted maps are rare in the series preserved. When it survived, colour took refuge in certain glyphs, unless it served only to suggest the landscape as we perceive it, as if the painters had bartered their perception of the environment for a Europeanized vision. The running water that in 1599 had already become the blue ribbon familiar to us, 30 years later ran between two crude earth-brown banks.[27] There are doubtless several reasons for this renunciation. The sudden or progressive loss of a knowledge of colours; dead or fragmented memories; the impossibility, or just the difficulty, of obtaining colouring agents in a society and economy disorganized by the colonization; finally and especially a concern with rapidity and appropriateness to European requirements, which had no sense of chromatic signals, as appears from Spanish maps drawn in similar circumstances. It is obvious that, according to the place and time, these factors had a distinct effect.

In its overall structure the Indian map adapted itself to the western European vision of space. Apart from certain examples that recall the diagrammatic maps of the prehispanic period, in general the disposition of topographical elements tended to reflect more or less approximately their distribution on the ground. There we can see the colonial ending of a prehispanic hypothetical prototype or the victorious influence of European and Spanish models, or possibly a response to the pressing need to produce documents readable to the eyes of the Spanish, where they could find their bearings without too much difficulty. It is probable that prehispanic precedents, western European models and the force of circumstances combined at the expense of stylization and geometrism.

A series of adjustments came to be grafted on to this spatial organization, which accentuated western European influence. First, orientation in space: ubiquitous as the representative of the *pueblo*, the church frequently opened to the west (Plate 9) in keeping with the Christian tradition that directs the choir towards the east. As the church was always represented frontally, it tended to imprint its own orientation on the map. More rarely, a sun at the top of the page marked the east. Elsewhere, distances indicated on the map in steps or in leagues (Plate 10) sketched a rudimentary scale. Oriented, space was thus also measured. Measurement and orientation are not incompatible with conservatism in drawing. If it is true that indications of distance and the cardinal points generally correspond to the intervention in the map of a

Spanish writer, it is also true that this intervention would have been impossible if an Indian hand had not prepared the medium (Plate 9).[28]

The arrival of landscape – most often in the form of mountainous contours planted with trees, which strangely recall Dürer's gouaches (Plate 8) – or even the suggestion of distant bluish and colour-gradated horizons betray the influence of European engraving and painting, and still more of the numerous frescos that decorated churches and convents. This innovation, which we have picked out in other pictographic documents also executed around the 1570s, is not incompatible with the retention of chromaticism and the old conventions. One even feels that, more than a 'photographic' perception of the surroundings, it often constituted a supplementary sign to mark borders. Conversion to landscape or adoption of a neo-glyph? The question arises more than once.

On the other hand, another emerging tendency threatened the old style with disintegration to a far greater extent. Indigenous maps gave up colour, rejected all working drawings, any finish of outlines and curves, reducing themselves to a crude, extremely economical drawing, sometimes close to clumsiness (Plate 10). However, these maps are not sketches of more developed 'paintings'. They are the Indian version of Spanish maps drawn up in the same period, and have an undefinable air of more or less botched sketches: vague flecks mark relief, the rapid zigzag of the pen indicates a stream, a quick hatching signals the existence of a *pueblo*. The incisive line, the elementary schematic quality and, when colour appears, the daub, take us a thousand leagues from the calligraphic sophistication of the prehispanic 'paintings', in the elusive domain of the sketch. More personal, more subjective, the bearer of summary and direct information, drawn with a quill and no longer with a brush, the Spanish sketch represented a form of abstraction from reality that had recourse to a play of conventions less standardized and far less easily identifiable than those of the indigenous map. The choice of pertinent elements was variable, from large configurations to tiny parts. The Spanish sketch associated immediately readable data with optional variants that depended on the context or the personal style of the author. It is a matter of a 'weak code', which makes the individual intervention obvious, to the point that one would sometimes be lost if it were not for the legend that comments on the line. For the Spanish, sketch and alphabetical writing were quite obviously inseparable, as if they were but two modulations of the same stroke of the pen. At times the legend merged with the drawing even to producing the 'written map', in which legends drawn in *cartouches* placed in the geographical spot that corresponded to them invaded the whole document and determined its composition. Writing in some cases even replaced drawing completely. A paradoxical conjunction, unforeseen as much as involuntary: does the written map, an extreme variant of the sketch, not offer the European counterpart to the most traditional indigenous map? Rather than disposing glyphs on the perimeter of a rectangle, alphabetical inscriptions were distributed along the axes and the four sides. All things being equal, the degree of abstraction is comparable, even if there is no question of making the glyph the equivalent of Latin writing. Above all, it would be useless in these cases, as in others, systematically to associate western European influence with a 'realistic' vision of the environment. There was formalism and convention on both sides – which does not mean that it was a simple matter to pass from one system to the other, for many reasons.

Technically, the making of the Spanish sketch presupposed a perfect mastery of alphabetical writing and an assimilation of pictorial conventions that existed only in an empirical and implicit state, mixed with a not negligible dose of improvisation and subjectivity. The sketch was a given in a society and culture that tolerated, up to a certain point, the individual's play with codes, while the indigenous tradition appears to have imposed the uniformity of its conventions more rigidly. Following this hypothesis, access to the sketch by Indian painters would correspond to a profound transformation of relations to themselves and society. But have we not already pointed out the possibility of this change in the representation of the human figure?

At the same time, there was another major obstacle, more insurmountable. The passage to the sketch was never posed in terms of the substitution of one system of conventions for another more or less equivalent system. On the Spanish side, if one sketched, if one wrote, one sought exclusively to record the essential at the expense of peripheral, religious, mythical, or ecological notations, and apart from any aesthetic considerations. Pictographic expression, on the other hand, was polyvalent: for example, the glyphs *Coatepec* (Plate 6) – a serpent on a mountain – or *Citlaltepec* (Plate 10) – a star on the same mountain – not only identified places but mobilized a knowledge of their origins and a whole cosmology. At the same time, the Spanish sun, a circle surrounded by rays, which marked the orientation of the map (Plate 9), was a convention of weak value, essentially geographical and decorative. Moreover, while the glyph was autonomous, that is to say, a bearer of meaning by itself, the Spanish drawing demanded a written commentary or it might well remain ambiguous or unreadable. A slightly curved line marked a mountain only when associated with the tag *serranía*, while the 'mountain' glyph was absolutely intelligible, *even to a Spaniard*. Perhaps now one has a better grasp of the distance sparating these two cartographic processes: a distance which is at the same time of an intellectual, technical and practical order. If the Spanish sketch was economical in means, quickly drawn, and without any trace of embellishment, that is because it had a limited objective: to locate an estate, a donation of lands, in space; while the traditional indigenous map related, in an antithetical and complementary way, to the whole of the territory. The latter therefore conveyed far more information and often expressed complete familiarity with the places painted. In other words, the Indian painter who adopted the sketch must have acquired a different view of himself and his land at the same time as an accomplished mastery of alphabetical writing: so many elements that were not easy to combine, and which presupposed an extensive acculturation. But it is permissible to imagine that the Spanish sketch exercised a more superficial and harmful influence on indigenous style, simply by inspiring modifications of line and drawing, by suggesting more rapid execution and setting aside whatever appeared superfluous – colour – or too complex – glyphs. One feels that far more than the inclusion of landscape, the adoption of, or rather the evolution towards the sketch contributed greatly to the disintegration of the indigenous style, by removing from it whatever specificity still remained.[29]

We must take care not to imagine a linear evolution of modes of expression that would enable us to date with precision the renunciation of a process or the diffusion of a new technique. At most we can detect overall trends. It is not just the relative weakness of our store of documentation that is at issue. It is necessary to note that the modifications of spatial composition, of the play of conventions, of elements judged to be relevant, proceeded at quite different rates that varied with places and painters. A map made in 1601 at Tepejí del Río in the present State of Hidalgo testifies by the severity of its line, use of colour and 'classic' conventions, by the absence of landscape, to the relative persistence of a traditional style at the dawn of the seventeenth century. Three years later, in the region of Puebla, on the other hand, the map took on the style of a rough sketch, from which the old signs were practically absent and a landscape of woods and mountains took over. But 20 years earlier, near Malinalco, the map was already sketched and the hills planted with trees. These variants rule out a precise chronology and draw attention to the coexistence of different modes of cartographic representation, one of which was more traditional and the other more Europeanized. These two styles could coincide in the same land, in two neighbouring *pueblos*, but they also met on the same map, when glyphs were mixed with lines indicating ridges, or churches were represented frontally, and thus in the old way, or in three-quarters view in a rudimentary perspective.[30]

But these two styles are far from having the same weight: the

Europeanization of space was a virtually definitive experience, while the old language tended to be distorted and pictographs to disappear from most maps produced after 1620, at least from those drawn at the request of the Spanish authorities – a symptom of the loss of a technique and knowledge that must be pointed out, although with qualifications. This drying up should not conceal the continuation of a truly indigenous cartography until the end of the colonial period, based on compromises, borrowings, adjustments conceived and carried out in the last decades of the sixteenth century. A shrunken pictographic repertory often rough and irregular in treatment, glyphs lost in a landscape, a perspective sometimes sketched out, but also a continuing concern with the geometric and formal, indeed sometimes the return, or the preservation, of a native structuring of space figure in these maps, whose apparent resistance to change resulted in careful copies being made by successive owners.

The associated use of two iconographic or cartographic codes by the Indian painters of the second half of the sixteenth century is just one aspect of a prodigious capacity for assimilation and adaptation, examples of which we have sought to adduce. But it is a subject already touched upon several times, when this talent left the familiar terrain of pictographic expression to embark upon another adventure. Let us reopen the *Códice Sierra*. Pictographs strove to represent the graphic innovation introduced by the conquerors: writing and the act of writing. They painted in turn paper, the empty book, the bound book, the breviary, the music book, the deed and the Spanish *escribano* in the process of writing. The acute perception of alphabetical writing on the part of this Mixtec or Chocho *tlacuilo* eloquently expresses the extent to which the colonial history of pictographic expression is inseparable from the assimilation of alphabetical writing. According to the friars, learning reading and writing did not pose major difficulties. The experience began at Texcoco about 1523, where the Franciscan Pedro de Gante taught the young nobles 'to read and write, to sing and to play musical instruments, as well as Christian doctrine'. The undertaking extended progressively to the children of the nobility of México-Tenochtitlán (1524–5) and the environs, to the regions of Tlaxcala (1527) and Huejotzingo (1525), while the first Franciscans undertook the alphabetization of the Nahuatl language. From alphabetization to the writing of works in Nahuatl was just one step – probably taken by Pedro de Gante in composing his *Doctrina cristiana*, perhaps the first Nahuatl book printed in Europe towards the end of the 1520s. During this period, the missionaries gathered the first fruit of their teaching. About 1531, the bishop Juan de Zumárraga noted that 'many of these children are well able to read and write'. Some years later, towards

1537, the Franciscan Julián Garcés painted just as enthusiastic a picture for Pope Paul III. In January 1536 the college of Santa Cruz of Tlatelolco was established, offering an education of exceptional quality to the Indian elite under the direction of the most distinguished Franciscans. The progress of the young Indians was such that some settlers were soon alarmed, recalling that 'reading and writing are harmful as the devil'.[31]

According to the accounts, the Indians easily mastered the graphic mode, becoming 'very great specialists of all the letters, small and big, broken and Gothic', skilled at 'imitating the models presented by their masters'. It is true that learning Latin – the 'grammar' of the period – which began about 1533 under the rod of the Frenchman Arnaldo de Basaccio, was a problem to the extent that Nahuatl had no terms for grammatical rules. The obstacle was overcome after several years of effort, since the pupils 'showed themselves to be such good Latinists that they made and composed quite well scanned verses and long and congruent speeches'. We shall not attempt in these few remarks to reconstruct a history of the education of the Indians, which others have dealt with in detail, but simply point out the extent to which, from the end of the 1530s, the Latin alphabet infiltrated the Indian élite as it began to fix the various indigenous languages, beginning, as we have recalled, with Nahuatl. It is not easy to draw up a quantitative balance of this undertaking of alphabetization. Nevertheless, we consider that it was far from negligible, since each Franciscan foundation was at that time coupled with a school where the Indians learned catechism or more, according to their rank. The instruction of the indigenous elite progressed, then, at the rhythm of the expansion of the order. Let us add that the Augustinians pursued a similar policy. At the beginning of the 1530s, there were perhaps 600 young Indians already initiated to writing. Indians boys, and even some girls, learned from the friars to read and write. They also discovered at the hands of their masters or in the still modest libraries of the convents that strange object, the book. They contemplated the engraved pictures decorating the pages of the volumes. They perhaps already wondered about a technique – printing – in which some of them would later win renown.[32]

It would certainly be wrong to imagine that Latin writing immediately supplanted pictographic expression. The *tlacuilo* painted glyphs during the three centuries of the colonial domination and pictographic expression was still almost untouched by any influence when the nobles mastered reading and writing as early as the 1530s and 1540s. Neither immediate nor inescapable, the passage from the glyph to writing did not take the form of a substitution, but rather that of a meeting on the indigenous space of the 'painting'. It is significant in that respect that in the sixteenth century the terms *cuiloa, tlacuilo, tlacuilolli* and many others which referred in Nahuatl to the painter, the act of painting and the painting, were also applied to the world of writing. But let us look first at the example of the Mixtec.

The Mixtec 'paintings' of the region of Oaxaca have been preserved in sufficient numbers for us to be able to draw some precious indications from them. Although prehispanic in origin, the *Codex Colombino* – which revealed the biography of a personality called 8-Deer – was annotated on two occasions between 1522 and 1541. But its owners, the lords of Tututepec, were not concerned to transcribe or annotate the contents. They used it to record in Latin letters the limits of their territory. This entirely pragmatic objective gave greater importance to the authenticity and antiquity of the medium at the expense of the content, and modified the function and meaning of the *Codex*, which became a kind of equivalent of a deed of ownership. The *Lienzo of Jicayan*, painted in 1550, on the other hand, already illustrates quite a different process: in the margin of traditional pictographs, it bears alphabetical Mixtec inscriptions which constitute a partial gloss on the glyphs. But this gloss is several decades later than the execution of the painting. This distance disappears on the *Lienzo of Ocotepec* (1580), which was annotated in Nahuatl at the time of its execution. But was it not already done away with 25 years earlier, when the *Códice Sierra* was produced? Later, the 'Genealogy of Tlazultepec' (1597) also shared its space between alphabetical writing and the old signs (Smith, 1973, pp. 15, 13, 170, 147, 161, 170–1). Contemporary with or later than the painting, discrete or invasive, relevant or not, the alphabetical gloss impinged on the pictographic space, following quite different procedures, whose counterpart we discover in Nahua society. The gloss concerned toponyms (*Mapa de Sigüenza, Mapa Quinatzin*), characters (*Mapa Tlotzin*), or all the pictographic information (*Matrícula de tributos* and *Codex Mendoza*). It was generally a later addition, attributable often to a European hand, conceived to make the document intelligible to the Spanish. It did not disrupt the organization of the painting unless space for the gloss was not reserved in the conception of the work. However, the inclusion of alphabetical writing could go beyond simple commentary, as is illustrated by the *Historia tolteca-chichimeca*. Developed at Cuauhtinchan in the environs of Puebla, between 1547 and 1560,[33] this work reveals much about the range of possible relations between the glyph and writing. There we find, as earlier, a written gloss applied to pictographic documents reproduced by the painter: the written preceded, followed or surrounded the pictographs that it limited itself to commenting on, or to which it offered a pendant, thus creating a real duplication of information.

But the gloss could also refer to 'paintings' that the painter had not reproduced but that the writer had used as sources of information. The step was thus quickly taken from a commentary on documents outside the work to the composition of autonomous writing, devoid of any figural representation and any pictographic reference. What the alphabetical tale won in continuity, the pictographic material lost in consistency. Broken into scattered fragments, isolated from their original context, the pictographs submitted to the demands of the commentary as to the constraints of the format even to the point of pulverization, until only glyphic islands remained, reduced almost to the role of decorative vignettes (Plate 11). Preserved, they became illustrations where a landscape slipped in, unless they took on the ornamental function of a European frontispiece. The *Historia tolteca-chichimeca* requires an infinitely more detailed analysis. There we see many comings and goings between two modes of expression, but also sometimes hesitations and regrets that allow us to imagine that the author was not insensitive to the loss of meaning implied by the dismembering of a pictographic panel.

The successive stages in the work of the Franciscan Bernardino de Sahagún followed similar paths. In the *Primeros memoriales* collected between 1558 and 1560, pictographs dominate the written commentary, no doubt a sign of informants already adult at the time of the conquest and still completely familiar with pictographic expression. On the other hand, in the far more developed survey found in the *Florentine Codex* (1578–9) the text, written in Nahuatl, relegated not only the Spanish summary that was made of it, but also the pictures, to a subsidiary role. They have ceased to be true pictographs, to become coloured or monochrome illustrations, subordinate to the writing. There we see with no difficulty the hand of a new generation of informants trained by the friars, writing an alphabetized Nahuatl, accustomed to books and engraved pictures. Truly indigenous texts written in the last 25 years of the century corroborate this decisive change: the *Diario* of Juan Bautista, an Indian of the city of Mexico, *alguacil* and collector of tribute to His Majesty, unfolds as an unadorned text, and the same is true of the later chronicles and Indian reports.

We sometimes forget that the discovery and conquest of America were contemporary with the diffusion not only of the printed book but also of the illustrated book. We cannot then dissociate the penetration of the written text from that of the engraved image, as decisive if not more so.[34] Moreover the two fields were closely interwoven. The books opened by the friars, and very soon by their Indian pupils, had their historiated letters disposed on backgrounds of foliage, figures and symbols. The letter merged with the picture somewhat like the glyphs, but the tie linking it with the decoration generally remained arbitrary, the ornamentation, the effect, prevailing over the meaning to be imparted. The equivalent can be found in the sculpted anagrams decorating the façades of churches built by the mendicant orders. Engravings offered the Indians, whether they knew how to read or not, images as strange as those that the Spanish noticed in the pictographic manuscripts. Covering a principally religious repertory, they presented scenes of the life of Christ as well as a symbolism of the divine, disconcerting to the indigenous eye. They opened the gates of the western European *imaginaire*, drawing fabulous monsters from its bestiaries. They strung together a profusion of decorative motifs, friezes and roundels, replicas of which the Indians found on the recently painted walls of cloisters and churches. One might wonder about the meaning that the Indians could have attributed to these ornaments that they contemplated or even painted. With what feelings did they perceive the chimeras and fantastic creatures? How did they understand the 'demoniac', the 'decorative' and what their own tradition suggested? But engravings also reflected the defeated, when they showed them praying, marrying or confessing: such was the vision that Spanish and Flemish art nurtured of them and the image that they sought to inculcate in them. Beneath the themes and iconography ran the fundamental elements of the European iconographic codes of the Renaissance, the representation of the human figure, of gesture, depth and perspective, and even exceptionally a representation of logic and modes of reasoning as visualized by the schemata engraved at Mexico of the works of the Augustinian theologian Alonso de la Vera Cruz. As in western Europe at the same period, it was the engraving that fixed the image that expressed the world. Like others, the Indians were prey to this enterprise of visual domination, a first skirmish in our modern wars of images. Nor did they escape the curiosity that it aroused: the Indians who stole books seized by the Inquisition claimed that 'they wanted them not to read, but simply to look at'; in fact, to study the images of the saints that they contained. The diffusion of European engraving had at least three major specific implications: it imposed a monochrome vision different from the Indian 'paintings', which relied on colour; it offered the example of a linear syntax and texture, without relation to the contour line that delineated the pictographs; it maintained a specific relation to writing based on the juxtaposition of a visual code and an alphabetical code, while the pictographs mixed or rather merged these two types of information. In other respects, engraving could apparently approach the indigenous mode of representation or distance itself radically from it: in the first case it organized the disposition of objects over the whole space of the sheet, somewhat like the scattered-attribute space of the prehispanic tradition; in the second, it worked with perspective, landscape and three-dimensionality to compose a vision that must have deeply disconcerted the Indian observer.

Even though apparently more accessible than the alphabet, based as it was on a total abstraction of the sign, the engraved image still required of the Indians a learning process about which we are, moreover, informed. It favoured the copy, the imitation. Very early on, the Indians showed themselves to be capable of producing remarkable replicas of engravings and all kinds of documents, from the bull to the musical score. This aptitude explains how Christian symbolism could so easily creep into pictographs to express the saints' names or liturgical feasts, or how Renaissance motifs came to invade the *Codex of Tlatelolco*. But, however faithful it might be, the copy does not imply comprehension of the overall organization or of the principles ordering the composition of the whole image. It permits the extraction of isolated elements far more than the conception of new images. It is this difficulty with extracting a structure coupled with ease in reproducing the parts that seems to govern the chronology of the borrowings that the Indian painters drew from the western European repertory. The phenomenon of two or three generations living through changes that Europe took centuries to inaugurate – changes imposed from without and not spontaneously experienced and lived – raises the old question of a cultural, intellectual and even sensory dependence between western Europe and the worlds it dominated. If only there were time and space enough to compare the Flemish, Italian, and of course Spanish experience with the process at work among the Indian artists, to contrast the stages of a reconstruction of reality and space, to extricate the chaotic passage from a flat space without shadows (in its Plotinian or Mixtec conception) to depth, relief. But it would be too long a detour, implying a knowledge of Spanish art that is lacking and a range of studies that hardly exists.

The last Renaissance

One might believe that images and letters served only to duplicate and disrupt modes of expression that still managed to justify their existence. Or, on the contrary, one might maintain that by the expedient of phonetization and the enrichment of iconographic repertories, letters and images contributed to their preservation, conferring on them unpredicted aspects and unsuspected orientations. But that would be once more considerably to underestimate the receptiveness of the indigenous world to colonial society. Without the tremendous task,

begun by the missionaries and their informants by 1533, we should
know little about prehispanic cultures. Writing up the 'antiquities'
helped to preserve whole sectors of these cultures from oblivion. A
catalogue of this work would be too long. It was dominated on the
Spanish side by the work of Andrés de Olmos, Toribio de Benavente
(known as Motolinía), Bernardino de Sahagún, Diego Durán, Juan de
Tovar, Mendieta, Torquemada, Alonso de Zurita, without overlooking
for Oaxaca the works of Francisco de Burgoa or for Michoacán the
Relación de las ceremonias y ritos ... To this should be added the
writings of *mestizo* historians as well known as Alva Ixtlilxóchitl or
Muñoz Camargo. But we should remember that the Indians themselves
shed their role of informants to take up the pen, interpret the 'paintings'
and 'write' the speeches and stories of bygone days, as did the authors
of the *Anales de Cuauhtitlán* towards 1560–70,[35] taking inspiration
from the old 'books of the years' or *xiuhamatl*, or the anonymous
author of the *Códice Aubin*. At Tenochca, Alvarado Tezozómoc went
as far as producing two chronicles, one in Spanish and the other in
Nahuatl, the *Crónica mexicana* (*c*.1599) and the *Crónica mexicayotl*
(1607). The recent history of the conquest inspired accounts from
perhaps 1528 at Tlatelolco. In 1548 the Tlaxcaltec Thadeo de Niza
produced his history of the conquest of Tlaxcala even before the famous
Lienzo was painted, and five years later a first Indian version of the
Historia de la conquista de Tenochtitlán appeared, which Sahagún
would later incorporate in his *Historia general*. Just like the 'paintings',
the new writing recorded events of the conquest (Baudot, 1977, pp.
119–57, 395–429; Gibson, 1975; Garibay, 1971, II, pp. 267–313).

The substitution of alphabetical writing for pictographic expression
was much more than a simple matter of translation or transcription.
While the *cantares* (hymns) and *huehuehtlahtolli* could easily be recorded
in Latin characters – at the expense, it is true, of a crystallization and a
Christianization of the oral tradition (Bierhost, 1985) – the process of
writing down the 'paintings' seems to us to have had a far more decisive
significance, even if at first it was not perceived. We recall that the
'paintings' had a specific dimension in belonging to the perceptual as
well as the conceptual realm. Was not the *tlacuilo* 'a possessor of many
colours, a colourist, a drawer of shadows, a maker of feet, a maker
of faces'?[36] In bringing into play relations of form and colour and
spatial effects, offering modes of reading and multiple approaches, the
'paintings' show an intuitively and immediately perceptible specificity,
only partially able to be verbalized by virtue of their 'iconicity', to
borrow the language of the semioticians. The 'paintings' are images as
much as texts, and words cannot offer the exact equivalent of an image.
In other words, it appears that writing down pictographic knowledge

necessarily involved a loss of substance, a loss all the more disquieting as it was irremediable and ineffable. The process extended beyond the realm of intellectual or aesthetic categories to become a question of the implicit basis for any representation of reality. It concerned the principles of selecting and coding elements relevant to the environment. Here we are touching on the deepest and least explored sediments of a culture, those which, never explicit and never questioned, make up the singularity of a cultural configuration. The retention of pictographic expression in the sixteenth century is probably attributable to the roots of this relation to reality and its representation far more than to ideology (the 'idolatries'), pseudo-cultural reasons ('the inertia of tradition') or the intellectual or technical inability to master writing. But relinquishing the pictograph in favour of writing not only signified giving up a preferred way of grasping reality, it sanctioned other disengagements: a break with the ritual, public, ostentatious use of 'painting' and of *amate* paper, which was offered in sacrifices. No more images of the gods or ancestors *to be seen*, no more paper to be ritually consumed, but sheets covered with writing *to be read*. Even if the transcriptions, or rather alphabetical versions, made by the Christianized Indians preserved a certain sacred resonance – a sacredness no doubt demoniac for the most convinced neophytes – they broke radically with the materiality of the *painted* object and instituted a probably much more neutral relationship to the medium. It will be objected that the Spanish also had sacred texts, the holy scriptures, for example, that the Indians saw them treat with the greatest respect, and that these same Indians had first observed with stupefaction the magic of the 'paper that speaks'. But this astonishment did not last, and the ordinary relationship of the Spanish to the material form of the written, even if it consisted of religious or magic texts, was more detached or more sporadic. When in 1558 a Mexica Indian committed to writing the *Legend of the Suns*, he was, as well as keeping an essential tale of Nahua cosmogony from being forgotten, recreating it by extracting the 'paintings' that he had under his eyes and the poems that he had in his memory.[37] Even better, he conferred a new status on it, by giving greater significance to its documentary character at the expense of its hermeneutic significance and its ritual functions. In other words, writing down the paintings involved not only selection, censorship, and the synthesis of several traditions – an exercise that the old *tlacuilo* engaged in – but also a secularization and a dematerialization of knowledge which was no longer *shown*. The distance taken by the Christian Indians from their past could not have found a more concrete illustration.

But this distance was also a recomposition, to the extent that alphabetical writing imprinted its linear continuity, its one-way reading on the story, marked necessarily by a beginning and an end. In that respect the 'paintings' appeared more flexible. And without a doubt the impact was stronger still in so far as writing broke the old distinction between the spoken and the painted, substituting a common and unique mode of expression, the alphabetical text. It was the business of the new writers, with no precedent and no guide, to organize, combine and link interpretations of the painting, the oral fragment, the curious anecdote, the amazing detail, the witness's testimony. Which they did, often with surprising skill.

Must we conclude that the impact of writing completely disrupted the indigenous memory and vision of things? Throughout the sixteenth century, as we have seen, alphabetical writing and 'paintings' coexisted, sometimes in the same space, and without a necessary loss of oral traditions. Moreover, not all the manuscripts were produced to the order of the Spanish, who guided the writing. Some sought to perpetuate prehispanic customs like, for example, the keeping of local annals. In this case the break was less, the objective analogous, the custom unaltered; only the medium was different. But can we say as much of the short notes that an author devoted to his career, to the details of his existence? Did writing encourage self-examination? Did Christianity contribute to giving to individual lives and experience an interest that is hardly recognized? In destroying, or raising questions about, traditional hierarchies, did colonization at the same time weaken old loyalties, to the point of promoting personal expression at the expense of insertion in the domestic group and the community? It is quite possible that all these social, ideological and technical factors can explain the appearance of texts such as the *Diario* of Juan Bautista, in which this collector of tribute from the 'vagabond' Indians of Mexico tells about his ills, speaks of his circle, describes bull runs and holidays, gathers fragments of sermons, notes the price of Castilian paper and hens. And it is not unlikely that the Christianized authors of the *cantares* so busy with introspection and their personal destiny felt the twofold influence of the new religion and the new writing (Bierhost, 1985). Even when it did not encourage the birth of new forms but limited itself to recording the old patrimony, the act of writing was by no means an innocent exercise. It altered the content of the inheritance and the nature of the relationship that the Indians maintained with it. By accommodating it to an exotic means of expression practised by acculturated Indians, thus subjected to a Christian and European education, alphabetical writing assumed an ambiguous, surreptitious function: it ensured the safeguarding of 'antiquities' at the expense of an imperceptible transformation that was also a colonization of expression.

Nevertheless, we cannot dissociate the transformation of expression from the more immediate stakes. Writing was the instrument of assimilation, or more precisely of a less subtle and more generalized subjection to the demands of colonial society. If it is true that the Spanish authorities gave a legal value to pictographic testimony, it still had to be glossed or accompanied by an interpretation in Nahuatl or Spanish. In fact communication with the viceregal bureaucracy required writing as much as recourse to an interpreter. Orders, lists of *barrios* in Mixtec, Zapotec, Matlaltzinca and above all Nahuatl became more and more numerous in the second half of the sixteenth century. Indigenous writers and interpreters – the *nahuatlatos* – wrote petitions, wills, deeds of sale and gift. Complaints at law, accusations, were addressed to ecclesiastical judges, to the viceroy, to the *corregidor* or to any *visitador*.[38] One grasps the ambiguous significance of this adoption. The Indians accommodated themselves to forms that were strange to them, but they also learned to use them to their advantage. Thus they acquired knowledge without precedent and the means to exchange it, to the point that 20 years after the conquest, in 1541, the Spanish were worried: '[The Indians] have such good writers, in such numbers, that I cannot say how many there are, and they write letters that, not without risk, reveal to them all the business of the country from one sea to the other, which before was impossible for them.'[39] The same attitude prevailed when in 1545 they got hold of the text of laws that favoured them, or every time they wrote or had written complaints denouncing their fate. The best known of these manifestations probably remains the letter that the Indian nobles of Mexico and its environs wrote in 1556 to the king of Spain.[40] The greatest names of the Indian aristocracy did not hesitate to subscribe to this dark view of the indigenous condition and to ask that the Dominican Bartolomé de Las Casas – whose deeds and most likely writings they obviously knew – should become their appointed protector.

In other respects, religious literature in Spanish or translated into a native language – Nahuatl and more exceptionally Huastec, Totonac, Tarascan, Mixtec, etc. – began in the 1530s to circulate in certain indigenous circles. It consisted of biblical texts – the epistles, the gospels, Ecclesiastes, the Proverbs, the Book of Job, the Book of Tobias; catechisms, sermons, confession manuals, devotional works – *Corona de Nuestro Redentor, Horas de Nuestra Señora, Espejo divino*; lives of the saints. At first there were manuscript works, then printed texts distributed by the friars and intended specifically for the indigenous public, as the Franciscan Alonso de Molina explained in the introduction to his *Confesionario mayor* (1565), which he sought to fill with 'useful and necessary subject-matter for penitents, so that they will know how to confess and declare their sins'. Again, in 1607, Joan de Mijangos

revealed that he had written his *Espejo divino* in the form of conversa-
tions 'so that the natives who read it would understand it more easily'.
But the Indians remained in no way passive readers. They copied for
each other everything that passed through their hands, so well that in
1555 the First Mexican Council was concerned, considering it 'extremely
detrimental to give sermons to the Indians [written] in their language,
on the one hand because they do not understand them and on the other
because they make errors and mistakes in copying them'.[41] The Council
not only ordained the seizure of all sermons in the Indians' possession,
but demanded very close monitoring of the texts that were given to
them in future, 'so that they could neither falsify them nor corrupt
them'. It went so far as especially to forbid the sale to Indians of a
'book of fates' that was circulating in Castilian. In 1565 the Second
Mexican Council again took up the manuscript literature in the Indians'
possession, requiring that all the collections of sermons and texts drawn
from scripture should be taken from them, so as to leave them only the
catechism approved by the ecclesiastical authorities. These steps reveal
not only the spread of reading among the Indians but also the existence
of circles that reproduced the texts without taking any notice of the
Church. While the clandestine transmission of ancient ritual 'paintings'
was hardly a surprise, these 'unauthorized' copies a little more than
30 years after the conquest are disconcerting. We would give a good
deal to discover examples of these works and to determine if the
'corruptions' and 'errors' with which they were studded were not the
fruit of a first Indian interpretation of Christian texts – and thus a
first heresy, which the Church seems to have mistrusted as much if not
more than 'idolatrous survivals'. Perhaps, too, we see a glimpse of
these deviancies in the Christianized versions of the famous *cantares
mexicanos*?

Whatever the progress of writing, it could not stifle oral expression;
but it probably altered its status appreciably. Indians continued to sing
the ancient *cantares* at home or in noble houses throughout the sixteenth century, despite the prohibitions of the Church and the provincial
councils. To be sure, it consisted of no more than a clandestine or at
least suspect activity. Far from suddenly fossilizing, the oral tradition
was able to remain lively to the point perhaps of expressing a revival of
ritual centred on exaltation of the warrior ethic and past sovereigns. But
for the nobles it had ceased to occupy the exceptional place it had had
before the conquest. In addition, like all oral transmission, it was
difficult to dissociate from a public 'production' that combined it with
other elements, visual, acoustic, ludic or dramatic. Often shorn of the
complement and support of the hidden 'paintings', mislaid or burned,
cut off from the institutions that ensured their diffusion, monitoring

and expressiveness, the songs and speeches of old had to coexist with other compositions inspired by the missionaries.

Taking advantage as best they could of the Indians' taste for singing and oral expression, the friars taught plain chant and Gregorian chant at the same time and with the same success as writing. Cantors and masters of chapel proliferated in the *pueblos* to such an extent that it was claimed that the least hamlet had three or four Indians who sang the Hours of Our Lady in their church every day. But the Church also took care to exploit traditional forms, to rework the old *cantares* to sing of the Christian faith, the 'life of Christ and the saints', casting a new content in a familiar and tried form. The friars tried their hands and, even more interestingly, the Indians composed poems that were sung for the great religious feasts. Works produced throughout the century told of the creation of the world, the Annunciation, the Nativity, the Redemption. They took over the images and stylistic conventions in use before the conquest – flowers, butterflies, *quetzal* feathers; they reworked pagan themes, conferring on them a Christian colouring. But it is not unthinkable that this formal continuity masked a decisive break in composition. Without making a systematic rule of it, it appears that the songs received a written form from their conception; in other words, the process of creation was no longer able to be confided to memory alone, but gave rise to a written elaboration, which betrays the infinitely complex and new intertwining of old themes and Christian borrowings. There again we detect the penetration of another technique of expression and organization of thought without, it is true, being able to seize its exact significance. The theatre of evangelization, whose extraordinary success in indigenous circles is known, encouraged an analogous process: it was the Franciscan written work that served as canvas for the oral expression of indigenous actors, and for their attempts at composition. Theatre, like colonial singing, was based on the primacy or at least the anteriority, of the written (Horcasitas, 1974).

It would be wrong to generalize, even if we encounter other examples of this retreat of the old orality and the advance of writing. The very adverse circumstances lent themselves to it. Concerned to verify their contents, the friars gathered transcriptions of what the Indians sang, while for their part the Indians preserved the songs in writing, sprinkling them with Christian terms to thwart the censors. The checks of the extirpators of 'idolatries', the secret efforts of the guardians of the past, the enforced immersion in a society that linked temporal and spiritual power with writing, curiosity for this new technique, all conspired to deprive the oral of the authority it had enjoyed at the time of the *cuicatl* and the *tlahtolli*. This was obviously true within the leading circles, who dealt with the clerks and the administrators; much less so among the *macehuales*. There was a progressive decline of the oral, doomed for the nobles of the seventeenth century to be no more than the instrument of historical reminiscences and to be identified more each day with the culture of the rural and urban masses. Or was it more precisely the agony of an aristocratic orality, tied to the 'reading of the paintings' and prestigious settings, to the profit, perhaps, of more modest and less supervised forms?

We have difficulty in defining with the desired precision the circles where these new forms, these unprecedented compromises, were developed. Anonymity generally cloaks the painters, witnesses of the condemned past as well as observers of the colonial present. It conceals the creators and the sculptors of glyphs, the readers of books, the lovers of engravings and sketches. How many were concerned with building bridges between the two worlds, hesitating between modes of expression with no common frame of reference? It may seem paradoxical to study the product, the practice, before examining the author, but even the nature of the sources hardly leaves us a choice. Nevertheless, it is possible to take several soundings. It will be recalled that in January 1536 the college of Santa Cruz of Tlatelolco opened under Franciscan direction. From the first years it welcomed about 60 young men from the country's Nahua nobility, who 'came to study all the subjects of the art of grammar, to speak Latin, to understand and write it, and even to compose heroic verses'. For some 20 years, from 1546 to 1565, the Indian students trained by the friars even took in hand the direction of the institution and some of the teaching. It is often stressed that during this period bad administration almost destroyed the enterprise, while the significance of the temporary but exceptional autonomy that these Indians enjoyed is neglected. However, in the same period numerous forms that have been described here made an appearance: grammar, rhetoric, poetics, philosophy and medicine were taught. Pliny, Martial, Sallust, Juvenal, Livy, Cicero, Boetius, the Fathers of the Church, Nebrija, Erasmus, Luis Vivés, etc. were read. From the college of Santa Cruz emerged an indigenous group brilliantly initiated into the lettered culture of the Europeans. Indians from Mexico, Tlatelolco, Azcapotzalco, Xochimilco, Texcoco and even Huejotzingo in the valley of Puebla were encountered there. They were 'scholars' who also knew how to be men of power, since many occupied the functions of governor, and the most notable, don Antonio Valeriano, a 'good Latinist, logician and philosopher', even governed the Indians of the capital for 30 years. Often informants and collaborators who guided the investigations of the friars, especially those of Bernardino of Sahagún – Martín Jacobita, professor and rector of the college, Antonio Vejerano, also a professor, Pedro de San Buenaventura – were recruited from their numbers. It is remarkable that these Indians, who had received a particularly sophisticated European education, also continued to preserve the ancient learning. Was it not Pedro of San Buenaventura who explained to Sahagún how to calculate the beginning of the prehispanic year, and who copied or wrote out the *Hymns of the gods*, one of the richest and least revised texts on the old cults?[42] But it was these same Indians who recorded in the *Coloquios* a version of the only great debates that opposed the Franciscans to the indigenous priests,[43] or who painted the narrative of the Spanish conquest, the *Historia de la conquista*. We have the feeling that these privileged witnesses between 1550 and 1580 managed to dominate two cultural spaces, Indian and Christian, and what is even better to express and reconstruct the initial encounter.[44]

There were also remarkable translators who corrected or established the Nahuatl versions of Latin or Spanish texts that the Franciscans gave them. There they rendered an incalculable service. Thus Hernando de Ribas, who died in 1597, came to participate in the drafting of the *Diálogos de la paz y tranquilidad del alma* of Juan de Gaona, don Francisco Bautista de Contreras to work with the Franciscan Juan Bautista on the Nahuatl version of the *Contemptus mundi* and on the book of *Las vanidades del mundo*. Not only did they handle an exceptionally rich Nahuatl, in the fashion of Estebán Bravo, but they wrote a Latin that astonished Spanish readers. It was said of Antonio Valeriano, who died in 1605, having long been governor of the Indians of Mexico, that 'even in the last years of his life he spoke Latin *ex tempore* with such elegance and pertinence that he seemed to be Cicero or Quintilian'. The 'so well composed' letters of don Francisco Bautista de Contreras, written in Latin, were admired. Translations were also made from Nahuatl into Latin. The most spectacular example remains the work on indigenous medicine attributable to Martín de la Cruz, translated into Latin towards 1552 by the Indian Juan Badiano de Xochimilco with the title *Libellus de medicinalibus Indorum herbis* (Garibay, 1971, II, pp. 180, 221–4).

This mastery of languages was accompanied by the development of a linguistic reflection that from then on made possible the alphabetization of Nahuatl (Mignolo, 1989). By permitting the isolation, decontextualization and notation of all the words, the alphabet made possible what remained completely outside the scope of pictographic expression: the compilation of indigenous grammars and 'vocabularies', the most accomplished of which undoubtedly remains the *Vocabulario* of the Franciscan Alonso de Molina with whom the Indian Hernando de Ribas collaborated. Don Antonio Valeriano made his contribution in the field of etymology and semantics. One can easily guess the patient research carried out on the borrowing and translation of European categories, on 'the niceties of concepts and language', of which more than one resulted in the creation of neologisms to which Nahuatl easily lent itself. Weeding out of terms too charged with pagan resonances, Christianized interpretations of traditional notions, devaluing of words calling to mind conduct become unacceptable in the new order, but also a quest for elegance and a concern with exactness: rarely has intellectual collaboration been taken so far. It was in effect thanks to the work of these linguists and these Indian informants that the friars were able to develop church Nahuatl to govern the relations of the Indians to the clergy and to dogmas throughout the colonial period. Student, then rector of the college of Santa Cruz, don Pablo Nazareo confided that he had undertaken tirelessly night and day to 'translate from Latin into our language all that is read during the year in the churches of the land: the gospels and epistles of Sundays, saints' days, Lent and the feast days . . .' Even typography did not put off the intelligence or the handiness of the Indians of the college. Diego Adriano, originally from Tlatelolco, 'learned to compose and composed in print in any language, as well and as quickly as a master of the art'. The same was said of Agustín de la Fuente, who died in about 1610, and to whom we owe numerous illustrations in the *Florentine Codex*.[45] These activities of the translator, language expert and even printer put this group of Indians in close contact not only with texts intended for preaching, catechism and confession, but also with works whose translation into Nahuatl suffices to testify to the slow but sure assimilation of the culture of the European clerks: let us mention, among others, the *Contemptus Mundi*, that is, the *Imitation of Christ* of Thomas à Kempis, the *De Consolatione Philosophiae* of Boetius, or the *Fables* of Aesop.

Beyond a doubt we detect there the appearance and constitution of a strongly Christianized lettered elite, whose principal characteristic was to be intimately linked to the mendicant orders and especially the Franciscans. We know that the first, but soon relinquished, objective of the college of Santa Cruz had been to train Indians for the priesthood. The project fell through, in the face of the hostility of one Church party and even of its promoters, disappointed by the weaknesses of some of their students. None the less, the Indians of the college provided the Church with the intellectual and linguistic means to penetrate the indigenous world more effectively by furnishing the knowledge that they had and supporting the conversion of the populations by all means. Let us simply recall the Augustinian college of Tiripitío, where the Tarasc nobility could learn Latin, Greek and even Hebrew, repeating – on a smaller scale, it is true – the example of Tlatelolco. Its most famous pupil, don Antonio Huitziméngari Caltzontzin (died 1562), who was governor of Michoacán, had numerous works in Latin and enjoyed the friendship of the chronicler Cervantes de Salazar. Quite far from there, in the region of Oaxaca, the most powerful Mixtec *cacique* listed only two books in his will of 1591, even if they were the *Flos Sanctorum* and the *Contemptus Mundi*. European lettered culture thus extended beyond Nahua territory to penetrate more distant lands, to touch other ethnic groups (López Sarrelangue, 1965, pp. 173–5; Spores, 1967, p. 242).

But educated Indians of the college of Tlatelolco or elsewhere did not limit their action to supporting the enterprise of Christianization. They applied themselves with as much energy to defending their privileges and their rank. A number were linked to the princely families of Texcoco, México-Tenochtitlán or Tlaxcala. That was the case at Texcoco of don Antonio Pimentel Ixtlilxóchitl and his father don Fernando; of the *mestizo* Juan de Pomar and Fernando de Alva Ixtlilxóchitl; of don Alfonso Izhuezcatocatzin Axayacatzin, son of king Cuitlahuac, who was governor of Texcoco and wrote the history of his past in Spanish and in Nahuatl. Don Pablo Nazareo, the tireless translator, was the husband of a niece of Moctezuma, from whom the author of the *Crónica mexicayotl*, Fernando de Alvarado Tezozómoc, was also descended. Pedro Ponce de León, author of a *Breve relación de los dioses y ritos de la gentilidad*, joined himself to the line of the lords of Tlaxcala. Antonio Valeriano was thus an exceptional figure, for it seems that he did not belong to the nobility, which did not prevent his son Diego from marrying a noble woman of Azcapotzalco. Without belonging to these aristocracies, the provincial nobles or those of more modest domains, the *principales*, took part in the development of this new culture, while preserving their inheritance, trying their hand at writing, consigning to it the history that was being made before their eyes. Francisco Acaxitli, governor of Tlalmanalco, wrote a book about 1550 on the expedition of the viceroy Mendoza against the Chichimec. From Tepeapulco and Huexotla, near Texcoco, from the region of Chalco and Amecameca, came archivists, compilers, informants, who collected pictographic manuscripts, preserved them, annotated them, circulated them, wrote reports in Nahuatl and read Spanish. In the Mixtec highlands, don Gabriel de Guzmán, *cacique* of Yanhuitlán from 1558 to 1591, had complete mastery of Spanish. And Michoacán, we have seen, was not outdone with don Antonio Huitziméngari or those Indians from Taximaroa who in 1560 received from the French Franciscan Mathurin Gilbert assurance that the works seized by the Inquisition would be restored to them (Garibay, 1971, II, pp. 228–30, 299; Spores, 1967, p. 179; Fernández del Castillo, 1982, pp. 14–16).

We can detect in these various attempts the tenacious will to reconquer an identity that had been roughly treated, to fill the gaping abyss, the 'net' burst by the conquest, to adapt to new conventions, whether religious, political, social or economic, while trying to save the essential: the status, goods and privileges of the old ruling groups. The Indian nobility learned to know its conqueror better, and to conform to the model held out to it by the Spanish Crown, that of the Spanish *hidalgo* whose clothes, emblems (arms, heraldry, horse) and ostentatious piety it would take over, without for that reason breaking with a past that concealed 'the origin, the basis and the genesis of the domains'. Whence the jealous care to gather the 'paintings', to keep them for the lineage, to make copies and transcriptions to provide evidence of a legitimacy that the upheavals in the wake of the conquest sometimes rudely put to the proof. Whence also this rush to take on the functions of *escribanos* and interpreters (or *nahuatlatos*) who ensured the coming together of the two societies. To survive socially by reconciling what was no more than a partly forbidden past and the inevitable colonial reality was, it appears, a continuing process that took the form of the interaction of painting and writing among the nobles, defeated but still conscious of being indispensable intermediaries between the conquerors and the native populations.[46]

The objective of this long detour to 'painting' and writing was to examine the emergence from the 1540s among the old ruling circles of a radically new culture. The study of the coexistence of modes of expression and different codes, the analysis of the passage from one to another, the manifestations of old forms and their preservation, the often groping working out of original solutions, was made in the image of the transformations, the choices and the compromises of the indigenous nobility of the Nahua lands, from Michoacán or the region of Oaxaca. When the Italian quattrocento juggled with modes of representation, using old or new systems according to the objects being painted, it drew from the same cultural source, in the same society; it took its inspiration from different but, despite everything, related sources. The exceptional interest of the Mexican experience resides in the conjunction of practices that one could believe to be irreducible, bringing together traditions developed without any earlier contact. There was a multiplicity of expressive media: glyphs rubbed shoulders with the alphabet and musical notation; the painted picture met the engraving; oral transmission oscillated between prehispanic or Christianized forms; plain chant, polyphony followed upon ancestral dances. Multiplicity also of languages: Latin and Spanish were added to the Indian languages, dominated by Nahuatl, which served everywhere as *lingua franca*. Multiplicity of calendars in the Annals, which recorded the Indian and the Christian year at the same time. Or in these 'paintings' – the *Codex of Tlatelolco*, the *Codex Mexicanus 23–24* – which discreetly marked the correspondences, in the secrecy of memories, under Christian images or by the re-use of old symbols. Or again, on these 'repertories of times', which initiated the Indians to the European zodiac. Multiplicity of spaces, which in monastic complexes joined the enclosed, covered precinct of the churches with the vast empty expanse of the squares inspired by the great prehispanic platforms. More prosaic multiplicity of dress, of which the *Codex of Tlatelolco* provides very good examples. Multiplicity, finally, of economic practices, which was able to add to the exploitation of traditional resources – the tribute in men and in kind, the obligatory gifts of subordinates – the revenues of the cattle farm or the products of silkworm breeding. It is not, however, a question of revealing a stable complex, within which each feature would come to occupy an established place. On the contrary, we have had several examples of complex configurations in gestation, where the old was modified, decomposed, to be integrated into improvised creations, or to accommodate exotic elements. Relations were reversed according to contexts, convergences and places: western European iconography was predominant in the convents, its indigenous counterpart prevailed at the same period in the 'paintings'. Comparison, juxtaposition or connection, two modes of representation and of making reality intelligible coexisted, which also implied two distinct systems of cautious approach and convention, governing not only the image of reality that one put together for oneself but also more directly the codes of perception themselves. It was as if these Indians had taken a double look at things, as sensitive to the aesthetics and canons of old as they were open to new relations, different pasts: 'They have managed to know the origin of our existence thanks to the books that they read, [namely] where we come from and how the Romans subjected us and converted us at the time of the pagans that we then were, as well as all that has been written on the subject'.[47]

It remains to be determined if this duplication of schemata, categories and perspectives could result intellectually in establishing a new 'ideolect', a structuring of the whole, homogeneous and durable, with the association in some 'paintings' of landscape and indigenous cartography (unexpected prefiguration of what Holland perfected in the seventeenth century) or the pictographic aspect of the botanical plates of Martín de la Cruz's *Libellus de medicinalibus* . . . providing remarkable examples. Or was it no more than instances of individual synthesis and local initiative, the compartmentalized, tentative experiment with collecting samples that is sometimes recalled by monastic architecture, when it accumulated borrowings of the most diverse styles. Did not the quattrocento itself also falter in the beginning? (Vargas Lugo, 1969.)

The cultural, social and political experience, some manifestations of which we have followed, failed to institute a dynamic capable of mastering the irruption of the European west, of assimilating and combining it with the autochthonous inheritance. The 'miracle' aborted. Or more precisely the experience was diverted from the course it had taken towards more modest circles, where it took other forms, doomed to a marginal existence and a minority cultural status in the colonial universe. There are many reasons for this. The ranks of the Indian nobility had been decimated by the wars of the conquest, distant expeditions, massacres and executions. When it survived and was able to negotiate changing sides after the humiliation of defeat, it had to learn to perpetuate itself in a hostile and unforeseen colonial milieu, which subjected indigenous customs to the law of the king and of God. First to be affected and condemned to obliteration were the children of mothers repudiated by the spouses whom the Church abjured to renounce polygamy. Women and bastards were brutally shorn of the rank that was their due. The structure of marriage found itself in confusion. It is true that the Crown demonstrated concern to protect the status of the nobles, to grant them privileges, favours and goods. It did so as much through respect for the established order – whatever its origin – as because it could not do without these all too precious intermediaries on whom depended the collection of the tribute and the obedience of populations. The Crown gave the descendants of the prehispanic lords and those who had infiltrated their ranks the title of *cacique* and admitted them to the functions of governor (Gibson, 1964, pp. 166–72; López Sarrelangue, 1965, pp. 83–108, 123–4). Often the innovations introduced the greatest confusion, since the conditions of accession related less to local tradition than to the good will of the colonial authorities, when they were not subject to the hazards of intrigue and corruption. The favour of the Spanish, of an *encomendero* or a clergyman, was a precious asset and the accusation of idolatry a sure means of neutralizing or brushing aside a rival that custom would have supported. There was the possibility for *macehuales* who were ambitious, able and rich as a result of business to take possession of lands once attached to temples or to the Mexica ruler, to escape tribute and to become one of the *principales*. These many and daily usurpations, combined with the pressure of the Spaniards, fostered a feeling of insecurity and uncertainty that did not spare the aristocracy. The echo of it can be found from 1545 in the will of don Antonio Pimentel, *cacique* of Texcoco, and in the correspondence that the aristocracy of the capital exchanged with the Crown in the second half of the century. From 1570 on, the demographic crisis took on such dimensions that the nobles lost numerous *macehuales* who were attached to them. The survivors preferred to lend their arms to the Spaniards, while the Crown endeavoured to reduce to the rank of tributaries as many Indians as possible, even those of noble blood, and to restrict the rights of the *pipiltin* over the plebeians. These difficulties ended, to take up the terms of Charles Gibson, in 'a loss of income, power and prestige for *caciques* and *principales*' (Gibson, 1964, pp. 156–7; López Sarrelangue, 1965, p. 144). The cumulative effects of marriages with the Spanish, cross-breeding, the sale of hereditary goods, the constant strengthening of the European presence, and above all the ravages of epidemics, hastened the decline of a nobility that the authorities had no longer, from then on, to handle carefully. To which should be added the disintegration of net-works of dependence dominated by the indigenous nobility: at the same time as it lost control of the division of tribute, it ceased to constitute hierarchical groups where each had to keep his place. And the increase of individual links with Spanish society probably only accelerated the process. It is significant in this regard that the historian Chimalpahin, although a passionate bard of the grandeur of the domains of Chalco and Amecameca, chose to add to his indigenous name the patronym of his Spanish protectors don Sancho Sánchez de Muñón, master of the school of the archbishopric, and don Diego de Muñón. The practice was very common. Thus, in the process of coming closer to the Euro-peans, the nobility was dissolving the links on which it had constructed its power even if it retained, in the manner of Chimalpahin, the precious memory of its origins.

Worried about reaching the elite and for lack of resources, the Church was particularly concerned with educating the nobility in the first decades. In the second half of the century it tended to neglect all social distinctions, partly because the stratification of indigenous society became more blurred and the populations less numerous. At that time, nobles and plebeians often learned together to read and write,[48] and the latter progressively gained access to important functions in the com-munity, becoming *alcaldes*, *regidores*, *escribanos* and even governors. But there were other breaches, also opened by the Church. Around the convents founded by the mendicant orders, from the end of the 1530s, clustered a crowd of Indian servants who were exempt from the payment of tribute and in effect exclusively dependent on the friars, who exercised a still unquestioned jurisdiction and discretionary authority over them. Most had no qualifications: they were porters, gardeners, cooks. Even so, they discovered and learned new practices, from the cultivation of fruit trees to the rudiments of monastic cooking.[49] Some acquired greater familiarity with ecclesiastical matters, for example the sacristans who accompanied the priests and who were entrusted with the cult objects, or the *topiles* and *alguaciles* who undertook to keep order in families and to gather the faithful for Mass; or the musicians and cantors who took part in the office. Cantors and musicians, organists, flautists, players of trumpet, pipe, sackbut and hurdy-gurdy even became so numerous that the Council of 1555 was alarmed. Generally there were about a dozen for each *pueblo*, even to the most modest hamlet. This increase exemplifies a process that affected all the Indians of the Church. For the ranks of cantors and *fiscales* of the nobility were swelled relentlessly by newcomers happy to avoid paying tribute and to acquire a status that they would never have dared to claim before the conquest. The stakes were considerable, for they involved spiritual leadership of the community in the largest sense. The cantors and *fiscales* prepared the dying for confession or death; helped them to write their wills; administered baptism in the absence of the priest. They taught catechism and announced the feast days. They kept the register of alms and offerings, and watched over the cult objects and ornaments of the church with as jealous a care as that which others used to have – or still did have – for the 'idols'. It is highly probable that from this group came the Indians who on their own initiative copied the manuscripts left by the friars or composed *cantares* on Christian and para-Christian themes, fashioning a Christianity that might already have partially escaped its propagators.

Another circle, not far from the foregoing, maintained close links with western European forms. These were the masons, sculptors and painters who, under the direction of the friars, built churches and convents in more than 300 places, carving façades and capitals and painting thousands of square metres of fresco. Insensitive – and for good reason – to the chronological succession of European styles, they invented the *tequitqui* style and gave their work the appearance in turn of Romanesque, Gothic, Manueline, Mozarabic, Renaissance or plateresque style (Reyes-Valerio, 1978, pp. 133–65). We can no doubt detect among them the same distinction that set city aristocrats apart from small provincial notables: trained on the job, the artisans who worked in isolated villages could not be confused with those of the workshops of San José de los Naturales in México-Tenochtitlán, Santiago Tlatelolco or Tlaxcala (who received orders from the whole valley of Mexico), or those of Puebla, Michoacán and the Oaxaca region, strongly influenced by western European styles.

It is certainly not easy to distinguish among the painters and sculptors, among the Indians of the church and the civil authorities, the nobles and the *macehuales*. All the same, we can consider that in the second half of the century, far from confining themselves to subsidiary tasks, the plebeians invaded all the steps of the hierarchy, becoming cantors, *fiscales* or governors. In the *altiplano*, at Michoacán and Oaxaca, the result was the education of a group of notables whose power had no prehispanic roots, which was no longer connected to domains or to lordly houses, and above all whose horizon was limited to the territory of the community. These progressive modifications of the social fabric raised questions about the cultural process that we have surveyed. The sophisticated education intended for the nobility lost its meaning and efficacy to the extent that the power and social influence of the group was weakening irresistibly. The irruption of new notables broke the chain of learning that once held the *pipiltin*. The projected alliance between the tradition of the nobles and the Christian and European contribution was condemned to more or less brief duration while *principales* who owed nothing to 'blood' or to 'antiquity' proliferated. But the redistribution of social cards, or rather their jumbling within the indigenous world, is not enough to account for this impasse.[50]

The diffusion of writing and the written, the study and partial preservation of indigenous cultures presupposed on the part of the Church and the Crown (on which the former was closely dependent in the form of the *patronato*) a climate of openness and curiosity that was demonstrably compromised in the years following the abdication of Charles V (1556) and the closure of the Council of Trent (1563). Spain became the champion of the Counter-Reformation. This hardening showed itself in New Spain by the establishment of the Tribunal of the Inquisition (1571) and by increased supervision of the printing and circulation of books and writings – and in particular, of those in an indigenous language (Fernández del Castillo, 1982, pp. 1–47, 247, 81, 513). Another decisive step was the Church's closing the priesthood and religious orders to the Indians, who were also removed from the jurisdiction of the Inquisition: the Indian people were set up in the state of eternal neophytes and spiritual minors, even if much later some would accede to the priesthood. These steps condemned the college of Tlatelolco, which progressively reduced the number of teachers and lost students in epidemics, so that at the beginning of the seventeenth century it was no more than a school where reading and writing were taught. In 1585 the archbishop of Mexico pronounced against the teaching 'of Latin, rhetoric and philosophy to the Indians'. But beyond these steps and these relinquishments, we cannot forbear to recall the retreat of the mendicant orders and especially the Franciscans, to understand better the withering of experiences tried during the course of the sixteenth century. The Franciscans had dreamed of a New Spain where they and the Indians alone would lay together the foundations of a new Christianity (Phelan, 1956), they strove to interpose themselves between subject populations and conquerors, they tried to spread the techniques of western Europe while preserving what was acceptable of the old cultures. They inspired, as we have seen, many steps, attempts, compromises, that surrounded the working out of an Indo-Christian culture. While remaining a considerable economic power and enjoying extended privileges, the regular Church (i.e. the religious orders) had to learn to deal with other competing powers: the administration of the viceroy, the *audiencia*, the secular clergy (priests and parish priests), the bishops; it had to measure itself in a colonial society where the weight of the Spanish, the *mestizos*, the blacks and the mulattos grew while the Indian population was diminishing to a considerable extent and at an accelerated rate. More than useful, irreplaceable auxiliaries of the conquest and the colonization, the mendicant orders (like the Indian nobles) in the second half of the century became partners who imposed themselves far less. The progressive desertion of the college of Tlatelolco was contemporary, let us recall, with the halt in construction of great monastic buildings, the abandonment of the immense *atrios*, whose useless space welcomed only sparse populations (Gerhard, 1972, pp. 181–2; Kubler, 1948).

The demographic decline which struck the Indians and the confusion in the relation of forces that flowed from it thus contributed to check the blooming of an original culture, which was successfully integrating the Christian and European contribution with a native base and tradition. For it was a culture that was dying as it was coming to life:

> As of today [the last years of the century] in the most famous cities and *pueblos*, by a miracle there has not remained a single *principal* Indian or Indian of a certain rank, the palaces of the old lords are ruins or about to crumble, the houses of the plebeians are empty and dilapidated, the routes and roads are deserted, the churches empty on feast days.[51]

It is thus not the irreducibility of the cultures that were coming into contact that brought the defeat of the emerging syntheses. On the contrary, despite the 'traumas' of the conquest and the trial of colonization, we are surprised at the precocious apprenticeship in writing or the ability to record the new society with the brush. These reactions, this receptivity, show that communication and exchange were not only possible but flourished at the expense of sometimes subtle adjustments. To what point were they viable, to what extent could they function with two apparently irreconcilable ways of approaching the real and the person, and keep an equilibrium between two languages to draw an original synthesis? The question invites us to examine other contexts in which the native elite also faced an upheaval in its modes of expression under the imposition or influence of a monotheistic religion, coupled with external domination. The reactions of local cultures among the African peoples penetrated or touched by Islam and faced with an imported literacy come to mind. The originality of the Mexican experience stands out better: it enables us to renew the debate, substituting for the duality oral/written a more complex confrontation of the alphabet, the painted image and the oral, and beyond the preoccupations of the anthropologist and the historian, it illustrates the course of a culture which suddenly shifts from the image to writing, the reverse of what we can observe around us today. Nor shall we neglect to compare the reactions of the Mexican nobility with the behaviour of the Chinese won for Christianity, to measure the decisive importance of relations of force and to appreciate more fully the degree of malleability of Catholicism (Goody, 1968; Gernet, 1981).

Let us be content with emphasizing that the Spanish conquest, conceived in the largest sense, did not manifest itself exclusively in prohibitions, destructions, and abolitions. It had implications less spectacular, although as corrosive in the long term: latent, silent implications, that took the form of disqualification (of the oral), decontextualization (of pictographic language in relation to its usual references, or of elements of this language in relation to the whole that organized them), singularization, withdrawal of connotations from the field, or distancing. These inflections, these displacements, were not mind games or products of an abstract confrontation between great entities that for convenience we call cultures, but concrete outcomes of practices as diverse as the painting of glyphs, writing, map-drawing or plastic creation. By means of these practices the revolution of modes of expression and communication launched by the Spanish colonization took place. An incomplete, because too quickly stifled, revolution, the Mexican experience prospered so long as the equilibrium of forces favoured it. For this whole evolution must be explained in terms of social factors, epidemics and collective death: the decline and decimation of the old nobilities, social mobility, the fading of the 'empire of the mendicants', the rise of the *mestizos* and the whites. Moreover the 'paintings' did not omit references to the epidemics, or the sick and dead that they left, from the *Codex Telleriano-Remensis* to the *Códice Aubin* or the *Códice Sierra*. However, if the immediate social and economic effect of the slaughter of the Indian populations was quite perceptible (and relatively well known), it is still necessary to discover its impact on memories before observing the emergence of new cultural alternatives in other circles, as the indigenous nobility plunged into an interminable twilight.

2
Memories to Order

The originality of the forms that we have seen appearing in the indigenous world of sixteenth-century Mexico can hardly be dissociated from what must be called the 'modernity' of conquering Spain and that of the empire of Charles V. Even though there had been the Morisco precedent, we know that it was in New Spain that Church and State launched the colossal undertaking of subjecting sizeable populations to a 'civilization', to a uniform style of life; that there too practice imposed a precise definition of Christian marriage, or a pedagogy of confession on a large scale; that it was also there that the Crown precluded feudalism. Also astonishingly 'modern' were the encyclopaedic questionnaires conceived, rethought and worked out before being launched throughout the Iberian peninsula and upon the vastness of a barely known continent.

From 1578 to 1585, throughout the New Spain of the period, the *corregidores* and the *alcaldes mayores* convened the responsible officials of the Indian *pueblos*. For they had to complete a questionnaire developed by the chronicler and cosmographer of the king, Juan López de Velasco, in 1577. The undertaking was by no means new, since it was inspired by investigations and questionnaires prepared by Juan de Ovando y Godoy, who until his death in 1575 had set out to gather as much information as possible on the territories subject to the Crown. Questionnaires of 37 (1569), 200 (1570), and 135 (1573) questions were successively revised and finalized by the famous legislator. A similar survey had been carried out in Castile beginning in 1574. It produced the considerable mass of *Relaciones topográficas de los pueblos de España*. A printed questionnaire was then sent to New Spain in 1577, addressed to the viceroy, who transmitted it to the *corregidores* and *alcaldes mayores*. It was composed of 50 sections, themselves subdivided into several questions, which together tackled almost all aspects of the colonial world. Physical geography, toponymy, climate, agricultural and mineral resources, botany, languages, political history, population, diseases and business are some of the numerous themes touched on by these questions. The range alone testifies to the ambition of the project nurtured by the Council of the Indies and the cosmographer of the king. The undertaking was carried out to good effect, the *Relaciones* were sent to Spain, but they were never exploited: a fine example of the gulf separating the curiosity of the State from its capacity to 'process the data' that it had gathered.[1]

The surviving 168 *Relaciones* of New Spain focus on about 415 *pueblos*. They make up an exceptional corpus, even if it is incomplete. Some *Relaciones* were stillborn, others were destroyed, some are yet to be unearthed. A significant number of those that have reached us, in accordance with the instructions for the questionnaire, are accompanied by maps, many painted by Indians. Together they make up a practically inexhaustible body of material of considerable interest, only partly exploited thus far. Here we shall study a quite limited aspect: namely, the way the Indians, or more precisely the indigenous informants, described their own past in the light of the orientation of the survey. Before tackling the investigation, it is perhaps not superfluous to mention the flood of questions to which these informants were subjected. They had successively to give an account of the significance of the name of the *pueblo*, the circumstances of its discovery or its conquest; the physical characteristics of the land; the number of inhabitants and their variations; their living conditions and ways of life – *inclinaciones y manera de vivir*; the languages; the roads and distances; the circumstances and foundation date of the *pueblo*, the number of its first occupants; its site; its status and political regime in the prehispanic period, the tribute, the 'adorations and rituals and customs that they had, good or bad'; the forms of government, of war, the modifications of clothing, nourishment and physical condition; the healthiness of the region, the diseases that were rampant, the remedies to deal with them; the geography, fauna and flora, mines and quarries; trade, and so on. The list, as we note, is staggering. The answers are generally equally amazing. In other words, the investigators called for numbers, dates, facts, comparisons, interpretations, value judgements and objective comments. A considerable task, for which few Indians were prepared, complicated by the particular circumstances that the survey set up.

Far from arising from within the community or the lineage in the context of a teaching, festival, litigation on succession or even clandestine rituals, the indigenous answers were thus the result of external constraint, completely foreign to the environment and the group. Summoned by the *alcalde mayor*, the indigenous governors of the land, the *principales* and all the old men of the *pueblos* who came under his jurisdiction had the questionnaire explained to them before they made inquiries about all the necessary points with a view to 'confiding to their memory' as many answers as possible and producing a veracious declaration that would state the 'essential', that is, 'the *truth* of what all and each of them could know and understand, whether by *experience* or by hearsay'.[2] Communication of the information was thus the subject of a sometimes brutal constraint, and could not be dissociated from the groups involved. The investigating commissioners of this survey, like the intermediaries, belonged to the dominant fringes of indigenous society – we shall return to this point – or of colonial society. Thus, beyond the interpreter and the notary, the Indians spoke to the *corregidor*, the *alcalde mayor*, sometimes in the presence of a member of the regular or secular clergy who assisted or even participated in the investigation. It is obvious that the abundance and density of the data that were gathered depended on the relation of forces and the quality of the links built up between the Indian notables and the Spanish authorities, as well as on the presence or absence of a clerk sensitive to the musty smell of idolatry. To which were added personal factors: the time devoted to the survey, the curiosity shown by the investigators and the familiarity they had with indigenous matters. Naturally it would be possible to hold forth indefinitely on the trust-worthiness and the quality of the information collected in these conditions which, like most of the sources about indigenous worlds, quite obviously ran the customary or unexpected risks of social, linguistic and cultural communication, its misunderstandings and its approximations.

It seems that the specific circumstances of each survey had the greatest influence on the answers recorded and the extent of the reticence and omissions. There is nothing to indicate that the informants, officially Christian for some 40 years, *systematically* sought to remain silent on the question of idolatry. Even where, in certain regions of the bishopric of Oaxaca, recent memories abided of the campaigns of extirpation, the Indians described the origin of the sacrifices and the nature of their practices; which does not rule out more or less authoritative statements, depending on the context. On the other hand, it is more difficult to evaluate to what extent the Indians tried to dissimulate the nature of the resources and the number of men living in their region. We know that the fiscal burden depended directly on the number of declared tributaries for each *pueblo*. To some *Relaciones* was added a supplementary device that further complicates the analysis. Thus those of Texcoco and Tlaxcala were written by two *mestizo* historians well up on local traditions, Pomar and Muñoz Camargo. Despite the great interest of their work, I have preferred to set it aside, since a study of the acculturation of indigenous memories through a *mestizo* rereading mixed with historiographic and political ambitions presents too many pitfalls.[3]

Without claiming to have circumvented the obstacles of filtering and interference, it may even be possible to take advantage of them, on two conditions. First, to keep as an object of the study the inflections, indeed the distortions that the Indians imprinted on their words in answer to the Spanish requirements, instead of seeking to carry out systematic research in prehispanic material. The second condition, a corollary of the first, is to accept that the Spanish survey should not be reduced to a more or less apt set of questions and answers, but to remain aware that it set up confrontations so subtle and hidden that they escaped all the protagonists. A request for data which the indigenous people answered or did not, the survey at the same time imposed a conception of knowing which was perhaps not that favoured by the Indians. For example, for Indian informants, what could this twofold requirement that suddenly confronted them signify of going to the *essential* and of speaking the *truth*? Could the criteria of the statement be the same for colonizers and colonized? Did not everything depend rather on the manner in which each group perceived reality and evaluated the correctness and the meaning of a piece of information? We might equally wonder about the relevance that the Indians attributed to data that flowed from personal experience – the *espiriencia* – or transmitted from mouth to ear. Is that not to suppose and impose a conception of knowing and communicating that tends to appeal as much to the individual as to received tradition, whether painted or spoken?

But the survey did not stop there. It projected on to the Indian world an approach to society, politics, religion and economy; in other words, it imposed a cut-out of reality with its infrastructure, its presuppositions, its explicit and implicit logic, its tacit axioms, its unconscious organization. It forced all Indian informants to provide data examined closely under categories and associations that were not necessarily their own.[4] Moreover the process was not one way, since the Spanish investigators were forced not only to translate in the literal sense of the term, but also to interpret what the Indians wanted to say to them. Indeed, the essence of the undertaking rested on the shoulders of the informants. If the situation was not new, since it dated back to the first moments of contact, the survey of 1578–82 contrasted strongly with all earlier ones. For perhaps never had the Spanish required so systematic and encyclopaedic an exercise, since it extended to the whole of New Spain and tackled practically all fields of knowledge, from geography to economics, from demography to history, from religion to nutrition. For

the first time, all the Indian *pueblos* were invited to describe themselves
and to do so in the language of the rulers.

From this point of view the question is no longer, or not only, to
gauge the authenticity or incompleteness of the indigenous accounts, to
examine the impact of relations of power or the zeal of the servants of
the Crown. It raises more basic points. It concerns the conceptual
matrices that organized the information and the manner in which they
could alter it. We suspect that perception of time and relations to
the past were one of the domains in which, pressed by the Spanish
investigators, indigenous memories had to say '*lo más esencial y
verdadero*'. They did so between 1579 and 1582, from the valley of
Mexico to the mountains of Oaxaca, from the gulf of Mexico to the
shores of the Pacific. As in Spain some years before (1575), other
memories answered to practically the same rubrics, also concerned with
separating 'the true from the doubtful'.

The *Relaciones geográficas* have often been used as inspiration for
writing about the past of Mexican societies, for lack of other accounts
or to fill gaps in knowledge. However, there is nothing to indicate that
the Indians of the *Relaciones* perceived their past in the way the Spanish
of the sixteenth century conceived it or, *a fortiori*, as we claim to
apprehend it today. It is thus necessary at the same time to analyse the
contents and to study the organization and strengths and lapses of the
indigenous memory. From the valley of Mexico to the region of Oaxaca
or to Michoacán, oral tradition seems to have played a major role
everywhere in the looking back to which the Spanish survey gave rise. It
was the old people – *los antiguos viejos*, who seem to have been
confused most of the time with the local nobles and notables, the
principales – who excavated their memories to find something to answer
to the colonial authorities. Their disappearance was several times cited
to account for the amnesia or confusion and uncertainty of recollection
and knowledge. To these old people the sources attributed advanced
age: those of Ixtepejí, northeast of Oaxaca, were between 65 and 90.
The margin of error or approximation hardly matters. Let us rather
recall that the old people who at the time of the survey (1579–82) were
80 years old had been born before the Spanish conquest (1519) and had
thus been brought up in a prehispanic environment still free of any
European influence. These were the last witnesses of a bygone world,
who retained not only earlier information but also techniques that
ensured its preservation and transmission, whether it was a question of
learning the oral tradition, recollection, as practised by indigenous
societies, or study of the 'paintings'. We understand that their death
could affect the memory of the group as well as the means of preserving
and communicating it.[5]

Further, we know how closely orality was associated with observation of the 'paintings', and that the preservation of the whole of the information depended on their subtle interplay. Consultation of the 'paintings' was sometimes explicitly mentioned by the Indians who were questioned. Sometimes only the nature and the density of the accounts allow us to hypothesize their existence – an existence that implies not only the material preservation of the object but also that the ability to interpret it had been retained. And, we might add, to reproduce and even to elaborate new ones on the basis of old documents and more recent information, as suggested by the dates of production of the indigenous maps that still accompany quite a number of *Relaciones*. The report on Mexicalzingo even provides the name of one of these painters, Domingo Bonifacio, from whom the *corregidor* ordered the map of the *pueblo* in 1579. When these 'paintings' still existed, they established the memory of the foundation, the succession of *caciques*, the toponymy, the computation of time and the feast days, like the *Tira of Tepechpan* that the informants from that *pueblo* probably consulted. They 'showed bygone things' and were 'the memory of those to come'. It is impossible to establish – except for the maps – to what extent these documents were traditional in conception or if the gloss in Latin characters had already invaded them, which was probably often the case at the end of the century. Did the informants already have at their disposal texts in Latin writing that recorded local history in the form, for example, of annals? It is difficult to say, although we know at least that at Tepeaca, Mexicalzingo and Huichapan the Indians kept these records. It is true that if the Nahua (and even Otomí) *altiplano* is rich in documents of this kind, they are scarcer at Michoacán and practically nonexistent in the region of Oaxaca.[6] However that may be, the *Relaciones* remained terribly discreet on this subject, restricting themselves to revealing the diffusion of the signature, which was common practice among Indian governors, more irregular among the *principales* and *alcaldes* who served as informants, and with alluding here and there to schools and Indians who knew how to read and write.

As the sixteenth century ended, the supports for indigenous memory confronted the combined assaults of widespread death and deculturation: the death of informants who had memorized the 'words of the older people'; the loss of techniques of reading and making 'paintings'; the disappearance, finally, of these documents, lost, confiscated by the friars, destroyed by the Indians themselves, or neglected as they became indecipherable. But the situation was more critical still when local cultures had hardly developed pictographic language and it is probably to this handicap that we owe the poverty and rarity of the memories of Michoacán. Thus in the difficult and precarious conditions of the last decades of the century emerged memories completely different from what they might have been.

Could the many 'histories' collected from Michoacán to the region of Oaxaca be confused with an indigenous vision of the past and a factual dynamic? Beyond a doubt they were indigenous statements, even if clumsily written up by the Spanish *escribano*. But the questionnaire invited the Indians to recall their past in a fragmentary way and in a heavily linear perspective, without worrying about cyclical references that were still quite common in European societies of the sixteenth century. The informants were even intellectually constrained if they wished to offer the elements of a satisfactory answer, by which I mean intelligible for the interlocutors, who knew nothing of the mysteries of indigenous thought. The questions demanded of the *pueblos* that they go back to their origins, dating the year, recalling their political and military history until the Spanish conquest, and above all that they compare numerous aspects of the past of 'infidelity' or 'gentility' (paganism) with the Christian present of the colony. Subjected to the procrustean bed of an essentially linear history, the informants were led to extract from their past episodes that met the criteria of a survey that gave importance to indications of date, identity and quantity.

It is true that the old Nahua and no doubt other groups – the Mixtec, for example – knew and practised the register of unique facts when they had to mark in an unimpeachable manner the origin and justification of acquired or conquered rights, the borders of a territory or the distribution of *calpulli* in a region. But this factual and linear approach seems to have been subordinate to the return of cycles, since it ended by sustaining with its substance what, for lack of a better term, we call the 'myth'. The event was catalogued, interiorized and understood to the extent that it could be inserted in a pre-established matrix, in pre-existing schemata. The assimilation of the unforeseeable arrival of Cortés to the expected return of the god Quetzalcoatl offers a remarkably eloquent example. The computation of cycles (of the day, the 13-day period, of the month and the years) thus had uncontested primacy within a perception of time that we have glimpsed before. It culminated in the *xiuhmolpilli*, that is to say the period of 52 years at the end of which, having gone through all the names of years (which resulted from the combination of 13 numbers and 4 signs), it was believed that the universe could come to an end. As these cycles of 52 years followed each other without receiving identifying names, chronological pinpointing in the European manner becomes extremely difficult (López Austin, 1973, pp. 79–106).

On the other hand, the Spanish survey changed the meaning, the forms and the substance of indigenous recollection: the meaning, because it was not interested in an exegesis of this order; the forms, because it set up a situation of listening, of bringing the past up to date, in a quite unusual and artificial way; the substance, finally, because it set up the event as the single milestone of a trajectory leading to a colonial and Christian outcome. To respond to it, Indian informants had to outline a veritable historical construction, articulating a *past* and a *history* (more or less) in the sense of the representatives of the Crown. Starting from an indigenous date – which was not a date for the Europeans – they had to discover an equivalence with the Christian calendar. More precisely, they had to decide on a point of departure from which years elapsed would be counted and to discover how many 52-year cycles separated the date of the 'painting' from the present of the informants. So it was that at Tepeaca, southeast of Puebla, two foundation dates were successively produced.[7] The first, probably extracted from a 'painting', agreed with the old calendar: *Ce-Tecpatl*, 1-Silex. Made up of a number and a name, they allowed no chronological dating but at least gave an indication of position within a cycle of 52 years and of a series of 13 numbers and four names of years. They were thus devoid of relevance in the eyes of the Spaniards. The second date took the form of a count backwards: 'It was 313 years ago that this city was founded.' And this count, which started from the year of the survey (1580) made it possible to measure a period, but without ever coming up with the apparently absolute and universal form of dating that is familiar to us. The Indian reflection thus travelled part of the way down the road which separated it from European chronology without going so far as to produce a Christian date, since the lapse of time indicated – 313 years for Tepeaca – could have meaning only in relation to the precise time the survey was in progress. The process was the same at Chimalhuacan-Atenco (320 years), Coatepec (415 years), among the Otomí (of Tornacuxtla, 160 years; of Hueipoxtla, 360 years; or of Tezcatepec, 300 years), among the Nahua and the Totonac of Jonotla, some of whom even plunged much further into the past. An account from Ixtepejí exceptionally describes this process: 'There could be 9 or 10 ages or times, counting by ages of more than 100 years, such that there could be 900 years more or less, that three lords came out of the province of Yoloxonequila'. It was thus a calculation of the number of ages – here probably of 104 years, which would correspond to two indigenous cycles of 52 years – that corroborated the trip back through time and fixed the foundation date.[8]

It emerges that Nahua, Totonac or Zapotec and still others were fully capable of establishing a bridge between their computation of time and that of the Spanish, and of performing what was at once a conversion and a complete modification of the apprehension of the time and date of an event. For if it is obvious that the two systems were not irreducible, they none the less expressed radically different concerns, one putting emphasis on measurement, chronological pinpointing, while the other gave greater importance to the quality, the nature of the moment. 'Ce-Tecpatl, 1-Silex' did not refer to a past *century*, to a unique temporal segment, but to a type of year, to a range of influences felt or to other years with a similar name. And putting two 52-year cycles end to end at Ixtepejí to make up almost one of our centuries cannot make us forget that these two units – the cycle of 52 years and the century – emanated from quite dissimilar conceptions of time. This is not to mention that the two worlds diverged on a complementary level: while the Christian calendar was unique and had pretensions to universality, the indigenous computations were multiple, their point of departure and the initial year of the cycle of 52 years varying according to groups and domains. Instead of following the flux of a uniform chronology, some dynastic genealogies and histories cut off segments of time that each had their own coherence, duration and substance. Probably the uniqueness and universality of Christian dating were all the more disconcerting to the populations for being immediately perceptible.

The time that had elapsed between the foundation date and the year of the survey was also grasped in a colonial perspective when conceived as a succession of periods. For the Spaniards and the questionnaire, the conquest and especially Christianization must constitute the major break about which the recent and distant past would be organized. Everything implicitly and explicitly led the informants to think of their past according to this cleavage, which also took the form of a dichotomy – obvious, banal for the investigators and for us – between the *antes* (before) and the *ahora* (now). Thus these Indians were forced to ask themselves about changes in eating, clothing and sanitary habits that appeared to have accompanied the colonization and hence to come up with an account that was based on a potential opposition between the time of the 'gentility' and the society after the conquest, as if it went without saying that an essential and permanent break had taken place.

Also it was necessary for the Indians to take the road that the Spaniards were opening for them more or less implicitly. But as usual indigenous reactions were astonishingly diverse and complex. Some grasped the pole that was offered them out of simple convenience. It was in fact convenient to consign to an already distant past, more than 50 years old, all that could have to do with idolatry, with 'rituals and ceremonies that they practised and did of old in the time of the infidelity', which made it possible at the same time to dismiss the somewhat thorny question of the retention of paganism. Thus the spotless present of the Christianization followed upon the long past time of the idols, as if the formulation of the Spanish question, centred on the old days, and the prudence of the informants converged quite involuntarily to compare the two periods. Does this mean that the Indians adopted as such a chronological articulation based on the Spanish conquest and that they accorded a crucial resonance to this episode? Paradoxically enough, on this section their answers remain vague and allusive. In that respect the account of Tamazula, which recalled the irruption of an 'other world', was rather an exception. It is true too that the Indians were not invited to give their feelings about the conquest, but simply to furnish the name of the Spaniard who had discovered or subjected the land. When the conquest was mentioned, it was generally in the course of a chronology, 'at the time the Spanish arrived to conquer this land'. Similarly, the evangelization appeared only here and there, such as on the baptism of a *cacique*. It is none the less true that the informants did not dwell on these events, as they did on others, moreover without the Spaniards having suggested them. It is probable that, while the Spanish conquest made an undeniable break, it did not rule out older breaks just as brutal and perhaps perceived as just as decisive. For the Indians did not neglect to introduce in the account of their past sequences completely foreign to the diachronic and binary scheme postulated by the Spanish. Rather than restricting themselves to partitioning their past between a *before* and an *after* the conquest, the informants of some *pueblos* showed themselves able to recall distant and completely differentiated phases of which the Spanish could not have had the least idea. In so doing, they outlined, without any cyclical aspect, a linear history composed of a chain of more or less unlike periods: the autochthonous origin (Zapotec, Mixtec) or the distant migration (Nahua); the foundation of the *pueblo*, the succession of *caciques*; the campaigns and invasions; the cultural transformations in the largest sense of the term. Periods followed each other a little like the different plans of the landscape, and three-dimensionality invaded indigenous maps at the end of the sixteenth century, as if the dissemination of historical depth accompanied the adoption of depth of field. Of course, this was so only in the best of cases.

Highly complex processes seemed to invigorate this effort to produce the past. First, there was an implicit recourse to basic prehispanic schemata: I am thinking, for example, of the theme of the original migration from Chicomoztoc, the primordial cave, the 'Place of the Seven Caverns', common to a number of Nahua accounts (Duverger, 1983; López Austin, 1973, pp. 56, 80 and *passim*); the theme of the chthonic origin at Oaxaca;[9] the tale of the meeting of a wondrous

animal, a future protective divinity, on the site of the *pueblo*, or the
introduction of agriculture, or accession to complex ritual forms. But
other measures are mixed in, born, it appears, of the need to respond
to the Spanish question. These could, to varying degrees, combine a
refusal to answer, expurgation of the data, a political and ideological
manipulation of facts, and removal of the censorship once practised by
a powerful neighbour, a touchy metropolis or the emissaries of the
Triple Alliance. These measures were conscious and calculated.

But they mask still other factors, more difficult to detect. Gathered
about the *alcalde mayor* or the *corregidor*, questioned by interpreters or
charged with passing on the Spanish questions to their communities, the
informants were in a way obliged to search their memories and to
extract from them facts abstracted from their cyclical context, cut
off from their insertion into pre-established and recurrent sequences,
converted, reduced to unique events. On this point the *Relaciones* are
quite obviously silent. How otherwise could they have registered a
process of pruning that completely escaped the Spaniards, who were
incapable of conceiving that the past could be evoked and history could
be thought out in ways other than theirs. This decontextualization
of information was a corollary of, and even completely indissociable
from, the return to categories that answered to the criteria of the
Spanish authorities. It was the case, among others, of questions on the
'ceremonies and rituals' established in specific areas, cut off from their
social, political and economic extensions. It was also true of those
foundations attributed to *individual* initiatives, although they actually
reflected cosmogonic schemata or repeated archetypal episodes. The
Indians were thus induced to select from their memory material that
could fit into the blanks of the Spanish questionnaire, at the expense of
original configurations that once gave them their meaning. Let us add
however that, far from remaining passive, some informants knew how
to turn aside and exploit these riddles to highlight the distant past,
without idols, with a view to diverting attention from the presence of an
embarrassing paganism. In other words, if it imposed on indigenous
memories acrobatics and often impoverishing exercises, the Spanish
survey neither paralysed nor stifled them.

The difficulty arises elsewhere. The most recent past witnessed a
dramatic break whose intensity surpassed the multiple impact of the
invasions of the Triple Alliance or even the Spanish conquest: a break
experienced everywhere, whose unprecedented proportions hardly gave
rise to the recurrent matrices of a cyclical history, unlike the conquests
that followed each other on Mexican soil. More than the 'coming of
the Marquis [Cortés]', this catastrophe that defied comprehension,
interpretation and comparison gave the Indians the feeling of having

entered upon a shattering era, having nothing in common with what they had lived through until then. Modern estimates with their dry figures show how right they were: from a population of perhaps 25.2 million inhabitants, central Mexico had fallen in 1532 to 16.8 million, then to 6.3 million in 1548, before reaching 2.6 million in 1568. In 1585 the country numbered no more than 1.9 million indigenous inhabitants and yet the nadir was far from being reached. Still more crucial, on the eve of the exercise of the *Relaciones*, indigenous populations had been decimated by an epidemic of *cocoliztli*, the most fatal of the century, whose multiple symptoms still hide its exact nature. Their new conditions of life together with the absence of systems of defence adapted to the diseases introduced by the Europeans explain this incredible mortality (Cook and Borah, 1971–9, and Borah and Cook, 1960; Florescano and Malvido, 1982).

From reading the indigenous accounts, epidemic death appears most often to have been experienced as an unprecedented phenomenon. Although the Indian populations had known the ravages of epidemics, memory of them was blurred and they had perhaps not taken on the generalized character and greater frequency of those that accompanied and followed the Spanish conquest. Confronted with new or recrudescent illnesses such as smallpox, measles, and typhoid fever, the accounts could only denounce the impotence of the *curanderos* – when death had spared them – and of the old pharmacopoeia: 'against diarrhoea they had taken many herbs but to absolutely no effect', 'no kind of remedy, herb or purge can deliver us from this so violent danger'.[10]

Consciousness of the extent of the catastrophe breaks through the statements made by the informants to the Spanish. The Indians of Chimalhuacan-Atenco admitted having gone from 8000 to almost none, those of Coatepec-Chales from 10,000 warriors to 700 tributaries and 400 children, mostly orphans; Cuzcatlán, on the borders of the bishoprics of Puebla and Oaxaca, collapsed from 40,000 to 900 tributaries; Xalapa, in the present State of Veracruz, from 30,000 to 639 tributaries. The Mixtec *pueblo* of Mitlantongo lost three-quarters of its population in the epidemics and the province of Chinantla counted no more than 1000 tributaries, while before the conquest it claimed to have dressed ranks of 100,000 warriors. Whatever the margin of approximation, panic and sometimes calculation that taints these numbers, they reveal in their dryness the view of a population in the course of witnessing its own disappearance. Acknowledgement is given on all sides: 'once there were masses of people', 'on the contrary, the region was full of people'. Once, according to the Nahua of Coatepec, the Indians lived to be old, up to '80, 90, 100, 110 and 120 years, and others even more', 'plagues were rare', while for 40 years sicknesses and epidemics 'that had not existed at that time' proliferated, decimating the *pueblos*. At Coatepec, at Chimalhuacan-Atenco, at Chicualoapan, at Tepoztlán, the morbid inventory was established of those 'thousand kinds of illnesses': measles or *matlalçagua*, 'the spot on the side', *cocoliztli*, typhoid fever or *matlaltotonque*, sleeping sickness, mumps, haemorrhoids, smallpox, haemorrhages.[11]

But the questionnaire also asked the Indians to interpret the phenomenon and to explain the changes that affected their physical condition. Now this query came at the end of a long question that dealt with forms of government, customs of war, eating patterns, clothing practices and their transformations: 'How were they governed? Against whom did they make war and fight? The clothes and outfits that they wore and the ones they wear now? The foods they lived on before and those they live on now? *And* if they were in better or worse health before than now and the reason they gave for it?' As it was phrased, the question did not necessarily imply links or relations of cause and effect between the first part (government, war, clothing, food) and the second (health). It seems, on the contrary, to be content with juxtaposing subjects with no connection between them (politics and clothing, for example). But by a strange phenomenon of shift in meaning and collision, a number of Indian informants sought to answer the last question by relating it to all the preceding subjects and giving the conjunction 'and' (*y*) a value that it probably did not have.

That it was not always done proves, if need be, that we owe more to indigenous reflection than to the wording of the question the setting up of a link between mortality and the evolution of ways of life. In many places ignorance and disarray prevailed over any attempt at interpretation. In amnesiac Chiconautla, north of Mexico, 'the natives let themselves die like animals without bringing succour'. At Tepexpan, not far from Teotihuacán, 'a little before the arival [of Cortés], about a year before, they caught a kind of smallpox that took over their whole body and many died of it and since then they have diseases without respite without understanding why'. The replies were the same at Totolapan in the present State of Morelos, among the Nahua and the Tepehua of Huejutla in Huastec, among the Mazatec of Ixcapuzalco in Guerrero, at Michoacán, or again among the Chontal of Toltepec. Other Indians seem to have taken refuge in an idealized vision of a past without ills at Tezcatepec or at Teloloapan also in Guerrero. The Indians of Oaxaca made similar responses. Although the Zapotec from Ixtepejí must have been quite conscious of a considerable drop in longevity and of having lived in better health, 'despite all the difficulties that they endured', they admitted understanding nothing about what was hitting them. The same incomprehension was found among the Indians of Teotitlán del

Valle, among the Mixtec of Tilantongo or of Nochixtlán, Acatlán or Chila.[12]

Overcoming their disarray, other informants tried to provide answers by reverting to the questions that preceded the one dealing with health. These answers are far from uniform. Each in its way revealed the attempt of a society striving to account for the unprecedented, to conceive the unique. Some approaches seem to take the line of a traditional explanation. At Coatepec, it was recalled that the death of young people, in its possibly exceptional nature, used once to have to be interpreted. 'It was seen as a miracle [agüero], it was marvelled at, and it was said that they must have committed some sin to die young'. In other words, premature deaths were attributed to the breaking of a prohibition that one might imagine was of a ritual and sexual order. The observation of the Nahua informants of Coatepec is taken up by those of San Juan Tututla, near Tetela in the Sierra de Puebla. In both cases death struck the individual who had become *tetzahuitl*, a creature from whom emanated noxious forces and who inspired fear, disquiet and scandal. If one reviews the sequel to the response of Coatepec, we find an apology for the old order, which banished idleness and limited the consumption of alcohol, and an awareness of living through a generalized breakdown of traditional standards, although without going so far as to link this state of things to mortality. These Indians thus put side by side, but without linking them, the notion that premature death is the sanction for a transgression, the loss of rules of life, and the demographic catastrophe. How were they to impose this old interpretation that concerned individual and exceptional deaths on collective, incessant death? The neighbouring *pueblo* of Chicoloapan did not venture along this road either, restricting itself to adding to the list of lost and relinquished standards the late marriage of the old days (at 30 years of age for men and 25 for women). 'Appalled' by the fall in population, the Chontal of Coatepec in Guerrero limited themselves to comparing the two ways of life, the old and the new, without making it the key to mortality. In the same region the Tepuztec of Utatlán contented themselves with pointing to the paradox of a past existence that associated precarious conditions of life with a longevity and robustness far greater than in the present but, they claimed, without understanding the reasons for it.

In contrast, the old men and notables of Chimalhuacan-Atenco took the step of denouncing what they considered to be the 'cause', 'the great idleness of the natives, who have become lazy, and the great vice of their drunken binges. For although they have lands to work, they do not want to put them to good use. That is why they die as soon as they catch the slightest illness'. We hear the same reasoning in the region of

Teotihuacán, or towards the south in the *pueblos* of the region of Cuernavaca or the State of Guerrero.[13]

Whether the Indians directly related mortality to changes in their conditions of life, or whether they sketched only prudent parallels, nevertheless in quite a number of *Relaciones* they produced an apparently paradoxical analysis, since it exalted the trying life of bygone days and denounced the idleness of the present as if the colonial exploitation had no weight in their eyes. The picture of a trying and laborious existence that the informants called to mind seems to have sought less to express an exhausting task than a cluster of activities, regulated, organized by the traditional authority and even including war. It implied resistance and being accustomed to effort, acquired through constant and regulated training: according to the Otomí of Jilotzingo, 'they never stopped but exercised themselves in many things, which made them agile'. This characteristic rhythm of the old days was compared with the *regalo*, the 'easy and convenient life' that prevailed from then on, and which substituted for this intense regime an unbearable idleness and laziness, coupled with a clear quantitative and qualitative improvement in the food the Indians ate, 'cooked bread, chicken, beef and mutton'. Others added the transformation of sleeping arrangements (raised beds) and of clothing ('Spanish shirts that they were made to wear'), indeed the giving up of sanitary practices such as those twice-daily baths taken at Tepoztlán or at midnight at Ocopetlayuca. Another paradox: the colonial peace was perceived as an additional factor in the decline of indigenous populations because it put an end to the periodical conflicts and thus to the military activities that kept the Indians busy.[14]

The analysis is surprising. Austerity, frugality and incessant work would thus appear to be linked to a healthier, longer life, while the 'greater convenience' of conditions of life under Spanish domination ended up in this stupefying slaughter. One might at first think of seeing in this evaluation of the colonial regime the imprint of a Spanish investigator, inclined to minimize the exploitation to which the Indians were subjected and to present his administration to the Crown in a flattering light. If there is no doubt that the investigator often imposed on the colonial period stereotyped formulae ('the dearth of activity and the great comfort') and that he could not but welcome favourably the comments that gave a hard and severe picture of prehispanic times, if it is clear that he even sometimes gave free reign to a profound contempt towards the dominated populations, he was far from systematically substituting himself for those he was questioning. First because the reasoning was rather uncomfortable, which led to making these 'benefits' of material acculturation and the Spanish regime the origin of a demographic rout that filled the Spaniards as much as the Indians with trepidation. Also because the Indian interpretation was often too circumstantial to have been articulated or fabricated by the colonial administration which, for example, had no reason to suspect the lowering of the age of marriage – how could they have known? – as a cause or the cause of indigenous mortality!

In fact, in the mixture of Indian statements and Spanish transcription, it is no doubt necessary to distinguish two quite dissimilar languages. On the one hand, the European view, moralizing and sometimes 'racist', which deplored the laziness, the idleness, the vice supposed to prevail in New Spain. On the other hand the Indian analysis, less inclined on the whole to moral evaluation in the European sense of the term, but rather to a more comprehensive judgement concerned with acculturation as a whole or, to repeat the explanation of the informants of Ocopetlayuca, to 'the fact of having changed customs'. What can appear in isolation as a notable improvement of dwellings, clothes, food (and which perhaps was for the Indians), was above all grasped by the informants as the breakdown of a way of life, the upheaval of an organization, a totality of practices and habits – the *costumbres* – as diverse as war, the age of marriage, or grooming. Let us take the case of drunkenness. The Spanish deplored its diffusion and the contemptible impression it gave. The Indians themselves dwelled on a more profound aspect, more sociological in a way, denouncing the giving up of social rules and the rigorous repression that governed, without forbidding, the prehispanic consumption of alcohol, whether it was a case of temporary prohibitions (festivals) or proscriptions tied to a social class or an age group. Norms were observed – 'the law that existed among them' – and those who infringed them were punished, if necessary with the death penalty. Other domains met with similar scrutiny: the consumption of food that in colonial times ceased in part to mark distinctions of rank and status, or again the matrimonial practices that increasingly escaped the traditional regulations.[15] It was thus often – the *Relaciones* of Oaxaca on the whole corroborate this feeling[16] – the disappearance of a continuous tension, a demanding regulation, that seemed to preoccupy the informants as if the plagues that repeatedly struck proceeded from them.

The explanation of mortality by the collapse of standards constituted a particularly original approach, even if Nahua thought already established relations between cosmic, social harmony and the state of equilibrium assured by physical health. The approach was new to the extent that, constrained to purge references to prehispanic 'idolatry', they confined themselves to the domain of social and material life and depended on a reconstruction of the old way of life that was stereotyped and often even idealized: the standard would have ruled without excep-

tion, all of an individual's activities would have been guided by it. That
was a reconstruction, an extrapolation, that carefully avoided touching
the chapter of rituals and beliefs as well as raising questions about
the colonial regime. Some communities, however, were not satisfied
with this analysis (which I should almost like to characterize as pre-
positivist!) and ventured forth on more conformist tracks or sometimes
more dangerous ones.

Although a simpler interpretation compelled recognition, it was,
quite surprisingly, rather exceptional. It sufficed for the informants to
take the ecclesiastical line, which made epidemics the divine punishment
for idolatry. That is what the Chontal, the Nahua and the Itzuca of
Teloloapan did, judging that their physical decrepitude was accounted
for by the 'sins of their ancestors', or the Mazahua of Temazcaltepec,
who invoked 'the will of God', the Tarasc of Pátzcuaro or again the
Zapotec of Amatlán. But this interpretation was rare, and it even seems
sometimes to have been plastered over the more indigenous theme of
the collapse of the standards of old.[17]

There remains the inexpressible, the 'anticolonial' and sometimes
even anti-Christian explanation, certainly in a minority, but at least as
frequent as the Christian interpretation that the Indians appear to have
internalized relatively little. We find it in lands as distant as the Sierra
de Puebla (Tetela), the Guerrero of Taxco and Chilapa, or the heart
of the valley of Mexico. The informants of Mexicalzingo, south of
the capital, did not hesitate to implicate the growth of hard work
(más trabajo) and in a slightly more veiled way Christian monogamy.
Zumpango incriminated the weight of colonial exploitation and Taxco
complained of the deportation of Indian manpower. It was the same
story at Tepeaca and at Tetela in the Sierra de Puebla, whose
encomendero Pedro de Escobar was notably taken to task. The Zapotec
of Tehuantepec denounced the 'congregation', in other words, the
enforced round-up of populations in the county town or cabecera. At
Epazoyucan and Zempoala, it was 'personal services', bearing tamemes,
work in the mines and poor nourishment that were said to have increased mortality, and even, at Yuriria in Michoacán, the construction
of the Augustinian monastery. Throughout these accounts, the term
trabajo seems to have been taken in its European and colonial sense of
oppressive task and no longer, as at Coatepec, as regulated and significant activity. Moreover, we sometimes suspect the beneficent presence
of a corregidor or friar who shared the sorrows of the Indians enough
to join their voices. In the region of Oaxaca, the Mixtec and Zapotec of
Guajolotitlán also recalled that in the time of Moctezuma the tribute
was lighter and they were then exempt from being employed. Depending on the pueblos the denunciation of exploitation could take a virulent

tone or be limited to certain glimpses in the course of a sentence, such as the mention of those Chinantec who died extracting gold from their rivers or after their deportation to cold lands.[18] But it was on the decimated coast of the Pacific that the Nahua Indians dared a frontal attack on Christianization: 'they were separated from their gods, who used to indicate what they should do to get well when they fell ill; and since afterwards they became Christians their gods disappeared; it was then that they began to die'. The Zapotec of Ocelotepec were moved to act in 1577, after an epidemic that took 1200 victims, reverting to their old sacrifices so that their gods would put an end to the sickness.[19] These two accounts reveal that half a century after the conquest, Indians could and still dared to apply a traditional response to an illness. We know, for example, that the Nahua understood the origin of illness as the breaking of prohibitions, in the event of certain signs of the calendar, the baleful action of sorcerers and the intervention of the gods. These same gods could cure the ills that they sent. That the Indians were able to hold to this blasphemous reasoning in the presence of officials of the Crown says a good deal about the entrenchment of this interpretation, the superficiality of the Christianization and, especially, the profound disarray of the local populations. It is quite obviously impossible to know how far what the Indians of Huatulco said out loud reflected the thoughts of other groups who had taken refuge in silence, the Christian explanation or the apparently – just apparently – more neutral invocation of the upheaval in ways of life. Again, it was a question of an interpretation of impotence in confronting sickness. The informants of Coatlán brought to bear a more precise version of the aetiology of the plague: 'Since the day the Spaniards disembarked, Our Lord began to punish them . . . the first sickness they had was brought about by fear at the arrival of the *teutl* – which means the people from heaven – for that gave rise to considerable fear and dismay; from which came to them this sickness.'[20] We recognize the importance that the Indians ascribed, and still do, to fear, *susto*, *espanto*, in the origin of sickness (Aguirre Beltrán, 1973, pp. 109, 224; López Austin, 1980, II, p. 246). The mention of 'Our Lord' may indicate the introduction of Christianized reasoning, but the absence of a precise motive – the punishment of sins for example – suggests rather a veiled allusion to the wrath of an ancient divinity. However that may be, the tale of Coatlán, just as that of Huatulco and the clandestine practices of Ocelotepec, flows from a region difficult to penetrate, long agitated, shaken in 1544–7 by the messianic revolts of Tetiquipa. Their cross-checking attests that still in 1580 all the elements of a traditional interpretation of sickness and death were preserved south of the bishopric of Oaxaca.

But perhaps we should ascribe less importance to the longevity –

commonplace after all – of a prehispanic system of interpretation than to its censure in a colonial and Christian world, and to the related need to have recourse to new explanations of the demographic catastrophe. It was essential to account for its *singularity* and, possibly, to compare it to a comprehensive evaluation of the transformation of societies. It is, we believe, by the acknowledgement of this singularity, doubly inscribed in the epidemic death and the establishment of radically different ways of life, that a linear perception of a time without return and without recurrence could infiltrate indigenous consciousness, at least that of the informants who, to answer the questionnaire, had to show 'what they understand and clarify and communicate to others'. Such was the singularity of a present which often left them without a voice, unless it was to outline an interpretation of a cultural and material order that could seem in many respects more 'modern' and more sophisticated than the providentialist reasoning that the Church gave out. We would thus have in the constraining and completely unusual context of a Spanish survey – and involuntarily aroused by it – the original manifestation of thoughts confronted with intellectual exigencies and mental schemata based on a quite different apprehension of time, the event, and reality. This was an invitation to make up a past reduced to a linear chain of singular facts separated from its cyclical horizons.

Was all that remained of indigenous time only a flattened temporality, reduced to the pure and simple expression of a linear succession? Far from it. In the margins of this past cast in the bureaucratic mould there appear, surreptitiously, other glimpses and perceptions of a time that seemed to be reiterative and predetermined. It was the question about 'rituals and ceremonies' that paradoxically provided an opportunity, although the Spanish had by no means sought to explore a temporality that dealt neither with the immediate scope of the survey nor even with their thought structures. To answer this question, some Indians mentioned their old calendars, thereby revealing that these were neither all lost nor all forgotten. On the contrary, informants sometimes referred to them with such remarkable freedom that they could well have exposed themselves to the accusation of idolatry. Starting from the 18-month calendar, the *xiuhmolpilli* or *xiuhpohualli*, informants from Teotihuacán reported that they had 18 feast days a year, one every 20 days. Informants from around Acolman described the rituals to which these festivals gave rise with a wealth of detail otherwise found only at Teotitlán del Camino. Linked to the vigesimal system that was omnipresent in Mesoamerica, the 20-day cycle left a deep impression in memories: it was found among the Nahua of Cuetzala in Guerrero, among the Otomí of Ajacuba or Tecpatepec. The Chontal of Oztoman in Guerrero explained that 'they counted the months from 20 to 20 days and every month they had a feast day . . . Then they followed a 360-day year'. In the region of Oaxaca the Mixtec of Tilantongo recalled having celebrated 10 great annual feast days, the Chinantec four, while the Cuicatec of Atatlahuca also had a year of 360 days at the end of which they sacrificed to their principal god. Longer rhythms were indicated here and there: the service of seven years fulfilled by the priests of Atatlahuca; the custom of having one's hair cropped every four years among the Mixtec of Mitlantongo; the collective fasts every eight years at Texcoco, etc. The regular recurrence of periods of fasting marked the passing of life so strongly that numerous informants mentioned them, from Guerrero to the mountains of Oaxaca, from the valley of Mexico to Michoacán, distinguishing periods of 3, 4, 9, 40, 80 or 140 days during which the Indians refrained from consuming certain products or from having sexual relations. The day also had immutable scansions: punctuated by six sacrifices among the Mixtec of Tilantongo or by two ritual baths at Tepoztlán, while the night at Epazoyucan, near Zempoala, resounded three times to the call of a seashell. Finally, birth, marriage and death opened periods of varying duration whose obligations the Indians of Tepoztlán and Ixcateopan described to the Spanish investigators.[21]

Other informants dwelled on the periodicity of tribute and sometimes even that of war. Every 80 days, Acolman handed over the tribute that it owed to its lord; Chila followed a similar rhythm; while Taxco sent the products that México-Tenochtitlán demanded from the *pueblo* every 20 days and once a year. Elsewhere this withdrawal of local bounty took place 3 or 10 times a year. It is true that in the region of Oaxaca the periodicity of 80 days was maintained until the year 1555. Cycles of tribute related to work cycles. To alter these regular rhythms resulted in disorganizing daily activities, creating dead times. From this arose the apparently paradoxical feeling of prehispanic overwork and colonial idleness, although one should not identify all the cycles as a happy equilibrium, troubled or progressively undone by the conquest. The Indians of Ucila observed that the Mexica domination had also signified the imposition of ritual obligations (a fast of 140 days and two sacrifices a year), as if the power of the conqueror had gone as far as subjecting this Chinantec population to its own cycles.[22]

Let us not try to make more of these fragments of cycles that the Spanish editors collected indiscriminately. They belonged to a comprehensive conception of temporality that orchestrated all human activities, which reaches us only through the accident of irremediably shattered and profoundly impoverished responses. What the Indians could really rescue from it in 1578–82 depended, as we know, as much on the preservation of painted calendars as on the survival of specialists in the *tonalpohualli*, the divinatory calendar. Chontal, Mazatec, Tepuztec or Cuitlatec accounts mentioned them. The Nahua and Otomí of Epazoyucan, southeast of Pachuca, described the activities of their 'herbalists', who, 'thanks to the calculations they made and thanks to their paintings interpreted every day and said to each the day of his birth, the difficulties that he would encounter, whether he was going to become rich or poor, or if he was going to die in unhappiness. They called them *tonalpouhques*'. Among the Tepuztec of Utatlán, 'those who were born each received the name of days'. Elsewhere too they had not forgotten that divinatory practices paralleled the great moments of political life, telling the fate of a war, the outcome of a sickness or the appropriateness of a marriage. But, they hastened to add, 'those who knew it are dead'. Which was contrary to the statement of the Spanish commissioner, who explained that if the Indians said little more, 'it was because they had been punished for it'.[23]

Whatever practices were still in effect at the time of the *Relaciones*, it is beyond a doubt that the Indians still had in mind the diurnal and nocturnal cycles, the sequences of 13 and 20 days and the annual periodicities that structured the traditional temporality and conferred on it a depth, a substance, for they governed, it will be recalled, the arrival and the combination of influences that came down from the heavens or rose from nether worlds. We have already mentioned its persistence towards this date, emphasizing the significance represented by the preservation of this custom. It went far beyond the realm of religious confrontation, the narrow field of rituals and beliefs, and that is no doubt the reason for its deep entrenchment. Rare were the friars who showed themselves sensitive to the profound specificity of Indian time and were scandalized by it like Bernardino de Sahagún, who about 1578–80, thus in the same period, recorded this indigenous dictum: 'What used to be done a long time ago and is done no longer will be done again. It will thus be once again as it was in the past. Those who live today will live again, they will be anew', to add, 'this proposition is Plato's and it is the devil who taught it here for it is wrong, completely false and contrary to the faith!'[24]

It was however this conception which implicitly showed through the accounts that aimed less to locate a moment on a chronological scale than to penetrate its political, religious, social meaning, as if Indian societies – in the manner of the Balinese described by Clifford Geertz (1973, pp. 391–4) – had sought to decipher, file and describe the various manifestations of reality more than to measure a time or to locate an event. That is what the indigenous date (*Ce-Tecpatl*) suggests about the foundation of Tepeaca. We can understand better how the

Indians – who admitted and claimed to be Christians – could have continued to cherish a cyclical perception of time if we recall that not only did it escape the sermons of the Spanish clergy (who generally contented themselves with the visible manifestations of paganism) but also that the Church had imposed a liturgical calendar that itself was cyclical, just to confuse things further. Nevertheless to keep its meaning and its functions, this temporality required the availability of technicians who could well have disappeared, and the constraints of society and colonial life, of which the survey is an example, pressured the Indians to establish correspondences between their approach and the Spanish chronology.

Invisible to the Spaniards, another time was concealed in running water, inside mountains, in the depths of forests. Where the investigators saw just an anodyne reading of the landscape, the Indians revealed fleeting glimpses that went considerably beyond toponymy or geography. From this misunderstanding a body of data was conceived that will be sought in vain under the chapter of rituals and ceremonies. The indigenous perception of landscape was not at all innocent, even though it escaped the vigilance of the Spaniards. Not only did the Indians 'believe that all high mountains and elevated sierras participated ... in divinity', but they considered that lakes, caves and mountains were favoured points of contact between the world of the gods and the terrestrial surface. They were the accesses linking the ever-present time of the creations and the gods to that of humans, the passages that divine powers, men and shamans could take, whose 'perplexity when they regained the terrestrial surface at a time different from what they thought they would find was often mentioned'.[25] Sites of evolution from one time to another, objects by nature indestructible, unlike temples, pictures and 'paintings', secret landmarks and lairs of the gods, these elements of the landscape showed and preserved in their immutability an ancient relationship to weather and the environment. It can perhaps be better understood now why the introduction of western European landscape conventions in indigenous maps could, depending on the case, signify something quite different from decorative choice and 'progress towards realism', but rather conceal the inclusion of another immanent reality in the woods and mountains.

Nestling at the foot of the mountains in the warm and luminous mists of the north of the State of Morelos, Tepoztlán perfectly illustrates this sacred geography of places, this inertia of landscapes. The *pueblo* took its name from the god Ometochtli Tepuztecatl, who was revered there; to the east the *estancia* of Santa María Magdalena was designated Amatlán 'because once it had an idol that they adored and called Amatecatl, which obeyed the devil Tepuztlán'. The rocks that encircled the village still held the memory of the sacrifices of children and of the gods who occupied them: Cuahutepeque, the 'Mountain of the Eagle'; Chicomocelotl, the 'Mountain of the Seven Tigers, for so the demon called it'; Tepuztecatl, 'because of the demon who had his headquarters there'; Tlahuiltepeque, 'where they went to make sacrifices and fire, whence its name of Mountain of Light'. 'These names', observed the Indians, 'came from those of the idols who were in these mountains, where once they climbed to celebrate their sacrifices': the Mountain of the Wind, the Garden of the Monkey, the Mountain of the Precious Stones, the Mountain of the Crow, the House of the Night.[26] Sometimes it was a whole region that kept its divine significance: the Otomí region of the north of the valley of Mexico continued to be designated with the term Teotlalpan, for 'long deserted by men, it was once dedicated to the gods'; and above all the land of the origins, the caverns of Chicomoztoc, from which the Nahua groups emerged on to the surface of the Earth. There was nothing mythical or legendary there for informants who saw it as, on the contrary, an essential aspect of their own reality. Sometimes the allusion concerned only a local feature and hardly revealed the way in which the Indians apprehended their environment: the apparition of a miraculous snake on a mountain (Coatepec-Chalco and Coatepec of Guerrero), a ball game (Taxco), a sacrificial stone (Tetela del Río), an idol hanging or suspended on a hook (Pilcaya), a mountain of light that illuminated the whole area (Tequisistlán), lagoons for offerings, caves dedicated to the wind god (Texcaltitlán), a tree of the gods 'at the foot of which once appeared numerous demons'.[27] At Coatepec-Chalco, even more than at Tepoztlán, the mountains still reverberated with happenings supposed to belong to a past gone for ever. A bare mountain of average appearance, Tonaltepec, the 'Mountain of the Sun', concealed on its flank a 'dark, deep and disquieting' cave where the Indians once began to sacrifice to the demon while their priests consulted a rock god who answered them. On the higher sierra of Quetzalcoatl the famous divinity showed itself once in the form of a serpent with green feathers, 'passing from one sierra to another ... and making loud hissing sounds and cries that spread terror'. The informants of Teotihuacán could not but describe the grandiose site where rose and still rise the 'temples of the moon, of the sun Tonacateuctli and of the Lord of Hell', city of the gods where in the past the *pueblos* of the surroundings and the Mexica sovereign came to lay their offerings, divine ruins that dominated the Great Mountain of the Mother, Tenan. Finally, Michoacán and the region of Oaxaca could lengthen the list of examples.[28]

Like a vast indelible canvas, landscape and toponymy kept alive the memory of an inescapable presence that reflected the indigenous commentaries, referring to the profound nature of places as well as to the significance of their names. For if toponymy everywhere concealed cosmogony, this was because they could not be dissociated. For a good number of Indians, a mountain or a spring could not be just the physical and ephemeral setting of a bad superstitious story, but possessed an incommensurably perceptible, affective, even sonorous density. They were still imprinted with this disquieting presence which spread fear, with this *tetzahuitl* so tied to the native perception of the divinity – without mentioning the theophanies of which the several Coatepec preserved the traces and rehearsed the memory. It will be understood that, starting from distinct approaches to the environment and reality, each pursued his aims; and that the past according to the Spanish could often have been the present of the Indians – which goes without saying, since it formed part of the same immutable reality. Their accounts moreover did not make a distinction between 'myth' and historicity. Furthermore, they sometimes kept silent about too overtly embarrassing aspects. However, even pruned, the narrative retained its coherence, setting in the same register 'legends' and politics. At Chimalhuacan-Atenco, at Coatepec-Chalco or at Alahuistlán, old people reported the intervention of the protective numen without a rhetorical or corrective precaution of any kind: 'Teotonoc appeared to them quite frequently in human form. He spoke and conversed with them, he told them what they ought to do'. They even showed the traces left by the god on the mountain, the mark imprinted on the rock by the divine rod.[29]

It would be another form of imprecise expression to reduce landscape to a setting humming with sounds, saturated with colours and presences. It is a microcosm where the Indian fitted in, defined himself, where life took its meaning, an oriented universe that the missionaries and representatives of the king shattered when they insisted on moving populations and massing them on other sites. One need only come back to the Indian maps of the end of the sixteenth century to rediscover in a glyph-landscape, in a horizon line, this presence that words are powerless to suggest.

Rather than delving about in the *Relaciones* to try to get to know prehispanic societies better, it was probably of some value to linger over the images that the Indians retained some 60 years after the Spanish conquest, at the risk of getting lost in the labyrinth of cultures and the accidents of memory that configure a land as fascinating as it is chaotic and heterogeneous. This pluralistic vision is none the less ruled by ubiquitous recurrent constraints: the informants were plunged into the unaccustomed and exotic context of a European survey; they were obliged to produce for the whole extent of New Spain information that could be adapted to a linear and decontextualized perception of their

history; they were led by the logic of the survey to make an abstraction
of any cyclical dimension, or rather to isolate it as such, confining
it to narrow spheres (the rituals) newly circumscribed by European
categories; finally they were led to reflect on the whole of past indigenous society and by that very exercise to distance themselves from
it. There is nothing close to a spontaneous movement, or even the more
confident and more personal relations that obtained in surveys carried
out by the Franciscan friars. The informants found themselves confronted with local representatives of the Spanish authorities and these
representatives only sporadically shared the curiosity of the friars.
Confronted with an analytical grid of time and society that for the
Spaniards was in the order of evidence, the informants reacted in
different ways. Not all responded to it. But when they did, it was often
by preserving a considerable margin of manoeuvre, whose many manifestations we have been able to follow, whether they took the form of
political censure or an original periodization.

Did the experience of the questionnaire have a real impact on Indian
memories, throwing into confusion or dislocating their conception of
time and their vision of the past? This would no doubt attribute a
disproportionate significance to a too brief encounter and to often
superficial exchanges. Or rather did the exercise simply precipitate or
deepen an acculturation whose degrees, it goes without saying, varied
according to the groups and regions? That seems rather to have been
the case, particularly in the regions most exposed to Hispanization: the
valley of Mexico, the region of Puebla, Pátzcuaro to Michoacán, the
mining areas. Nevertheless, during these surveys informants of all ethnic
groups without any exception could familiarize themselves with the
conception of the past dear to the investigators of the Crown. They had
to provide a 'truthful' account, that is to say, one that conformed to the
criteria of the Spanish administration, woven from remarkable events,
constructed on a break between the past of the 'gentility' and the
Christian present. Everywhere the Indians – and not only those who
had been interrogated by ecclesiastics curious about 'antiquities' –
discovered the right way to speak of the past, to make 'history' of it in
the Spanish sense of the term, that is to say, to furnish a version
receivable by the colonial authorities, a 'flat', 'one-dimensional' reading,
where time was no more than a succession of facts and space a banal
landscape and a toponymy.

On the degradation of indigenous memories, made perceptible by the
hints provided in the answers and more often by their silences, it is
easier to agree. In the margin of rich memories which are declined – for
the Spanish commissioners and for us – according to the three prongs of
the linear, the cyclical and the perennial, how many confused and

especially inconsistent accounts are not all to be attributed to a rushed administrator or to a refusal to give information? The loss and destruction of the 'paintings', the stifling of the pictographic tradition, the slight diffusion of alphabetical writing – perceptible, among others, in the region of Oaxaca and at Michoacán – the disappearance of witnesses, and above all the decimation of human memories, appear to have strongly affected the snapshot quality that the surviving *Relaciones* provide. It seems that in the last decades of the sixteenth century began the threefold eradication of categories, media and men, as well as a complete destructuring of the perception of time or a recomposition of the past in the indigenous consciousness.

Many, unequal, diverse to the point of contradiction, these memories still shared a common feature that marks its seal on all these constructions. The schematic images that they offer us, the choices that they make, the accents that they emphasize, are ruled less by the accident of reminiscences than by the social origin of the informants. Recruited among what remained of the nobility, among the *caciques* and *principales* and sometimes the direct descendants of the prehispanic lords, Nahua informants built up by successive touches a picture of ordered societies where power was indisputable and unquestioned. The political independence once enjoyed by these *pueblos*, the education, the rigidity of justice and laws, the respect and absolute obedience due to the *caciques*, work conceived as a social imperative, made up, according to them, a remarkably stable whole where each remained in his place. But the situation had indeed changed and more than once the nostalgic bitterness of the informant shows through when he describes the etiquette of the old days, when he compares the memory of the *caciques* with their sumptuous finery of feathers that called to mind 'tigers, lions or birds' to the *macehuales* covered with a simple loincloth and a cape of *henequén*. The alimentary prohibitions, now overturned by new foods and the confusion of hierarchies, contributed once to separate those who ought to be set apart, since 'at the time of their gentility not one common Indian could eat anything but *tamales* and a little *atole* and no chicken', while 'the lords used to eat cocks and hens [in fact turkey hens and cocks] as well as game and human flesh'. For it will not be forgotten that, apart from its ritual and 'dietetic' functions, cannibalism served as a social marker, since the plebeians did not have the right to eat the flesh of the sacrificed nor thus to absorb the divine force that it harboured. By abolishing it and introducing the consumption of pork, beef and mutton, the Spaniards substituted for the traditional socioreligious distinctions criteria of an economic order, which were applied entirely differently.[30]

The indigenous thinking on authority was thus not at all innocent.

Whether among the Otomí, or in Chontal and Tepuztec Guerrero, we hear the same vindication of the old order, of the prohibitions and strict supervision under which the individual lived, just as one did not forgo recalling that the old funerary rituals, now banished, signified the distance between the Chontal, Tepuztec and Mazatec commoner and the elite.[31] It is true that in the Oaxaca region, the past was idealized far less. It is perhaps not immaterial that one of the *pueblos* most involved in exalting the old society was the Nahua domain of Teotitlán del Camino. The informants even ventured partially to rehabilitate the sacerdotal environment, indicating that the priests of old 'lived like saints', after having mentioned their mortifications, their chastity and their sobriety, as if Nahua cultures and their zones of influence had lived in an obsession with a well-ordered existence that other Zapotec or Mixtec *pueblos* seem to have escaped. These accounts suggest political organizations less complex or at least more flexible than those of the Nahua. Let us add that the frequent intervention of an external domination – that of Teozapotlán at Macuilxóchitl, for example – probably contributed to nuance or smother the nostalgia of the informants. The memories of Oaxaca were often memories of dependence, as satellites of more powerful neighbours. It is possible too that some accounts emanated from new sectors that had broken with the old ruling circles.[32]

Beyond these regional diversities, whose examples could be multiplied, let us say that these dependent memories were confused with those of the once hegemonic *pueblos*, that they mixed together the knowledge of the last witnesses of bygone days with that of the Indians who were the most exposed to acculturation, as allusion to their signature reveals. They thus reflected locally the emergence and the diffusion of a culture whose genesis we have followed and whose impact, dynamism and limits throughout New Spain can perhaps be better appreciated. To these notables of the end of the sixteenth century fell the task of reconciling two conceptions of time: that of the Spanish administration, with its chronological landmarks, its periodization, its sense of event, its criteria and its requirements; and that of the indigenous tradition, more concerned with the parallelism of facts than with an analysis of their succession and for which, with the passage of human time, the strata of events were superimposed, 'enhancing a blurred image that wise and ordered men succeeded in focusing better with each revolution' (López Austin, 1973, p. 97). Between these two approaches there existed meeting points none the less: Spanish liturgical time was cyclical in its way, while Nahua tradition not only knew a minor linearity but still more cherished the idea that a cycle was inscribed in a temporality irremediably doomed to degeneration and disappearance: the Fifth Sun was perishable, and it was the last. Let us add the most unforeseen effects of ubiquitous death, which made populations familiar with the singular and unprecedented. The inability to take account of the unhappiness of the time, the loss and relinquishment of divinatory techniques and thus of the means of reading the present and foreseeing the future, must have urged an awareness of a temporality that, without really being grasped as irreversible, was now experienced as aberrant and unbearable, as this excruciating account of the year 1582 suggests:

Many Indians hang themselves, others let themselves die of hunger, others poison themselves with herbs; there are mothers who kill the children to whom they have just given birth, saying that they are doing it to spare them the trials that they are undergoing.[33]

3

The Primordial Titles or the Passion for Writing

Is it possible to pursue the analysis a century later, and even to adjust it, giving up a panoramic view in favour of a closer study? No doubt, provided that one bears in mind the origin and limits of the only available sources, in the absence of the surveys carried out during the seventeenth century. In the accounts recorded in the *Relaciones geográficas*, Indian leaders of the end of the sixteenth century were constrained to review what they had retained in their memories. They often represented a socially threatened environment, a nobility plunged into demographic torment but which preserved direct, often human links with the pre-conquest past. A century later, when the population had ceased to decline, new groups in the small or medium-sized *pueblos* were occupied with recording other memories, which appear to have assimilated part of the lesson spread by the *Relaciones*. To explore them, we have available sources that are noteworthy in two ways, for their conception as well as for the richness of their contents. Probably since the nineteenth century, we have been accustomed to call them the *Títulos primordiales* or 'Primordial Titles' (Gibson, 1964, pp. 271–87 and 1975, pp. 320–1; Lockhart, 1982). Written in the indigenous language in a community or a *pueblo*, these anonymous documents record the borders of a territory, urging the local Indians to defend them with determination. They are in some respects like a family of documents frequently produced during the colonial period and even these days, namely title deeds. In the event, they were more or less thick files composed of deeds of gift or sale, grants of jurisdiction, expert reports made in the field – the *vistas de ojo* – and intended to define the limits of lands, contradictory interrogatories, and finally certificates of confirmation, sanctioning taking possession. The collection, recorded and authenticated by a Spanish notary, was meticulously preserved by the interested parties, invoked and produced in case of dispute and litigation. The authentic Titles have considerable interest for the study of indigenous property but to the extent that they conform to the Spanish norm, they leave little leeway for the intervention of the Indians or the expression of a vision different from that of the representatives of the Crown. That is why I shall not dwell upon them, bearing in mind that their presence constantly confronted the Indians with what the Spanish administration judged to be formally and physically admissible. The *Títulos primordiales* can be said to be fakes, in that their composition is as a rule much later than the events that they claim to establish and especially later than the dates that they bear. They are fakes in the way they report historically incorrect events – some even made up out of whole cloth – fakes entrusted with replacing authentic Titles that might never have existed or could have disappeared, whether destroyed, mislaid, sold or neglected by communities and *pueblos* that had become unable to decipher documents originally written in Spanish in the course of the sixteenth century. But quite obviously, the incomparable value of the Titles resides in the 'forgery' itself, since they show in a relatively autonomous indigenous context a considerable creative effort combined with a perceptible mastery of writing. Thus one should from the outset avoid confusing our view with that of the Spanish, emphasizing that what is *fake* according to the criteria of historiography and colonial law can express a different apprehension of the past, a singular grasp of the event and of history. It is, among other things, what distinguishes the *Titulos* from the *falsos cronicones* that flourished in Spain at the same period, making their analysis terribly difficult. For they raise problems of chronology which in most instances can only be approximate; innumerable difficulties of reading due to disconcerting palaeography or arbitrary written forms and transcriptions, especially because of the use of Indian languages – Nahuatl, Zapotec – in a way different from their classical form, and the bad state of preservation and dispersal of the documents.[1] The few examples that I have used cannot do justice to the exceptional richness of this source, as only a large collective study could.

Our Titles seem to have been worked out and drawn up in the second half of the seventeenth century. Their written form, the dates of their presentation in legal proceedings, the mastery of writing that they exhibit, the nature of their contents and their references, the errors that show up and the comparison with documents of the sixteenth century and the beginning of the seventeenth century suggest this approximate date. But it is no less important to point out that in the eighteenth century and sometimes up to the end of the nineteenth century they constituted the memory of the *pueblo*. They thus correspond to a crystallizing of memory, and to the outcome of a process set in motion by the Spanish conquest. Most of the Titles cited here are of Nahua origin. Two come from the valley of Toluca: San Bartolomé Capulhuac and San Martín Ocoyoacac, from *cabeceras* some 10 kilometres apart. The remainder lead us south and southeast of the valley of Mexico, to the neighbourhood of Mixquic, Chalco and Amecameca. Cuijingo, Zoyatzingo and San Miguel Atlautla describe a triangle southwest of Amecameca; Cuacuauzentlalpan also belongs to this zone; Santiago Sula is located further north between Chalco and Tlalmanalco, not far from Los Reyes; to the west, San Nicolás Tetelco occupies the immediate outskirts of Mixquic, San Gregorio Acapulco those of Xochimilco and Santa Marta those of Milpa Alta. Let us add the *pueblo* of Santo Tomás, to the southwest, on the mountain of Ajusco. Finally, removed from this southern group, more to the northeast near Texcoco, is located the *pueblo* of Tetzcotzinco. Physically these pieces take up one or several dozen folios. They may be accompanied by drawings or even maps.[2]

'Whoever you are . . . if you know how to read and write, you will discern the reasons of the elders that are inscribed here' (Santa Marta). The Titles insisted obstinately on the crucial importance that they attached to writing, which they even went so far as to make a categorical imperative: 'I order that this writing be made . . . I order that this be inscribed and written on this paper'. This was so for several reasons. First of all, a piece of information had to be recorded and transmitted so as to make up a memory, 'so that you are not ignorant of what happened'. This piece of information, it is obvious, was intended to protect the interests of the group, to 'defend those of the *pueblo*' (Sula), 'to serve as a shield and example of the way you come to find yourselves now, fully surrounded with a wall' (Santa Marta), 'to be able to know how to speak and answer to defend your lands' (Cuijingo). Writing was thus clearly conceived as the form, the model of discourse to hold, the procedure to be followed in case of litigation before the tribunals of the Crown. We understand from this that these papers could have taken on almost sacred importance, that they were the 'royal papers to preserve' at Santa Marta, 'the paper written by God' at Atlautla, to the point that their conservation constituted a crucial task entrusted to certain members of the community: the *guardapapeles*, who were sometimes designated by name. These most precious 'papers' thus formed part of the patrimony of the community in the same way as territory, and the Indians dreaded lending them to the Spaniards as much as letting land to them. The value accorded to writing matched the respect that surrounded the 'paintings' before and after the conquest. Beyond the vital concern with preserving a title deed at all costs, one discovers that they deliberately linked it to an ancient tradition, as is shown by the care taken to underline its antiquity: 'This writing is not new nor made yesterday...because it was done an immemorial time ago' (Cuijingo).

The Spanish easily spotted the naive trick of a document that proclaimed its own antiquity. Here we detect the affirmation of a kind of timelessness that placed that Titles in a distant past as easily as in a recent past or an immediate present. Memory and source of information, instrument of defence in the service of the community, the 'paper' had to be protected by secrecy. Its communication to the Spanish was thus forbidden. Only the highest authorities were fit to know its contents, only the 'famous people of Mexico', 'the great king' would read its translation. Dedicated to proving the authenticity of acquired rights, recalling privileges granted, the Titles were thus addressed at the same time to the community and to the masters of New Spain.[3] In effect, in the second half of the seventeenth century, modest indigenous communities handled writing with an acute sense of its many uses, assigning to it the preservation, transmission and demonstration of information. And, of course, its manipulation. Measuring the weight of the instrument that they had appropriated and fashioned, they made of it a highly valued object, whose prestige merged with that of the old 'paintings'.

Before examining prehispanic or indigenous sources, it is appropriate to take the Titles for what they claim to be: documents like those drawn up by the colonial administration. It is indisputable that the authors of the Titles were familiar with the most common forms of colonial writing. Their mastery of writing leads us to see them as the local Indian employees who preserved, read and disseminated the instruments emanating from the colonial authorities, and indeed in certain cases took part directly in their composition. It is revealing that the Titles of Sula were followed by authentic deeds sanctioning purchases of lands made by the local Indians, three *cartas de venta* or *de concierto* dated 1593, a 'petition' addressed by the Indians to the judge-governor, an 'order' of the latter, a 'transfer of ownership' carried out by the *alguacil mayor* in the presence of the *escribano de república*. There is a whole collection of formulae, dates, an accumulation of signatures, lists of witnesses, a terminology that employs the administrative and legalistic language that inspired the Titles of Sula and of other *pueblos*. Everything points to an attempt to give the document a date, including constant references to the colonial authorities, recourse to a judicial vocabulary, and this acknowledgement at Cuijingo, which could not be more explicit: 'I give you the form to be able to know how to speak and answer'. Administrative rhetoric, the model of writing, was taken as a means of defence. The Indians took it over as they had appropriated writing, to ensure the protection of their territory.

Another type of colonial writing circulated in Indian country in the seventeenth century, which the Indians limited themselves to reading and above all listening to: that Christian word spoken by the parish priests and their Indian *fiscales* in sermons, prayers and masses. In the Titles it took a sizeable place in the form of the invocation to the Trinity that open them, or this short prayer that precedes the *Mersed de Zoyatzinco*: 'Oh my Lord and God, for you have given us light and we enjoy the clarity of the stars that are the creations of the Divine majesty of God, Lord of the whole world . . .' Other Christian formulae close other Titles. It even happened that recourse to Christian language and discourse played an intimate role in the conception of the text and in the train of thought, in the fashion of this meditation on death provided by Sula: 'And if God left us the example of his death, even if he is dead, he is not dead as God, he is dead because he had our human flesh; and so it is that our ancestors, even though they are dead, never died, they shall revive on the Day of Judgement. So all of us shall revive'. The Christian theme of resurrection served at a given point to support the affirmation of the continuity and everlastingness of the *pueblo* in the person of its oldest founders.

Let us add a particular kind of document that belongs to administrative procedure as well as to the realm of spirituality: the will, with which the Indians were promptly familiarized. The Titles of San Bartolomé Capulhuac were presented as a succession of wills quite different from the traditional form, but which retained several clauses from them and especially the participation of the narrator in the first person. The choice of testamentary model personalizes the discourse, in apparently adding to it a rare touch of subjectivity and feeling:

> Now I have already established what belongs to the saints and what I have promised before Our Lord God, in weeping melancholy tears when I saw what was happening to me, since there was no one, and I was alone, in pain but happy . . . (Sula, fo. 20r°)

However, let us refrain from generalizing. In other pieces the speaker retains his anonymity, and even energetically insists on it.[4] Such was the paradox of the Titles, which presented themselves as the expression of a collective voice and sought to give it a name, to *affix* a signature, constrained as they were to *identify* a tradition to make it acceptable to the Spanish.

To compare only the Indian Titles with documents written by the

Crown and the Church would box us into a problematic of reproduction and falsification, even of distortion, to use a term that may appear more neutral. In this field, as in many others, the Indians were more than the skilful or clumsy recipients of the products of colonial domination. They had their own resources, whose inventory I shall attempt to draw up. The Titles were presented in the form of oral narratives, speeches, or more tangentially as dialogues between several protagonists, some of whom could have been Spanish. Even if the old people were sometimes questioned, interrogated, and taken as witnesses, the speech was invariably addressed to future generations designated by stereotyped formulae, periodically inserted in the course of the tale. They were 'those who begin to stand, those who walk on all fours . . . , those who lag behind . . . , those who are beginning to turn onto their stomachs . . . , those of the stomach who are not yet born . . .' (Atlautla). These were not the only formulae nor the only pictures decorating the Titles. One could cite many many others.

These speeches often took the form of warnings, advice, or protests. They articulated principles of conduct for the use of the notables and nobles of old, exalted the respect due to the word of the elders, regulated the exercise of justice and power, and threatened the downgrading of those who did not know how to merit the obedience of the *macehuales*. Several texts also contained apparently premonitory exhortations, strongly counselling the Indians against keeping company with the Spanish, who sooner or later would steal their lands and their Titles. These give us poignant denunciations of the perils of acculturation:

> By keeping company with those who wear their hats pulled down on their heads and their swords under their arms [the Spaniards], by joining them and eating what they eat, whoever also goes on horseback will be lost, for these people seek to take away his lands . . . Do not allow your sons to listen to the advice of the Spanish, for they will try by trickery to take away their lands, they will bind them with kindness, they will give them what they eat. The natives will see it as a gift. But when they wake up, the Spanish will already have added up the bill for all that they had given them to eat and the money that they had provided them and, in this way, they will take their papers; and when they regain their forces, they will find themselves shorn of their lands. (Cuijingo)

The 'premonitory' exhortation, located in an ill-defined past, only reflected the practices that the authors of the Titles could have observed directly and even suffered from. To articulate this plea, they assumed anew the tone of a standardized oral tradition and even a genre whose importance we have seen in the prehispanic period, the *huehuehtlahtolli*, the 'ancient words', whose metaphorical style and rhetoric break through. Other passages – the appearance of the miraculous quail of Sula or the story of the water demon – have more about them of narration (*tlaquetzalli*) or of the 'tale of ancient things'. Among the Titles that the Indians of the *pueblo* of Santo Tomás Ajusco produced in 1710, there is one dated 4 February 1531 that astonishes by the virulence with which it attacks the Spanish conquest. The tone has an unequalled harshness and despair: the intensity of emotion, the attachment to the old gods – which leads to Tezcatlipoca being spoken of as 'the veritable and true god' – the recall of the ancestors' prophecies and the fatal fulfilment of the 'ancient words', all combine to make this text the equal of the famous *cantares* of defeat, and the anti-Christian imprecations attributed to the *cacique* of Texcoco or the subversive statements of the Indians pursued by the Inquisition of Zumárraga in the course of the 1530s. But we also find explicitly formulated in it the policy of constrained accommodation that I mentioned:

I have decided to set up a sanctuary where we shall place the new god that the Castilians have brought us. They want us to adore him. What should we do, my sons? We must be baptised, give ourselves up to the men of Castile to see if in this way they will spare us.

It is probable that this exceptional text was composed after 1531, towards the middle of the sixteenth century, if we accept the date (1551) suggested by the Nahuatl version and several other indications. None the less, we do not know how the Christianized Indians of the end of the seventeenth century read or heard it. It is not impossible – we have seen examples in the Oaxaca region – that the antiquity of the text gave it all its value, independently of its after all embarrassing contents if produced, as was done, before the Crown tribunals. These few examples reveal that the Titles drew upon the indigenous oral tradition of forms, recipes and formulae on which they depended in part. But it is not to be ruled out that some elements of this tradition had been transcribed earlier and that they had therefore remained only a rigid memory: as was probably the case of the song of lament of Santo Tomás Ajusco – which raises the still more complex question of written sources.

It is likely that the Titles were not the first alphabetical texts drawn up in the *pueblos*. Given the contents of the information that they record, and the diffusion of writing in the sixteenth century, it is hard to imagine that they proceeded directly from the oral tradition or were composed entirely on the basis of authentic deeds preserved by the communities. One thinks immediately of the Annals that numerous *pueblos* began to draw up in the second half of the sixteenth century. We would still have to find traces of them in the Titles that have reached us. Several texts present similarities here and there that suggest the existence of a common source, or rather of a common heritage on which they might have drawn. In respect of the Spanish conquest, the Titles of Atlautla, those of Santa Marta and the Annals of San Gregorio Acapulco contain close enough details and observations about the beginnings of the conquest, the battles of Mexico and Tlatelolco, the duration and the date of the hostilities.[5] We are comparing the Annals of San Gregorio with these two texts intentionally, since they were integrated in the Titles of the *pueblo*. The Annals of San Gregorio, whose relations with the *Códice Aubin* and the Annals of Tlatelolco have been stressed, constitute a catalogue of events that mixes in episodes of general interest – the arrival of Zumárraga (1529), the striking of the first silver coinage (1537), the execution of the *cacique* of Texcoco (1539) – with regional or local data. They allow us to surmise that a common written report was circulating in the sixteenth century in the *pueblos* of the valley of Mexico, and that this memory began perhaps to weaken, at least in this form, at the brink of the seventeenth century. That is so with our Annals, which were interrupted in 1606 after having covered, rather badly, the last two decades of the sixteenth century. It will be noted that from 1580 they were hardly sensitive to any but natural catastrophes and had totally left the field of politics proper. There was a frequent discontinuity of the indigenous memory probably corresponding to the cumulative effects of the demographic crisis and the social decline of the Indian nobility that traditionally kept up appearances.[6] But we can also see it as a gap, open to the development of another memory. In fact, the Titles did not take over from the Annals, even if they were undoubtedly inspired by them, drawing on their material. Thus they permitted themselves great liberties with dating and chronology in the sense that we understand and practise them. The Titles of Zoyatzingo, for example, signalled the year of the events that they described in the margin of the text, with the most surprising dates (1945, 1947, 1005, etc.). These dates were accompanied by an extreme contraction of horizons. Let us compare the Titles of San Gregorio Acapulco with the Annals that precede them. The authors of these Titles focused almost exclusively on events related to the history of the *pueblo* – the demarcation of borders, the choice of patron saint – and it was the same with other Titles. In a general way, even though the form of the Annals was more or less respected, the internal organization of events, the choice and succession of dates leave us perplexed to say the least. It would thus appear (but this is just a hypothesis) that the authors of the Titles used the old Annals only to recall an event with major repercussions – the Spanish conquest – and to recall its date, as if they did not know what to do with the other material that must have appeared to them without interest and relevance in the context of a strictly local 'history' of the territory.

Apart from the indigenous Annals, we cannot dismiss the existence of models that would have guided the composition and drafting of the Titles far more directly. These were rather like models that would have circulated widely and been recopied and plundered by numerous *pueblos*. At least that is what is suggested by a reading of the Titles of Atlautla, Santa Marta and San Gregorio. The three documents describe in similar terms a period of troubles and civil war in the course of which the Indians appear to have established themselves on their lands before receiving *mercedes* from the Crown, before the institution of 'congregations' and the formal establishment of the *pueblos*. The analogies of structure and contents cannot be fortuitous; but this does not mean that there must have been passive reproduction of a pre-existing text. On the contrary, the exploitation of this written material gave rise each time to more or less extensive revisions. It is revealing that these encounters occurred in places as far removed as Atlautla, south of Amecameca, and Ocoyoacac[7] in the valley of Toluca, a distance of about 80 kilometres as the crow flies and much more by the paths that crossed the mountains and forests that separated them. They reveal, like other sources to which we shall return, that in the course of the seventeenth century writings circulated, were recopied, were exchanged in the indigenous world of the *altiplano*, texts that could have been local and regional Annals, authentic or fabricated Titles, or transcriptions of the oral tradition. And why not 'paintings'?

At first sight the Titles present themselves as entirely written documents, without links to the old 'paintings'. A less superficial analysis quickly refutes this impression. Some Titles (San Francisco Cuacuauzentlalpan, Santa María Nativitas Tetzcotzinco) were visibly inspired by pictographic documents, from which they appear to have more or less skilfully extracted maps or genealogies. But without neglecting these indications, perhaps it suffices to stay with the Titles themselves. It appears that many of them were 'illustrated'; and that their images sometimes carried information that the writing did not take up or at least did not comment on expressly. This explains the perplexity of the interpreters of the *Audiencia*, confronted with drawings unaccompanied by a written counterpart in the indigenous language.

Several types of representation can be distinguished easily. Some lead straight to the Christianized pictographs when, for example, figures of saints or the drawing of a church designate the names of the *pueblos*.[8]

Others recall prehispanic images, like scenes where the old people of the *pueblo* and the representatives of neighbouring localities face each other.[9] In still others we see the right hand of the viceroy encircled by an alphabetical inscription spread out on four sides of the sheet, appearing quite freely inspired by European engravings.[10] The same diversity appears in styles. If the saints of Ocoyoacac are just reproductions or interpretations of Christian iconography, other representations are more disconcerting. In fact the line of the human body, the profile heads, the interaction of conventions and the use of space testify to undeniable autochthonous relations. It is particularly perceptible in a last type of representation that comes from Cuijingo. In one (Plate 12), the Spanish interpreter thought he recognized the delineation of the descendants of the conquerors of the *pueblo*, proclaiming their possession of the territory under oath. In the other (Plate 13), he identified eight *caciques* who gave their names to the borders and boundary stones of the territory.[11] The rectangular format of the two sheets governs the overall distribution of the figures. Inside these rectangles a kind of St Andrew's cross appears, with five horizontal bands defining the subgroups. In each case, the centre of the rectangle and of the composition is occupied by a noteworthy element: the church of Cuijingo, a date, a cross. A constant concern with balance and symmetry seems to prevail over the obvious clumsiness of line. Everything leads us to believe that we are looking at indigenous maps, whose placement on the page continues to be inspired by prehispanic cartography. The figures of one (Plate 13) are related to localities or neighbouring *pueblos* that correspond to the borders of the territory and follow each other on the page, with one exception, in the order of the route and the enumeration set out in the written text. In the other, four figures appear on foot, each associated with a neighbouring *pueblo*, as if it was a question of locating Cuijingo in a very summary fashion in relation to neighbouring territories (Tenango, Xochitepec) (Plate 12). If it is true that the space is Christianized to the extent that it is centred on the church, one cannot but point out the extraordinary 'archaism' of the conception, or more precisely the fidelity to a precolumbian representation of space, based on the diagram and a succession of places, indifferent to the landscape and the consideration of real distances. This is a space itself basically conceived as the distribution of four planes about a centre, in accordance with what had been established by traditional Nahua thought (López Austin, 1980, I, p. 65). These two 'maps' differ considerably from those drawn up at the end of the sixteenth century for the Spanish administration in that they express space in an older style, with a minimum of concessions. As the Titles are first and above all documents drawn up in and for communities, it is probable that these maps reflect a less acculturated (although later) indigenous perception and even that they suggest indirectly what Nahua 'cartography' had been before the conquest.

It is still necessary to agree on the meaning of the term with which we designate them. These 'maps' are more than geographical devices. The most schematic is closer to a symbolic figuration of the *pueblo* in the 'sworn' statement of its borders, as is revealed by the words spoken by the figures: 'my demarcation / here is my *pueblo* / here are my borders' (Plate 12). The second, if it offers the essential locations in relation to the borders, none the less retains the value of a comprehensive sign that expresses, exalts and visually ratifies the indigenous ascendancy over the community's space (Plate 13). In turn, this map probably constitutes the condensation of a more complex document mentioned and commented on elsewhere by the interpreter, but today disappeared or lost. A 'figure' in it 'pointed to' the name of each spot; 'paintings' – an eagle, mountains, a cross, an eagle with mountains, a mount crowned with a bird and a nopal, etc. – designated the inscribed borders, while the neighbouring *pueblos* appeared in the form of chapels and churches; finally other 'signals' marked the roads. In that this map also showed the communication roads and *pueblos* of the region, it attained a greater degree of precision than that of the two preceding documents. But to the extent that we can judge, depending on the perplexity of the interpreter, it obeyed the same canons. In other words, these three documents would each correspond to a different degree of abstraction and schematization, without failing to echo a prehispanic apprehension of space.

Can we say as much of the forms of expression that accompany them? Alphabetical writing occupies a considerable place, since it serves to record the names of figures, the localities, the *pueblos* of the neighbourhood, the acts and even the dates. The same was true of the large map if we believe the description of the interpreter. But all of them also welcomed 'figures', that is to say pictographs that are still quite detectable on the two preserved works. They have an onomastical or topographical value: A serpent (*coatl*) and a hummingbird (*huitzil*) are drawn behind the head of Clemente *Huitzil* Mizcoatl, a shield (*chimal*) appears behind that of Miguel Te*chimal* (Plate 13), etc. The most customary ideograms were added, the volutes of speech blossoming into flowers, footprints marking movement or communication roads, beside signs just as familiar, introduced by the colonization, the church, the cross. Reduced to the congruent portion, scribbled more than drawn, and never painted, despite the term *pintura* that designates them, constrained to share expression with writing, the glyphs seem to pursue the retreat that we have seen them begin in the sixteenth century;

but without disappearing, or ceasing to integrate themselves in compositions of prehispanic inspiration. On the contrary, these documents convey a movement opposed to that which we have detected in the second half of the sixteenth century. While the glyph of that period was preserved almost intact, but isolated in an already Europeanized space, almost a century later the 'maps' of the Titles are scattered signs of debased line in a traditional context.

This reversal is actually not a reversal. This time it is probably a question of productions from inside the Indian group, which emanated from sectors less directly exposed to Spanish demands than were the indigenous nobility of the sixteenth century. Rather than a paradoxical and regressive evolution, I would see the preservation in more modest circles of a tradition of native inspiration, oriented towards the *internal* transmission, copying and reinterpretation of prehispanic pieces. That in no way rules out that there, as elsewhere, the glyphic repertory was progressively curtailed, the lines debased and the colours lost, and that the sketch map in the Spanish manner inspired the quickly traced line. I shall maintain that the preservation of a traditional representation of space can also be explained, or explained much better, by deep-seated conditioning linked to the cultural structuring of perception, rather than by a fragile mastery of knowledge and a technique. Observation of the drawing of the human figure invites analogous considerations. At Cuijingo, figures are represented in profile like the 'paintings' of old. However, the features are all carefully individualized. Look at the shape of the nose, the drawing of the eye, the fullness of the beard. Similar European influence characterizes the costume of the figures on foot, dressed in the Spanish manner, whose bodies are seen in three-quarters view, still or in movement. In the two documents from Cuijingo, the representation of the human figure is thus undeniably composite (Plates 12, 13). It is obvious that in moving towards a greater personalization, in piling up borrowings, the Indians sketched a new language, devoid of or cut off from a part of its old conventions: colour, continuous line, stereotyped stylizations. But the emphasis on the head, the breaking down of the body into independent parts, the dominance of the profile, remain traditional. The overall structuring thus again points to prehispanic models. It denotes a perception similar to that which associates the impoverishment of the glyph with the maintenance of an indigenous approach to space.

Still, one has to make distinctions depending on the Title and the *pueblo*: some only rough out the bodies of the figures, while others are broadly inspired by Christian iconography. At the same time, even in the latter case the old canons remain perceptible, as two pages of the Titles of Ocoyoacac in the valley of Toluca demonstrate. Against the background of a mountain, one produces several episodes of the establishment of the borders of the *pueblo*.[12] The diversity of attitudes, gestures and drapery, the detachment of a foreground set against a mountainous backdrop, the sensation of movement that emanates from the scene, are at the opposite extreme from the Cuijingo style. But the absence of a true perspective at the top of the page leads us to a traditional perception, still more pronounced in the sort of small picture that calls to mind the celebration of a Mass in the *pueblo* (Plate 14).[13] Colonial features abound: elements of clothing (trousers, capes, hats) and architecture (the church vault, baptismal fonts), symbolic acts (prayer on the knees); and references to Christian iconography (Christ, the Holy Ghost), the writing of the protagonists' names, reveal the indisputable mark of the Christianization and the colonial domination. But if the structuring of the composition sketches a vague foreground, it ignores perspective, and above all places the figures and objects in an empty space without horizon line, recalling the native tradition of scattered-attribute space. The representation of the Adoration of the Magi of the *barrio* of Los Reyes prompts the same observations, although this time the European model is still completely detectable (Plate 15).[14] The figures appear to have been extracted from the original canvas and disposed against a ground composed of blown-up pictograms of the church and the village houses. Whatever their style, the Titles maintain notable elements of the pictographic tradition, integrating them with a text. The Titles are not written commentaries added or referring to pictographs, but more precisely the late heirs of the long drawn out shift from the glyph to writing, whose first stages in the sixteenth century we have followed. They constitute one of the successful outcomes of the encounter, whose other modalities remain to be discovered.

Reviewing this group of sources, however superficial and hypothetical this highlighting may be, it is obvious that the Titles embodied and established several practices that associated, sometimes inextricably, orality, writing, and 'painting'. Among these three media practically any union, any exchange, seems to have been acceptable: a transcription of the codified oral *huehuehtlahtolli* or a simple borrowing of their form; setting in of *cantares* composed in the first decades of the colony; oral gloss on the 'paintings' inserted in the text; reproduction or production of 'paintings' integrated in the document; appropriation of the juridical and religious writings of the Spanish; modification of Annals into Latin characters or partially painted and glossed, etc.[15]

The Titles would thus appear to constitute variegated collages that set side by side the most diverse borrowings and genres, materialized the clumsy and muddled attempts of groups who appear to have been trying their hands at writing outside the control of the clerks, without models and previous training. There is nothing here of the more or less standardized conciseness of the *Relaciones*, or even of the sometimes heavy prose of the Indian historians of the sixteenth century. At any rate, this judgement is hasty, based once more on the chaotic appearance of a narrative that is disconcerting and on forgetting the name they bear: *Títulos*, Titles. As the plural clearly indicates, far from corresponding to a unique narrative, the Titles usually combine texts of unequal length and different contents. Let us set out, for example, an inventory of the writings juxtaposed in the Titles of Zoyatzingo:

A first document belongs to the genre of Annals, since dates inscribed in the margin punctuate its progress. But the comparison stops there, for these dates make up an extremely discontinuous and incomplete series of years. After having run through the events of a troubled time – the entrance on the scene of the Spanish, the announcement of the Christianization and the arrival of Cortés, the 'Great Marquis' – the tale mentions the origin of the construction of the church, the affirmation of ancestral rights over the territory and the recognition of borders; it refers finally to the visit of Cortés, to the *merced* that he wished to grant to the *pueblo*, to the enumeration of the borders and the fixing of the boundary stones of the territory, to close practically on these words: '*y pusimos estas memorias*' 'we have drawn up these statements'.

Next we read a much shorter text, by another hand, entitled *Mesed Cihuatzincon (Merced of Zoyatzingo)*, which is nothing other than an exhortation to the construction of a church and to conversion: 'we ought to become Christians'. The Indian *mesed* has kept only the title of the Spanish deed of gift and in a vague way allusions to certain legal clauses.

After this comes a piece of writing that notifies neighbouring *pueblos* of the rights of Zoyatzingo before registering their appearance and their agreement.

Then a text edged with black ribbons, by still another hand, entitled in the Spanish of the Indians *Formalidad de la fundasión*..., which takes up in turn the struggle against the pagans, the construction of the church, the choice of patron saint, the subduing and conversion of the scattered pagans, the 'congregation' of 1555, the measuring of the lands of the *pueblo* by a Spanish judge; it embarks on a new list of borders, the partitioning of lands among the Indians, mention of the founding pagans, the defence of the *pueblo* against the attacks of

the Chichimec Indians, the choice, again, of a patron saint, the baptism of the Indians who had remained pagans, the demarcation of borders.
Finally the last section, by a still different hand, takes up the theme of the measuring of the territory and the enumeration of its borders.

We have the impression that all these various texts, beyond their variations, their additions or their contradictions, are endlessly tackling the same subject by repeated touches and successive approximations: the foundation of the *pueblo* and the marking of territorial boundaries. It is as if this set of additive themes progressively made up the subject of the Titles, as if the memory of the *pueblo* resided more in a cloud of data and cross-checks than on the rigidity of a synthetic version. The Titles of Cuijingo confirm this observation. They are made up of three 'signatures'. The Titles of Ocoyoacac bring together at least two texts that deal with the description of boundaries and are each introduced by the invocation of the Trinity and closed by the formula 'may it be so'. The Titles of San Bartolomé Capulhuac are organized, as we have seen above, around a series of wills, and so on.

This composition by superimposition or piling up of autonomous texts made possible the redundant approach of the same episode appearing in different lights or again in enlarged or transposed versions. In the case of Sula, for example, the election of the patron saint, the invasion of the Mexica, the threat that intrusions on the territory of the *pueblo* left in the air, were thus treated from multiple and sometimes barely reconcilable angles. No homogeneous tale, then, with a linear unfolding and precise connections, but rather repetitions, a multiplicity of illuminations from which emerges the orientation common to all these tales: the affirmation of the rights of the *pueblo* to a clearly circumscribed territory. This constant recourse to the repetition of themes, the reiteration of formulae contributed to moving the narrative line of the Titles close to the movement of an oral statement. It generally does not exhibit the rigour of a linear progression, nor does it follow the implacable or simply ordered march of a systematic argumentation, preferring to put the accent here on the emphasis of an exhortation or there on the flight of a religious digression. In other words, in a general way, the construction of these texts seems to a large extent to flow from the practices of orality. This is not surprising, not only because these Indian societies continued to immerse themselves in oral expression, which is too obvious to deserve to be emphasized; but above all because some of the available compositional models pointed to speech. One thinks of Christian preaching but also of the proceedings of the colonial administration, which were read and especially explained in public, and which involved oral and repetitive procedures. One even thinks of transcriptions of the old oral corpus, whose writing down need not have upset the ordering. This fertility of orality, but of a carefully codified orality, is what undoubtedly led the Indians to take apart or mutilate the structure of the Spanish proceedings that inspired them or to relinquish the regular chronology of the ancient Annals.

The oral model is even more directly apparent in the way in which the Indians presented their Titles. They conceived them at the same time as speeches, harangues addressed to an audience, and as 'interrogatories', to judge from the terms that were often used to designate them in a strongly hispanicized Nahuatl: *Telocadorio, derocadorio, delogadorio*, while in Spanish procedure, the *interrogatorio* corresponded essentially to the judiciary inquest that gathered declarations of witnesses or of the parties to a litigation (Lockhart, 1982, 389–90).

The indigenous narrative did not limit itself to flowing into old forms or to colonial terminology (*merced, posesión*) – composite borrowings. It also innovated, by transposing and adapting. Thus it developed a new type of tale, which marked a decisive moment in the appropriation of Christian discourse: 'the invention of the patron saint'. At Sula, seized by divine inspiration, the two principal notables, Miguel Omacatzin and Pedro Capollicano, were wondering about the choice of saint that would serve them as patron, and consulted the 'sons' of the *pueblo*, i.e., the local population, about the question. In the course of the following night, a very handsome Spaniard appeared to Miguel and called his name three times. He told Miguel of his desire to extend his protection to the *pueblo*. The following morning, Miguel told his vision to Pedro, who had had a similar experience. Both of them were sorely troubled. The divine protector showed himself once again to Miguel to indicate that he was none other than the apostle St James, 'who came from Persia ... from the direction of the East'. Miguel announced this to the *pueblo* and with a common voice all resolved to build a sanctuary devoted to the apostle. The Titles of Cuijingo and Milpa Alta record episodes in the same vein, which denote an unorthodox appropriation of the Christian supernatural, other manifestations of which we shall see. In other words, even if the production of Titles apparently was a matter of do-it-yourself and patchwork, we should be wrong to infer from their disconcerting and often 'chaotic' composition an inability to master the story and to convey information. On the contrary, we shall recognize a remarkable effort of shaping and creation relating to their vital function, the defence of the land.[16]

This undertaking took place in a favourite arena, rereading the past; a rereading developed in the course of the seventeenth century and finalized as a whole in the space of three or four generations, almost a hundred years after the period of the *Relaciones geográficas*. We are from the beginning struck by the profound transformation of the representation of the past, and particularly of the origins. The founding of the *pueblo* tends from now on to fit into a framework that breaks with local or regional prehispanic traditions to attach itself to Christian cosmogony:

> Understand or know that when God created the world, he did all he wanted to do, he did it and wanted it because he could do it. The Most Holy Trinity created all the heavens and the earth with the whole firmament of the world. God also created the heavens and the earth and the stars and all that there is in the world. God created them for he is [all-]powerful. And now I shall speak and explain and declare and tell in what way the *pueblos* were founded and how they received official form. (Sula)

Though Sula mentioned precolumbian episodes – the checked invasion of the Mexica – the origins of the *pueblo* were based on an indigenous interpretation of the Christian Creation myth. Ceasing to be the more or less abstruse and appliquéd reference of the preachings of parish priests, the Christian cosmogony made its entrance into local memory and from then on the centre of ancient space, as we have seen in the 'maps', can be confused with the Christian sanctuary.

To this was added a decisive constituent element of the foundation of the *pueblo*, the arrival of the Spaniards, an event indissociable from the Christianization: 'It was the will of God that the Spanish came... Came the commandment of God and of our king of Castile, came those who ought to govern since they give and convey the grace of God in all parts of the world and take care of the *macehuales*.' The crucial stage of the foundation ceased to be lost in the distant times before the conquest, even if the Titles still took account of a distant origin and occupation. The essential now resided in the Christian history of the *pueblo* to the point of being confused with it. The light that in the time of the *Relaciones* of 1579–82 sometimes illuminated centuries past, now only, or almost, swept over the decades just before the Spanish conquest, say from 1521 to the end of the 1550s. A similar scenario was played and replayed in the texts, around the same protagonists: the king-emperor Charles V, the two viceroys Antonio de Mendoza (1535–50) and Luis de Velasco (1550–64), the bishop (then archbishop) of Mexico Juan de Zumárraga and the elders of the *pueblo*. Among these few figures took place the ceremonies that punctuated and organized the foundation of the *pueblo*: baptism, confession, profession of faith, erection of the sanctuary, choice of patron saint, enthronement of new local authorities, demarcation of borders.

Between these Indian and Spanish protagonists, agreement could not be more complete. The second brought faith and hastened to reassure. The first, the elders of the *pueblo*, welcomed them with gratitude, even with enthusiasm, sometimes in tears and contemplation. The military shock, the political upheaval that the Spanish conquest represents to us were generally pushed into the background or completely erased. It is none the less true that when the community preserved the traces of Annals relating to the invasion, dark images of the downfall and death of the lords could still come to the fore. However, even in this case the conversion to Christianity remained the event that outclassed all others: 'We have put into your most holy hands our lives and our souls ... we have received our salvation with the water of holy baptism by which we all became Christians in our *pueblo* of San Francisco Cuazezentlalpan'. There as elsewhere, converted in the first hour, the elders actively took part in the Christianization of the Indians who were still pagan, when they did not exhort future generations to follow the example of their piety. In the same spirit the new power was not questioned for an instant. It was from distant Castile and the enforced relay of Mexico that all authority flowed, it was Charles V, the 'great lord king-emperor' who conferred on the elders 'the domination and the patrimony' and it was the capital of New Spain that constituted the 'matrix of the lords' and the origin of the faith. In this pacific or pacified context, drained of drama and Christianized, on this touched-up stage the *pueblo* received its lands 'in the name of His Majesty and of the grace of God'. Official sanction took the wholly Spanish form of a *merced* granted by the new authorities to the elders of the community and, let us emphasize, repeated elsewhere 'in all parts of the universe'. It was only then that the *pueblo* became the Indians' thing, the '*cosa propria*'.[17]

A reading that could hardly be more colonial and colonized, the story was also one of a pact. In exchange for the *merced*, for these lands granted to them, the Indians undertook to pay tribute to the king and to adore the God of the Christians. The indigenous discourse then seems to have been completely penetrated by colonial ideology. Radically alienated, Indian memory would thus appear to have adopted the reasoning of the conqueror, his logic and legitimizing rhetoric. The colonial authorities seem to have succeeded with a remarkable efficacity in inculcating their official version. The defeated would appear to be reduced, more than a century and a half after the conquest, to trotting out the good words of their masters, to whom they seem to be indebted for everything. But when we examine things more closely, the Indian attitude appears more complex and more ambiguous. Let us recall those 'maps' of which Cuijingo and Zoyatzingo preserved examples. In some a hand (whose middle finger bears a church) proclaimed that the *merced* was accorded by the very hand of the viceroy. This shows, beyond a doubt, the wish deliberately to bring out the intervention of the highest representative of the Crown. But the text itself corroborates this preoccupation with an emphasis too excessive to be gratuitous or simply rhetorical. At Zoyatzingo, it was Cortés in person who 'gave possession', set the obligations of the *pueblo* and recognized the limits of the lands and it was even a Spanish judge assisted by a *teniente general e intérprete* who baptized the borders of the territory with Indian names, all under the order of a fictional viceroy, Antonio de Valdes y Montolla. It was the same story at Cuijingo. In all the other *pueblos*, the emperor Charles V, the viceroys or Cortés (in fact often assimilated to a viceroy, which he never was) were designated as witnesses of local rights, when they did not intervene directly in favour of the *pueblo* to which they extended their sovereign protection.[18] Everywhere the highest Spanish authorities and the Catholic saints appeared as guarantors of order, or rather of the new established order and the legitimate rights of populations. Now we can perhaps better explain the insistence with which the Indians sought to place the foundation under the most noble auspices. That was an attempt to establish and protect territorial rights, by setting against possible infringements the memory of illustrious patronage. By reproducing the rhetoric of the Spanish, the Indians no doubt counted on taking advantage of the weight of royal authority. That explains the constant and in principle unimpeachable retrenchment on the part of the king and his representatives behind a rampart (often imaginary) of official measures. Not that the Indians deliberately chose this Spanish language of legitimacy rather than another. In the colonial and Christian Mexico of the seventeenth century there was no other way of formulating a discourse that would be at the same time comprehensible by the Indians and able to be ratified by the representatives of the Crown and the Church. But however narrow their margin for manoeuvre, in taking back responsibility for the formulation of colonial and Christian credentials, the authors of the Titles endeavoured to make them an instrument of protection and, beyond the shadow of a doubt, the basis of a communal identity.

Finally the Indians of the Titles were never passive and silent witnesses of official colonial recognition. Far from preserving their distance from Spanish intervention, they took over a role in the foreground. They were the conquistadores and the *fundadores del pueblo*, 'it was they who laid out the *pueblo* and built the houses since that was the will of the Most Holy Trinity ... They were the first to found the *pueblo*.'[19] They would have known no better way to appear as actors fully engaged in the story, by the same right and to the same degree as the Spanish. Their participation was shown at crucial moments such as on the occasion of the building of the local church, universally linked to the granting of lands. In the accounts the Indians moreover ended by arrogating to themselves the paternity of this step, to the point of leaving the Spanish and authoritarian origin of the construction in the dark.

The church undeniably symbolized a new era, the Time of the Most Holy Trinity, by becoming the centre of a ritual life that sanctified the continuity of the community. Look at what the Titles of Ocoyoacac have to say about it:

> We have established the temple of God our father and of our mother the holy Church so that *San Martín Obispo*, Bishop of Ocoyoacac may find a worthy welcome there, the centrepiece of the *pueblo*; it is his well-loved and honoured house of congregation, where the beloved ministers and priests of the Lord will receive the honoured and well-loved body of the most holy sacrament; so that they may implore him in his house of prayer and his holy church; so that Mass may be celebrated there; so that children and grandchildren may be born there; so that they may receive baptism and kneel; so that they may take the body of the most holy sacrament; so that they may be decently buried when they die.

Similar declarations appear in the Titles of Zoyatzingo, Cuijingo or Acapulco.[20] All alike made of the sanctuary not only the favoured place of contact with the divine presence manifested in the form of the holy sacrament, but also the focus of a body of religious practices, Masses, baptisms, funerals, which accompanied the evolution of the group and its members from birth to death. It also enclosed an image, which was a saint and whose house it was. It was an excellent intercessor, the glory (*el blasón*) and the new lord of the *pueblo*, since it became the proprietor of community lands by virtue of a true transfer.[21] We have seen above that the selection of the saint arose from an initiative emanating from the indigenous people, more precisely the 'fathers', the 'founders', in fact the notables. The episode was so important that it took the form of a miraculous account freely inspired by Christian hagiography. This was a way of arranging for a divine guarantee – since 'nothing can contradict the word of San Bartolomé' – without for that reason breaking with a more distant past, since all the prehispanic communities kept up singular links with the protectors who inhabited the mountains, springs and rivers of their surroundings. We are not unaware of the importance that the Indians accorded to the 'heart of the *pueblo*', bearer of divine will, reason for the group's being and driving force of its existence. We know that the installation of the first occupants of a site was accompanied by apparitions which signified that 'the god ceded the cultivable lands to the emigrants' (López Austin,

1980, I, p. 78) and then came the conclusion of a pact between the *pueblo* and the protecting power, which seems to have been a constant of the Mesoamerican past. But unlike the prehispanic divinities, who were directly at the origin of the appearance of the group, the patron saint appeared more as a being who came *later* and *from elsewhere*, 'from Persia ... from the East' (Sula) or from Tlaxcala (at Cuijingo). It was now the church that served him as sanctuary and not some mountain of the environs. However, despite this foreign origin that he shared, it is true, with the Spanish, the king-emperor or Cortés, the *pueblo* took him over completely. Everything took place as if the saint was perceived simultaneously in his exotic nature and in his full identification with the place, thanks to an ambivalence characteristic of many syncretic processes.

The Christianization of the *pueblo* was pursued by the introduction within the community of Spanish institutions, 'the forms of our government, which ought to include the functions of governor, *alcalde* and *fiscal*' (Zoyatzingo). According to the Titles, before the Spanish there were only neighbourhoods (*barrios*) with elders at their head. Some Titles even dated to the Spanish domination the division of the *pueblo* into four *barrios* and the designation at their head of a responsible official or *merino*. The Titles generally attributed to the viceroy Luis de Velasco the Elder the merit of having set up new local authorities, even if at Cuijingo, for example, Cortés was said previously to have established the *república*, that is to say a government in good and due form. The establishment of the local administration, of civil (and spiritual) charges, was conceived at the same time as a right to fame for the *pueblo* (*para mayor honra y corona deste pueblo*) and a stabilizing gesture, a factor of order and justice embodied in the rods of justice rendered to dignitaries. Finally the accession of the *pueblo* to institutional existence was coupled with a true transformation of the settlement. The *pueblo* was the object of a complete remodelling based on the Spanish *traza*; its houses and roads would from then on be governed by the regular design of the grid plan. Urbanism, politics and religions were inextricably mingled.[22]

After or before the construction of a sanctuary, a supplementary episode sometimes complicated the foundation of the *pueblo*: the 'congregation'. Then conceived as a measure of universal scope ('they indicated everywhere the limits for the congregation of the *pueblos*') and as an inescapable event, this enforced assembly of populations on the site of the *pueblo* often appeared as a prerequisite for the foundation. Once the operation was concluded, the elders of Santa Marta had only to proclaim that 'they have won the land'. None the less, the deportations of the Indians who had been scattered sometimes left burning memories. The Titles called to mind the existence of these populations in the isolation of the 'plateaux, mountains, caves and rocks', before giving details of the episodes of their submission, the reprisals of the Spaniards, and sketching the agitation of a troubled period: 'The elders knew violent confrontations, the *pueblos* fought one another . . . when they regulated the lands, when in the presence of God they indicated on all sides the limits for the congregation of the *pueblos*.' These 'congregations' thus not only seem to have affected relations between the *pueblo* and the populations dispersed on its territory, but also to have unleashed brutal struggles between neighbouring *pueblos* whose jurisdiction and borders were put in doubt as a result.[23]

After the shock and the repression came the calm. At Cuijingo the text describes how in six days the Indians

> installed all their houses, to the astonishment of don Francisco Chicontecatl, to whom the rapidity of the construction appeared unbelievable. The carpenters and the woodcutters installed a very big holy cross, they cut many trunks or branches and rapidly built the church or the chapel . . . Then they built their property and the lands were divided up in an instant; they established their houses according to the conventions and they completed everything in six months.

The role of these first converts or neophytes was not insignificant since it was they who undertook to draw in the pagans so that they would be baptised, receive lands and set themselves up in the *pueblo*. This time, unlike the brutal interventions of the Spanish, the method was peaceful and consensus (*la conformidad*) was the rule. But if in a general way the account of 'congregations' first stressed the Christianization of the populations and the ordering of the country, displacement and deportation were despite everything felt as a humiliating event and the opposite of permanence and putting down roots. The perceptible contradictions, the peremptory affirmations sprinkled through the accounts perhaps betray the embarrassment of memories confronted with an episode that was difficult to bring into line.

More than the construction of the church dedicated to the patron saint, still more than the troubled episode of the 'congregations', the marking of borders was the keystone of the foundation of the *pueblo*; it was even the principal subject of the Titles. It was the most notable act of the foundation, a spiritual act, almost sacramental. Following the course of the borders had all the appearance of a liturgy. Concretely, the operation consisted in following the limits of the territory to recognize and mark them by common agreement with the bordering *pueblos*. For the elders who took part it was an exhausting walk, a long

excursion of several days, a succession of climbs and descents to the
bottom of vales. The Indians were then engaged in marking the limits,
'we made with our hands two mounds ... two mounds made by hand
with stones [we placed here] a stone serpent ... a stone face that we
carved ... there a stone with an inscription' (San Bartolomé Capulhuac).
At Cuijingo the placing of boundary stones was carried out 'by
attaching the tips of the tall grass to each other'. The operation cannot
be dissociated from gestures of appropriation that the elders of Sula
accomplished in the Spanish way, 'by spitting, throwing stones and
pulling out grass and scattering it everywhere as a sign of ownership'.
These gestures tirelessly repeated were punctuated by outdoor banquets,
stops where Mass was celebrated, stops to spend the night. They were
accompanied, to the sound of trumpets, with embraces and exchanges
of flowers with the neighbouring *pueblos*, unless trouble broke out and
meetings degenerated into confrontations. It is probable that clubs, or
other arms such as those shields, obsidian swords, bows and arrows
drawn on the Titles of Ocoyoacac, were also an integral part of the
demarcation rituals, that they symbolized the strength of the *pueblo* and
recalled the memory of distant expeditions of conquest.[24]

But here is the heart of the matter. The course was a circuit as well
as a discourse, a kind of film and litany of localities, markers, natural
and artificial boundary stones, a series of toponyms that ended only
with return to the starting point. The route followed and the list tell of
the inscription of the community on its territory and its enclosure on
itself. The 'boundaries on all sides' drew a closed circle. The borders
were as impermeable as they were impenetrable. The Titles proclaim the
major cleavage, that of *outside* – the others, the bordering *pueblos*,
the Spanish administration and *hacendados* – and the *within* – 'we, the
elders, those who will be born ...' The within: a circle whose centre
would have been the church. We think of the maps glimpsed above and
now grasp better their 'cartographic' limitations and their intentions:
they showed the unity of the *pueblo* and the boundary markers of the
world that counted, at the borders of an elsewhere located somewhere
off the sheet, of an environment not represented because not relevant,
nonexistent, or potentially hostile and threatening. We shall therefore
not be astonished that the Indians of the Titles never appear as Indians.
They are above all the 'people of ... Cuijingo, Zoyatzingo, Atlautla',
etc. All these data reveal a withdrawal into itself of a community
besieged by the Spanish and also in some cases, for nothing is simple, a
redefinition and new departure for a territorial collectivity.

The construction of the church, the choice of patron saint, the
sharing out of lands, the design of the village and especially the marking

out of borders, were episodes whose memory had to be preserved and whose true value ought to be recognized by generations to come when the elders had gone: 'Now we are leaving, weary of walking for you. And we shall penetrate within our borders until Judgement Day, where the good and the evil of our actions will be judged'. But mention of the weariness of the elders was often mixed with more dramatic memories where the terms of the *Relaciones* reappeared almost verbatim. Some fixed the Christian foundation before the epidemics in a kind of golden age. Others associated the 'congregation' and the baptism of the Indians with an outbreak of sickness, 'gripped with fear the survivors became good Christians on the side of God; for girls and boys, men and women died, there remained no more than five or six houses'. Some Titles referred to epidemics that broke out between 1530 and 1560, others expressly to that of 1576. All testified that the demographic apocalypse remained in the seventeenth century an inevitable landmark, an unforgettable wound, unable to be healed, as had already been expressed by the informants of the *Relaciones geográficas*.[25]

Composed well into the seventeenth century, and probably after 1650, in the form that has reached us, the Titles constructed a past focused principally on the first days of the Spanish domination: a coherent and *real* past in the eyes of the writers and members of the community, who could have had access to it. The better to appreciate its originality, we must now come back, by way of a short detour, to the domain of history as modern research reconstructs it. The Titles put together facts that correspond on the whole to what we know: the setting up of an indigenous administration reproducing the Spanish model, the construction of the church, the choice of a patron saint, the 'congregations', the *mercedes* of land granted by the Crown to the *pueblo*, constitute the essential features of the history of the Indian communities in the course of the sixteenth century. As we have seen, the Crown first dismantled the ascendancy exercised by the nobility over the indigenous populations, to respect only the local level of the *cabecera* or principal town. The *cabecera* was a town on which depended more modest nuclei, scattered hamlets, the *sujetos*. *Cabecera* and *sujetos* composed the *pueblos*, which were thus dissociated from the tribal, ethnic and political groups to which they had originally belonged. In the middle of the sixteenth century, the Crown introduced the *cabildo* in the Spanish style, with its offices of governor, *regidores* and *alcaldes*, elective offices subject to confirmation by the viceroy, who granted the 'rods of justice' to the newly designated office-holders. This introduction took place under the viceroy Luis de Velasco the Elder (1550–64), often mentioned in the Titles. 'The 1550s and 1560s', as

Charles Gibson observes, 'appear as the period of greatest prestige, confidence and affirmation on the part of the Indian governments' (1964, pp. 190–1). Successive viceroys granted *mercedes* of land to the *pueblos*, which moreover amounted to sanctioning a situation, since the donations were located within their borders. The formalities that accompanied these steps were for the rest faithfully enough recalled by the Titles. The construction campaigns of chapels and churches began in the 1530s, to be completed at the end of the century. This process was accompanied by a remodelling and reorganization of the settlement along the lines of the chequerboard plan (Kubler, 1948) that combined prehispanic tradition and the Mediterranean experience. Nevertheless, contrary to what the Titles suggest, these transformations were not simultaneous.

It is undeniable that the 'congregations' had a considerable effect on a number of *pueblos*. For lack of time and means, the Spanish first limited themselves to leaving the indigenous environment as they found it. At most they built a monastery or a church at the site of the principal town or the *cabecera*, while the Indians continued to live scattered in the environs. Then the growing need better to monitor the populations who fled the demands of the conquerors and refused to be converted incited the Crown to institute stern measures and to undertake several campaigns of 'congregations'. The first followed the epidemic of 1545–8. It sought from 1551 to 1558 to constrain the Indians to regroup themselves in villages designed in the European manner and to shift the *cabeceras* to sites that had the consent of the authorities. By force or persuasion, populations had to give up their dwellings for new settlements. These first steps thus responded to particularly pressing administrative, economic and spiritual concerns, but they did not succeed in putting an end to the dispersal of the Indians. To remedy it and to make better use of a population that was literally melting away, a second campaign entrusted to 'judges of congregation' began in the last decade of the century (Cline, 1949; Simpson, 1934); 'The new towns were built by the Indians themselves in the traditional Spanish grid pattern surrounding a central plaza with church and market. The *estancias* were abandoned, their chapels razed and Indian dwellings burnt' (Gerhard, 1972, p. 27). From 1593 to 1605 thousands of localities were struck from the map, although the Indians did not fail to set up a tenacious resistance and to multiply efforts and pressure of all kinds to resist. It is thus not astonishing that the 'congregations' imprinted on indigenous memories such varying recollections where the justifications put forward by the Spanish (Christianization, administrative network) were confronted with the echoes of the clashes to which they gave rise. Finally, we have reviewed the trace of epidemics already dealt with at length above. In other words, the Titles did not fabricate; in their own way, which remains to be described, they dealt with well-established facts and events.

With some exceptions, they unquestionably emphasized the colonial sixteenth century. Will it be concluded then that prehispanic times had permanently evaporated from memories? Probably not, if only in the form of the periodization that cut through the Titles and distinguished the 'Time of the Gentility' and the 'Time of the Most Holy Trinity', the 'Period of the Catholic Belief' or again the 'Period of the Christian Faith'.[26] The Titles would have taken up and their authors interiorized the dichotomy introduced by the Spaniards and broadly disseminated by the survey of the *Relaciones*. But the informants of the *Relaciones* conceived the 'gentility' in precise terms. Practices, norms, events and dates were drawn to the attention of the Spanish investigators. The 'gentility' of the Titles, on the other hand, was thought of as shrunken, reduced to a few dry words, a few clichés (already so close to our own!). It was the memory of a pre-Christian time when idols were adored, sometimes (but rarely) a cluster of notations in which float paganism, cannibalism, scattered settlements, names so different from Christian nomenclature. Exceptionally, precise and isolated facts emerge: a Mexica invasion at Sula set before the foundation of Mexico, Chichimec raids at Cuijingo that sowed terror, confrontations with bordering *pueblos*, a migration and the displacement of a settlement, etc. Again it was a question exclusively of events with a local bearing in the politics and evolution of the group, unlike the colonial references that were inserted, as the Indians are well aware. However that may be, and this is essential, the prehispanic period was no more than a back-drop, a setting. Recalling a pagan past served in general to support the claim to ancient local roots but never to give an account of the origins and founding, as did numerous informants of the *Relaciones*. When the Titles nevertheless called to mind a prehispanic foundation, it remained, without exception, a precedent, a kind of general rehearsal in relation to the Christian foundation, whose principal moments have been described. That was so for two main reasons: the effect of time, of forgetting precipitated by the hazards of pictographic tradition and oral transmission; and above all the quest for a Christian and Spanish legitimacy that, in tactically serving the interests of the *pueblo*, induced distancing from the 'Time of the Gentility'. The consistent absence of dating of this pagan period should probably be attributed to forgetting as much as to indifference and lack of interest, as if the 'Time of the Gentility' did not have the same status or the same substance as the 'Time of the Most Holy Trinity'.

The dual vision of the past seemed to occupy memories everywhere.

It appears to obey criteria of Spanish origin and more precisely a Christian vision of the passage of time: it was the arrival of the Catholic faith and not the military conquest that sealed the difference, that made the old days shift into the other time. It is undeniable that in this second half of the seventeenth century the authors of the Titles accorded to the evangelization a favoured place in the economy of their past. Can we suggest that they conceived it as the succession of two profoundly different periods in the axis of a linear perspective directed towards an end that the Titles moreover mentioned in several places: the end of the world (Cuijingo), the Last Judgement, and the resurrection of the dead (Sula, Zoyatzingo)? Should we, to explain it, call upon the success of a century and a half of Christian preaching that succeeded in inculcating the unfolding of a history that would entail the Creation, paganism, and Christianity to culminate in an apocalyptic ending? That would be to work quickly. As always the Indians refuse to subside into the hypotheses that we make available to them. However, it would be convenient to leave aside a certain number of embarrassing details. Can we accept, for example, that the caesura, the passage from one time to another, was not uniformly dated and especially that it varied within the same document? How to explain that the placement of prehispanic events in relation to the colonial era differs considerably from what we expected from the pure and simple adoption of a Christian system of periods? The chronological organization offered by the Titles was at the same time varied and variable, the prehispanic era and the colonial period not always taking up on the scale of our time the place that we assign them. Some Titles limited themselves to allusions to the old days so blurred that we can hardly speak of the constitution of a dualistic past. That was the case at Ocoyoacac, Atlautla or Santa Marta. At San Bartolomé Capulhuac, the relations maintained with the pagan past were quite different. The Titles described a paganism awaiting Christianization, a time of latency and of preparation, where the saints already offered help by their intercession, where the place of the new faith was already indicated. It was the same story at Cuijingo, which made baptism precede the construction of the church or the choice of patron saint. The infiltration of Christian elements into the prehispanic context – the will of God, the intervention of the Trinity – contributed to producing a similar effect, just as some correspondences lent the same Indian name to the prehispanic founder and the colonial founder. If Christian time at San Bartolomé Capulhuac overflowed into pagan time almost to the point of annexing it, at Cuijingo, the 'Time of the Gentility', without losing any of its specificity, was knit together with the Christian epoch rather than being marked off from it. The organization of the two periods took forms as unusual and diverse as the intentions to which they responded. In the case of San Bartolomé, the text so well Christianized a past that was not Christian, that the 'first founder' appeared in an irreproachable light, while Cuijingo followed a different strategy that consisted in 'putting together', accumulating episodes and data that corroborated the antiquity of the rights of the *pueblo*.

The disconcerting permeability of eras can take on still more surprising, and even incomprehensible forms. It happened that analogous events unfolded symmetrically before and after the 'arrival of faith'; or that an episode initially dated to the colonial period was temporally diverted to run aground on the banks of the 'gentility'. Or again that events were telescoped: a Mexica invasion was superimposed on the Spanish invasion, the troubled times of the Chichimec aggressions were dissolved in upheavals caused by the conquest, etc. It is true that some of the *Relaciones geográficas* also concealed accounts that appeared to aspire to the Spanish colonization without ceasing to depict that of the Mexica. They were cautious accounts, since they were addressed to the Spanish, and inserted in a linear chronological framework that would perhaps suggest analogies but excluded any confusion. The tale of Sula, on the other hand, followed a course that was capricious in a different way. The same events were reported twice, in different versions and a muddled temporal context, as if they belonged simultaneously to the prehispanic and the colonial periods. The involuntary confusion this time apparently prevailed over the subtle play of implicit comparisons. Was it confusion, or rather the expression of another relation to the past or, more precisely, the development of a past that had nothing to do with what we mean by the term? Related episodes in the Titles of Zoyatzingo are marred with a like ambiguity. One of them concerns the sharing out of the lands of the *pueblo* among the *principales* of Zoyatzingo. Stuck on to the account of surveying the territory and the confirmation of the *merced* by the viceroy, the episode at first appears to transport us to the colonial epoch, as is moreover confirmed by the Christian names (Joseph, Juan) of some of the *principales*. But the end of the account refutes this interpretation, since it makes of the protagonists pagans of a more distant time and then deprives them of their Christian names. A little after this episode, the tale provides another example of temporal drift. A *cédula real* of August 1537 introduces the description of the battle that led the founder Xohueyacatzin against the Chichimec. At first linked to the colonial era, after 1557, the event ends by being dated to the prehispanic period: 'And that took place before the coming of Christianity'. Was it the clumsiness of the writers, their ignorance of chronology and of handling Christian dates that resulted in these events travelling between periods? Or a demonstration of another understanding of time? Do we not constantly make out in the colonial context the emergence of anterior events as if prehispanic time lived on beneath Christian time, to the point of surfacing here and there? Strata of events appear to come together to superimpose themselves. The troubles, the displacements of population of the first half of the sixteenth century would be mixed up with older upheavals; the episodes of an agitated local life would merge rather than being inscribed in a rigid succession. The names, some pagan, some Christian, appear to illustrate this process of aggregation, superimposition and setting up correspondences: Ahuacatzin and Juan Ahuacatzin, the founders of Zoyatzingo, can be at once two different people and the same figure through time. The same figure in the course of a tale could thus appear as a foreigner with a helping hand or a neighbour with exorbitant claims. In the same way, the frequent 'confusions' between the great figures of the Spanish domination, Cortés, the viceroys, the emperor, reveal that the identity of the person was less important to the writers than what it signified, in this case power, colonial domination. If the Titles juggled history, they none the less followed their own logic. Everything took place as if events acquired meaning by reason not of their singularity but by their recurrence and their insertion in a common matrix that enfolded them and stirred them all up to make them significant. A matrix that appeared to welcome a multitude of variants whose accumulation seemed in the eyes of the Indians to constitute history, the past.

An examination of the dates that mark out the second time, that of the Most Holy Trinity, poses other problems that lead to similar reflections. Absent from the epoch of the 'gentility', dates were attributed exclusively to Christian reckoning as if only this calendar could measure colonial time and all memory of the old systems had vanished. The dates were applied to the great events of colonial history and to episodes of a strictly local order. With few exceptions, they describe a temporal arc extending from 1520 to the end of the 1550s. However, although they provide overall chronological references that are relatively satisfactory in defining these first decades of the colonial domination, they are on the whole inexact, downright false or even – to our eyes and those of the Spaniards – completely absurd: at Zoyatzingo some events are dated 1005, and others 1945 and 1947! In fact the dates did not really serve to date the events in relation to one another by locating them on a common scale. It happened, on the contrary, that the same event was dated differently, that the same date could correspond to events that were temporally irreducible, according to our criteria. Look at the apparent 'chronological chaos' that constantly muddles the reading of the Titles of Sula. Though the introduction of baptism was dated 1532, the arrival of the faith went back only to 2 June 1607 and Christianization to 1609. A text from Atlautla dated at the beginning and end to the year 1552 referred to the Spanish conquest of August 1521, which appears natural to us, but also mentioned the *cocoliztli* epidemic of 1554, which is less so, the delineation of borders of August 1556, and even a meeting with the viceroy Luis de Velasco that was said to have taken place on 14 October 1676! At Cuijingo, the image of the patron saint was carried into the *pueblo* in 1555, four years exactly before the choice of this saint was made. The same 'congregation' was successively located in 1555 and in 1559, and so on.

Still the dates are not incoherent. Apart from its role of approximate temporal index, it seems that dating served above all to confer a seal of truthfulness and authenticity on the writings and deeds reported. In the manner of the Spanish, the Indians knew how to associate the validity of a document with the *presence* of dates, and that is probably why they did not hesitate to multiply them. But it was not a question of just borrowing a label, an empty form (the year, the month, the day), indeed one of the uses of a date, and not a logic for the measurement of time. That could be characterized as inexactness, experimentation or a wild fluctuation, unless we read it as an original use of the European calendar, which would give greater importance to a derived significance – the mark of historicity – at the expense of its primary function of chronological siting. Finally, is it necessary to read in the erratic diachrony of these texts, which in turn go backward and forward in time, the still potent influence of a thinking close to orality, ready to embrace all its digressions, stops and returns, concerned with producing the most information rather than articulating it chronologically?

The Titles defined information and the event by building up layers, reproducing data, telescoping them if need be. Periodization could distinguish or confuse periods, and dates could mark acts that followed one another or simply give them a veneer of authenticity. It is even less surprising that the narrator could in the course of a tale project himself into the future or travel about in the past as if he belonged simultaneously to different temporal sequences. The authors of the Titles retained of European time what bolstered their statements and left aside what could hardly make sense in their eyes. They kept a framework, a kind of 'after the manner of . . .', which was supposed to confer on the Titles the armature and authenticity of an official document of the Spanish administration. They took up a binary periodization that affirmed their profound adherence to Christianity: it was to maintain an attitude appropriate to their feelings and to the values of colonial society. They developed certain favourite borrowings, for example, that of belief in the resurrection of the flesh. The topic made possible the expression of the coherence of the group through time, the cohesion of a human group comparable in its homogeneity to the spatial whole defined by the minute and exhaustive enumeration of borders. The Christian formulation also corresponded in its overall perspective to the telescoping of different periods in favour of a divine timelessness analogous to the time of the gods of the ancient Nahua. They agreed finally to a cyclic conception based on the return of time and of persons: 'Even though they are dead, they are not dead . . . they shall revive on the day of the last judgement'. A divinity of the old days who appeared in the Titles of Cuijingo illustrated the same proposition: 'Acne in the morning was a creature of low age, at noon a finished man, very upright, and at sunset became Acne once more, which . . . means that he returned to his being which was that of a very aged old person'.[27] Unlike the subject of the sphinx's enigma, the indigenous 'demon' passed through the categories of age to return to the departure point instead of undergoing a one-way evolution. The Indian cycle ignored the singularity of destiny, as Sahagún had once complained.

On other points the authors of the Titles showed themselves more reticent or more embarrassed. For the Indians brutally caught hold of by our sixteenth century, the Christian and western European past could offer no consistency, no reality, whether it was cyclical or linear, oriented or not, repetitive or irreversible. If it was possible for them to interiorize and interpret the idea of a common outcome – Judgement Day – it was more difficult for them to locate themselves in relation to that distant point of departure constituted by the birth of Christ. The importance of the European segment of time, its contents, its nature, its placement in the past and not in the present (in the manner of the countdowns at which the informants of the *Relaciones geográficas* were virtuosi) to a great extent escaped the Indians as if they had been given a present and a future suspended over the gaping abyss of a doubly inconceivable past, for what should be put in it and how could it be understood? It was an enormous gap that the authors of the Titles busied themselves, as we have seen, with filling in their way – but not by resorting to old computations like the informants of the *Relaciones* nor, consequently, by turning to equivalences between indigenous dating and the Christian calendar, and still less by calling to mind in a precise and coherent way the prehispanic period. In contenting themselves with scraps set side by side and with a more or less respected Christian calendar, the authors reveal that they belong in a general way to a group detached from traditional historiographic learning, a different sphere from the nobility that we have seen at work in the sixteenth century and in the *Relaciones*. It is true that the authors of the Titles are anonymous and that the Titles themselves are fluid material, copied, completed and interpreted through the years. But if we designate as nameless those who finished these texts in the second half of the seventeenth century in the form that we know, we can attach them to a circle of country notables, without direct links to the old days, unlike the nobility, and who filled in what they no doubt never knew by reading the ancient Annals, official documents, wills and alphabetical writing. Their access to pictographic and written material of the sixteenth century joined to their mastery of writing sets them indisputably in the ruling circles of the community, those charged with the duties of *escribanos*, who pass for having a knowledge and tradition that inspire trust. In the same way the local figures that they put on the stage were far more likely to be holders of *cargos*, or charges created by the Spanish, than representatives of lords and princes.

In this respect a comparison with the writings of Chimalpahin, the Indian historian of the region of Chalco and Amecameca, where many of our Titles come from, is enlightening. The historian died about 1660, at a time when the Titles were taking their definitive form. A noble educated in his traditions and steeped in Christian culture, Chimalpahin gave details at will of the old genealogies, the conquests, the noble domains from the most distant beginning, citing his sources and informants, and handling all the computations skilfully. The Titles revived only bits of strictly local history, with no chronological framework or real temporal depth. Chimalpahin wrote in Nahuatl a history of Spain, flaunting his knowledge of the European past.[28] The Titles lose themselves in the names of conquistadores and viceroys and see no further than the borders of the territory. It is not a question of developing a comparison which would make no sense, but more simply of suggesting the cultural and social abyss that separated two environments: one, of the indigenous nobility, in decline; and the other, far more invigorated, of small town notables, who had succeeded in infiltrating into local positions of authority at risk from social upheavals, the death rate, the extinction of families and splits of communities. It is perhaps not irrelevant that some Titles insisted on maintaining the rank of *pueblo* and claiming an antiquity that history seems to deny them: an eagerness that betrays the ambitions of the newcomers to doubtful legitimacy? No doubt.

Does that mean that what distinguishes indigenous memories according to the *Relaciones* from the memories preserved in the Titles can be reduced to a social gap? That would imply that the content of the memories differs because they proceeded from different social groups. But it was not only a difference of class, but also the passing years, the decline of the old nobility over time, the mass accession of the notables to running communities and the cumulative effects of mortality – the demographic nadir was reached in the middle of the first half of the seventeenth century. To a certain extent the memory recorded in the Titles took over from the memory of the nobles, where it had disappeared, by developing quite a different approach and relationship to the past. It cleared a space for itself on the indigenous stage and became the memory of communities, since the Titles were the texts that they presented and that represented them to the authorities. None the less, the emergence of new memories in the second half of the seventeenth century, completely accepted by broad sectors of the indigenous population, did not exclude certain continuities with the Indian past. But these continuities belonged to the overall scheme, concerned principles of organization rather than the identity of the elements tackled or retained. These principles meanwhile remained in an implicit, latent state, and would have ceased to be systematically and didactically transmitted or conceptualized as they had been in, *inter alia*, the prehispanic mythologies. For a long time there had been no schools to teach the canons; there remained a common, specifically indigenous way of structuring time and space. As a result the treatment of time in the Titles calls to mind the treatment of space in the pictures that accompany them. They teem with borrowings from the western European patrimony, while continuing to observe a traditional deployment. Did not the diagram of the borders included in the matrix configured by the rectangle of the page echo the redundant and cyclical narrative organized by other matrices? In both cases, the writing of the conquerors was adjusted to indigenous ends, the invention of an origin, and the definition of an identity.

Are the Titles exceptional evidence? Isolated productions? Because we know them better, I shall not dwell on another category of documents known as the *Codex Techialoyan*, from the name of the first manuscript that was the subject of study (Robertson, 1975; Galarza, 1980). Like the Primordial Titles, these works go back to the seventeenth century, but present themselves as documents drawn up in the sixteenth century. The dates that they bear are approximate or wrong. The events related and themes addressed are practically identical: military and spiritual conquest, 'congregations', the patron saint, the baptism of populations, local leaders, the intervention of the viceroys Antonio de Mendoza and Luis de Velasco and of the *cargos* that they conferred; finally, and again the principal subject matter, the description of the *pueblo* and the list of borders. These documents were addressed to the inhabitants of the *pueblos* but were also destined to furnish information to the Spanish. Like the Titles, they were also designated by the term *altepe-amatl*, 'book of the *pueblo*'. They were distinguished from them, however, by the considerable role that they reserved for the image, to the point that they were once able to be considered as a renaissance of the pictographic tradition in the middle of the seventeenth century. As in the case of the 'illustrations' of the Titles, these images painted on *amate* paper are quite different from a decorative manifestation or an ornamental digression. They constitute true glyphs which, despite their enlargement, appear to have managed to preserve their character of toponymic or anthroponymic sign. In any case the ever more pronounced stylization of the lines, the fusion of decor and phoneme in the midst of what J. Galarza has called the 'phonetic landscape', the now minor role of colour, the rendering of perspective by the interplay of volumes, the suggestion of relief and the succession of planes, highlight the dynamism and originality of this form of indigenous expression. And the subtle and close relationship that was achieved between the written text and the image reinforces this impression: 'the text completes the pictographs, links the different thematic contents in them like a hyphen and shapes the pictographic unity of the page' (Galarza, 1980, p. 128), but it is the drawings that dictate the order in which the texts are read. Unlike the Titles, which conveyed the predominance of writing, the *Codex Techialoyan* explored a different path, subjecting writing to painting and knowing how to exploit its plastic potential according to requirements, as if the image had succeeded in domesticating the word, as the pictograph did with perspective since, again according to Galarza, it appears to be the very contents and significance of the glyph that determined its use. It followed naturally that pictographic expression could then free itself from the oral discourse that had once been closely associated with it: a silent revolution, intellectually exceptional, but without a future since it went against the flow of history, that is, against the colonial privilege of alphabetical writing. Less innovative, the authors of the Titles believed that they were playing this last card – that of writing – but without really following all the rules of the game or entirely sacrificing the pictographs.

Whether Titles or *Codex Techialoyan*, it is not their authenticity that makes these documents precious but the creativity to which all bear witness, their skilfulness in fusing together an experience and a native understanding of the past with what the Indians believed, could or would grasp of the colonial world, their aptitude in renewing and inventing modes of expression. They constitute a phenomenon of major importance in the history of Indian cultures and that of culture in general, a phenomenon of which the catalogue of D. Robertson or the Titles itemized to date offer but a dim reflection. It can be surmised that in the valleys of Mexico and Toluca, of Puebla perhaps, all the *barrios* or hamlets of any importance were capable of having, acquiring or

fabricating them. Between the constraints of the colonial model, those
of writing, of oral tradition and the old schemata of the perception of
space and time extended empty or abandoned spaces on which the
indigenous *imaginaire* worked in the seventeenth century with abundance, invention and diversity. That of the Nahua notables at least.
These approaches at once unlike and complementary developed probably at the end of the demographic low point (1610–50) and in any
case accompanied the slow rise in numbers of Indians. They blossomed
even in modest villages, profiting from the circulation of an astonishing
variety of manuscripts, official writings, 'old paintings', originals or
copies, Annals, maps, authentic and forged deeds, to which were added
the documents of the family of the *Codex Techialoyan*. It is true that we
still do not know the paths taken by the models, the 'schools' of
painters or the groups of writers that gave to the body of these productions, Titles or *Codex Techialoyan*, their relative homogeneity. But here
and now it is obvious that the history of the indigenous cultures of New
Spain cannot be separated from that of the appropriation of writing.
We must therefore once and for all give up the stereotype of communities immersed in orality or deprived of memory. And yet never had
large-scale death left so many voids.

Did all the pre-conquest 'painting' societies become writing societies
in the seventeenth century? Limitations of space rule out legitimately
extending this analysis to the Otomí, Zapotec and Mixtec Titles, which
reveal insights as fascinating as the works of the valley of Mexico.
Nevertheless, let us take up an example that tackles anew the tale of a
conquest and a foundation. This time it is not a Title but an indigenous
account translated by Otomí Indians at the request of the Franciscans of
Querétaro (a city located less than 200 kilometres northwest of México-
Tenochtitlán) who wished to gather information on the evangelization
of the city and the origins of the miraculous cross venerated there.
The circumstances in which it was composed remain obscure. At most
we can attribute its paternity to Otomí *caciques* from Querétaro, and
date the writing to the middle of the seventeenth century.[29]

The account, whose slips and careless style Spanish readers hastened
to point out, is precious in several respects. It reveals the image that
some *caciques* had retained of the conquest and the foundation of their
city. It emerges from an ethnic group that had populated the *altiplano*
well before the arrival of the Nahua, then had been subjected by
them, without for that reason having lost its language and culture
(Carrasco Pizana, 1950). However, the Otomí were from then on
reduced to a peripheral existence, exposed to the contempt of their
Nahua masters before being subjected to that of the Spaniards. They
served as auxiliaries to both the Nahua and Spanish. Under Spanish

domination, they participated in the colonization of vast areas of the Mexican north, and in the struggle against the Chichimec nomads who harassed convoys on the routes to the silver mines. Minor skirmishes preceded what it has been agreed to call the 'Chichimec war'. They took place in the zone of San Juan del Río and Querétaro, where Otomí Indians had come seeking refuge shortly after the fall of México-Tenochtitlán. Around 1531 some of them, led by a merchant named Conní, settled in the area of Querétaro and formed ties with the Chichimec who occupied the territory. Some time later a Spanish *encomendero*, Pérez de Bocanegra, made contact with Conní, who agreed to be baptised and submitted to the Spanish Crown. Conní took the name of Hernando de Tapia, won the Chichimec over to the Christian faith, and began a brilliant career in the service of the conquerors: an exemplary collaborator, he became governor of Querétaro, waged war against unsubjugated groups, and founded numerous *pueblos*.

This is the 'official' Spanish version of events that are known to us from other sources. Our Otomí text is considerably different, locating the events in May, June and July 1502, or almost 30 years before the 'historical' date; putting the emphasis essentially on the role of a certain don Nicolás Montañez, captain general, at the expense of Conní, alias Hernando de Tapia; and finally offering an astonishingly remarkable version of contacts with the Chichimec. The text most likely reflects the preoccupations of local politics, which are difficult for us to untangle. The persistent endeavour to minimize the role of the historical founder don Hernando de Tapia and, on the other hand, the concern with highlighting the *pueblo* of Tula and its *cacique* Nicolás Montañez, suggest that the account arose from a ruling group that exploited the progressive eradication of the powerful Tapia family from the local scene to impose its own version of the past. An attempt would have been made to establish a narrative more in keeping with a new partition of influence and power. There was nothing very original in that. Numerous Nahua Titles seem to respond to similar motives. But at the same time as it redrew maps, the account dealt fully with the conquest and the colonization, even though in a disconcerting light, since it told an exclusively Indian tale from which, with certain rare exceptions (Charles V, the viceroy), Spaniards were absent. Not only were they excluded from the terrain of confrontations with the Chichimec, but from the very territory of New Spain, although we know with what prudent care the Spanish supervised and often accompanied the expeditions of their Indian auxiliaries (Powell, 1952; Gruzinski, 1985b; Super, 1983).

More disconcerting still is the realization that the protagonists never appear with the features of Otomí Indians. They are described as and call themselves *Catholics*: Catholics whose conversion goes back to an uncertain date, at least prior to 1502. We understand in these circumstances that the Spanish conquest and its political and military aspects were missed out. In a Mexico practically devoid of Spaniards and occupied by 'Catholics', there was no need to refer to this episode. We recall that certain of our Nahua Titles avoided or turned aside this dramatic reference, reducing it to the spiritual dimensions of the arrival of the faith. We can guess that some did it to erase a painful memory, and that others did not consider it relevant to call to mind an event that had no local repercussions. The attitude of the Otomí who composed the account appears to belong to the first interpretation. But it adds a rare subtlety. The protagonists of the story in effect enjoyed a doubly remarkable position, since they arrogated to themselves the titles of Catholics and conquistadores. Laying claim to intangible privileges, they recognized as masters only the king and the viceroy. They used all their energy to spread among their Chichimec adversaries 'what Christianity consists of'. The very real difficulties of these expeditions were systematically not mentioned in favour of a fanatical idealization of the past, which enabled them to merge into the group of real victors, the Spanish masters. In this scenario of the sixteenth century, the Otomí became the Catholics, which amounts to saying that the account strives, and succeeds in the attempt, to combine the prestige of native arms and the fruits of an acculturation without tears and without humiliation. Without constituting, properly speaking, a flagrant inversion of the past, but rather the fiction of what could have been – as if the Indians had received the place promised to them by the Crown – this glorious memory broke with the mediocrity of a dismal present. In the middle of the seventeenth century, Querétaro had ceased to be a frontier post defended by the Otomí, to fall into the hands of Spanish cattle breeders and merchants. The Otomí had become an ethnic minority lost among other minorities, Nahua, Tarasc, *mestizo*, blacks and mulattos. Their identity was then reduced to the constricted scale of an urban subculture, fallen back essentially on language and ties of kinship. Seeing their influence and their fortune dwindling, the *caciques* fixed up a prestigious past for themselves, furnished with a fictional identity. But this idealization is not what distinguishes the account, and neither is the conjuring away of any pagan or prehispanic reference.

The interest of the account resides rather in the unique way it tells of another conquest, that of Querétaro. For the whole text is constructed around a warlike confrontation that is curiously missing from the narrative. The preparations for battle and its immediate aftermath are described in detail. On the battle itself, however, there is not one line. The event is not denied, it is completely evaded: a disconcerting process that comes down to eliminating from the conquest its bellicose aspects and those that were humiliating for the defeated. Everything takes place as if the report had wanted to transform the confrontation into an encounter without victors or vanquished. There is every indication that this muted tone is implicitly linked to the silence maintained about the Spanish conquest. If it is true that the account deals explicitly with a war between Christian and pagan Indians (the Chichimec) the Otomí memory seems in fact to be engaged in constructing a pacific *archetype* of the conquest in which behind the 'Catholics' we make out the Spanish, and the 'barbaric' Indians would refer to the Otomí themselves. Of the conquest, there would remain just an operation based on equality and reciprocity, practically concerted and even partly 'programmed' by the Chichimec adversary, which would provide indigenous memory with the framework of an 'acceptable' past. In other words, the Otomí were not unaware of the Spanish conquest; they accepted it provided that its essential was erased: the aspects of conflict. This is an extreme scotomization of reality, while it remains embryonic in the Nahua Titles, which tended to see the Spanish conquest as simply the arrival of the faith.

At the same time, the Otomí account offers quite a different interest – that of its writing. Like the Nahua, Mixtec and Zapotec Titles, its sources appear to have been many: Annals and 'paintings' perhaps dating to the sixteenth century could have provided material. But the account also draws inspiration from the baroque festivities that periodically enlivened the city of Querétaro. Its colourful descriptions of troop movements, costumes and martial music call to mind the fictional combats in which from the sixteenth century Indians took part 'dressed as Spanish' and false Chichimec. They recall unmistakably the feast days celebrated at Querétaro at the height of the seventeenth century in honour of the Holy Cross. It is not impossible that the account itself was inspired by one of those indigenous canvases which directed the steps of the 'extras' who then invaded the streets of the town. But it is equally the product of a reading of the official proceedings that accumulated in Indian archives. From them it borrows a ponderous rhetoric, a vocabulary, a taste for figures and dates used above all in a formal way. But for the author (the authors?) of the account, as for the writers of Titles elsewhere, writing has become the favoured instrument of recording the past. A gauge of authenticity, it required accumulating signatures and testimony, multiplying *escribanos* and notaries at the risk of lending these Otomí an improbably early mastery of writing, but which attests there again to the value that certain indigenous circles, of whatever ethnic group, accorded it in the mid-seventeenth century. Better still, the account goes beyond this stage in aspiring to literary creation, by including a sizeable fragment of one of those bombastic dedications that works of the period abounded in. With its rhetorical effects, its affected style, this passage introduces a discordant note that quickly lapses, it must be admitted, into the most confused gibberish and an avalanche of ill-understood or badly copied formulae. Still the choice and the borrowing, however clumsy, reveal the presence of a stylistic preoccupation and thus of an author in control who had wanted to personalize the text. It is an author who also claimed to address himself to the 'virtuous readers' and who did not hesitate, compelled by his erudition, to give the name of the Italian Bramante as the master architect who accompanied the 'Catholics'. Of course the attempt only set off the mockery of Spanish readers. The Otomí memory was thus desperately engaged in constructing a Mexico without Spaniards, a conquest without victors, with all the more illusion and dream as the tale was no longer tied to a territory, a *pueblo* to defend, borders to guard.

One could pursue the analysis with other Otomí, Zapotec and Mixtec Titles. We shall limit ourselves to certain examples chosen in the bishopric of Oaxaca. Two Zapotec texts from the mountains of Villa Alta de San Ildefonso give rise to comments that could be applied to the Nahua Titles of the valley of Mexico.[30] Located at about 1400 metres, dominated by the crest of Zempoaltepetl (3300 metres), extremely hilly and wooded, the region had been difficult to subjugate. The Zapotec and still more the Mixe rose up several times in the course of the conquest and the sixteenth century (1550, 1552, 1570). In 1527 Gaspar Pacheco and Diego de Figueroa founded Villa Alta de San Ildefonso, which became the third Spanish settlement in the bishopric of Oaxaca and the capital of the Province of the Mixe, Zapotec and Chontal (La Fuente, 1977; Whitecotton, 1977). The Dominicans undertook to evangelize the land, assisted by a mercenary by the name of Olmedo. The *caciques* were baptised and as elsewhere Spanish conquistadores served as godfathers.

Presented and translated in October 1715 at the request of San Juan Juquila in a trial that set it against the village of San Juan Tanetze, the Titles of the *pueblo* consisted, in the words of Zapotec Indians, of the 'account of our first foundation and of all the lands that we had won since our gentility'. They concerned the territories of the two *pueblos*, Juquila and Totolinga; the first, in the middle of the seventeenth century, had absorbed the second. The close relationship of the two texts in written form and content suggests a common origin and composition contemporary with the agglomeration of Totolinga to Juquila.

Both are presented as *memorias probanzas*; they are dated at 'five hundred and twenty-one year', 1521, and at the end bear the names of their presumptive authors: 'I Pedro Binopaa, I Pedro Marthin Laa, I Juan de Bilachinaa', who proclaim themselves to be the ancestors of the natives of the *pueblo* of Totolinga. As in the case of the Nahua Titles, it was the elders and ancestors who expressed themselves, recalling past events: 'We took the lands and regions which our children and grandchildren could benefit from and cultivate'. The narrative merged with a scenario that is already familiar to us. If no allusion was made to the military conquest, although it was particularly agitated in the region, the evangelization, on the other hand, was fully treated. As the three 'signatories' recalled, 'we had been to await the arrival of the law of God at Oaxaca. The father minister arrived first and baptised us. He was called Fray Bartolomé de Olmedo'. The welcome reserved to the friars was warm, embellished with standards deployed, the music of drums and bugles. The usual episodes followed: the construction of the church, the baptism of ancestors, the distribution of *cargos* (*alcalde*, *regidor*, *fiscal*), the designation of the Indian governor, ending with taking possession of lands in the accustomed form of the recognition and enumeration of the borders of the territory.

As in Nahua country the dating is false. The date 1521, barely plausible for the Spanish conquest, too early for the evangelization and impossible for the distribution of *cargos*, served to concentrate and combine a series of events founding the colonial and Christian order. A certain number of features none the less distinguish the Zapotec Titles from their Nahua equivalents. The Spanish intervention – of the evangelizer Fray Bartolomé de Olmedo, of the *alcalde mayor* of Villa Alta, of an ancestor of the Spanish and even of a godmother, doña Catalina de Media – was far more pronounced. There were, for example, the *alcalde mayor* and the friar who decided the choice of site for the church and that of the *pueblo*. The foundation of the Spanish village of Villa Alta de San Ildefonso served in some way as a prototype for that of Totolinga and Juquila. The geographical background was more vast. Not only Oaxaca, the capital of the region, but Villa Alta and the whole territory were the site of important episodes, and there is even a trip to Spain. After being reunited with the 'ancestor of the Spanish' don Ypolito del Baye (= Valle) de Comania, the four ancestors of Juquila appear to have reached Spain to ask for royal mercy. On their return to Mexico they appear to have passed through México-Tenochtitlán and Puebla before returning to Oaxaca and Villa Alta de San Ildefonso. This setting, congruent with Mexico and the Spanish empire, is closely linked to the assertion of an ethnic identity that would have been sought in vain in the Nahua Titles. The return and baptism at Villa Alta of the representatives of the Zapotec *pueblos*, the parallel between the ancestor of the Spanish and that of the Zapotec, express in their way an enlarged indigenous consciousness, far beyond the narrow circle of the borders of their *pueblo*.

But, first paradox: this consciousness was offset by a considerable loss of autonomy, for the widening of horizons could only come up against the geographically ubiquitous Spanish, ecclesiastics, representatives of the Crown, or colonists. None the less, recognition of the Spanish presence did not imply recognition of defeat. The drama of the conquest was discharged, the conquest expurgated of its humiliating and brutal aspects: we recall, for example, that in this region the Spanish threw the Indians to their dogs. Second paradox: where we would expect a more acculturated writing, in accordance with the reinforced presence of the Spanish, we discover an expression quite thrifty in its means – at least to judge from the Spanish translation, which we owe quite obviously to an Indian. This involves a limited vocabulary, a restricted and repetitive syntactical repertory, a minimum of borrowings from the phraseology of the colonial administration and the language of the Church. In the midst of this extreme economy, which contrasts with the variety of effects and styles disclosed by the Nahua Titles, recurrent elements prevail: the list, the enumeration, the juxtaposition, milestones of an itinerary, borders of a territory, functions assumed by the elders, names of founding ancestors:

> Uno de nosotros se llama Laa; el otro se llama Bilachinaa, el otro Binopaa . . . Su antepasado de los de Juquila ttumó la bara de alcalde y ttanbién su antepasado de los naturales de Ttalea tumó la bara. (One of us is called Laa; another is called Bilachinaa, another Binopaa . . . The ancestor of those from Juquila took the *alcalde*'s rod and so did the ancestor of the natives of Ttalea.)

This mode of stereotypical and standardized construction is perhaps not very far from what the gloss of a pictographic manuscript would look like, describing the arrival of the Spanish and fixing the borders of the *pueblos* of the region. We would thus advance the hypothesis of an alphabetized environment, but devoid of the mastery shown by the Nahua Titles. Should the form of writing then be compared – more than in the valley of Mexico – with oral expression? Does it remain profoundly derivative of the gloss of pictographic documents, whether traditional or as Europeanized as the *Lienzo de San Lucas Yatao*? (Glass, 1975, pp. 75–6.) Or would it rather be under the combined influence of 'painting' and oral transmission? We note that we find ourselves in lands difficult of access, barely penetrated by the Spanish, where acculturation in all its forms remained a more superficial and later phenomenon. This is true, although the manifest existence of written texts and 'paintings' (which do not fail to call to mind the *Codex Techialoyan* of the valley of Mexico) would lead us to correct the cliché. But the spread of the alphabetical medium does not necessarily imply that of the message and rhetoric associated with it, at least in these regions.

A Mixtec account dated 8 February 1523 and translated in 1696 also tackles with notable precision the episodes surrounding the arrival of the Spanish in the region.[31] It concerns the account of Don Diego Cortés Dhahuiyuchi, *cacique* of the *pueblo* of San Juan Chapultepec in the district of Quatro Villas, that is to say, the part of the valley of Oaxaca which came within the sphere of influence of the del Valle marquisate. This text too was produced in the eighteenth century, in the context of a trial that opposed the Indians of San Juan to those of San Martín.

As usual, relations with the Spanish were depicted in a peaceful and confident light, but war broke out between the 'Mexican' allies (thus Mexica or Nahua) of Cortés and the local Mixtec. Naturally, as it is a Mixtec text, the Mexicans were defeated by the Mixtec, who magnanimously offered lands to the defeated 'of their own free will' so that they could settle there. We recognize the usual sleight of hand, which transformed a rout into a generous victory and attempted to explain why the *cacique* don Diego had to divest himself of half his possessions in favour of the Mexicans who settled at San Martín. The text follows with the traditional enumeration of borders. It was dated 8 February 1523, and bequeathed by don Diego, 'so that the tributes of the lord Marquis will be paid'. To this writing in the Mixtec language, whose style is close to Nahua texts of the valley of Mexico, is added an 'ancient painting', also described as a map (*mapa*), and a 'Title-will' of 1565, together making up a group analogous to those encountered in Nahua country.

Set against the Mixtec version was that of the invaders, this time not Spanish but their Mexican allies, founders of the neighbouring and rival *pueblo* of San Martín. According to the latter, a Zapotec Lady, who had got into trouble with the Mixtec, asked Cortés for help. The conquistador speedily sent her 'Mexican' troops, who in exchange for their loyal services received from the Lady lands to settle on. The same version did not hesitate to report a confrontation between 'Mexicans' and Spanish, which turned to the advantage of the former. Conquerors, the 'Mexicans' condescended to accord to Cortés a little piece of land 'to found the city'. As in the Mixtec tale, the roles were systematically reversed, the same process erased the defeat and made victors of the vanquished without ill feeling. At this juncture the limits of the territory and the *barrios* were established, the rights inscribed on '*papel*' (paper), the solidarity of the community affirmed. Everything leads one to believe that these Nahua Titles, like the preceding ones, date to the second half of the seventeenth century.

These two Mixtec and 'Mexican' documents show that in the same place completely contradictory versions of the history of the *pueblos* can coexist. The *Relaciones geográficas* of the 1580s had moreover already taught us this. If we compare them to the Zapotec Titles, we cannot but be surprised by the vaster horizons revealed by these writings of the bishopric of Oaxaca. Zapotec go to Spain. Mexican followers of Cortés fly to the succour of a Zapotec Lady and confront the Mixtec. To this change of scale corresponds the emphasis on the Spanish invasion and endless references to the ethnic group, as the context did not permit evading or pushing the Spanish conquest to the background. Two possibilities appear open at this point: acknowledging the conquest, while removing its traumatic significance, as did the Zapotec of Juquila; or overturning the past without regard to history (San Juan Chapultepec), or indeed plausibility (San Martín). These Titles have at least one point in common with the Nahua texts of the valley of Mexico: the Spanish conquest, military or spiritual, was now perceived as the major event of the past, the necessary point of reference, tied to the origins, while the memories of the end of the sixteenth century gathered in the *Relaciones geográficas* reflected a quite different vision. That probably explains why the text of San Martín dated to the Spanish conquest doubtless more ancient confrontations, since the Mexica had been established at Oaxaca from the last decades of the fifteenth century.

It remains to us to extend this study to the end of the eighteenth century and to examine what became of indigenous memories at that date, to gauge the impact of the end of the baroque period and the repercussions of the 'enlightened' policy of the Bourbons in the twilight of their domination over Mexican lands. It is necessary to mention the Nahua *lienzos* from Guerrero and Morelos, to present texts from the region of Tlaxcala, Puebla and Cholula, to review those from Michoacán, the better to gauge the extent and density of the phenomenon.[32] And to the so often cited Nahua, to the Mixtec, Zapotec and Otomí, one must add the Matlaltzinca, the Tarasc and obviously the Maya of Yucatán and their *Chilam Balam*, even if it is clear that the Nahua were pioneers in the matter. We have the feeling of having hardly penetrated a teeming, badly understood or disdained universe, a proliferating underground, where modes of expression were worked out that united alphabetical writing and 'painting' in a highly variable but always original way. The innovation did not reside, obviously, in the creation of a graphic, objective memory, inscribed on 'old and ruined notebooks'. The *calpulli* from before the conquest had their own archives and they could be substantial and embarrassing enough for the then powers to think of destroying them. The innovation was in the use that the Indians made of writing, which was always quite different from simple borrowing, a passive copy in the manner of the administrative texts, the deeds of sale or gift, the wills that the Indian writers drew up. It corresponded to intense creative work that affected the contents as well as the expression, depending on whether the Indians had chosen to accentuate the text or to subordinate it to the image.

First, the diversity of the image: in the seventeenth century, in the same region and for the same tribe, 'painting' could include a minimum of glosses in relation to conventional signs or open itself to figurative scenes that call to mind so many small pictures. It suffices, to convince oneself, to set side by side the *Lienzo of San Lucas Yatao* and that of *Yatini* among the Zapotec. Just like the Nahua of the valley of Mexico, the 'school' of the *Codex Techialoyan* treats the image differently from that of the Primordial Titles. The preservation and circulation of models from before the conquest or of the first decades of the colony weighed undeniably on the inspiration of the painters, although always in altered or reinterpreted form. In other cases the contemplation of works of European style seems to have influenced the Adoration of the Magi of Los Reyes, the landscape of the *Lienzo of Chinantla* or the scenes in the *Codex of Chalchihuapan* of the surroundings of Cholula and Puebla (Castro Morales, 1969). But here again as borrowing implied rereading, the landscape became emblematic.

There was the same diversity in the writings: from the disjointed narrative of the Zapotec Titles, the juxtaposed tales of the Nahua Titles with their literary flights, to the disconcerting erudition of the – or rather one of the – Otomí authors of the Account of the Conquest of Querétaro (Gruzinski, 1985b). This re-use of the most diverse material in the service of an abounding inspiration was unequalled in the villages of Mediterranean Europe. Thus no underground tradition or secret legacy would maintain the prehispanic inheritance intact. No linear evolution either would lead from the unstoppable degradation of the traditional pictographs to the irresistible victory of European 'realism' and the conquerors' writing. These Indians take us elsewhere, to a time and place that are no longer those of before (the conquest) but not ours either, nor those of the Spanish. They mark out paths that, if they remain dead ends, still each constitute fascinating alternatives to the culture of the Church and the Crown.

Difficult to date, these works are for the most part anonymous. They were believed to be objects emanating from modest *pueblos*, indeed hamlets, *barrios* that aspired to the status of *pueblo*. A number of them no longer exist and their origins are difficult to identify. In the same way, their authors have been located within a stratum of small notables without prehispanic pretensions, of too recent lineage for its history to be told, and who based the identity that they proclaimed on the *pueblo* and the colonial past that they recreated. That we have spent a long time on this group does not mean that the seventeenth-century Indian memory found its only expression there. Let us rather say, to simplify grossly, that this manifestation had to occupy an intermediate position between a profoundly Europeanized memory and the memories, far more difficult to grasp, of the peasant masses or the Indians absorbed by the *mestizo* groups and urban circles. The survivors of the great noble families of the sixteenth century, the *caciques* of the city of Mexico and its environs, of Oaxaca or Tlaxcala, for example, also continued to maintain their memory. But in the second half of the seventeenth century, they seem to have given up any vague historical impulse. It was for them no longer a question of writing and still less of rewriting history as Alvarado Tezozómoc, Chimalpahin or Cristóbal del Castillo were able to do. They contented themselves with keeping the accounts of their loyal services, accumulating wills and tracing the line of their genealogies. They collected *mercedes*, privileges and royal schedules, coats of arms and devices, 'lineage papers' and death certificates. They put away at the bottom of their trunks paintings and maps (*mapas*) to support their statements (Fernández de Recas, 1961, pp. 18, 77–80). Their task was strictly to serve the family, or more precisely the lineage. Their close relations with Spanish and *mestizo* society, which took the form of incessant marriages, explain that their apprehension of time and the past were adjusted to what was expected of any *hidalgo*; to the point moreover that some would not hesitate to place their indigenous ancestors among those of the conquistadores whose names they bore and whose descendants they sometimes were. To the indigenous memory was then added or substituted that of the 'genealogical books' imported from Spain.

There is one point on which these memories differ profoundly. Those of the nobles and *caciques* are for the most part fossilized memories, authenticated, cumulative, memories on the defensive that cling to often contested rights and privileges. Ruin, family quarrels, the loss of papers moreover often left these families adrift. On the other hand, the memories of the Titles and the *Codex Techialoyan*, those of the *pueblos*, while taking on this protective function, simultaneously constituted new incongruent memories, which constructed, crystallized and fused an often contested identity. Confronted with the dispersed memories of families, these living memories posed the question of the origin of the group and its roots in the territory, and were able to profit from the margin of autonomy that the crisis of the Indian nobility and the policy of the Crown left to the community. Their escape in large part from the stifling yoke of the Spanish administration that held the fallen aristocracies at its mercy was attributable to this leeway.

That is to say that access to writing and the written, far from entailing a homogenizing of Indian cultures by crystallizing, censoring and making their heritage uniform, seems to have had the opposite effect. The Hispanicized true copy appeared almost as the antithesis of opening up an original and autonomous space, producing texts that were accused of falsification, of 'chimeras and contemptible fictions'. In the eighteenth century we shall see other movements setting up a distance that separated the Europeanized Indian elite from the indigenous masses and even the notables. This cultural differentiation was probably far less tied to the extent and the variety of learning suddenly become accessible – as we have seen, still limited to Spanish religious practice and law – than to the exploitation of a technique in liaison or not with other native media. In fact it was more a mode of expression than a literate culture which penetrated the world of the Indian notables, even if it is difficult to distinguish the medium from the message. That is no doubt one of the reasons why autonomy was preserved.

This multitude of painted and written memories reveals that the indigenous cultures hardly died with the sixteenth century. The astonishing flexibility that they demonstrated in drawing from all sources, multiplying borrowings and innovations invites us to think of two concepts whose repeated use ends by concealing the complexity, the processes and the objects that they designate: I am speaking of *syncretism* and *tradition*. We have already seen that *syncretism* covers subtle phenomena affecting the modification of contents as well as the evolution of modes of expression, with incessant differences of phase, false returns to the beginning and chaotic advances. As to *tradition*, we know that we cannot remain unaware of the social diversity, the concurrent and complementary media (written, painted, oral), the multiple roads, the sudden impasses, the unforeseen awakenings, the incessant movement. After having discovered writing in the sixteenth century and succeeded in joining the written text to pictography, the nobility appear to have given up these methods to fall back on the minute reproduction of the European model. It was another social environment that in the seventeenth century took this route in creating the Primordial Titles or the *Codex Techialoyan*, as if the petty notables had taken over from this 'Mexican renaissance' in a role that they were to keep until the nineteenth century and sometimes until the present. 'Invented' (to take up Hobsbawm's term) and thus fixed at the end of the seventeenth century, this tradition was in turn concealed and still persists in the twentieth century, often reduced to the state of ruined panels whose meaning the Indians have progressively lost, or that they venerate on a par with the saints on their altars. We would have liked to pursue this study by defining in what way these groups, these individuals adopted and diffused new canons that could not receive the support of the colonial authorities who ignored or disdained them. How can one explain that sectors of the ruled, deprived of the leaders who once established the norm, nevertheless managed to produce 'models' of expression (Titles, *Codex Techialoyan*)? That would involve investigating not only the degree of autonomy which was left to them or that they had been able to preserve, but also the relations and networks of power that continued to unite them even outside colonial society.

By means of painted and written memories, the 'torn net' of the first decades of the sixteenth century began to be rewoven in the second half of the seventeenth century. From Oaxaca to Querétaro, the Spanish conquest (it is hardly surprising) became the major event for all who had a piece of power. Many found the means to 'bypass', deal with or reinterpret the break of the conquest, to take into account the institutions, structures, managers and schemata put in place by the colonial domination. Many constructed a plausible reality for themselves, which was first a past but also an instrument to deal with the present and confront the time of generations to come. We recall the formula: 'I am giving you the form so that you will be able to know how to speak and answer to defend your lands . . .' Thus coherent and synthetic visions emerged, no doubt anecdotal for us but which expressed what some groups considered to be the essence of their reality and which in most cases was connected with the space of a territory. A word in conclusion about the *pueblos* that held Titles in good and due form. They certainly possessed an official memory, corresponding to that of the Spanish and above all to that of the acculturated nobles, but it was superimposed on an apprehension of the past similar on the whole to that of the Primordial Titles. If not in the details of the events, at least in principle, in the accents given, the scansions marked (the primacy of the conquest and the Christianization, the rootedness in the land), this deep-seated apprehension must be close to what I have tried to describe. This in no way erases the distance separating the notables guided by authentic documents, prisoners of the official line, from the Indians constrained to invent a history, to knock together a past. But we should be wary of contrasting too stringently the false and the true, since between these two poles there existed a broad range of nuances that made possible all shifts, any straddlings. The difference seems to me to reside in the degree of spontaneity and inventiveness at work as much as on the contents or the form used. Still the nobles of the cities and the countryside, the notables of the villages (with or without authentic Titles) do not by themselves stand for indigenous societies and cultures. They make up only a minority sector, perhaps 5 per cent (Israel, 1975, p. 44). There remains the enormous mass of population that never had access to the written text, still less to 'paintings', those whom we call for the sake of convenience *macehuales*, peasants, artisans, agricultural workers, miners, household staff. I have not referred to them until now, apart from mentioning that they had been stricken by death on a vast scale.

4

Colonial Idolatry

The more or less sincere rallying of the ruling classes to the society of the conquerors, the active role of the Indians of the Church, the disappearance of the ceremony of the old cults, replaced by Christian institutions, colonial exploitation in its most varied and brutal forms and, to crown it all, the colossal demographic collapse overwhelmed the daily life of all the indigenous people. The policy of 'congregations' for its part contributed to weakening the sense of rootedness in the land of the groups that death had spared. In the course of the 1620s the Indian population of central Mexico reached its nadir – 730,000 persons – representing no more than 3 per cent of what it had been on the eve of the conquest (Cook and Borah, 1979, III, pp. 100–1). If one adds to this the effects of the anomy implied in questioning traditional norms and hierarchies, if one considers the impact of the cultural disorientation produced by the introduction of new models of conduct (Christian rituals, weddings and marriage, work), all the elements seemed to converge towards the end of the sixteenth century in a vertiginous human and cultural agony. The chronic drunkenness denounced in the *Relaciones geográficas* would be but one of the most flamboyant symptoms of the irresistible drift of the *macehuales*.

But can we ignore the other side of this debacle: a progressive acculturation following in the footsteps of the Christianized nobles, in the framework of the colonial *pueblos*, centred on churches and convents, and under the leadership of a clergy ever more numerous in relation to the faithful practically in the throes of extinction? The 800 mendicant clergy of 1559 numbered 1500 by 1580 and about 3000 by 1650. The acculturation gave rise to triumphalism very early on, but the lack of resources and staff at the disposal of the Church and even more the great distances that separated the cultures in confrontation were underestimated. In fact the apparent dilemma of anomy and conversion masked more complex attitudes among the Indians. It camouflaged depths apparently insensitive to change, whether undergone under the still relatively manageable form of Christianization or, more damaging and uncontrollable, of epidemic death and colonial exploitation. Observers of the second half of the sixteenth century as perspicacious as Sahagún or Durán were not mistaken. They suspected under numerous almost insignificant features the persistence of something threatening, still insurmountable.[1] While the Council of 1585 again called for (briefly, to tell the truth) the persecution of the 'dogmatizers', the destruction of the temples and idols and the eradication of the 'vomit of idolatry', they still considered the question more from the angle of a possible relapse than as a silent continuity. It is true that the prelates only muttered imprecations against the old practices, and from 1571 the Indians were removed from the competence of the Holy Office, to be submitted exclusively to the jurisdiction of tribunals (*provisoratos*) of each diocese or still more directly of the district ecclesiastical judge (*partido*). It seems that these authorities never undertook so systematic and strict a campaign as that which the Inquisition claimed to deploy.

It is true too that the Church seemed to be completely absorbed by quite different tasks: conflicts with the civil authorities, incessant rivalry between regular and secular clergy, tensions between orders and within them between creoles and peninsulars exhausted the energy of more than one. Locally the dissensions that opposed parish priests to the *encomenderos*, then to the *hacendados* or to the *alcaldes mayores*, the fear of scaring off populations ready to flee too demanding pastors (and thus to pay neither tribute nor parish dues) frequently defused any impulse to root out ancient practices. These difficulties or these considerations inclined the priests to observe the *status quo*, to content themselves with supervising morals or enclosing themselves in an inveterate pessimism, contemptuous of the Indians and justifying any exploitation. Finally, others preferred peacefully to attend to their affairs like that priest from the Puebla region who was more engaged with his relatives, his maids and his 200 head of cattle than with his indigenous flock. Routine, contempt or indifference, had the Indians ceased to take pride of place among the Church's preoccupations? In fact the post-Tridentine Church, considering that the evangelizing phase had ended, pursued other aims and deployed other strategies, which we shall examine below (Llaguno, 1963, p. 55; Greenleaf, 1965; Gruzinski, 1990).

This relative indifference would condemn us to ignorance if exceptions had not come happily to confirm the rule. After all it does not matter much that the few parish priests who were engaged in denouncing and extirpating idolatry encountered only a feeble response. Their testimony remains. We know that neither the work of Sahagún nor the decisions of the Council of 1585 were published; nor did the treaty of Ponce de León or the considerable body of work of Ruiz de Alarcón (1629) and of Jacinto de La Serna (1656) have the honour of being printed in the seventeenth century.[2] Only a few authors of lesser calibre were more fortunate.[3] However, despite the cry of alarm that they raised, there were no concerted campaigns of extirpation like those insistently demanded by Jacinto de La Serna apart from some temporary commissions circumscribed to certain regions. And, irony of fate, far from concerning themselves with the Indian sorcerers pursued by Ruiz de Alarcón, the Holy Office accused the extirpator with having sought unduly to play the inquisitor with his flock. This was a more unpardonable crime in the eyes of the tribunal than all the falling back into bad old ways of the untutored populations taken together!

Hernando Ruiz de Alarcón was for five years charged by the archbishop of Mexico Juan Pérez de La Serna with learning 'about the pagan customs, the idolatries, the superstitions that persist and remain still today'. It was in the torrid parish of Atenango del Río that he had to end his days, before 1646. Jacinto de La Serna was a more considerable figure. Born in 1595, doctor in theology, parish priest of Tenancingo, then of the parish of the cathedral of Mexico in 1632, three times rector of the university, under two archbishops *visitador general* of the diocese, La Serna in 1656 finished writing his *Manual de ministros de indios*, which took over the essentials of Ruiz de Alarcón's treatise, adding to it information drawn from his predecessors and his personal experience. Sign of the times and of the decline of the orders, Ruiz de Alarcón and La Serna belonged to the secular clergy.

The interest of these two investigations is exceptional since, above all preoccupied with efficacity, the two authors reworked relatively little the material that they had collected. On the contrary, descriptions of specific cases abound. Facts are situated in their original context. Men and villages are identified. Dates and circumstances are provided for the curiosity of the reader. Concerned to lose nothing and to draw everything to the attention of the other priests to 'affect a tireless curiosity' the better to trap the 'dogmatizers', Ruiz de Alarcón and La Serna expanded in a remarkably detailed manner on the gestures, the rituals and, it is worth emphasizing, the invocations pronounced by the Indians that they were pursuing. Ruiz de Alarcón even systematically recorded the Nahuatl text. The treatises thus offer Indian testimony that, unlike that gathered by the great chroniclers of the sixteenth century, is not arbitrarily and systematically dissociated from the circumstances of its production to be integrated into the explanatory grid used by the author. That does not mean that the extirpators avoided developing a theory of indigenous paganism and of its persistence, but they did so to a large extent in the margin of the information that they recorded. The method saves the Indian informant and quite often the pursued *curandero* from anonymity. Far from being excluded, it was he, much more than his discourse or gestures, who was the object of interest and of the repression undertaken by the two ecclesiastics. This scrupulous attention in fact reflects a twofold conviction. On the one hand, La Serna and Ruiz de Alarcón believed in the dissemination, the danger and the partial reality of the universe of pagan forces that they were hunting down under the appearances of Christianity. On the other hand, they were convinced that they had to do with a complex that permeated the least aspects of daily life. That explains the scrutiny that, far from limiting itself to the spectacular and the exotic, investigated the trivial, noted the episodes of the inquiry, the origin of the informants and the position of the investigator, with a care that one seeks often in vain in the recent anthropology of the Indian societies. One will point out in any case – and one will be right – that no more than their predecessors did they escape errors of interpretation, an obsessive fear of clandestine conspiracy and hidden leaders propagating error and lies.

This precious documentation forces us to limit our attention, as we have done in reading the Nahua Titles. What the inquiry gains in depth, it unquestionably loses in breadth. Governed by their informants and their obsessions, Ruiz de Alarcón, Jacinto de La Serna and to a lesser extent Ponce de León introduce us nevertheless to three regions that, if they are far from exhausting the variety of New Spain, offer a field diversified enough for us to be able to carry out numerous cross-checks and put forward certain conclusions. The most northerly and the coldest is without a doubt the valley of Toluca or more precisely the south and centre of that region dominated in winter by the snowy peaks of the Nevado. Not far to the east the Morelos outline a rich basin that slopes down to the foothills of Ajusco and drops towards the south, passing from a temperate climate to semi-tropical and tropical heat. Further south and still lower, the north of Guerrero where, scattered over these sun-parched lands, the Nahua populations mixed with older groups, Chontal and Tlapanec. A common feature to all these regions at the beginning of the seventeenth century was the demographic rout, far more lethal still than that described in the *Relaciones geográficas*. And there were variants linked to ecclesiastical presences more pronounced (the valley of Toluca, Morelos) or more slack (the often deserted reaches of Guerrero), as well as a more or less marked penetration of the colonial economy with its *haciendas*, its stock breeding and its exploitation of sugar cane, and finally its mines around Taxco or at Zacualpan.

How to apprehend this secret dimension invading – if one can believe Durán and later Ruiz de Alarcón – the core of Indian life? To choose the word idolatry to designate it might seem paradoxical to the extent that it appears to defer to the grids and obsessions of the sixteenth-century missionaries. I have none the less used it because, on the one hand, certain extirpators of idolatry were able to sense the considerable significance of a phenomenon that by far overflowed the cult proper of idols, superstitious practices or secret games of magic. Also because, without being fully satisfactory, it enables one to avoid vague, apparently neutral and all-purpose terms such as cult and belief and, even more, the old debates about magic, witchcraft and religion that might well further cloud an already complex subject. It was above all necessary to refrain from presenting the process of acculturation as the confrontation of two 'religions' that would symmetrically gather dogmas, beliefs and rituals. That would have been to project on to the indigenous world overlays with pretensions of clarity but which were really reductive and perhaps without much relation to the configurations offered by these cultures. It would have been to falsify the nature and the comprehensiveness of the phenomenon and to enclose it in a space considerably too small for it. Just as, moreover, it would not be possible to restrict colonial Christianity to a catalogue of prayers and gestures or to the ideological veneer of colonization. To speak of idolatry is also to attempt – through its reference to the matter of the object/idol and to the intensity of the affect (adoration) – not to restrict oneself to a problematic of 'visions of the world', mentalities, intellectual systems or symbolic structures, but to consider also the practices, the material and affective expressions from which it is completely inseparable. It is finally and above all a convenient and immediate way of drawing attention to the specificity of a domain that it now remains to explore and define.

It is obvious that societies brought together by the conquest faced each other not only on the level of religion, politics and economy but also and more comprehensively in the area of their respective approaches to reality. In this perspective, it seems that prehispanic idolatry was more than a 'religious' expression, that it conveyed a distinctively indigenous understanding of the world, that it showed what constituted objective reality and its essence for the Indians. Prehispanic idolatry wove a dense and coherent network, conscious or not, implicit or explicit, of practices and knowledge in which were inscribed and deployed the whole of daily life. It made plausible and legitimate the reality that these cultures and societies constructed, proposed and imposed – a reality that clashes and conflicts did not raise doubts about. However brutal the aggression and the demands of the victors of old – think for example of those of the Triple Alliance – they respected the equilibrium of the local cultures in their relations to reality, time, space and the person. At most they superimposed observances and customs that continued to emanate from the same cultural group or from the same Mesoamerican source.

With Christianity it was different. Like the old invaders, the Christians burned the temples and imposed their gods. But they refused to share or superimpose, demanding the annihilation of local cults. Not content with eliminating the old priests and part of the nobility, the Spaniards kept for themselves a monopoly of the priesthood and the sacred, and thus of the definition of reality in its natural and supernatural expressions. But especially working in a different language, so exotic and so involuntarily impenetrable that we might doubt that most Indians could have understood its exact significance, Christianity and the Church upset the game board along with the rules of the game. Christianity made its mark and cut into the monopoly of idolatry first by external manifestations: by the occupation of space at the outset, the construction of chapels, churches and convents; by its celebrations, its Masses, its feasts, the rhythm of its calendar; by the rallying of the nobles and the Indians to the Church, and so on. The old temples razed, the old cults forbidden, the church and the cemetery became the new religious poles of the *pueblo* as the maps drawn up by the Indians themselves illustrate. The patron saint chosen by the evangelizers or by the natives succeeded to the *calpulteotl* in conditions that the tales of the second half of the seventeenth century tell in their way. Defeated, exhausted by sickness, the Indians had no means to ward off a Christianity that moreover brought them substitute rituals adapted to their necessities for survival. From the 1530s the Franciscans celebrated the rogation liturgy in the valley of Mexico and the region of Tlaxcala to check epidemics or make rain fall. Christianized space, Christian time, the once uncontested ascendancy of prehispanic idolatry was watered down through the decades of the century of the conquest.

However, we are not going to consider the collective domain as that of an accomplished Christianization from the sixteenth century, even if public observance and group ceremonies could hardly escape Christian forms. The rituals of the Church coexisted in very numerous places with native practices. That is the case, for example, with the collective drunkenness that punctuated any celebration, or the ritual baths that the new authorities of the *pueblo* took soon after their designation, under the direction of the 'old and the elders'.[4] The ubiquitousness of these mysterious upholders of tradition, dissimulated everywhere under an anonymous plural (*los viejos, los ancianos*), implies persistences that it would be absurd to want to ignore or to deny. However that may be, the public domain is revealed to be more open to Christianization than the individual and domestic sphere, for many reasons: because evangelization in the sixteenth century was a massive and global undertaking; because, apart from the unequally distributed auricular confession, apart from baptism and marriage, the Church had no means to approach the individual; and because if the language barrier had more or less been overcome in the second half of the sixteenth century, that of concepts and categories impeded the influence that the Church claimed to exercise. We are thinking of the accent put on the individual's free will and personal responsibility, of the insistence on the nuclear family faced with cultures that reasoned and societies that were otherwise organized. We are thinking also of the silences of the Church on sickness and childbirth, on relations to nature and the elements, but also on the domestic group. It is true that the altars of Indian houses were early open to Christian images,[5] but the borrowing was made in native frameworks that gave a new meaning to the acquisition.

To these difficulties must doubtless be added the modifications and the perturbations of the social fabric as a result of the conquest. It is undeniable that Christianity and colonization competed to stretch and sometimes break the ties that united the domestic group to the community and not only to more vast groupings of an ethnic or political order. In imposing a system of canonical obstacles and a uniform matrimonial custom, the Church weakened traditional marriage practices everywhere. It wished to remove from the nobles and notables the control that they once exercised on the circulation of women. It sought to remove from the soothsayers the prerogative of directing or postponing marriages. It is true that it is extremely difficult to distinguish the fallout of this endeavour. Still, to the extent that the introduction of the Christian model corresponded to a crisis of social hierarchies, past norms and the old order, to a demographic collapse, to redistributions of the population, we can assume that, without completely disappearing, the symbiosis that existed between the individual, the domestic group and the rest of the community often found itself altered. It suffices to go through the *Relaciones geográficas* to be struck by the social or pathological manifestations – chronic drunkenness – that might call to mind the disintegration of consensus. All the more since at the same time and for the same reasons, the nuclear family acquired a new prominence. Not only was it the only form recognized by the Church, but the fiscal policy of the Crown contributed to strengthening it by modifying the tributary unit, partitioning the domestic group and making widows and single people full-scale taxpayers. Finally, the introduction of the practice of making a will and of auricular confession, the spread of private property and of a salaried group sowed in the long term the seeds of an individualism without precedent before the conquest (Gruzinski, 1988).

This package of undermining influences and of more or less effective constraints had an undeniable impact on the social and cultural coherence of the indigenous communities. Rather than encouraging their acculturation and their Christianization, it seems at first to have introduced disparities of evolution, differences of phase between once contiguous and complementary domains. In these conditions we understand better that in the margin of the penetration of a public, collective and ceremonial Christianity could subsist, relatively unscathed, contexts within which people continued to draw from idolatry meaning for their activities and the answer to the continuous assaults of unhappiness, sickness and death.

The persistence of idolatry is shown first of all in the heart of the home, and in a quite concrete way. From the centre of Guerrero up to Morelos, Indian men and women concealed on altars or in the 'heavens' of the Christian oratories the 'idols of the lineage', the *tlapialli*.[6] In little baskets, in sometimes locked hampers, they kept carefully tied up gourds, statuettes and especially small objects, bracelets, children's toys, half-consumed copal, embroidered cloths, coloured stones, often also hallucinogenic plants, *peyotl* and *ololiuhqui*. These collections, heterogeneous for us, must, like the 'paintings' be able to be read meaningfully in a way that escapes us. They conceal in any case a force whose emanations were feared. They could be opened or touched by no one, so much so that they were left to fall into dust with time. The domestic baskets do not fail to evoke the *tlaquimilolli* of before the conquest, those reliquary 'bundles' that served to seal the union of the *pueblo* with the tutelary deity, with the difference that they had been chosen by the founder of the line and remained in the hands of his descendants and not of the community. In the beginning these objects served for the rituals and sacrifices offered at any moment of life of the members of the lineage: domestic fire cult, new year's gift of new fire and of *pulque*, inauguration of a house, childbirth, etc. Their transmission followed male or female lines of relationship and not the track of marriages, since each spouse remained the exclusive holder of the *tlapialli* belonging to his or her forebears and usually to those of the same sex. After the extinction of the line, the *tlapialli* were supposed to receive the same attentions from the new occupants of the house and were under no condition to be moved from where they were. They thus constituted a kind of material and symbolic capital that expressed the continuity and the memory of the lineage, the solidarity of generations, and, but more indirectly, the commitment of the whole group to respect these objects. Finally and above all they ensured that the household would prosper.

The 'bundles' reveal two primary focuses of idolatry: the preservation of the links of ancestors that Christianity systematically denied, stating that pagan ancestors were being consumed in hell fire; and the trick of an object that is not an image, not apt to be noticed, but which still gives rise to a passionate attachment. In the eyes of these Indians from Morelos and Guerrero, in the first decades of the seventeenth century, the *tlapialli* retained a power far beyond that of Christian images. Their keepers competed in ruses to keep them from the requisitions of the ecclestical judge. Let us not imagine for this reason that their holders were pagan Indians rebelling against Christianity. *Fiscales* like cantors were able to reconcile their church functions with scrupulously keeping these objects until the extirpator surprised them and forced them to confess. It was in any case the manifestation of a memory of lineage that favoured relations and the common dwelling at the expense of the couple and marriage, and kept itself removed from the community as well as from the Christian family. An analysis of the *tlapialli* could not better confirm the persistence of idolatry in a domain that, more easily than the couple or the community, escaped the direct influence of the Church.[7]

The home moreover remained the setting for rites of passage and marriage, which were far from secondary survivals. These included indigenous 'baptism', in the course of which the newborn was bathed before being given a name drawn from the old calendars and having the ears pierced. The bath, the choice of a name referred to the introduction into the child of its *tonalli*, i.e., the force linking the child individually to the cosmos and giving it 'vigour, warmth and value, while permitting its growth'. If the *tonalli* corresponding to the day of birth was good, the bath took place immediately; if not, it was put off until a less unfavourable date. In the meantime the child was placed under the protection of the fire of the hearth, from which it received light and force. That takes us back to the Nahua conception of time, cycles and the cosmos, which saw in each day and each moment the confluence on the terrestrial surface of divine forces and influences whose nature had to be identified and dangers sometimes averted. The *tonalli* exercised two considerable effects. In the short term it ensured the survival and growth of the child; in the long term it oriented its personality. We understand that the loss of the *tonalli* was considered an extremely serious blow to the integrity of the being, and that in the seventeenth century it was still the subject of complex practices and therapies destined to localize, recover and reintroduce the *tonalli* into the sick organism. This is the interpretation, among others, that was hit upon to account for the sicknesses and death of very young children. Marriage also gave rise to old gestures, and it would be interesting to study at length practices centred on the domestic fire because of the divine energy that it radiated, its warmth and its luminosity, which related it to the *tonalli*. That was the origin of the libations of *pulque* and the offerings made to it on the occasion of a sickness, the construction of a house, or the first fruits of the harvest. Domestic idolatry, in other words, was not limited passively to filling the voids left by the partial penetration of Christianity. The physical architecture of the house and lofts, the nooks that it concealed, the objects that it accommodated, the fire maintained in it, brought their immediate, familiar support to an incessant evocation of the vital dynamism that structured what was quite different from a collection of 'survivals' or 'superstitions'.[8]

But to confine idolatry to domestic rituals or to make it a duplicate of certain more or less Christianized communal rituals would be to fail to understand its scope and nature. In fact we find it rooted at the heart of most activities of the indigenous people, who applied themselves to detecting and acting on the favourable or unfavourable divine forces that circulated on the terrestrial surface and overshadowed all their acts. That was true of the hunter, the fisherman, the farmer, the Indian who manufactured lime or collected honey, the one who collected wood on the *monte* or who devoted himself to a small business or peddling. All that affected production and distribution had to do with idolatry. These activities were conceived and practised in the framework of a reality that to us appears transfigured but which in fact corresponds to the way the Indians dealt concretely with the constraints and difficulties of work and production;[9] at least traditional work. It is notable that the new activities introduced by the Spanish were absent from the field of idolatry. Neither the mine, nor work on the *haciendas*, nor the *repartimiento*, that obligatory tapping of indigenous manpower, seemed to awaken a specific echo in the preoccupations and observances to which the extirpators called attention; no more than, on another level, conjugal relations in the sense of the Church definition.

This inability to account for constraints that were a growing burden on indigenous existence is doubtless revealing about the decline of idolatry. None the less, idolatry could not have been reduced to a body of knowledge monopolized by small circles, lost in the midst of the ignorant and uncultivated masses. To believe their own accounts, the Indians who sowed *camotes* or gourds, those who raised agaves to produce *pulque*, the fishermen who threw their nets, possessed all the words, the objects and the gestures that were supposed to ensure the success of their undertakings, to punctuate their successive phases, and to orient their progress. Under this form, there is no doubt that idolatry was not only intimately associated with the activities of production and trade, but also represented a knowledge still quite broadly disseminated among the Indian populations.

However, in certain fields the bearers of a specific knowledge made an appearance. There were, for example, the *conjuradores de nubes* who made it rain or made the hail stay away, and ruled the mountains – those boundless reservoirs of water and winds –[10] as if the vast space of the sky and the winds and their capricious mechanisms remained within the competence of idolatry. When we know the crucial importance of the regular alternation of dryness and rains for the fate of the harvest in New Spain, we understand how recourse to these conjurors reflected an old adherence to a sacred geography, an interpretation of 'natural' forces, and tireless combats on which the survival of the group could depend.

The struggle against death and sickness, as well as the perils of childbirth were other fixed points of idolatry, once again by means of men and women who knew the words and the plants. Women were in the forefront here. As midwives, they looked after preparations for birth, coming into the world, the care given to the mother and the newborn. It was they who kept the child's *tonalli* from the attacks of bad or anonymous powers. There were at least 20 in Morelos and Guerrero made known to us by Ruiz de Alarcón. Four of them appear to be socially distinct from the others; two were married to Indians called by the Spanish *don*; another was called *doña* Catalina Paula (in colonial society *don* was an indication of the upper status of *principal* or of *cacique*). But nothing permits us to assign any kind of rank to the remainder of these Indians, and it seems that their functions had little to do with their social extraction. The same with their age: some are old but not all; or their condition: some are widows, others are married. Apparently just one knew how to read or write: Petronilla de Tlayacapan. It seems that women took up divination in greater numbers than did men. Most of the time it was women who found lost objects and animals, discovered lost friends and re-established the troubled balance of the domestic hearth. The importance of these women should be emphasized: they took part as the equals of men in the transmission of the ancient cultures. It is moreover the first time that we see them taking part so openly in the process of acculturation and counter-acculturation.[11] Their jurisdiction was generally identical to that of their male counterparts, like them called *ticitl*. 'Doctor, soothsayer, sage and sorcerer', specialist in all ills, the *ticitl* provided care with plants, instruments, manipulations and invocations. In laying on hands or scrutinizing grains of corn, he identified the origin of the ill and discovered the means to ward it off. While ordinary *curanderos* generally lived in modest conditions, those who practised divination were 'greatly esteemed, covered with gifts and provided with the necessities'. In fact the distinction between those who harboured a once priestly knowledge and modest practitioners trained on the job was often blurred and that was no doubt the fruit of a century of Spanish domination and Christianization. So it was that certain healers succeeded in acquiring great notoriety and even in eluding the suspicions of the clergy.[12]

These men and women are known to us. They confessed their practices. On the other hand no wrongdoing 'sorcerer' spoke ('they never admit', reports Ruiz de Alarcón), none of those whose harmful undertakings were feared, those who sowed death, the *teyolloquani*, 'he who eats the heart of someone', the *texoxqui*, 'he whose look fascinates', the *tetlachihuiani*, 'he who makes something happen to someone', the *tlahueliloc* 'the bad, the perverse', the owl-man, 'he whose heart is twisted', 'he who makes fun of people'. It is true too that the *curandero* could in certain circumstances, but without ever acknowledging it, take on this role; ambivalence played such a leading role in his practices. The 'sorcerers' nevertheless carried out a precise function, that of explaining and polarizing one of the origins of the evil, by embodying the aggression, devouring, trickery and anguish. Did the status of these figures become quite different from what it had been before the conquest? It is difficult to say. There existed then a marginal category, disapproved of and feared, of 'sorcerers, profaners, thieves and rapists', who made detestable use of their prodigious powers and whom the Indians did not hesitate to eliminate physically. Christianity in this field as in others muddied the waters, since in the eyes of Christian Indians, the traditional *curanderos* without any exception ought also to fall into the Spanish category of 'sorcerers'. If we add that their activities were more than once ambiguous, it will be understood that it is sometimes tricky to work out if the suspected Indian was a 'sorcerer' because he was heterodox in the eyes of Christianity or because he was an evil-doer in the eyes of the Indians. Criteria were superimposed without systematically confirming one another.[13]

We consider that from the midwife to the *curandero*, from the 'conjuror of clouds' to the Indian in his field, in his house, on the bank of a river full of fish, from the guardian of the domestic relic to the 'devourer of the heart', in this first third of the seventeenth century idolatry wove its old tapestry, discreet, transparent, protected (or almost) from the view of the Spanish, made up of a mastery of learning and observances that produced an indigenous reality, which marked out the field of experience and set up a specific relation to the Other and to the world. Idolatry not only brought an answer to biological and social unhappiness, to the precariousness of conditions of life but, even more, inculcated a manner of seeing and acting in contexts as distinct and complementary as ancestrality, production and reproduction, the sick body, the domestic hearth, the neighbourhood, the fields, and the more distant realm of the *monte* where one went off to hunt deer and gather wild honey.

The evocation of reality revealed by idolatry took the form of knowing and saying, expressed in songs and invocations (the *conjuros*) in a particular form, the *nahuallatolli*, a language 'of hidden words', a liturgical language indissociable from an action on beings and things, a statement which was confused and combined tirelessly with observance. *Nahuallatolli* was a secret and esoteric language whose apparent mystery resided in metaphors, the ambiguity and imprecision that characterized them. It is attested in vast regions of Guerrero, in the Morelos and the valley of Toluca. But it was employed also quite certainly in the valley of Mexico, in the capital itself and the other Nahua lands (López Austin, 1967a, pp. 1–36). The hermetic quality of *nahuallatolli* was the fruit of the exploitation of its metaphorical register rather than the complexity of its constructions. The same formula could designate the most varied references: thus *xoxouhqui coacihuiztli*, 'the dark green fatigue of the serpent', depending on the case, could be pain in the shoulder, the chest, the stomach, fever, sore throat, toothache or pain in the eyes, a fracture, the pains of childbirth, and so on. So it was that more than a dozen different expressions designated fire or water. Still despite everything it was a limited and extremely stereotyped terminology grafted on to a simple and repetitive structure: the speaker who pronounced the *conjuro* presented himself in the guise of a being gifted with unlimited powers / who called up the assistance of forces or entities just as powerful / to command the adversary that he fought to cease his aggression. The metaphorical expressions that designated the protagonists of the drama being performed were hooked on to this scenario. In other words, *nahuallatolli* left little room for improvisation, while tolerating within the thus circumscribed framework a certain latitude in the choice of metaphors or the length of the invocation, the more so in that the choice of metaphors was not closed: expressions borrowed from Christianity enriched and renewed the repertory; others were forged to designate what was unknown before the conquest: livestock, beef and sheep, for example.[14]

This union of flexibility, malleability and formal rigidity, where one finds the indelible mark of codified orality, explains the geographical homogeneity of a language that ran from the warm mountains of

Guerrero to the plains of Morelos and even to the cooler valley of Toluca, in lands physically quite different and *pueblos* several hundred kilometres apart. This unity assured easy memorizing and an oral transmission that could take place within the domestic group, the lineage – from father to son – and the community by the intermediary of the 'old and the elders', or which could accommodate itself to more episodic contacts with itinerant 'masters of idolatry'. Some of them traveled from *pueblo* to *pueblo* like peddlers or goods carriers, covering respectable distances, going from the south of Nevado towards Toluca or passing from Morelos to México-Tenochtitlán. They contributed to spreading and maintaining not only the 'language of hidden words', but also the gestures and techniques invariably associated with them. Still there should be no need to imagine clandestine and organized networks as did the extirpators, quick to denounce 'complicity', conspiracy and 'contagion'.[15]

Nahuallatolli is obviously prehispanic in origin. At least we have good reasons for thinking so. It appears to correspond to one of the many expressions of the indigenous oral tradition in Nahua territory. Following this hypothesis it would be appealing to compare with the written religion of the Christians the alphabetized culture of the authors of the Annals and the Titles, an essentially oral and thus 'popular' idolatry. But the prehispanic or colonial share is, as usual, far less clear. Didn't the *conjuros* several times mention pictographic media?[16] Should we deduce from this that the recitation of the *conjuros* required the support and knowledge of 'painting' and as a result that the latter was widespread in broader sectors of the population, even among the women? Probably not, to judge from the preceding chapters. The searches of the extirpators would not have failed to reveal many of these 'paintings'. But they were not seized. Everything suggests, on the contrary, that the conjurors limited themselves to learning by heart and reciting a variable number of formulae without undertaking the long apprenticeship of an art in regression.[17] What then to make of the reference to *amoxtli*, to 'painting'? Should it be read as a simple metaphor? Or rather as the resurgence of the priestly origins of the *conjuros*, as if, far from having been a marginal, second-rate knowledge, the invocations were the decontextualized heirs to the knowledge of the priests and the nobility? Other indices, which we shall examine below, would also support this view. Neglected by Indian leading circles now gone over to Christianity, sometimes retained by country notables, idolatrous knowledge and observance would have been gathered and preserved in part by more modest layers of the population, plebeians, peddlers, healers and midwives. Would this drop in status perhaps explain the spread, the success and the fragility of idolatry in the seventeenth century? But this second hypothesis would tend to deny the *macehuales* any cultural existence before the conquest. Now we might suppose that they retained, if not a specific patrimony, at least a personal approach, no doubt less formalized and less systematic than that proposed by the teachings of the *calmecac* and the *telpochcalli*: that, for example, of the *curanderos* and the midwives. And it seems that the *conjuros* also bear its mark. It is true that we know almost nothing about this, apart from a few scraps understood through the filter of the nobles and the old priests, who informed the friars of the sixteenth century. It remains true that the exemplary, essential knowledge remained in the eyes of all that of the priests and the 'paintings', which explains the references made to them by the *conjuros*. It will thus be preferable to assign a twofold descent to the invocations, seeing them as the perpetuation of a prehispanic cultural form, 'minor' and 'subordinate', as well as the colonial receptacle of old learning, drifting, deprived of other means of expression, taught by fallen local priests, converted into 'masters of idolatry',[18] and even by the *tonalpouhque*, who still counted the days of the calendars.

That implies that, if in certain areas the indigenous cultures borrowed from Christianity and European culture, in others they were prey to internal evolutions inaugurated, let us recall, by the brutal reduction of the old cults to clandestinity. While the nobles and then the notables discovered progressively a space, a time, an exotic writing, in the surrounding chaos, other Indians combined the learning and speculations of indigenous priests and old people with the ordinary knowledge, perhaps more pragmatic, of the *curanderos* and the midwives. In this case Christian and colonial influence had only an indirect effect, limiting itself to setting off a process of internal mixing before arriving at the content of the new arrangements. This double origin probably explains why the *conjuros* did not make up the corpus of a coherent cosmogony that would be an organization and an interpretation of the *teotlahtolli*, the 'divine words' that spoke of the origins of the world and the epics of the gods. The *conjuros* offered only fragments, quotes, allusions. Fragments, not only because the *conjuro* rescued shattered learning, but especially because outside the context of its use, apart from the action that it exercised on the reality that it called up, it did not exist. The *conjuro* was only produced in an isolated way and to essentially pragmatic ends. In other words, the *conjuro* was more a power over beings and things than a knowledge; it was more a praxis, a making of connections, than an intellectual speculation. That does not mean that it completely ruled out speculation: *curanderos* and others could be led to think of the body of *conjuros* that they knew, but that was not their immediate and customary goal.

That is why it is tricky to seek to extract from the *conjuros* a systematic representation of the world that we none the less surmise to be underlying, implicit, but which perhaps sometimes escaped the Indians that pronounced them, since their efficacity demonstrably took precedence over their significance. That does not prevent us – leaving the question aside for the moment – from exploring the reality created by these formulations, by an idolatrous speech that instantly created the conditions of its action.

A word that claimed first of all to proclaim a power: the user of the *conjuro*, whoever he was, entered fully into the reality that he called up by granting himself more or less complete entitlement. From the outset he portrayed himself as He who holds the knowledge, 'He who knows the Land of the Dead and the Domain of the Heights', he was the 'Priest, Lord of Charms' (or the 'prince of the *nahuales*'), Cipactonal, the inventor of the calendar. Unless he identified himself with Centeotl, the god of maize. The more the circumstances and the invocation resembled a confrontation, the more numerous were the titles invoked. We recognize the names of divine prehispanic powers: Xolotl, the god of Transformations, Quetzalcoatl, Xipe Totec, Cipactonal and Oxomoco, Xochiquetzal, Miclantecutli, the 'Lord of the Land of the Dead'. But we also see the many manifestations of the same power: 'the Young Man, the Adversary, the Mocker', 'He whose People we are', so many names that refer to all-powerful Tezcatlipoca, whose supreme power, knowledge of signs and of fates the conjuror thus appropriated.[19]

Absent however from these identifications were the primordial divinities, Earth, Fire, Tlaloc, but also the tutelary god of the *pueblo*, the *calpulteotl*, as if the first were not able to be 'personalized' and the second belonged to a communal sphere, distinct from the field of action of the conjuror. That being so, the choice and accumulation of titles did not aim to transform the identity of the conjuror to the point of making it the incarnation of power. That would be to lend to the prehispanic gods a personality, an individuality that they never had. It was rather more modestly to affirm the presence of a temporary power, required in a given context. Yaotl, the 'Adversary', enabled one to prevail in combat; Quetzalcoatl introduced the mythic reference on which he based his intervention; Cipactonal appeared in an interrogatory on fates. All were instruments rather than identifications. In this respect the conjuror could not be confused with the prehispanic man-god who received in his heart for a given period of time part of the divine energy whose *ixiptla*, receptacle, he became. The conjuror incarnated a quite different kind of relationship to the divine, more episodic, more pragmatic, if I may say so.

There was a common denominator to all these titles, that of *tlama-cazqui*, the 'Priest', the 'Officiant', which served to qualify the conjuror as much as those to which – beings or things – he addressed himself. Before the conquest the term designated a 'minister of sacrifices' but also the 'demon who is *present* in an idol or who makes an appearance'. Etymologically, he was 'he who offers something', an idea developed by one of the titles of Tlaloc, the agrarian god of the mountains and the rain: Tlaloc Tlamacazqui, which Sahagún gives as Tlaloc the Provider, 'he who gives men the means necessary for physical subsistence'. Everything thus leads us to believe that the term marks a connection with the divine, accession to the world of the gods, and enrolment in a network of exchanges and vital gifts, those of priests towards gods and of gods towards men.[20] In receiving the name of *tlamacazque* all, from the conjuror to the plants, animals, tools and instruments that he used, came to make up a sacerdotal collectivity whose presence, identity and nature were thus stipulated. La Serna confirms this reference to the prehispanic clergy when he reports on the *tlamacazque* of bygone days that they 'were divine, separate from the remainder of ordinary men, that they were generally old men recognizable by their big lock of hair'.[21] That corroborates the links suggested between the 'popular' knowledge of the conjurors of the seventeenth century and priestly circles. They had probably existed since before the conquest on a local scale in groups that seem to have been homogeneous enough. But the colonial domination contributed to reinforcing them by weakening the distinctions of status and function that separated pagan priests from healers and sorcerers, all rejected by Christianity in the same opprobrium.

From this self-affirmation, the universe in which the conjuror moved arises under our eyes. Everything takes its place, or rather it is the reality of things which is discovered there, made present, that of the forces which will help him like the powers which will threaten him in their respective identity, their invulnerability or their murderous irritability. Endowed with his in-humanity, the conjuror can now at will manipulate the inmost depths of things, seduce, intoxicate, pacify, repel or destroy. The *nahuallatolli* opens doors to him unless he chooses the parallel or complementary paths of sought-out drunkenness and hallucination, sleep and dream, or the ecstasy attained in exhaustion and penance.[22]

But it is not easy to delineate in words the world that arose from the invocation, even if it was based in part – and sometimes distantly – on the 'divine words' or, if we prefer, on myths, although the hackneyed term is hardly satisfactory. At Temimilcingo, in Morelos, at Tlaltizapan, we recognize without difficulty the tale of the descent of Quetzalcoatl to hell in the texture of the formulae used to reduce fractures. The invocations pronounced against scorpion stings put other 'divine words' to work (for example, the story of the priest Yappan), while some limit themselves to mentioning the divine name of the scorpion and others describe the rebuffs of the animal or even play out on the body of the sick person the episodes of the 'fabulous' drama.[23] But this canvas with the divine background appeared much more systematically and explicitly in the terminology used in the invocations. Beings and things were endowed with names from the calendar that corresponded to the sign of the moment of their appearance. Thus 1-Water designated trees and wooden objects, 1-Death things of the earth, 1-Silex mineral matter and objects, 4-Cane fire, 7-Flower the deer, 8-Silex the agave, etc. Other signs, again the combination of a number from 1 to 13 and one of 20 substantives, marked the phases favourable to the intervention of the gods and served to designate them. In all, the repertory offered 260 possible appellations which together made up, as we have seen above, the divinatory calendar. Far from being arbitrary, these appellations, on the contrary, expressed and made real an indigenous conception of time and of the divine presence: a time calculated by ritual computations, produced from the influences of divine time that made clusters of forces, varying according to the moment, come together on the terrestrial surface; a fluid divine presence, whose successive manifestations were punctuated by cycles that did not crystallize on concealed individualities (López Austin, 1980, I, p. 70; León-Portilla, 1980, pp. 157–61).

Through invocation, idolatry thus favoured the omnipresent time of the gods at the expense of human time. It made itself at home there. Rather than passively waiting for the forces to arrive, it snatched them up at the source. By mentioning the mythical name of a thing, idolatry brought about its irruption in the present and in daily life. Thus it broke away from the compartmentalization of time and did away with the complex calculations that made possible picking out the moment when a force, good or bad, surfaced on the earth. Idolatry in a way short-circuited the usual cycles in a concern with immediate efficacity and economy of means. We understand that it was able not only to foresee but also to affect the future, in deciphering the *tetzahuitl*, 'the miracle, the augury', this latent extrahuman force to come and yet already present, ready to manifest itself and meanwhile already active, even if its effect was only perceived later.[24] Idolatry discovered the emergence of what was already there, for it did not deploy itself in our linear temporality.

But the significance of idolatry did not stop there. At the same time as it propelled the conjuror into the time of the gods, it effected a complete transmutation of space. Or rather it deployed space as it was for the Indians: a double space that the *conjuros* ordered according to a vertical axis and a horizontal plan. The vertical axis joined two poles, *In Topan, In Mictlan*, 'the Above and the Below', or if we prefer 'the Domain of the Heights, the Land of the Dead'. To know was precisely to know and master 'the Above and the Below'. This axis was in turn subdivided into a series of planes: the 'Nine Beyond', where Tezcatlipoca came from; the 'Nine Lands of the Dead', where he sent his victims. It was on this vertical axis that the essential transmutations appeared, the transformations of state, the passage from waking to sleep, from life to death, from sensitivity to insensitivity, from consciousness to drunkenness, from illusion to experience or from experience to illusion. The axis was the site of the beginning and the end of things, it was the ascending and descending passage that the divine influences borrowed, the fire of fate, the cycles of time. Finally, it was a space covered instantaneously, indifferently and in all directions by the conjuror, 'not tomorrow nor the day after but immediately'.[25] Because the vertical axis was indissociable from the ground plan, the 'Nine Lands of the Dead' (or the 'Ninth World of the Dead' according to various modern interpretations) communicated with the centre of the Earth, which in turn was linked with the four directions, West, North, East and South. At the four extremities of the earth's surface, as a *conjuro* for the deer hunt recalled, the *tlaloque* (the clouds) supported the sky. What was found on the earth's surface? Teotlalpan, the Land of the Gods, the desert, the 'paradise' according to Ruiz de Alarcón's translation; Tollan, the place of bulrushes but also the end of the world; Teoatl, the ocean, the water, wonderful for its depth and vastness; Tlalocan, the watery stay of Tlaloc; the distant regions where the *tonalli* wander. Another primordial place, Chicomoztoc (the Seven Caves) which the informants of the *Relaciones geográficas* mentioned, whence emerged the different groups of humanity but which in the *conjuros* metaphorically designated the interior of the body. These places, these territories, configured a plan of space where fire occupied the centre. It was a close and distant space, present in daily life, visible in the home, the four corners of the granary or the mat one slept on, a space that inhabited the interior of one's body. A space that combined with time under the sign of instantaneousness and immediacy, as if idolatry discovered and made present the reality of things. The telescoping of time and the visualization of quadripartite space in the Primordial Titles of the valley of Mexico illustrate two or three generations later the fertility of these perceptions and of these old forms, even if they have lost substance and an openly pagan purpose.[26]

Still the content of the *conjuros* is distinctive because they were current in a less acculturated environment than that of the notables of the Titles, and also because they corresponded to a stage before the overall evolution that we are striving to define. Ignoring the constraints of human time and ordinary space, the *conjuro* combined the polysemy of phenomena, posed the fluidity of kingdoms, established the permeability of beings and things. Fire, water, wind, clouds, the sun, but also animals and plants, sacred sites and areas, objects, sicknesses and the divine powers acquired a common essence and unveiled their essential reality in the context of the time and space that idolatry constructed. Then the conjuror discovered for himself and others a universe of transformations, of metamorphoses where one slipped imperceptibly from the human to the vegetal kingdom, from the animal kingdom to that of things or gods, from the priesthood to the divinity, where the components of being were unstable and perishable.[27] It was a universe where three vital forces ensured the life of man and the body. Concentrated in the head, the heart and the liver, they connected man to the cosmos, making of him 'the ordered and stable synthesis of the universe' (López Austin, 1980, pp. 262, 285). But if two of them failed, then the equilibrium was broken and blemished; sickness or death intervened. It was thus a universe of extraordinary malleability, instability and mobility that overturned the categories and classes distinguished by the European mind, or at least that of the Spanish clerks who were frightened of what they discovered and recalled that the world of Nature could not be confused with that of free will, any more than Truth with the 'fancies, fictions, and diabolical representations' that the demon inspired in these wretched *curanderos*. For the Church 'there are no transformations',[28] borders were clear, unless Satan interfered to upset the order of nature. Confronted with these barriers, these distinctions which flowed from a fundamentally binary apprehension of a world where heaven was opposed to hell, nature to culture, being to becoming, and the spiritual to the temporal, idolatry spread out its many-dimensional, versatile, reversible reality, indifferent to dichotomies and rigid definitions without, however, sliding into chaos and the arbitrary. Idolatry had a specificity that the extirpators converted into irrationality; a plasticity quickly categorized as lightness and inconstancy. Once more, the logic of some became the folly of others.

The indigenous borders of the natural and the supernatural are not our own. Not only did they correspond to different thresholds, they also worked differently. They had a flexibility and a versatility that, without abolishing them, tended to remove much relevance from our distinctions, and made it impossible to dismiss idolatry to the paraphernalia of religion, myth, even the supernatural or some other place cut off from daily life. As we have seen, it defined relations to production, time, space. But in other fields it was anchored in the substance of existence, without for that reason limiting itself to reflecting it. The language of idolatry was in many respects a social language, to the extent that it regurgitated formulae in which were expressed the relations of kinship and class that predominated in Indian societies. Let us say, to be more precise, that it exploited particularly what they conveyed of deference and respect. In pre-conquest societies, just as in our ancient world, these manifestations took on extreme importance. So it is that, with the term *macehual* used in its strict sense of vassal, we meet a term that designated the nobles and powers of old – *tecuhtli, pilli, tlaçopilli* – and which applied to gods as well as to animals, plants, and even to whoever pronounced the invocation. This terminology made possible, among other things, defining the relationship of the patient to the healer or to instruments of healing, specifying in an indisputable way the dependence and hierarchy of positions. Thus the conjuror summoned *ololiuhqui*, a powerful hallucinogen, to 'console its vassal', who in exchange, 'will work in its service and sweep for it'.[29]

Likewise diverted from its current use, the vocabulary of kinship served to mark the distances, the attitudes of deference among the beings and things mentioned by the *conjuros*. Like the preceding Titles, it permitted the conjuror to set up a flexible order and to specify the rank that he occupied, whether he presented himself as the son, nephew or older brother of the one mentioned while the terms 'my father' (*nota*), 'my mother' (*nonan*) or 'my father, my mother' (*nota . . . nonan*) designated divine powers. It will be noted that 'uncles' and 'older sister' generally tended to occupy antithetical positions. They seem to have been contrasted on the level of gender (masculine ≠ feminine), number (plural ≠ singular) and relations maintained with the conjuror, who held 'his uncles' for adversaries and usually received the support of 'his older sister'. Numerous exceptions, let us admit, confirm the profound ambivalence of the beings and things that haunted indigenous reality, as well as the ambiguity of the links that the conjuror could build up with them. However, on one point things seem more firm.[30] In fact, we have the feeling that we must discover if not the principle, at least one of the organizing axes of the *conjuros*, beyond the terminology of kinship, provided by the two terms *cihuatl* and *tlamacazqui*. The first, *cihuatl*, 'woman', delineated a vast feminine domain associated with 'older sister' and 'mother'. *Tlamacazqui*, on the other hand, governed a masculine world, whether or not coupled with 'uncle(s)'. It alone designated the agent, but it applied as well to primordial divinities (fire), and to clouds or instruments of healing. If we recall that there once existed *cihuatlamacazque* alongside *tlamacazque*, that is to say priestesses, we can deduce that the conjuror was having recourse to a division at once sexual – underlined by *cihuatl* – and priestly, to distribute and order these appellations. Let us add that colours were associated with each term, for reasons that sometimes escape us.

But would it not be banal, after all, to conclude that the world revealed by colonial idolatry was ordered according to criteria that were those of the old society and sociability? Banal to observe that idolatry could not be dissociated from a social framework and that, far from occupying an external sphere, it constituted a way of expressing, informing, and playing upon social relations. That would amount to being too quick to forget a century of European presence. We note that colonial idolatry recalled models highly contested by the Spanish domination and Christianity, whether concerned with hierarchies, nobles and indigenous titles, priestly references or even relations of kinship. The nobles were in crisis, deprived of the prestige and the authority that legitimized the deference and the respect accorded to them. The title of lord (*tlatoani*) was very early banished by the Crown; that of *tecuhtli* (chief) fell progressively into disuse. The forbidden, persecuted indigenous clergy had vanished in their old form. The word *tlamacazque* had even come to designate the indigenous servants of the Spanish. The Christian family was spreading, with its insistence on the conjugal unit and the nuclear household, the determination of kinship by marriage, the equality between younger and older. Monogamy and canonical impediments tended to diminish the role of uncles, who had once frequently married the widow of a brother and thus the mother of their nephews. This does not mean that the old society had been swept aside, but more simply that idolatry appeared as a kind of conservatory of social relations and the codes that informed them, and that an ever more pronounced hiatus was opening between what they called to mind and the transformed society of the seventeenth century.[31]

In the *conjuros* there was a pragmatic aspect, noted several times, which made them *also* models of conduct to observe, steps to follow, feelings to experience. We have already observed the emphasis placed on deference, respect within the relations built up by the conjuror. That was unquestionably the mark of an indigenous expression of sociability and formalism, which however could not dissimulate the diversity of relations engaged. Certain *conjuros* broke out with a brutal violence that sometimes corresponded to sexual aggression. Others exploited a seduction that opened roads more peaceful but not less sure. Didn't the hunter or fisherman confine himself to bragging of the charms of his spouse, the better to attract and seduce his prey? Often too the design of distancing the adversary without provoking a violent confrontation shows through, in leading him 'there where there are many agreeable things and abundance of goods', or in asking him to hide to avoid destruction. The admonition, the recall of the task to be accomplished, inspired other formulae that demanded of the instruments a flawless efficacity, and allusions to shame, fault and infraction did not fail to evoke the ethics and the lines of conduct stated by the *huehuetlahtolli*. They confirmed, if confirmation was needed, that idolatry adhered to the daily life of the native, to ordinary experience, expressing and dictating manners of acting and behaving. But it was also able to express manners of being, by exploiting affective states. Anger, fury, affliction and disquiet were the familiar and powerful motivations of the scenarios developed by the *conjuros*. The anger and hatred of a god, of a hallucinogenic plant, could be the declared source of unhappiness and sickness. But it was also 'the sorcerer [who] wishes ..., provokes anger, disturbs'. Desire and covetousness set up threats to be avoided, defused or turned aside.[32]

Several registers are mixed up here: the way in which the Indians conceived the dynamic of emotional states, the specific tonality that they lent and the role that they attributed to them. For (we sometimes forget) feelings and passions, their representation and their mode of expression, are cultural productions in the same way as categories and concepts. It is therefore difficult to translate them into our language without betraying the specificity that is their own in the indigenous universe. Anger and hatred do not necessarily have for us, for the Spanish, and for the Nahua the same echo and the same meaning. We nevertheless understand, despite their opacity, that ardent desire and covetousness can enclose a strong charge of destructive aggressiveness, somewhat in the manner of the evil eye, if we recall that intensity of desire for the Nahua gave rise to a release of energies and of nefarious forces. Affliction, moreover, seems to have corresponded among the Nahua to a mixture of material frustration and physical suffering. An anthropology of feelings and passions would show that idolatry put into play affective states and psychological reactions that were the ordinary lot of indigenous existence, even it if meant projecting them on to the divine, when an unfathomable unhappiness was explained by the anger of a god. But it also contributed powerfully to organizing and making coherent the emotional experience of the individual. It accounted for the injuries that threatened him: anger, hatred, mockery, covetousness; it considered the trouble that they awakened; it defined and commented on the states through which the victim passed. Better, in implementing what La Serna calls 'the barter of passions',[33] idolatry manipulated and interpreted them. Finally, it proposed counter-attacks that ranged from seduction to sexual violence or destruction and that were supposed to re-establish joy, tranquillity, rest. In other words, idolatry, through its language, its scenarios and its practices, oriented the emotional structure of experience, which it made to correspond to the experience that the subject had of himself or the contexts and situations that he was faced with. Idolatry was rooted in a psychic, affective ground that it shaped at the same time as it expressed it. It articulated the feelings to be experienced, set out the states to pass through in contexts as common as sickness, hunting or fishing with a net. That is no doubt how, more than by the memory of 'myths' and the social echo of metaphors, it acquired a capacity to invent and incorporate that almost preserved it from time. Idolatry was not just the updating of norms, categories, representations, cosmogonic models – space and time. It was also able to follow the hazards of human behaviour in combining and articulating acts, sensations and feelings, in proposing and even imposing ways of experiencing and reacting. Finally, it is self-evident to say that idolatry made real and developed unconscious forces underlying conduct and passions, and that the images of woman and the mother that it used deserve a full study by themselves.

The *conjuro* made the link between forces, beings and things. It verbalized and put into practice another of the major axes of idolatry, the absolute interdependence of persons and the world. Contrary to the Christian preaching that since the sixteenth century attempted to explain free will and personal responsibility towards God and men, the meshes of idolatry were used, without resorting to words, inextricably to link individuals between themselves, and individuals to cosmic forces. That is revealed in particular by the threat of stain, which in Nahuatl covered the idea of dust, dirt, garbage. Deviance alone might well put in danger the domestic unit or that of the whole group. The man or woman who undertook illicit relations, projected their stain, their 'dirt' on to their circle, their spouse, the pregnant wife, the children, the animals and the plants. The symptoms of evil were then incalculable. Gonzalo Aguirre Beltrán stressed the critical importance of the notion of dependence in the Nahua aetiology of sickness (1973, p. 42). It would no doubt be necessary to extend it to the perception that the Indians harboured of the world around them and which they made an interlace of influences, exchanges or conflicts between anonymous divine powers (Tlacatl, the Person, Mahuiztli, the Wonderful, the Fearful) or identifiable but never personalized powers (Earth, Water, Fire) between sorcerers, healers, relatives or neighbours. It was an interlace within which personal initiative and the free will of the individual mattered not at all, given the external origin of the evil that emanated from gods, wood demons, clouds, unappeased desire for the other, the malevolence of a third, or even again loss of the *tonalli*. The (Christian) notion of sin, of a moral stain on the being, was not current here since it presupposed a personal autonomy that was not perceived as relevant. It was the same with the most common activities where, more than on himself, the individual depended on the activating of a *conjuro*, on taking into account a cluster of forces, on locating spatially and temporally, without which any action would be doomed to failure. It was up to him then to borrow the non-identity of the *tlamacazqui*, the finery of a title, the rosary of appellations that assured him that he would be strong, provided only that he ceased to be himself.

In these dense and homogeneous networks the individual and the group found the guarantee of their coherence, their interdependence that paradoxically crises and conflicts would only further reaffirm. Everything worked and ought to work in the context of proximity, right up to bewitchment. In exploring the reality of things, in reading the interaction of harmful dependencies, the *curandero* thus assumed an irreplaceable role. Master in the art of establishing and scrutinizing the field of possibilities to elicit plausible deductions and identifications, the *curandero* interpreted social relations using all the means offered by idolatry, its grids, its techniques, its scenarios, and basing himself on an intimate knowledge of the environment. In doing so, the *curandero* revealed himself to be the agent of a sporadic but precise control over the members of the group, the neighbourhood or the household. For he disposed of means to position and use the tensions that shook the group, by naming the perpetrator of an evil, transforming a suspicion into a certainty, working out an explanation.[34]

A package of beliefs, practices, gestures, words and objects, idolatry was nothing like an extra that would come to prolong or amplify reality or add its ritual security to the most diverse manifestations of human activity. It was far more, since it combined representation of the real with the manipulation of reality conceived as such. It was an *intellectual process* in the sense that it brought into play memory, interpretation, decipherment, prediction. It was in that way even a *knowledge* that served to conceive the body, time, space, power, domestic relations and sociability. It was in a more general way a group of codes, a cultural grammar that organized every relation to the real conceived and perceived by the indigenous people. It was thus logical that idolatry also ensured the *expression* and the *use* of *emotional states*, that it articulated possessiveness, hatred, frustration, dread, panicky fear, homicidal aggressiveness.

It would not have been all that if it was not also an *observance*, a repertory of actions, of conduct, even of deceptions that aimed to influence or transform reality perceived as such; a pratice oriented towards efficacity, the obtaining of tangible and immediate results: death, healing, luck; an observance capable of anticipating the future according to the combinations set up and the signs catalogued. We shall not be able to ignore the fact that idolatry used different techniques, those of the cure by the healer, of childbirth but also the gestures (and calls) of the hunter, the fisherman or the farmer and the lime-burner. The *conjuro* articulated a commentary that at the same time as it explained the action undertaken, foresaw its unfolding, gave details of its progression and the means it would employ, to the point sometimes of being a kind of instructions for use. The preparation of bows and arrows, snares and traps in the deer hunt, waiting for and locating game, the placement of nets and snares where fish and birds would be taken, corresponded to different and successive stages of the recital of *conjuros*. What they teach us about Indian techniques is often precious, but above all confirms the difficulty of claiming to distinguish ritual, magic and practical procedures.

For idolatry was also a panoply of often crude and banal objects: gourds full of water, kernels of corn and copal, lancets for bleeding; cupping glasses and plants for the healer; fishing rods, nets, traps, bows, axes, ovens, ritual objects as well as tools, whose invocation guided their use and guaranteed their efficacity. The objects formed an integral part of a set of gestures that associated the circles traced on the ground, the jet of kernels of corn, the rubbing of sick members to the often quaternary rhythms given by the succession of acts and movements of the actor.

As it was at the same time an intellectual operation, an affective experience and a material realization, idolatry did not need – like Christianity – to 'explain itself'. Far from having to be legitimized or to legitimize itself, it was enough for idolatry to exist. In the eyes of the Indians it was in the order of the obvious, constituted their objective reality, was the matrix that constructed *this* reality. The product was all the more plausible and indisputable if it corresponded to the individual and collective experience, if it was mixed up with the representation of the social body, with the demands of material life and the imperatives of production and reproduction. A superficial examination of the *conjuros* has shown in a specific field how idolatry could bring together all coherent cognitive schemata, social references, affective and emotional roots, the realization of the most trivial tasks and efficacity. This capacity explains idolatry's inherently compelling character without – and this is probably how it differs most from the Christianity of the missionaries – the problem of *belief* as an act of faith ever having been posed. Idolatry did not require personal adherence, it held together in a fluid network of dependencies, gifts and priesthoods multiplied to infinity.

Thus a native reality existed; that is, an indigenous field of possibilities and probabilities, which answered to existential contingencies – the survival of the individual and of the group – and was based on a specific approach to space and time, the human being and the divine, the connections between beings and things; a reality constructed on a perception and an interpretation of the real which is not ours, any more than it was that of the Catholic clergy. Idolatry expressed the reality of the Nahua Indians, including what they supposed to be explicit and implicit, conscious and unconscious, able to be articulated and ineffable. Let us recall in this connection the silent principles, the interiorized habits that organized the representation of space on the old 'paintings' or the drawings of the Primordial Titles or again the secret constraints that in these same Titles continued to produce a predominantly cyclical time in the seventeenth century.

Idolatry at issue

The preceding analyses are misleading. They might well suggest that a century of Spanish domination, epidemics and Christianization had hardly altered the old order of things. If the convenience of the exposition demanded that we banish almost all allusion to the colonial world, it cannot lead us, following other scholars, to fantasize an immobile indigenous world, miraculously preserved from the onslaughts of acculturation. We have every reason on the contrary to ask in what way idolatry could still account for reality as a whole, when so many new elements had troubled its order. We shall be wary also of the opposite extreme that would see in seventeenth-century idolatry just an amalgam of 'superstitions', an entanglement of 'aberrations of spirit' or 'vices of paganism'. Idolatry endured, not by some mysterious law of inertia, but first because it retained a cognitive, social and material function in the countryside we are covering of Guerrero and Morelos. The needs of the domestic group and for its reproduction had hardly changed since the conquest. The living conditions, techniques, work on the land had often evolved little, and the introduction of livestock, as we have seen, was 'registered' by idolatry thanks to certain metaphors created to order. The precariousness of existence, the fears and ills that struck beings and groups, were only aggravated by the colonial domination. As for the effect of the new colonial economy, it remained still marginal or indirect, even if raising sugar cane with its large windmills (the *trapiches*), its black and mulatto slaves became widespread in Morelos, even if the Acapulco road periodically came alive with the passage of merchandise in transit from the Philippines and Asia towards the capital of New Spain.

The change was elsewhere, in the gaping holes opened by the conquest: in the disappearance of the priestly and educational apparatus of the old days, which ensured the spread, interiorizing and reproduction of some of the indigenous learning. The phenomenon did not just affect the sons of the nobility, if we realize that in prehispanic times more modest schools, the *telpochcalli*, were also obliged to take the children of the *macehuales*. At best, in considering that, in the first decades, clandestine priests and the elders continued to ensure a semblance of training, the secrecy to which they were constrained for a century must have diminished their penetration. Unlike the *tlamacazqui*, who once taught at the foot of the sanctuary,[35] the *curandero* appeared as a more isolated being, driven to discretion, to a variable, sometimes precarious status, whose distinctive marks were more personal than social. One generally has the feeling that it was the use of *nahuallatolli* that now legitimized the position of the *curandero* and no longer his birth, rank, or belonging to a priestly circle. A power dependent on a knowledge of words . . .

We shall not conclude that the *gente popular* (ordinary people) of before the conquest knew only what the indigenous priests wanted to teach them. It is highly probable that a collective 'popular' knowledge existed then as well. But it seems that it was sufficiently integrated in the body of knowledge retained by the group to have to recall the authority of the *tlamacazque* priests and to define itself in relation to it. So it is that we interpret the allusions of the *conjuros* to the 'paintings' or to the ministers attached to the local sanctuaries, who lived surrounded by the consideration of the group and maintained by it. We understand that in this perspective idolatry could have suffered from an unquestionable institutional weakness as much as from a progressive blurring of the references that it offered.

The same distance, the same gap was driven between the colonial present and the references evoked by idolatry. The metaphors, for example, systematically mentioned the glyphs and the images of the gods represented in the 'paintings', but more often still sculpted on the walls of the sanctuaries that have disappeared. The colours whose use studded most of the *conjuros* – yellow, red, black and white, blue-green – refer not only to the 'paintings' but also to the stelae and painted walls that until their destruction the Indians had constantly before their eyes.

The repression of deviance was also modified or rather disorganized because, on the one hand, the predominant norms were now those of the Church and the justice of the king; and, on the other hand, indigenous justice lost a large part of its competence in favour of Spanish jurisdiction. It flows from this, for example, that deprived of its traditional extensions (the rituals of confession, corporal punishment, etc.), purging the stain was now much more connected to its material repercussions than to the pursuit and punishment of the deviant; impurity was ritually removed, if need be by committing another, while the perpetrator of the evil was, curiously, ignored.[36] It is not impossible that this reorientation was connected to a growing confusion of roles. Confined to the same clandestinity, once distinct or even competing spheres supported each other, the same Indians reading the signs, healing or causing sickness, exciting or appeasing desires.

It is true that not everything had disappeared at the beginning of the seventeenth century, that the Indian dances could be inspired by or repeat the old liturgies, that the 'paintings' were still preserved and above all – we generally forget this – that the objects of daily life survived everywhere. It is natural that their apparent insignificance protected them from the destructions of Christianization and later on from the curiosity of archaeologists and historians, very little concerned to investigate these obstinately present witnesses of the ancient world. This explains how idolatry resisted better in the domestic context, where it managed to preserve a constant link to the immediate environment, that is to say the essence of its plausibility. While sculpted calendars and 'idols' were broken and temples dismantled, these trivial objects, earthenware receptacles, gourds, snares, hearthstones, obsidian knives, censers, embroidered *huipiles*, trinkets and children's games continued to lend their discreet and omnipresent support to idolatry. It was a material, technical, we would say functional support, and much more, to the extent that the form of these objects, the colours with which they were painted, the acts that surrounded them, the orientation imprinted on them concealed a meaning, a capacity for evocation indissociable from the material use to which they were put. Everything, without any exception, was significant. The breaking of a pot, the cracking of a beam, the cinders of a hearth were so many signs to read, which joined the house to the universe of the cosmos.[37] Corn and *pulque* were food as well as a portion of divine power. Unquestionably idolatry owed to this material immediacy, this kind of 'immanence of the divine', its ability to maintain its efficacy and for a long time to master its course, despite the disappearance of the normative and political authorities who identified it with the language and expression of power. Nevertheless, we shall be wary of considering this 'material' domain (but is it really?) as the simple refuge of an idolatry deprived of its most 'noble' forms. That would introduce a scale of values empty of meaning, since it is a domain as essential as the sophisticated manifestations that ordinarily command attention, if not more so.

None the less, the loss of certain settings and certain components of the old idolatry, tempered with the preservation of a principally domestic substratum, in the end had an effect, at first through the growing fragility of knowledge and observance. The indigenous representation of the real that emerges from an examination of idolatry had neither to be legitimized nor made explicit. The Indians of common extraction sought in it the means of effective action towards people and things, not a speculation that had been the prerogative of the priests, the 'paintings' and the songs. It was sufficient for the conjuror to put into practice the network of relations and combinations required by the objective that he had given himself. Still the intelligence of the *conjuros* demanded the preservation of this knowledge and seems in large part to have foundered with the disappearance of the traditional clergies. We know that in the seventeenth century the conjuror did not learn the 'divine words'. On the contrary, his apprenticeship appears to have been quite cursory. The accounts concur in describing a teaching simplified by the rapid inculcation of all-purpose practices and polyvalent formulae 'for any kind of difficulty'. According to Ruiz de Alarcón the invocations that served to locate and recover *tonalli* that had strayed had often lost meaning even in the eyes of the Indians. The old computations, whose importance we have tirelessly recalled, knew the same oblivion: 'There are no more Indians who understand the ceremonial computation, or who know when the year begins or ends. They have retained in their memory only what they did on those days. Today they practise when they can and not when they wish; thus they practise outside the time of their ceremonies.'[38] As in the Titles, rather than an explicit, mastered and precise representation of time, it was a manner of perceiving it, a way of experiencing it, that continued to ensure its specificity.

The decay of the old institutions is quite obviously inseparable from the ravages of forgetfulness. And beyond the evolution of the memory of the notables, it would most likely be necessary to examine the evolution of the domestic memory, continually decimated by sickness, extinguished with the disappearance of the group, or dislocated in the death of generations or the disintegration of family ties. The documents are lacking. But we can perhaps better explain the role of the domestic 'bundles', the relics concealed in the houses, which assured a semblance of continuity but whose composition and origin we are also unable to explain.

With knowledge and observance in a fragile state, idolatry thus was neither inert nor intangible. It was fragile to the extent that it was more and more cut off from the religious, cultural and social environments that it had expressed, and a part of the structures that ensured its topicality crumbled or disappeared. It was fragile because its implicit and underlying axioms – the fluidity of space and time, the permeability and the interdependence of beings and things – was less and less nourished by the oral, liturgical, iconographic, even kinaesthetic memory of old. In this regard, reading the *conjuros* can be misleading. We would be wrong to confuse words with the mental operations that they designated and the observance that they appear to have governed. The observations of the extirpators of the seventeenth century lead one to believe that the distance had already been established. Idolatry thus ran the risk of ceasing to be an organized semantic memory, to become a succession of isolated formulae, esoteric because hollow, and the reality that it conveyed progressively in the process of cracking and disappearing.

Behind these injuries to idolatry, we have no difficulty in making out the consequences and the limits of evangelization. In repressing the most visionary forms of the native cults, the Church, as we have seen, dealt a difficult blow to the monopoly of idolatry, to the uncontested symbolic domination that it exercised. But in relentlessly attacking the idols, the rituals and the old priests, the Church failed to realize that it had to do not only with beliefs and observances but with an extra-ordinarily dense tissue of relations and combinations. At the same time, Christianity also meant Christianized Indians, and had done for a century, whatever the quality of their indoctrination, from the 'painters' who created Christian glyphs up to the faithful of the distant *visitas*. We have seen the part taken by Catholicism in the public celebrations, in the space of the *pueblo* and progressively in the communal memory, to the point of partially inspiring the composition of the Primordial Titles. In the course of the decades, the Indians became familiar with the rituals and liturgies and (we shall come back to this) with pictures, whose virtues they had the leisure to test, without always having grasped their meaning. In these circumstances their Christianity con-stituted a stock of new features, conduct and divine forces, which could not fail to 'contaminate' idolatry by taking up and reversing the vocabulary of the extirpators. It is still necessary to come to an agreement about the nature of this Christianity. Among the Indians one must, of course, distinguish degrees of evangelization: the Christianity of the nobles was not that of the notables who knew a bit of Spanish, as it was not that of the *macehuales* either. Among the latter and in the country there predominated a Christianity of the formula (the invocation of the Trinity), of the gesture (the sign of the cross) and of certain sacraments (baptism, marriage, more rarely confession), a Christianity in which sporadic attendance at Mass was more a measure of *allegiance* than an act of *belief*. We cannot stress enough how the personalized conception of divinity, the Christian conception of the individual and thus of the tie that binds them, seems to have considerably disconcerted the Indian people throughout the sixteenth century and still later. We shall thus not be surprised that the key notions of sin and the afterlife were often the subject of interpretations and misunderstandings which drained them of their original meaning, just as the exclusive empire that Christianity claimed to reserve for itself was hardly understood. It was doubtless elsewhere that the threat introduced by Christianity took more immediate form: in the disparities of assimilation and attitude that it gave rise to among the indigenous populations, in the consensus and continuity that it cracked, in the hesitations and contradictions that it engendered. We might think of those conjurors who agreed to give up their observances only to return to them later; of those Indians who accused others under ecclesiastical law; of those whole *pueblos* that followed the advice of a *curandero* before falling in with the completely opposed view of the ecclesiastical authorities. These prevarications, these reversals, contributed even within Indian societies to challenge, to undermine in many fields, the ascendancy of idolatry.[39]

A no less serious adversary lay in wait for idolatry at the beginning of the seventeenth century, paradoxically just because of the success of the *curanderos*, whose clientele was growing. The evolution was particularly spectacular for two groups of specialists, the fortune-tellers and the 'conjurors of clouds'. Very early on they had to answer to a demand coming from non-indigenous circles, but quite convinced of the efficacity of the procedures employed. A spouse or a *mestizo* neighbour, the *mayordomos* of the Spanish country estates, mulatto cowherds, black slaves who worked in the sugar mills, the Spanish of the large *pueblos* and the cities swelled the ranks of a disparate clientele who sought in New Spain as elsewhere healing, fortune, a reading of the future, mastery of climatic hazards, success in love. The apparition and then the development of an external demand uniquely concerned with profitability, immediate efficacity and as ignorant as it was indifferent to the body of presumptions, tenets and outcomes implemented by idolatry had an unforeseen impact. They opened up a 'second career' for idolatry, while overturning its meaning, impact and substance. They contributed not only to a diversification of words and acts but also to changing the nature of their deep implications. Idolatry in this form had to adapt to new contexts, take account of certain censures, know how to dissimulate itself with disguises when, for example, a *curandero* visited a convent to look after the nuns. Through commercializing itself, offering services, setting fees, the idolatry of the *conjuros* seemed to evolve towards the already heavily frequented areas of imported magic and witchcraft. Not that the prehispanic *curandero* did not also sell his help, but his intervention was inscribed in the context of a cosmogony, a quest for an equilibrium that had been broken. In *mestizo* or Spanish circles, he capitalized on a recipe, an expedient to which one had recourse out of curiosity or despair. It is true that the Spaniards, *mestizos* or mulattos did not hesitate to take the step that separated ordering services from personal participation; but without really penetrating indigenous reality, even when they adored idols, visited caves, financed the sacrifice of children or let themselves be seized by a collective panic.

The different forms assumed by the emergence of colonial society affected the integrity of idolatry by diminishing its field, partially erasing its references, directly challenging its plausibility. It remains to be established if in these first decades of the seventeenth century, in the areas of Morelos and Guerrero, these modifications entailed accommodations, partial adjustments, or if they already fundamentally challenged the body of representations and their organization. On these dates, and in most cases outside the cities and a public Christianity, idolatry seems despite everything to have preserved its control of the processes that we have described. It was not ruled by any principle of exclusivity, and could thus coexist, up to a certain point, with what the Indians 'made' of their Christianity. This apparent coexistence must have preoccupied the Church from the 1570s. The Dominican Diego Durán was worried at that time about the indecisive attitude of the indigenous people, as put in a nutshell by one of his interlocutors: 'They *believed* in God and at the same time *practised* the old ways and the rituals of the devil'.[40] In the mid-seventeenth century, equally scandalized, La Serna noted the twofold ritual observance among the Indians that he was pursuing: 'They wish to appear Christian while being idolatrous'. If La Serna lost his way in ascribing to them a machiavellian conduct fabricated of hypocrisy and duplicity, he closely questioned the capacity that idolatry retained of taking over all the features presented to it, to insert them in its reality: 'They are strongly attached to the things of our holy faith, vowing great veneration to them. [They want] most of the time in their invocations, their cures and their superstitions to imitate the ministers of the Church and to usurp their functions'.[41]

It remains to us to follow the process of misappropriation and absorption that constitutes one of the essential motivating forces of colonial idolatry. When the language of the *conjuros* borrowed terms from Christianity (the justice of heaven, the angels of God, etc.) it caught them in its nets, emptied them of their contents and integrated them in its compositions. Gestures, the sign of the cross, Christian formulae, the invocation of the Trinity underwent a like fate, as attested by the *conjuros* addressed to the clouds by specialists in rain and hail. Still more decisive was the inclusion of the Virgin, the saints or the angels among the possible sources of a calamity: 'We must know who you are, you the angry saint! If perchance you are Our Lady or perhaps Saint Gaspar or Saint John? ... Who is it who is angry: are they the masters of the earth, the angels of God?'[42] The Christian saint has shifted, or rather the Indians have opened to him the repertory of dangerous and ambivalent powers whose wrath is to be feared, a little like the way in which Christian images appeared in clandestine 'paintings' that took up the old rites. This step corroborates the faculty that the traditional modes of expression developed to capture new elements, to extract them from their context and to submit them to native organizations, with the difference that this time it was idolatry that governed the organization of these features. Other examples corroborate the absorptive capacity of an idolatry that was quick to annex new forces, bur also new rituals, above all if they were strangely related to old celebrations. Thus it was a good idea to sooth the anger of a saint 'by making a picture for him or if they already have one, making him a piece of clothing or a veil, or in adding a costume or making a feast for him'.[43]

Again, it is possible to discern – and this is the essential thing – degrees in the takeover. The Christian saint was often just a supplementary appellation bracketed with an old divinity in accordance with the traditional concept: 'These gods had these names and many others because they gave them their name according to the thing that concerned them or that was assigned to them'. So it was that the divinity of fire, the Old God Xiuhtecutli, was also called Xoxeptzin, Saint Joseph, and Ximeontzin, Saint Simeon, in relation to the great age of the two saints. In certain contexts the Holy Spirit came in the form of 'the bird, the spirit' (*in tototl in spiritu*) to designate the agent that attacked the sick person and made him impure. In quite another vein, idolatry at the beginning of the seventeenth century drew upon the diabolical repertory, at the same time distorting it to preserve only the principle of the pact with the devil. And this in the immediate surroundings of the capital of the viceroyalty.[44]

But it happened that the borrowing went beyond a borrowing to embrace a specific procedure, for example intercession, as when the conjuror implored the Virgin: 'Be my mediatrix for many things that are Your creations are being lost'.[45] The power invoked was doubtless more the Earth than the Mother of Christ, but the request for intercession introduced a perceptible evolution in the relationship to the divinity and in its personalized form. Let us not forget that the 'opening' of idolatry to other ethnic groups was complicated in the colonial

period by the disappearance of the authorities – pagan clergy, schools –
once able to exercise censorship. It follows that the permeability, the
proclivity to borrowing represents a strength as much as a potential
risk.

In quite another field, idolatry counter-attacked by borrowing the
vector of alphabetical writing: from the 1560s according to Diego
Durán. But unfortunately for us the Dominican considered it pointless
to record the '*conjuros* that circulate in written form'. In the seventeenth century sacristans copied other invocations and imprudently
signed their papers with their names. An Indian from Iguala was
accused in 1681 with having 'numerous books that were not good',
others hid 'papers written in their language about their superstitions
and their witchcraft'. Sporadic accounts thus reveal the existence of a
written idolatry as there had once been a painted idolatry.[46] We might
ask if putting the *conjuros* (and perhaps the calendars) into writing
could have had an impact on the content conveyed. Did the process
conceal a knowledge and/or contribute to safeguarding its transmission
at a time of epidemics and deaths? Isolated accounts speak of *conjuros*
transcribed on 'papers' and passed from father to son. Still the practice
of writing takes us towards the perceptibly more acculturated sectors of
the indigenous population, the cantors, *fiscales*, and musicians, who had
access to liturgical works from which they extracted formulae and
sometimes long passages as the need arose. This is probably where
those papers to combat fevers and to soothe anger and the 'justice of
heaven' came from, or that text that a conjuror at the end of the
sixteenth century (1587) preserved carefully in his oratory. It was an
extreme example of a *conjuro* taking up a Christian text (the Hours of
Our Lady) to monopolize, beyond the vocabulary and the references,
the essential competences (the intercession of the Mother of God,
salvation) and incline towards the realm of an Indian Christianity
considerably removed from idolatry. This invocation is accompanied by
a drawing that illustrates a similar movement: an eagle and a jaguar
joined back to back, in the manner of the devices granted to the
indigenous nobility; a chalice under a host at the centre; above at left a
banner imitating that of St John the Baptist; under the paw of the
jaguar a book, doubtless that of the Hours of Our Lady. This allows us
to see once again that the permeability of idolatry can harbour the seeds
of its dilution.[47]

We shall thus perhaps be less surprised to encounter among the
Indians arrested by the ecclesiastical judge representatives of the church
staff, these auxiliaries so fervent about the conversion of populations. In
other words, it was possible to reconcile *adherence* to portions of
Christianity, essentially observances, with a traditional apprehension of

reality, as did those cantors who were also elders and who placed beside the dead the traditional offerings of food, or those *fiscales* who kept the 'sacred bundles'. It was a question of two disproportionate registers, without common measure, which, understood and experienced in this light, were not contradictory. On the contrary, it seems possible and it is often imperative for the survival of the group to articulate them, at which the Church Indians were better than anyone. I am excepting, of course, a devout group (governors, sometimes notables), supporters of the parish priest, who went fiercely about accusing the others. Still it is probable that often their activities reflected conflicts of interest rather than the premeditated rejection of the universe of idolatry. There is nothing in fact to indicate that this group really conceived the divinity, belief, or the relationship to time and space in Christian and orthodox terms.

As to the remainder of these rural populations, it appears that their immersion in idolatry remained a fundamental fact of their existence at the beginning of the seventeenth century – with the nuances attributable to the varying quality of local memories, the relative efficacity of ecclesiastical supervision, the laxity of the parish priests. The Indians seem basically to have reacted to the context that attracted them. In general the context was decisive in the step, whether individual, domestic or collective, Christianized or pagan. It was the context that imposed its scenario, recourse to the elders, the cantors or the *curandero*, and not the origin of the features presented. And this context remained on the whole overwhelmingly that of idolatry, even if it was open to the agglomeration of new forces, to taking on and borrowing liturgies and images spread by the Church.

The idolatry of the early seventeenth century was not so much a survival since it retained an extensive empire, a solid credibility, a sometimes aggressive dynamism. Several elements however prohibit our making an inert structure of it: the loss of the context that supported it; its permeability, which in the long term opened the way to a transformation of the indigenous *imaginaire* and its perception of the real; and finally an adversary bent on systematically imposing its experience of reality, its supernatural, and to which we shall shortly return.

These conclusions could be examined in some detail. Do they apply, for example, in the same way to the Indians of Mexico? We should like to gauge the influence of the massive presence of the Spanish, *mestizos* and blacks, on the Indian groups that populated the capital, the role of contacts with *curanderos* from the country, the impact of a stronger Christianization. Candour constrains us to admit our ignorance about the period 1600–1650, the scanty sources authorizing only hypotheses already sketched above: loss of credibility, impoverishment, fashion for *curanderos* and diversification of their clients and, as we shall see, competition from a Christianity from Africa and Europe based on magic and the miracle. It is true too that memories were preserved better there than in the deserted villages.

On the other hand, we have a wealth of information about certain parts of the bishoprics of Oaxaca, the Zapotec of Sola, of Ocelotepec and Juquila, or the Mixe from Villa Alta. There we discover idolatry in proliferation, different in content since it corresponded to other cultures, but above all less injured by the colonial domination. It retained networks and hierarchies of priests who transmitted teachings, maintained the body of traditional rituals, organized penances and sacrifices, and made idols. Not that Christianity was absent from these lands; but it was completely subject to idolatry. The old computations decided the day offerings were left in the church, the altar that was chosen, the number of candles lit. The Christian sanctuary was hemmed in on all sides by idolatry, invaded by the smoke of copal and burnt feathers, spotted with the blood of chickens with their throats slit, pitted with hollows heaped with offerings. This presupposes, as was the case, the complicity and even the active collaboration of the local Indian authorities, *caciques*, *principales*, governors, *alcaldes* who celebrated the new year and the enthronement of new leaders in the old way. Mixe and Zapotec idolatry remained the favoured mode of expression of communal life, of holding power, of the hierarchy of responsibilities, and even the *mestizos* could not escape it. As for the church Indians, cantors, organists, *fiscales*, *alguaciles de doctrina*, they behaved like the heirs of the prehispanic clergy. They assured the cult of the sacred bundles of the lineages and communities, they perpetuated the knowledge of the 13 gods and the 13 months, they taught the handling of calendars and retained the mastery of a space still entirely marked with sacred connotations.

The maintenance of tradition, experienced as a continuity that the conquest could in no way interrupt, did not rule out borrowing. These Indians who lived in less acculturated lands difficult of access systematically used alphabetical writing and composed small notebooks of eight or so pages, in Zapotec, but also in Mixe, Soltec, Chatino. These *librillos*, of which some examples have been saved, are in fact calendars that fix the date of the sacrifices and ceremonies in the manner of the ancient 'paintings' (some of which were therefore still in the hands of the natives). Some communities bought these manuscripts from the Indians who preserved and copied them. The complete diversion of writing to the service of idolatry demonstrates to what point indigenous cultures in the seventeenth century retained an astonishing power of takeover.[48]

Let us look towards the Otomí Sierra of Tututepec, northeast of the valley of Mexico and north of Puebla, in about 1635. There we find pagan clergy and their acolytes, sanctuaries, offerings of paper, copal, turkeys, divinities of the mountain (Ochadapo), the waters (Muye), the harvests (Bez-Mazopho) (García, 1918, p. 301). In other words, a landscape much more 'ancient' than that of Morelos or Guerrero, which requires distinguishing the receptivity of the different social circles, the various ethnic groups and regions. Each group had its rhythms, its inertia or its fads. To give an account of these persistences is both simple and complicated. The isolation of the mountains, difficult communications, the barrier of local languages (Zapotec, Chatino, Otomí), the distance from the major axes of communications, the absence of Spanish settlement undeniably come into play. We might add, for the south of the bishopric of Oaxaca, the excesses of a Spanish administration of boundless rapacity. We are also aware that the intolerable burden of the *repartimientos* effected by the *alcaldes mayores*, *corregidores* and their henchmen provoked the famous uprising of Tehuantepec in 1660, and unleashed more or less violent unrest at Nejapa, Ixtepec, Yanhuitlán. But above all we shall point to the strength preserved by the indigenous communities who managed to save their essential lands and to close these regions of few attractions to the penetration of the European *hacienda*. Finally the Zapotec Titles, like the investigations following the uprising of Tehuantepec, show that a widespread feeling of ethnic identity remained, as well as ties between groups as distinct as the Chontal, the Mixe and the Zapotec. The Indian societies still showed a remarkable coherence, which found in idolatry an unequalled support and means of expression (Rojas, 1964).

5
The Christianization of the *Imaginaire*

Beyond the military, political, social and economic confrontations, the most disconcerting aspect of the Spanish conquest was probably the irruption of other apprehensions of the real, unlike those of the Indians, and not altogether like ours today. Colonial 'reality' spread out in a different time and space, it was based on other concepts of power and society, it developed specific approaches to the person, the divine, the supernatural and the afterlife. In fact the distances that separated the systems of representation or the systems of power reflected a more comprehensive, underlying and latent cleavage, tied to the way the confronted societies represented for themselves, memorized, and communicated what they conceived as being the, or rather their, reality.

However, it was to the strangest section of this exotic reality, without visible reference, without local links, that the evangelizers wanted the Indians to bring their adherence, namely, to the Christian supernatural. The undertaking was at the same time easy and practically impossible. Easy, because despite the considerable distances separating them, the two worlds agreed in valuing the supernatural to the point of making it the ultimate, primordial and indisputable reality of things. Impossible, since the way they conceived it differed in every respect. Misunderstandings proliferated: about belief, which in a general way the Indians interpreted as an act, at best a transfer of allegiance to a new, supplementary power; then about the 'reality' of the other. Each hastened to project his own grids on to the adversary. The Indians believed at first that they recognized in Cortés the god Quetzalcoatl returned from the distant Orient, surrounded with other gods, or else they discovered in the friars the incarnation of the monstrous *tzitzimime*, the creatures of their 'apocalypse'. For their part, the

PLATES

1 Prehispanic painting from the Oaxaca region: the *Codex Zouche-Nuttal*. London, British Museum.

Fragment relating to the story of the Mixtec Lady 3-Silex. Note the two-dimensional space systematically covered with signs, and the thick, continuous contour lines. One can imagine the palette of colours used: blue, violet, light red, dark red, yellow, black, grey, green. The human face is represented in profile; the body is simply a juxtaposition of parts with relatively few variations. Vertical red lines (above left) subdivide and punctuate the space. (*Facsimile of an Ancient Mexican Codex belonging to Lord Zouche of Harynworth*, Cambridge, Mass., Peabody Museum, Harvard University, 1902, Plate 17. Photo Editions Gallimard.)

2 *Lienzo of Tlaxcala*.

The conquistador Alvarado and the standard-bearer of Ocotelulco. In this episode of the conquest of Mexico the faces are still drawn in profile, although the charge of the conquistadores is undeniably of western European inspiration, as is the form given to the sun glyph above the mountain, or the succession of planes in depth. (In Alfredo Chavero, *Antigüedades mexicanas publicadas por la Junta Columbina*, Mexico City, Secretaría de Fomento, 1892. Photo Editions Gallimard.)

3 *Codex of Tlatelolco*. Mexico, Instituto Nacional de Antropología e Historia.

In the centre appear the viceroy Luis de Velasco and the archbishop of Mexico Alonso de Montufar, with the *caciques* of Mexico, Tlatelolco, Tacuba and Texcoco below them. All would have been present when the first stone of the new cathedral of Mexico was laid (1562). Near each head is an onomastic glyph. Renaissance and prehispanic styles are juxtaposed in a composition that remains native in conception. (In Robert Barlow and Heinrich Berlin, *Anales de Tlatelolco, Unos anales históricos de la nación mexicana y Códice de Tlatelolco*, 'Fuentes par la Historia de México', Mexico City, Antigua Librería Robredo de José Porrúa e hijos, 1948. Photo private collection.)

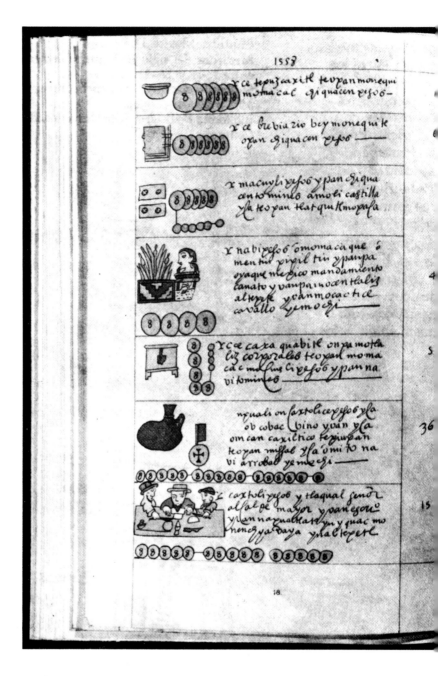

4 *Códice Sierra.* Puebla, Academia de Bellas Artes.

Left page: purchase of a metal bowl, a breviary, of soap from Castile, expenses of a trip to Mexico, purchase of a chest, of wine, cost of the meal given to the *alcalde mayor*, the interpreter and the notary. Right page: purchase of wooden planks for the roof of the chapel, a box for coins, acquisition of liturgical ornaments, of a salt-cellar, a silver bowl, and two saddles. (In *Códice Sierra,* ed. Nicolas León, Mexico City, Museo Nacional, 1933. Photo private collection.)

y cenpuali peços mocoba e çapaliy
ca omotla paço capilla en pate
qua requilcaro yoan ventanas
mochiuaz rey cali   20

y omocalaqui yntequitl yteopa
vino yntotlatoscani onlan
pella q ciame çona tiuj me3
tei junio ypan yn xvit 1556
cuyya xicuxt axiypam
cenpuali ona çona tiuj me3
tli agosto ypan xibitl 1557
cuyya caquao moquixticaxa
co yquac otlan tlaçona fran
val de vielfo unh mocaba o
caxao moçec teo cuytlath
ypença ynaxfan yx quichmo quixtia
yntequitl momaca cençontli ypan om
nali cepeço ypan cetomines hemi   çtã xL pí iLi
çoe yntequite

y moco ba el manpa cruz ye
tla axl thiltic yntecçmo
nequi mimique momacac
omenpuali matlactlixey   L uj eí
çço teopan onfa

y mocoba c mesçia ypta axtl
y van cubilete yvano camo
çaqua iztac teocuytlatl   xL buj eí
mochi momacac omenpuali
onchicome peços

y mocovac omesillas estradi
ote cavallos y tecçmone   xL eí
qui mo macac omenpalixe
sus

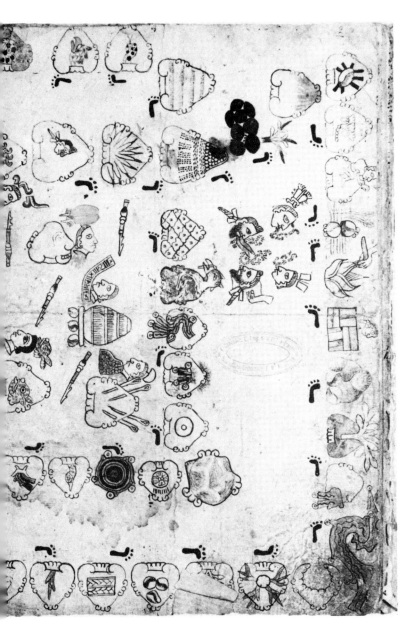

5 Map of the boundaries of Cuauhtinchan and Totomihuacan. Paris,
Bibliothèque nationale.

Although painted in the colonial period, this 'map' still illustrates the 'classic' diagram
style as defined by Robertson. It emphasizes the order in which the toponyms succeed
each other at the expense of the real distances between them. Mountains are delineated
exclusively by glyphs composed of elements that permit the various toponyms to be
identified. The footprints represent the routes taken by the figures. (In *Historia tolteca-
chichimeca*, with studies by Paul Kirchhoff, Lina Odena Güemes and Luis Reyes García,
Mexico City, INAH, 1976. Photo private collection.)

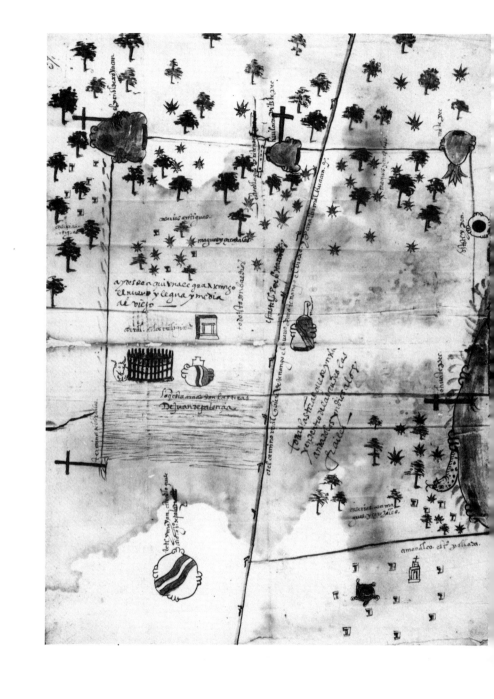

6 Tenango – State of Mexico. Mexico City, Archivo General de la Nación.

On this map of 1587 can be observed the crosses planted on the mountain glyph (*tepetl*) at the centre top and left of the map, as well as on the right side next to a serpent (*coatl*) at the place called Cohuatepec (*Coatepec*, mountain of the serpent), as if the Christianization of space coexisted with ancient survivals. In the lower right appears a water point surrounded by houses. In the centre, towards the left edge, the colonial glyph for a *corral* ('*corral de los religiosos*') with the drawing of a steer. The 'royal road' is marked with footprints and runs from the bottom to the top of the map. (Photo AGN.)

7 Tecualoya and Santa Ana, Malinalco – State of Mexico. Mexico City, Archivo General de la Nación.

Representations of *haciendas*, churches and a mill. The space is empty apart from the essentials. While a slightly elaborated traditional sign, the one for a house, designates the *hacienda*, the church with its bell is a colonial creation. On this map of 1594, alphabetical inscriptions now play an essential role in the identification of places. (Photo AGN.)

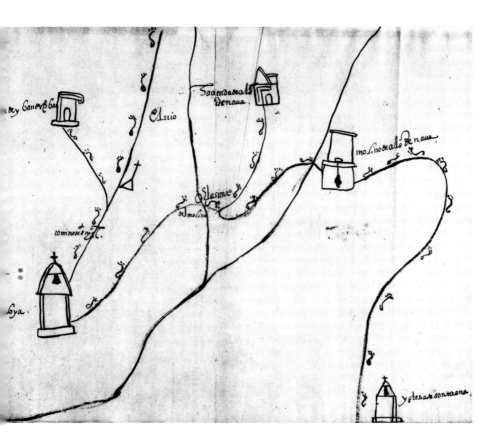

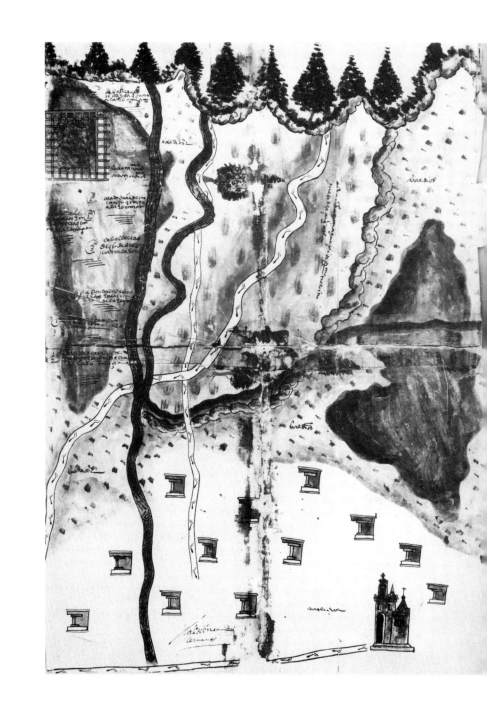

8 Coatlinchan, Texcoco – State of Mexico. Mexico City, Archivo General de la Nación.

There is traditional stylization below: the *pueblo* of Coatlinchan, its scattered houses and its church. Above appear the ridge line and the beginning of a landscape of mountains and forests. The whole is painted in warm colours that are hardly suggested by the range of the photo. Painters such as this are rare, continuing in 1578 to exploit a rich chromatic palette to distinguish the nature and intended purpose of pieces of land. (Photo AGN.)

9 Coatlinchan, Texcoco – State of Mexico. Mexico City, Archivo General de la Nación.

The *pueblo* of Coatlinchan figures as the glyph of a church surmounted by a bell; at the bottom in the centre, the lake is represented in a traditional stylized way, as are the fields, even if the line is sketchy. On the other hand, the landscape, where we still note the mountain glyph (upper right), with its fauna (a stag), its trees and its clumps of vegetation, calls to mind the landscape of the last map. But in this map of 1584 every trace of colour has disappeared. It is oriented (*oriente, norte, poniente, sur*), and annotated by a Spanish notary whose signature can be read lower right ('Alonso López'). (Photo AGN.)

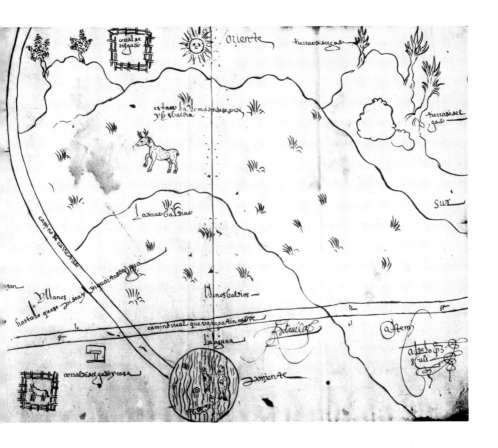

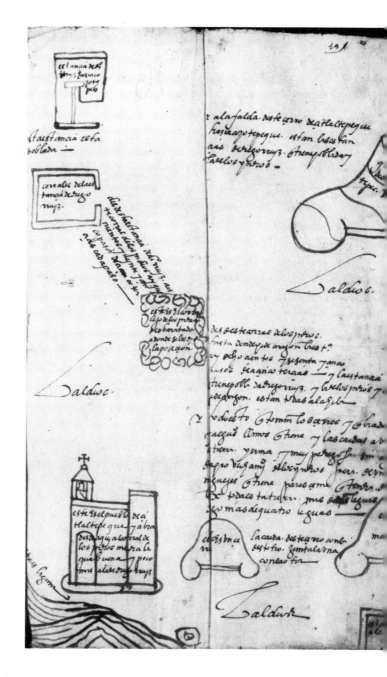

10   Citlaltepeque, Zumpango – State of Mexico. Mexico City, Archivo General de la Nación.

On this map of 1606, alphabetical writing invades much of the space, while the glyphs are roughly sketched: in the centre that of Citlaltepec (a star, *Citlali*, on a mountain, *tepetl*, *tepec*). The drawing of the vegetation and trees as well as the discontinuous line show the influence of the Spanish sketch map prevailing over the indigenous map. (Photo AGN.)

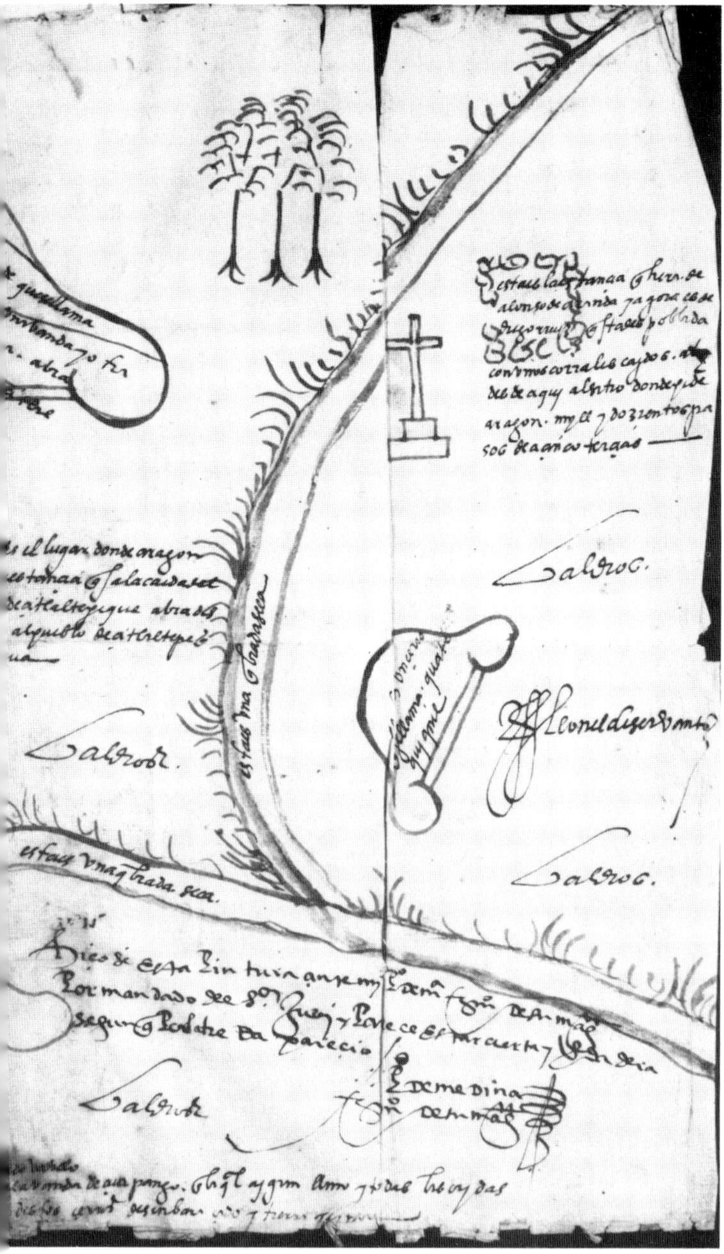

estaua la estancia a que se de
alonso de aujnsa ya gora co se
dizo muy de stauo poblada
con unos corrales caydos. a
des de aquj al ptio donde ysta
aragon. mjll y dozientos pa
sos de a nos teguas

Saldos.

es el lugar donde aragon
estauia la casa cayda se
de atl eltoque que abra 10
alquilo de atl etoque
ua

Saldos.

estaua vna estancia de l apalama guarapa

leonel dizer donto

Saldos.

estaua vna grada por.

Ajes de esta pintura an re mj escriuano fago de Animas
Por mandado de señor Juez y Porece es por cierto y verdadero
segun lo por el padre fra parecio

Saldos.

de Medina
de mjnas

11 *Historia Tolteca Chichimeca.* Paris, Bibliothèque nationale.

The narrative describes the migration of the Nonoualca Chichimeca. The toponymic glyphs are dissociated from the pictographic groups to which they belong (*Epatepec* at left, the 'mountain of the fox cub'). Still coloured, the glyphs have almost become decorative vignettes, illuminations decorating pages now invaded by an alphabetical text in Nahuatl. (Photo private collection.)

12 San Matías Cuijingo, XVIIth century – State of Mexico. Mexico City, Archivo General de la Nación.

In the centre is the church of the *pueblo*. At the four corners are the descendants of the conquerors of the *pueblo*, proclaiming their possession of the land under oath and in Nahuatl. The sketchy line, the drawing of the figures denote Spanish influence, while the stylization of space (a quadrilateral centred on the church) or the volutes representing speech are of prehispanic inspiration. This map was drawn by pen and ink in the second half of the seventeenth century. (Photo AGN.)

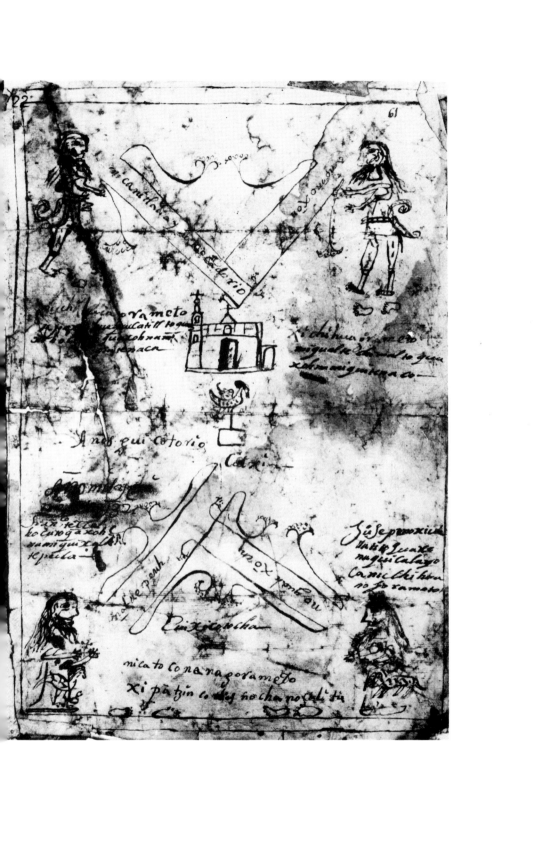

Ximeohui tlaqui
rrexihueyatilla
ю quaxinamiqui
kenaca

tpnoso
gna
hoбoта
rrereю
juaxi
namiqik
tacta

An to xal
xal Panahua
tilla юquaxona
miqui kenaca

AuxicoHa
togue

faVianterpan
rexiatyecuc
tcaxTa

ANO

fran.co rexcal

rexcal nepanti tla
toalexioquaxok
namiquixochikepee

Hi
tichina

ma Cuithualall — a Zacdeny

13   San Matías Cuijingo, XVIIth century – State of Mexico. Mexico City, Archivo General de la Nación.

On each side are the eight *caciques* who gave their names to the boundary markers and borders of the land. Once again the rectangular format of the page governs the overall distribution of the figures. Five horizontal bands define the subgroups, while the centre of the map is occupied by key elements: a church, a European date (1532). Each head is flanked by embryonic glyphs and inscriptions in Nahuatl that identify them. (Photo AGN.)

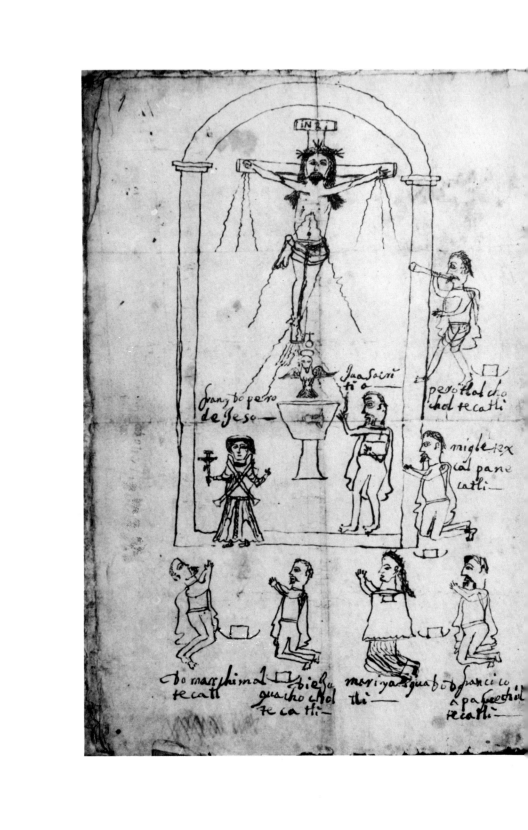

14 The church of Ocoyoacac, XVIIth century – State of Mexico. Mexico City, Archivo General de la Nación.

While colonial features abound (clothing, the vaulting of the church, baptismal fonts), and there are numerous references to Christian iconography (the Holy Ghost, Christ with his stigmata), the organization of the composition continues to ignore perspective: the figures are disposed in empty space devoid of a horizon line. (Photo AGN.)

15 The Adoration of the Magi, Los Reyes, San Juan Temamatla – State of Mexico. Mexico City, Archivo General de la Nación.

Facing the Virgin are the Magi, Melchior (*Sa Melchol*), Casper (*Sa Caçbar*) and Balthazar (*Sa Partezal*). This Adoration, inspired by a European engraving or a colonial painting, is in fact a toponymic glyph designating the hamlet of the Three Kings (Los Reyes). House glyphs surround an enlargement of the colonial church glyph onto which is imposed the memory of a familiar image spread by the art and religious drama of the colonial period. (Photo AGN.)

16 'Painting' seized in 1817 at Huitzizilapan – State of Mexico.
Mexico City, Archivo General de la Nación.

Acquired in Mexico City, this exceptional 'painting' represents the dance of precolumbian
origins of the Indian *voladores*, carrying out a therapeutic ceremony. Around the mat
from which the dancers throw themselves into the void are a church, a cross, a group of
musicians, natives disguised as animals and devils. This painting shows one of the figural
legacies of a prehispanic pictographic tradition, as well as the preservation of a ritual and
expressive recourse to 'painting'. (Photo AGN.)

evangelizers and conquistadores were not to be outdone and took the indigenous gods for the several manifestations of Satan. It was hardly surprising that the devil set himself to speak in the idols that he inhabited, that he took possession of pagans up to the very brink of baptism, or that he made spectacular escapes from the temples where he had been adored. Accused of pushing the Indian people to revolt, of setting them against Christianity, of deliberately provoking drought, devils were the inevitable protagonists of these first years. Far from being denied consistency, many aspects of the indigenous cultures were seen and interpreted by the friars as the threatening, black reality of the demoniac.[1]

Does that mean that by a systematic reversal the supernatural of one became the diabolical of the other? No, for that would be to attribute similar ways of thinking to the two parties. It is true that both accorded a crucial function to domains that we exclude in principle from our objective reality, but that was all that they had in common. The Church and the Indians did not assign the same boundaries to the real. The Church singularly restricted its territory. It excluded as a general rule states (the dream, the hallucination, drunkenness) to which the indigenous cultures conceded a decisive significance, since they encouraged the production and exploitation of images to which they gave rise and the contacts that they allowed to be established with other powers. While these societies showed themselves eager to decipher dreams, the Church fought the interpretation of dreams by denying them any importance, as it condemned the consumption of hallucinogens, sources of 'alienation, visions and delirium', indeed everything traced to 'madness and lewdness', as it denounced drunkenness in all forms, covering in the same reproof ritual and sacred forms close to ecstasy and possession. The Church limited the domain of significant reality by making what it excluded manifestations of the devil, vagaries of non-sense or simple trickery.[2]

Yet it was necessary to lead the Indians to understand the concepts and criteria that organized the reality that the Church defined. Catechism and preaching were the principal channels of the apostolate of the missionaries, who constantly came up against the limits of the word. How could one convey an understanding and way of seeing beings, divine figures, afterlives, without any equivalent in indigenous languages or local representations, if not by approximations that betrayed their substance and form? Everything led to confusion and misunderstanding: the Nahua *Mictlan* chosen to render Christian hell was but one of the abodes of the dead and what is more a freezing place; the Christian heaven designated by the term *ilhuicatl* had little in common with the indigenous Empyrean realm and its 13 levels; *In tloque in nahuaque* – 'the master of the near and the far' – that the friars took to signify God originally described Ometeotl, the Lord of the Duality of whom Tezcatlipoca and Quetzalcoatl were two of the many manifestations. *Tonantzin*, chosen as the name for the Virgin Mary, had once served to designate one of the forms of the mother goddess, and so on. The immense task undertaken by the friars met with insurmountable obstacles. The alternative was as simple as it was frustrating: was it necessary to use a European terminology completely impenetrable to the Indians or to build bridges by extracting equivalences, sources of infinite misunderstanding? Learning prayers in Latin perfectly illustrates the pitfalls of the first path; the linguistic work of the Franciscan Alonso de Molina, those of the second.

But even if it surrounded itself with commentaries that explained its contents and dissipated the confusion, Christian preaching hardly permitted visualizing the entities to which it made endless allusion. That accounts for the immediate recourse to visual supports of which Testerian catechisms were one manifestation. But the graphic visualization that they offered could concern only a minority of book owners. It was moreover so schematic and approximate that their impact remained limited. Frescos, paintings and sculptures, on the other hand, had a much broader distribution. We know that some missionaries supported their teaching with paintings that they commented on. In the second half of the sixteenth century, the Franciscan Mendieta 'painted in certain places all the mysteries of our redemption so that the Indians understood them better and many other things of the holy Scriptures of the Old Testament'. Before him, another Franciscan, Miguel Valadés, had systematically developed this approach.[3]

Besides the painted altarpieces and sculptures, in almost all the convents and churches monumental frescos spread out the essentials of Christian iconography before the eyes of the Indians. Some have come down to us. If we add the works of Spanish and foreign artists – first among them Simon Pereyns of Antwerp – it is clear that from the second half of the sixteenth century the Indians were confronted with numerous representations of European workmanship or origin, especially the inhabitants of urban centres and *pueblos* that accommodated large convents and churches. Of course it was different for the natives who periodically attended a parish church and generally had access only to poorly decorated chapels.

But the friars and European artists were never more than a minority. Indians trained from the end of the 1520s in the *atelier* opened in Mexico by Pedro de Gante reproduced and disseminated Flemish and Spanish paintings and even more the engravings that they had before them. Their works decorated the foremost churches and the homes of the Indian nobles. Numerous competitors in the city of Mexico and the town near Tlatelolco soon hastened to follow their lead, without always having received the same training. In fact quite early on, in 1552, the viceroy Luis de Velasco was concerned enough to want to subject them to the supervision of the chapel of St Joseph, where Pedro de Gante and his disciples were working (Toussaint, 1965, pp. 17ff, 218).

From the mid-sixteenth century, the infatuation of the Indians with European representations thus went hand in hand with the proliferation of what we would call 'primitive' copying. The official and faithful reproduction of Christian iconography that had spread to the churches of the valley of Mexico, the region of Tlaxcala, Michoacán, the bishopric of Oaxaca was coupled with an 'independent' production, whose often decried 'imperfection' is to be attributed more to an interpretation of European language than to native clumsiness. These works populated with Christian images the domestic shrines that since prehispanic times were set up in all Indian homes. We must emphasize one phenomenon that marked the whole colonial period. Partly removed from the control of the ecclesiastical authorities, the fabrication of Christian images, of paintings, statuettes and ex-votos filled the indigenous universe with representations that often scandalized the clergy. In 1585 voices were raised at the Third Mexican Council to demand the prohibition of depicting devils and animals alongside the saints, for the Indians adored them 'as before'. In 1616 a priest attacked 'statues of Christ, images painted on wood or on paper, whose traits were so ugly and whose appearance so hideous that they rather resembled puppets, scrawls or something ridiculous'. Again in the seventeenth century an edict of the Inquisition called for the seizure of images *de pilón*, graciously received by the Indians when they bought goods and piled up on their altars, 'images whose representation is to our eyes so removed and so different from the originals who live in the heavens'. But up to 1681 no order came to regulate the work of Indian sculptors. It is thus essential to keep in mind that Christian iconography was disseminated in the most modest circles through the distorting and regenerating prism of indigenous production, just as Christianity was spread by the intervention of Church Indians more than by that of the Spanish priests.[4]

More than the limits and modes of its dissemination, the style and canons of Christian iconography could make assimilation difficult. For the missionaries, the reduction of indigenous cults to the demoniacal implied simultaneous moral condemnation and aesthetic rejection. The local gods could not but be hideous. The indigenous icon was unmistakably reduced to the level of the proscribed and repulsive idol. But the disqualification and degeneration decreed by the missionaries rested on categories, classifications and premises unknown to the Indians: the more so since, convinced of the universality of their values, the Spanish clergy rarely concerned themselves with explaining them to their flocks.

Let us not deduce from this that the reactions of the natives were negative. On the one hand, the Indians had no choice in the attitude to adopt, but above all their conception of the divine was not governed by the principle of exclusive monotheism. Thus they most often contented themselves with adding the Christian icon to their own effigies, painting the Crucified in the midst of their divinities or, more prudently, hiding the old images 'behind a wall or inside the altar'. Since the Christian image was integrated into a native field – 'painting', the domestic altar – and the copy was usually made by an Indian hand with the adjustments that we can imagine, shocking to the Spanish clergy, this explains why the specificity of European canons did not suffice to hamper the reception of these images. In fact, the images were partially blurred under the projection of indigenous interpretations, which lent other meanings and other outlines to the images of the Christian faith. None the less, preaching repeated through the years and the multiplication of European images contributed to familiarizing the Indians with the European supernatural within the limits, it is true, imposed by the strangeness of the words, the exotic drawing and the filter of indigenous interpretations.

It was necessary not only for the Indians to be able to decipher these images but for some of them to become in the eyes of their community the witnesses of the new supernatural. If the first objective implied just gradually becoming accustomed to the iconic and iconographic codes of western Europe, the second required the Indians subjectively to experience what was sacred to the Christian. Now the early Church was hostile to the miracle which, it affirmed, played only a quite secondary role in the conversion of the Indians. The rejection of the miracle, explicit among Franciscans like Motolinía, Sahagún and the archbishop Montúfar, corresponded to an optimistic, even triumphalist conception of evangelization. It reflected and supported an indigenist bias, which claimed that the enthusiasm of the Indians to receive the faith had made any miraculous intervention superfluous. We might also perceive the secret but unquestionable influence of Erasmianism, some of whose concerns inspired the archbishop of Mexico Juan de Zumárraga. By leaning towards a religion without miracles, reserved on images and saints, animated with a concern to go to the essential and avoid confusions between the faith and paganism, one section of the Franciscan Church deprived Christianity of the means to materialize or visualize an *imaginaire* so removed from the Indians. At the same time, moreover, in the eyes of the Inquisition this trend verged on heresy.

However, miracles hardly waited for the closing of the Council of

Trent or the arrival of the Jesuits or even the installation of the Holy Office (1571) to occur in Mexican territory. The first Franciscans themselves had visions, practised levitation and revived some dead, contrary to the assertion of Motolinía. Many were the angels, saints, demons, the devil, to cross the paths of the evangelizers, to whatever order they belonged. But it was only at the very end of the sixteenth century that writers of history mixed with hagiography thought of making lists and seeking out the smallest miracle.[5] Still this hagiography, in spite of everything, respected the essence of the climate of the early sixteenth century, such that the miracle constituted an internal experience far more than an instrument of evangelization. It was only in the second half of the century that it systematically took its place in a pedagogy of evangelization and the supernatural, through friars whose exemplary life and miracles captured the attention of the chroniclers. One of the first and one of the most famous of those who were called the *venerables* remains incontestably the Augustinian Juan Bautista de Moya, who was the apostle of Michoacán and Guerrero, where he worked towards 1553. From 1550 to 1650, from Querétaro to the bishopric of Oaxaca, from the valley of Puebla to Michoacán, these holy men filled the Mexican countryside with the renown of their exploits, mastered the natural elements, kept away storms, attracted rain, ordered the clouds and plants, lit or put out fires at will, and devoted themselves to prophecy and divination. Above all they multiplied miraculous healings before and after their death, since their relics and their bodies (quickly dismembered by the over-zealous faithful) were themselves also endowed with miraculous powers. Without expanding on the role exercised by the *venerable* in the Spanish and *mestizo* society of the seventeenth century, we cannot fail to point out the strange relationship that blossomed between these friars, often of modest rank, who died in the odour of sanctity, of unimpeachable orthodoxy, and the indigenous *curanderos*, the soothsayers, the 'conjurors of clouds' whom we have met. All exercised the same therapeutic (the *gracia de curar*) and climatic function, the same faculty above all of communicating with the divine by means of a dream or a vision. One might object that the analogy is only superficial, but was it in the eyes of the Indians who interpreted these phenomena in their own language? Who saw 'sorcerers' in the *venerables* and 'saints' in the *curanderos*? If it is true that the *venerables* were the spokesmen of the baroque Church and, in a more general way, of the colonial apparatus, did they not also embody in their person and in an Indian environment an invisible world, a divine power, a direct relay, a constant connection with the Christian divinity? The *venerables* – and let us not forget their relics – thus became the immediate, physical, palpable, tangible expression of another reality, the one evoked much more distantly by the Christian images and more abstractly by the sermons.[6]

However persuasive they might be, the *venerables* still held the barrier of their body and their presence between the Indians and the Christian supernatural. To abolish this distance, the Indian had to accede to the subjective experience of the Christian miraculous. That was achieved as soon as they learned reading and writing. Attested from the first decades of evangelization, the indigenous vision was welcomed with circumspection by the Franciscan evangelizers, who conceded no more than that in the course of the 1530s, 'many neophyte Indians had numerous and diverse revelations and visions'. To recall examples: here in the course of Mass, a globe of fire had appeared above the holy sacrament; there a golden crown had placed itself on the head of a preaching Franciscan; elsewhere the heavens had opened before the eyes of a native devoutly awaiting the opening of the church doors. From this time moribund Indians were carried away to the beyond. About 1535 St Catherine and St Madeleine gave two neophytes the choice between the repulsive road of idolatry and the fragrant and flowered way inaugurated by baptism. In 1537 before dying an Indian of Cholula said that 'his spirit had been carried off towards the sufferings of hell, where he had been tormented with terror and seized with a terrible fear ... and that afterwards he had been led by an angel to a most agreeable and joyous place, full of delights'. But the Indians explored more than the Christian afterlife. They discovered in turn Christ, the Virgin, the angels, the saints, dead friars, the devil in person, who showed themselves to several Indians. Generally experienced on the threshold of death, these visions expressed a reprimand, a warning, a consolation or a message to the visionary or the living. The experience thus belonged to a pedagogy of sin, death and the afterlife. But it remained relatively isolated and sporadic. The indigenous vision existed, but still without participating in a deliberate strategy of evangelization.[7]

The dissemination of the Marian cult probably best illuminates the first stages of the Christianization of the indigenous *imaginaire*; and more precisely the little that we know of the origins of the cult of the Virgin of Guadalupe. The beginnings of this devotion certainly confirm the prudent attitude that the Mexican Church under Franciscan influence maintained towards miracles. At the end of the 1540s a Marian devotion had developed in a poor chapel north of the city of Mexico, at the very spot where once had risen a sanctuary dedicated to the mother goddess Toci. The devotion had received the encouragement of the archbishop Alonso de Montufar, of pious Spaniards and of ladies of quality who attended the sanctuary. But above all it encountered the favour of the Indians who continued to bring to the Spanish Virgin the offerings that they had once intended for the goddess. On the other hand, in the words of their provincial Francisco de Bustamante, and then those of Sahagún, the Franciscans violently denounced the devotion; didn't the Indians believe that 'this image painted by an Indian performed miracles and that she was thus God'? To this reticence towards miracles and the cult of images was added the fear of seeing the Indians continuing to adore under the name *Tonantzin* the old Mother of gods rather than the Virgin Mary. It is probable that the Franciscan Sahagún aimed accurately. He knew the Indians well enough to have learned that not only was it natural for them to conceive the Virgin as one of the manifestations of their old divinity, but also to mix up its image with the force she represented (= 'she was God').

The attitude of the secular clergy was quite different. They maintained that the devotion of the Spanish to the Virgin of the hermitage 'would turn to the advantage and the profit of the natives [who] in that way would come to be converted'. One could not more clearly signify the intention to exploit the Marian piety of the Spanish and the miracles of the image to attract that of the natives. The seculars prevailed. Creole and Indian devotion, the piety of the viceroys only grew towards the sanctuary of the Virgin of Guadalupe in the second half of the sixteenth century, even if there was still openly and officially no question of a miraculous apparition, still less of an image of divine origin, '*manu divina depicta*'. But already tales, an oral tradition, some echoes of which are found in indigenous texts, were taking place. Thus the *Diario* of Juan Bautista, that indigenous *alguacil* of Tlatelolco, indicates that 'in the year 1555 St Mary of Guadalupe appeared on the Tepeyac'; the *Anales de México* confirm: 'Year 1556, the Lady descended on the Tepeyac' (La Maza, 1981, pp. 30–1), a date held also by the Indian historian Chimalpahin in his *Relaciones*. It thus seems that from the end of the sixteenth century, literate indigenous groups collected the traces of one or several apparitions that they dated to the middle of the century, that is, the time when the cult was historically already well established. We might ask about the existence of Indian 'paintings' that would have recorded the Mariophany, of ex-votos that would have been placed in the shrine and would thus have contributed to its disclosure. But there is apparently no trace of any.

The third period and crowning of this development was opened by the intervention of the secular clergy in 1648 under the pen of Miguel Sánchez. His work, *Imagen de la Virgen María, Madre de Dios, de Guadalupe . . .*, collected and reconciled the tales then in circulation, giving them an almost definitive form as well as the theological basis that had been missing. According to Miguel Sánchez, the Virgin seems to have appeared several times in 1531 on the hill of Tepeyac to an Indian named Juan Diego. She appears to have ordered him to gather flowers and to take them to the bishop of Mexico Juan de Zumárraga. When the Indian opened the cape in which the flowers were wrapped before the bishop, the image of the Virgin appeared printed on the cloth. By publishing the same version in Nahuatl a year later (1649), the priest who was responsible for the sanctuary of Guadalupe, Luis Lasso de La Vega, deliberately proposed to reach an indigenous public 'so that the natives see and know in their language all the love that You [= the Virgin] have had for them and in what way was produced what has been much dimmed by the passage of time'. From then on texts, sermons, sonnets and poems dedicated to the Virgin of Guadalupe fed the outline of a creole nationalism while altarpieces, preaching and edifying theatre took on the task of broadcasting the tale thus established throughout the indigenous world: *autos sacramentales* drawn from the work of Lasso de La Vega were performed in the *pueblos* on the initiative of the priests and at the request of the natives.[8]

The recovery of oral traditions, their crystallization and return to circulation in a standardized form by Sánchez and Lasso de La Vega, the great survey of 1666 all testify, if need be, to the vigorous way that the Church took in hand the Mariophany of Tepeyac. It is not without interest that in the manner of the Primordial Titles the Church undertook to design a past, whose authenticity it too was convinced of, a past committed to becoming more real and more unwavering than the historical past. Again like the Titles but, it is true, on quite a different scale, the two priests established a memory and offered the basis of an identity and a new society. The processes were almost parallel even if they put into play quite unequal forces. They bear witness to the crucial weight assumed by the baroque seventeenth century in Mexican history. The Church was taking charge, by a manipulation both deliberate and unconscious, but not mere invention: one should beware of seductive short cuts or polemics. The devotion to the Virgin of Guadalupe progressively blossomed around an image, against the will of part of the Mexican Church, from the encounter of Spanish piety and the perpetuation of a native cult. It was later, only in the last decades of the sixteenth and the early seventeenth century, that the tradition of the apparition was added to miraculous healings realized by the image, and disseminated to all circles. It is necessary to come back to these decisive years, badly served by the sources, to discover the extent of the unprecedented process then affecting indigenous cultures, the Indianization of the Christian supernatural. That was indeed what it was when the Indians became convinced that the Virgin of Tepeyac appeared to one of them, leaving him a miraculous impression. This was decisive, but not isolated. In 1576, in 1580, Virgins appeared to Indians of Xochimilco and Tlatelolco in the environs of the capital.[9] Three years later the translation of the crucifix of Totolapan was accompanied by miracles that corroborated the sensitivity acquired by Indian communities in the capital to the Christian miraculous. At the passage of the image, amidst miraculous healings, the Indians saw the arms of the Crucified move, 'some thought that he was living and that he was giving them his blessing; others imagined that it was the true Christ, who fell into the hands of the Jews; still others believed that it was God and they adored it as such'. Faced with the Augustinians, who were determined to propagate the miracles of the crucifix, the Franciscans, on the other hand, worried as usual about the progress of the devotion and demanded the intervention of the Inquisition. But significantly it was no longer incredulity nor the paganism of the Indians of the capital that worried them, as had been the case 30 years earlier, but the possible vagaries of religious exaltation among 'people of limited faculties and whose intelligence does not soar'. That is to say, there existed in the 1580s among the Indians of México-Tenochtitlán and environs a receptivity to the miracle which was no longer an individual disposition but a collective affair. It seems that this represented a major break with the miracles catalogued in the first half of the century and an index of the degree of Christianization of the Indians of the capital, which we have already briefly investigated.

Other initiatives marked this decade. One year after the translation of the Christ of Totolapan, Dominicans inaugurated the sanctuary of Sacramonte at Amecameca, southeast of the valley of Mexico.[10] It was in this period too and throughout the seventeenth century that miraculous images of the Virgin, of Christ, of crosses proliferated and spread throughout New Spain. Under the threefold impulse of the baroque Church, Spanish piety and Indian devotion, the land of Mexico at that time was filled with local and regional devotions. The sacred and supernatural of the victors were implanted in the landscape, took hold on hills (Tepeyac, Los Remedios near Mexico), mountains, in gorges (Chalma) and mines; they took up residence on the coasts (Huatulco), they won over urban centres (Mexico, Puebla, Oaxaca) as well as more isolated regions (the Virgin of Juquila at Amialtepec). They imprinted a new significance on sites that until then, to go by the *Relaciones geográficas*, had been silent with memories of the ancient world. This penetration and local entrenchment of the Christian invisible, this tidal wave of images in the first decades of the seventeenth century corresponded unquestionably to the eradication of Erasmian tendencies, and to the end of the Utopian dreams that had sustained the missionaries. They followed the triumph of the Tridentine Church, within which the hierarchy, the secular clergy, the canons of the new cathedrals and the Jesuits began to displace the mendicant orders from the dominant position that they were occupying. The installation of the Tribunal of the Holy Office (1571), the arrival of the Jesuits (1572), the celebration of the Third Mexican Council (1585) accompanied the victory of mannerism and its baroque manifestations in monastic art, which died with the century. Too often this post-Tridentine Church was said to have abandoned the Indians, while actually it undertook to devote itself to them differently in a transformed context. The Tridentine Church had at its disposal a steadily growing manpower, since the regular clergy alone increased in number from 800 to around 3000 individuals from 1559 to 1650 for all New Spain, while the secular priests in the archbishopric of Mexico alone grew from a complement of 158 to 451 between 1575 and 1622. Nevertheless, if it is indisputable that the ecclesiastical infrastructure of the indigenous populations had filled out, it is more difficult to form an idea of its effect on populations often disrupted by sickness and 'congregations'. Let us limit ourselves to assuming that ecclesiastical policies had a better outcome, without wishing too quickly to make Christianization equal growth of clergy, and let us agree that the baroque Church was disposed to validate the devotions, cults and miracles that were current in the Indian, *mestizo* and Spanish populations of New Spain – provided that they were codified, channelled into celebrations where baroque ceremony occupied a crucial place.

Let us not forget above all that this policy belonged to a different New Spain from that inaugurated by the conquest. We know that in 1585 there were no more than 2 million Indians, while the Spanish, black and *mestizo* population, still in the minority, experienced constant growth. From the sixteenth century ever more numerous Indians left their cities and their *pueblos* to head towards centres with mostly white and *mestizo* populations. Founded in the sixteenth century, Puebla, the second city of the viceroyalty, accounted for nearly 17,000 indigenous people, while Querétaro, Celaya, Valladolid in Michoacán and Zacatecas, drew thousands of Indians. In closer contact with Spanish and *mestizos*, they were led further to integrate themselves into a collective, multi-ethnic religiosity, punctuated by the great annual processions – the processions of Corpus Christi – the *autos da fé* of the Inquisition, the sumptuous beatifications. There emerged a new, urban society, in the image of the cathedral, whose construction succeeded that of the convents and which welcomed into their naves all levels of the population: guilds and brotherhoods, civil and ecclesiastical authorities, rich merchants and indigenous *caciques*, without forgetting those mixed crowds of Indians, *mestizos*, blacks, mulattos and already 'poor whites'. Finally, if the Indian nobles were often no more than a shadow of what they had been, the Spaniards were not spared either by a society that rapidly burned out men and fortunes: didn't new generations of *pobladores* gradually exclude the ruined descendants of the conquistadores? In this more urban, more mixed world, is it surprising that the cult of the Virgin of Guadalupe, like the vast majority of Marian devotions elsewhere, associated all ethnic groups and that they flourished, like so many others, in the shadow of the cities or in their environs? (Israel, 1975, pp. 39–42, 45–79; La Peña, 1983, p. 237.)

But it is not enough to observe general phenomena to understand the way the Church attempted the conquest and colonization of the indigenous *imaginaire*. Too comprehensive or too meagre, the accounts that have held our attention thus far hardly make it possible to extract the practical methods of this progressive infiltration. It is not enough either to put forward the intensification of Christianization or the rise of cross-breeding to account for the phenomena. One must apprehend it on the level of the individual interiorization, the subjective experience – provided that we have the means to succeed. It happens that the Company of Jesus has preserved traces of a considerable number of supernatural phenomena – in the event, visions – experienced by the Indians and collected by its members during their apostolate. They are particularly abundant for the period 1580–1610, precisely the period with which we are concerned.

I have shown elsewhere in detail the way the Jesuits organized their preaching around visions had by the natives they were addressing (Gruzinski, 1974). They reported exemplary experiences, having recourse to a deliberate dramatization with the appearance of collective psychodrama, drawing all or part of the population into states of depression and great excitement (the *mocíon*, transport) where grief, tears, astonishment, terror and sometimes panic were mixed together. The Jesuits offered the Indians an incitation to the vision, a standardization of their delirium and models of interpretation. It is obvious that they imposed the same schemata on quite different states and disorders, whose specificity escapes us for the most part. But these models and these scenarios were broadcast and rebroadcast with such conviction that we have every reason to believe that the Indians ended by interiorizing them and sometimes reproducing them quite closely. Jesuit codification, Christian stereotypes and Indian delirium were superimposed to the point of being confused, if not always in the spirit of the visionary, at least in the spirit of the edified and 'transported' community. What do we find? Most of the Christian imagery: hell and its devils, paradise and its saints. The antagonism of good and evil took on all imaginable shapes and inspired even secondary oppositions, which underlined and supported the first: chromatism, luminous intensity, odours, sounds, materials were divided up into antithetical pairs that restated the duality in all keys and its ultimate resolution in favour of the Good, God, the Virgin, etc. Such was the imperturbable and rigid logic of a system that unmistakably relegated to a single and identical compartment the ugly, the sulphurous, the dark, the cacaphonous. We are at the opposite pole (but did the Jesuits suspect it?) from idolatry, where, as we recall, the ambivalence of the gods, the permeability of people and things, subtle transformations, multiple combinations, predominated. On the other hand, the Christian vision played on a simple and simplified schema (see the frequent exclusion of purgatory), dualistic in its structure, which encompassed the essential of the Christian supernatural and message. By counting on the interiorization of these associations and these repetitive scenarios, the Jesuit pedagogy of the *imaginaire* thus played on the most diverse registers. It went beyond the limits of speech and the painted image to anchor in the affective, the subjective, an Indian experience of this Christian elsewhere: by making use of emotions, fear, anguish; by integrating them into a problematic of sin and damnation; by dissipating them through ritual techniques (confession, penance) leading to the full assimilation of the Christian theme of salvation and redemption.

Let us say, to attempt better to define the phenomenon, that the Jesuits appear to have offered to temporarily disturbed Indians a structuring of their delirium in the form of a series of restorative symptoms borrowed from Christianity. And this with all the more success in that indigenous cultures at that time disposed with greater difficulty of means to take charge of, interpret and attribute a formulation to these troubles. I come back to this point in the pages dedicated to the crisis of idolatry. The Christian scenarios could be used, for example, as illustration and, let us not forget, in the resolution of delirious fits, hallucinatory psychoses or persecution complexes. Through this cultural reformulation, which appears essential in many respects, Christian beliefs about the afterlife and representations of it were lived as a *subjective experience* (still culturally structured) (Devereux, 1971, p. 25). In that way they could later be communicated and shared, although in another fashion, by the rest of the indigenous community. We understand that visions thus became a prop for the penetration of the Christian supernatural under the ardent and vigilant direction of the Jesuit fathers. We also understand that in these circumstances it constituted a favoured vector for acculturation, since it not only introduced images and patterns of conduct into the indigenous *imaginaire* – faced with the divinity, faced with wrongdoing – but also obsessive fears and a structuring of emotions and anxieties. The Jesuit example illustrates on a modest scale a much vaster process at work in New Spain at the end of the sixteenth century and the early seventeenth century, let us say between 1580 and 1650. It seems to me that it allows us to understand better the development of the Marian cults or miraculous images that flourished here and there. The directed adherence of Indian crowds to the Christian supernatural, the invasion of an exotic supernatural, its implanting in Mexican soil, were always at stake. In any case, it is not necessary to deny the existence and manifestation of truly indigenous experiences, without which the process that we have just described would have remained superficial, and without a future.

To go by this account, one could imagine that from the end of the sixteenth century the Church had undertaken the quiet and irresistible conquest of souls, aided by the difficulties and dilemmas of an ebbing idolatry. That would however be to forget that the Church, with a little more than 5000 priests by 1650, no more had a monopoly of the western European supernatural than idolatry held that of the demoniacal attributed to it. Spanish soldiers, artisans and farmers, African slaves, and even runaways introduced with them a mass of illicit beliefs and clandestine practices that the Tribunal of the Holy See endeavoured to contain rather than to eradicate. If we add to these groups the *mestizos* and mulattos, it was a population of more than 400,000 souls that in the mid-seventeenth century exhibited for the eyes of a good million Indians customs that were heterodox on more than one account.

The domination of the Church was never really threatened. However, quite early on it rediscovered on American soil its time-honoured 'adversaries', heretics and Jews. The first were negligible in number and probably never had a real hold over the indigenous world. Apart from a few Protestant pirates who had the misfortune to fall into the grips of the Inquisition, and pale replicas of Erasmianism, indeed of the Lutheranism that challenged the celibacy of priests or confession, attacks against the Church were limited to individual, sporadic and trivial outbursts. Let us recall, without exaggerating its impact, the presence of a clandestine Jewish community which alone embodied a religion different from Catholicism and by its very existence openly and radically questioned its origins and foundations. It was rather the uproar orchestrated by the edicts of the Inquisition and the *autos da fé* that could draw the attention of urban Indians to these Spanish and Portuguese who eluded the pressure of the Church by leading a double life, in which Christianity was only mask and appearance. On the other hand, it is unquestionable that the misconduct of the Spanish, the *mestizos* and the blacks, their subterfuges, their skill at distorting the obligations imposed by the Church, strongly influenced the behaviour of the natives, who discovered in turn the paths of concubinage and bigamy, faced with the indissolubility of marriage and the imperative of monogamy. It is not completely superfluous to recall that for the Indian people as a whole, Christianity was not only the religion taught by the clergy but also an interpretation and version proposed to them by the Church Indians and more sporadically by the Spanish, the representatives of the Crown, *alcaldes mayores* and *corregidores*, miners, *mestizos*, mulattos that they met in the city or the *pueblo*.[11]

One must turn rather towards colonial magic to discover the sphere that broke the hold that the Church claimed to have on the supernatural. By propagating pacts with the devil, better still, by 'constraining the devils to speak with them', and practising divination, Spaniards, blacks, mulattos and *mestizos* arrogated to themselves powers comparable to those of the indigenous *conjuradores*. Unlike idolatry and Christianity, colonial magic was not based on a relatively homogeneous approach to the world. It generally broke the ties that connected it to the circles and societies that had produced it, whether in the Iberian countryside or the African bush. To this irreversible uprooting were added disparity of origins, a chaotic evolution of components and a multiplicity of forms. Some practices were closely modelled on Catholic liturgy and 'misused the Eucharist, holy oil, altars and other sacred things'. Others distorted Christian prayers. Others took up just as it was, or with some adjustments, the model of the European witch, her pact with the devil, her nocturnal flights, the sabbath, even if the snake and the toad often replaced the cat of the Iberian peninsula. Iberian and Mediterranean influence mixed with beliefs, amulets and divinatory techniques of African origins. This heterogeneity did not rule out overlapping, superimposition and fusion of practices and beliefs. But they remained above all *practices* and *beliefs*, without ever leading to the establishment of a comprehensive or totalitarian apprehension of the world. The product was an unstable amalgam, comparable to these amulets that combine indiscriminately plants of indigenous origin, scapulars and magnet stones. It was a product whose use was limited to the resolution of biological or social misfortune, and whose components varied according to place and ethnic dominance, without ever attaining the range and coherence of Christianity or idolatry. Such a situation provoked a multiplication, a dispersal and a fragility of adherences and personal rejections, since no authority could guarantee the validity or the superiority of any form of divination or manipulation.

The meaning and function of colonial witchcraft and magic, of mixed origins, do not fall within our purview. While they set in motion concepts and practices of all kinds, their goal was far more unified. In a universe as institutionally rigid and hierarchical as colonial society, they often offered the means (illusory or not) of redressing the inequities to which the Spanish domination gave rise for the Indian masses that were in increasing numbers joined by African slaves and especially by hybrids of all kinds. In the seventeenth century there were black slaves who used all their strength to survive in an unknown and hostile environment, seeking revenge or to protect themselves from the oppression of their masters; *mestizos*, who found a place to occupy neither in the world of the whites, nor in that of the Indians; mulatto slaves, who could hope to see their progeny emancipated provided that they merged into, if possible, the *mestizo* and indigenous crowds; *ladino* Indians, acculturated enough to share the life of the *mestizos* and mulattos, but irrevocably condemned like them to occupy the lowest ranks of Mexican society. Finally, let us not forget the poor whites without a future, Spanish women, orphans, widows or abandoned, on their own or given over to prostitution. All swelled the ranks of a class unbearably excluded from power and the riches shared by all the powerful of the viceroyalty. In this rigidified society, it was often gender that made it possible to vault the social and ethnic hurdles, and erotic magic was obviously the indispensable instrument of these amorous strategies that wove among the indigenous *curandera*, the mulatto witch and the Spanish woman the secret complicity and powerful ties that Solange Alberro has admirably studied. To manipulate desires all cultures were drawn upon alike.[12]

Magic and witchcraft thus offered to all seductive visions of their learning and their efficacity. They opened access in a fantasy world to the values and goods that life denied. That explains the feeling that these practices had a pragmatic function above all, that immediate efficacity prevailed over coherence of beliefs and traits, as did the improvisation of means over tradition. The client (one must speak here in terms of the market and merchandise) is ready to do anything to attain his goals, even to the point that some Spaniards, doubtless more numerous than we think, did not hesitate to 'idolatrize' with the Indians to obtain the impossible. That explains this cascade of acts, substances, amulets, formulae, discreet routes that, as much as corruption, gave colonial society its dynamism and its malleability. Finally to pragmatism was added a concern with profitability, with commercializing practices and beliefs, for however modest it was or however vital it was considered, magic was a service to be offered for a fee, a livelihood for more than one man and woman. In this sense too magic was often just a system of defence, at the disposal of many rejected by colonial society. The rigid, strict categories and dichotomies that the Church was intent on imposing on the natives were thus pulverized to the profit of a multitude of beliefs and observances. It was this teeming and hetero-geneous landscape, contradictory in its rules and disconcerting in its criteria, that the natives discovered and learned to know. This addi-tional factor of disorientation added to the abstruseness of Christianity and the anomy prevailing in the sixteenth century cannot be stressed too strongly. One must be a learned man to understand that the *alumbrados* and *beatas* who in the sixteenth and seventeenth centuries knew the passing favour of the faithful were only dangerous heterodox souls. Furthermore, how could the Indians tell the European sorcerers condemned by the Church from those Spaniards who with the autho-rization of the bishops and the local councils could exercise the func-tions of *saludadores, ensalmadores* and *santiguadores*, that is, healers who treated sickness with prayers and blessings? While admitting that 'many superstitions' were mixed in, the Church accepted these practices. The same difficulty arises in distinguishing the *venerables* from the indigenous *curanderos* and even more from the wandering monks, the *frayles* who discovered mines, foretold shipwrecks, found fleeing slaves, and dubious hermits pursued by the Inquisition? But sometimes the borders of heterodoxy became still more flexible, when, for example, prayers were diverted to particular objectives or said in circumstances other than those ordained by the Church. We might think, finally, of those country priests who, not content to admit the reality of indigenous sorcery, had recourse to the assistance of a *curandero* or a driver-out of spirits. There was always something to baffle new converts, or rather to draw them still further along a slope familiar to them, that of borrowing, juxtaposition and confusion. The Christianity of the overwhelming majority of the white or mixed population of New Spain was a conglomerate, extraordinarily receptive to borrowings, faced with which the Inquisition limited itself to re-calling the norm, without ever succeeding in mastering it.

Varieties of colonial magic had the ability to 'contaminate' the lands where they were practised, were of a noxious stickiness that systematically voided of substance everything that approached, so that they became simplified schemata of short-term efficacy. If idolatry could much more easily deal with imported magic than with Christianity, it might just as easily founder in it. And the Indians might well lose their understanding of the world in a group of sparse and contradictory *beliefs*, which reflected the burgeoning of an unprecedented society.[13]

6
Capturing the Christian Supernatural

The progress of the Christian supernatural and the search for magic from elsewhere might have implied that idolatry was beaten in advance. But that would have discounted its permeability, that is, its still un-altered capacity to integrate exogenous features in the representation of reality that it presented. Once more we can hope to understand the process only by using microanalysis and by studying a number of specific cases, provided yet again by our extirpators.

Domingo Hernández was originally from Tlaltizapan, a Nahua village planted at the heart of the steamy, fertile lands in the region of Cuernavaca, on the right bank of the *río* Yautepec. He made himself a reputation for holiness (*era tenido por santo*) which gained ground after he received 'from heaven the gift of healing the sick'. It was in the early years of the seventeenth century.

> When he was at his worst, two people dressed in white tunics appeared to him and took him very far from there to another place where there was a sick person, and there they breathed air on him. Then they took him somewhere else, where he found another sick person and again they breathed air on him. Then they said to him: 'Let us return to your house, for they are already mourning; rest now, for the day after tomorrow we shall come back to get you'. At that moment, coming back to himself, he saw that his household was mourning him as if he were already dead.
>
> The two figures dressed in white came back three days later. As they had the first time, they took him to see the two sick people and they breathed on him just as before. Meanwhile they said to him: 'Hurry up if you want to see your parents, your grandparents and the rest of your kin, but if they find you, you must absolutely not answer them, if not you will remain with them and you will not get back to the world'. Then he saw

two roads, one very wide, which many took – it was that of the damned –
the other narrow, rough, congested with scrub, cane and thorns. It was,
they told him, the road of our Redeemer. He saw that few took it and
again that many people were going along the wide road. The figures in
white tunics ordered him to follow them and they arrived at the houses of
the marvels, where they said to him: '*Xitlamahuico*, etc., that is to say,
look and pay close attention to what you will see. Take note of what
happens to those who get drunk, take a good look, don't go back to
drinking . . . (and many other things of this sort), if not you shall undergo
the same punishment. Give up *pulque* immediately [or else] in three days
you will come back here. Let's go to your place now, for they are weeping
for you already and they must not put you in the ground'. Then they told
him: 'Listen, you who are poor and wretched, these are the means that
will give you something to drink and eat' in the world. They taught him
the words . . . with which ever afterwards he never ceased to heal and to
succeed in his cures, no matter how difficult. At that they took him back
to his house and, come back to himself, he saw that they were weeping
for him as if he were dead.

Then he related that that same night three ladies magnificently dressed
in white, without a hint of any other colour, came to visit him, and he
reported some of the words that they had exchanged. He said that the
three were the Virgin Our Lady, Veronica, and another lady whom he did
not identify. Our Lady said that Christ Our Lord had captured this sick
person and that she wanted to save him. Veronica obeyed her and fanned
air towards him with a veil. At that point he regained consciousness and
from that morning he was well.[1]

At first sight the visions of Domingo strongly recall those that the
Jesuits gathered and spoke about in their sermons of the same period.
Just at first glance: on the one hand, because it was clearly an initiation
and not a pious or mystical experience of an orthodox nature; on the
other hand, because these visions took place away from any interference
by the Church, in a context that recalls what it is convenient to call
shamanic initiation. Moreover, we can easily pick out the successive
moments: the sickness, the imminence of death, the apparent state of
death, the visit of supernatural beings and the voyage to the beyond, the
revelation of professional secrets, the return to the world of the living,
the healing and the birth of the 'shaman'. We are aware that the ancient
Nahua, and Mesoamerican Indians in general, cultivated shamanic
practices to varying degrees. For example, the Nahua believed that men
gifted with a vital force, an exceptional *tonalli*, could travel to other
worlds, enter into contact with gods and the dead, obtain revelations
there and bring back therapeutic secrets with them. Their *tonalli*, under
the effect of drugs and foods, then acceded to abodes closed to common
mortals (López Austin, 1980, I, pp. 74–5, 411, 415). In its develop-

ment and its objectives, Domingo's experience would thus correspond to this ancient tradition. Only on to this native scenario there came to be grafted a package of borrowings from Christianity that all have their precedents or their complements in pious visions familiar to us: the apparition of angels, the torments reserved for drunks, the two roads that lead one to salvation and the other to damnation, the intervention of the Virgin and the saints. Everything proceeds as if Domingo had experienced his initiation in a version strongly coloured by Christianity. One could stop there and limit oneself to noting the penetration of the sacred and the Christian supernatural into the indigenous environment at the dawn of the seventeenth century, and deducing the astonishing success in the affair of missionary preaching and Christian imagery. Meanwhile the existence at the same period and in the same country of a still quite lively idolatry leads one to look more closely and, in particular, to scrutinize the subjective and individual modalities for what seems to foretell a 'spontaneous' passage from one supernatural to another.

The vision of the punishment of drunkards opens a first path. As we have just read, the two figures in white tunics demanded that Domingo give up the consumption of *pulque* ('don't go back to drinking'). The importance attached to the episode suggests that Domingo was an inveterate drinker and that this inclination posed a serious obstacle to his healing, his salvation and the acquisition of the powers of a healer. We recall the spectacular dimensions that drunkenness seems to have taken at the end of the sixteenth century, as is abundantly revealed in the *Relaciones geográficas*. We have also seen that the colonial domination contributed powerfully to dismantling the network of 'divine words', of rituals, prohibitions and repressions intended to contain and regulate alcoholic consumption – in the event the fermented juice of the agave or *pulque* – before the conquest. It is permissible to think that long before the arrival of the Spanish, drunkenness was a worry to indigenous societies and that it constituted a kind of 'ethnic disorder', that is to say, a troubled state whose incidence and formulation belong to a given culture and society (Gruzinski, 1979). Far more than the consumption of drugs, that of *pulque* already tended to escape the norms of tradition and the community. But the Spanish domination intensified its disintegrative effects by the state of anomy that it instigated and, more immediately, by the new forms of alcohol, such as Castilian wine, that it introduced. Moreover, the Crown had no interest in effectively combating a tendency that brought in considerable profits, while the Church opposed to drunkenness only a moral reproof composed of assorted infernal threats, an unprecedented idea in prehispanic cultures, and some lashes of the whip. One was far from the infamous degradations and summary executions inflicted before the conquest.

The Christian answer (the Jesuits provide several examples) was also able to exploit the terrorized deliriums of drunkards who reported having visited the world of the damned. This was far from ineffective, since Domingo reproduced the same material in the context of his initiatory experience. The Indian appears to have succeeded in interiorizing the message of the Church, with its images and its fear of punishment after death, with its dualistic scenario of the afterlife (the two roads), in other words, its logic of sin and redemption. It was as if the Christian interpretation gave a convincing sense to Domingo's disorder at the same time as it dictated the means to put an end to it. The Indian would thus have come to conceive and above all subjectively to experience his drunkenness as a kind of sin punishable by posthumous divine sanctions: 'Don't go back to drinking... if not you will undergo the same punishment'. We would thus be inclined to consider the borrowing from the Christian theme of punishment of drunkards as a process that, far from being arbitrary, constituted a *defence mechanism* against a personal disorder. A process that would substitute a new answer for the features and modes of expression that native culture would have ceased to provide. Let us note that this borrowing simultaneously involves images (angels dressed in white, infernal torments), models of conduct, and affective states (anguish, fear).

On the other hand, the approach taken in the last vision appears to be a little more complicated. At first sight, Christian imagery – Christ, the Virgin, St Veronica – dominates the scene. In fact, as it is experienced and interpreted, the sickness of Domingo belongs to both idolatry and Christianity. The disorder did not fail to give rise to the calming intervention of the Virgin, but the Marian intervention was not yet mediation: the Virgin limited herself to having St Veronica act against the illness without personally intervening before her Son. Moreover, to the extent that emphasis was placed on the aggression committed by the divinity ('Christ Our Lord had captured this sick person') and where this attack was closely related to the capture of the *tonalli*, the disorder conformed to incontestably aboriginal schemata. The sickness followed a logic of persecution that, even if it was resolved in Christian terms, had no room for the theme of sin and forgiveness. It called to mind far more a representation of the origin of evil and a corporal experience pertaining to the Nahua world. This native dominance appeared equally in the recourse to therapeutic practices which, in a still implicit way, referred to indigenous categories, such as the invigorating and healing breath in which we recognized the *ihíyotl*, the vital force, the luminous gas residing in the liver. Unlike the episode of the punishment of drunkards, the interpretation of the sickness is thus Christian in its expression as well as indigenous in its spirit and content, as if the domain of the body and sickness belonged to a substratum resistant to acculturation.

It is not easy for the historian to give a satisfactory account of this process without falling into jargon or approximations. To speak, as we have just done, of the version (Christian), of the scenario (of sickness), of a scheme or logic (persecution) could quickly box us into a problematic a bit short on both container and contained. To attempt to escape, perhaps it would be worthwhile (in the manner of semiotics) to take inspiration from the distinction between *iconic codes* and *iconographic variations*: the former provide the basis for and create the intelligibility of reality, implicit and unverbalized; while the latter are explicit, more easily datable, as well as more consciously chosen and organized. In other words, like those of space and time, the representation of the body and the corporeal experience would together refer to a percept that would be, quite obviously, already a sociocultural datum, but one that would impose itself immediately on the senses, without the intermediary of any verbalization. This basic given, which operates without the subject's knowledge, would thus resist acculturation all the more tenaciously in that it would escape the conscious activity of the protagonist.

Must we add that this basic given is also psychological in nature, since it is connected with mechanisms of perception and more generally with the unconscious? Without a doubt, if we accept that the unconscious could not have transcended history and culture and that it mixed the personal and intimate history of the subject with that of its group. In the case of Domingo, the indices are so meagre that we can hardly outline an investigation. It is true that several hallucinatory episodes appear all to echo oral conflicts. Whether it is a question of the prohibition against drinking *pulque* (which the ancient Nahua associated with breast milk), of the prohibition against making oral contacts with kin in the other world, of the promise of material gratification of an alimentary order ('the means that will give you something to drink and eat in the world'), finally with the healing technique consisting of blowing air in the face of the sick person, it is possible that these coincidences are accidental, as it is possible too that they express the personal evolution of Domingo. Must we see in the relinquishment of *pulque* and the protection of the Virgin and St Veronica the overcoming of the oral fixations of infancy and the beginning of a relationship to the mother that would give Domingo a sense of security? It is plausible, if not altogether convincing. In this case, but also in that of a different problem, the vision would act as the cultural instrument of the expression and resolution of personal conflicts. In other words, it would also convey the workings of a psychological complex and more precisely the setting up of defence mechanisms that, together with a representation of the body and a corporeal experience, would determine the choice of cultural materials, their organization and their appropriateness to reality as conceived and lived by the healer.

But can we be satisfied with 'putting side by side' a sociocultural complex and a personal psychological complex? We cannot deny at the outset that the sociocultural substratum that we refer to depends on the manner in which the individual *personally* apprehends his culture, and thus the segments that he retains of it. On the other hand, and this is perhaps less obvious, it is probable that individual conflicts are in one way or another influenced by the conflicts of the group to which the subject belongs. I mean by this, without having more formal proofs to provide, that the psychological itinerary of Domingo is *a priori* indissociable from the tensions created and maintained by the acculturation and colonization of the Nahua populations in the area of Morelos. Understood in this way, the faculty of seeing dead parents again, in fact the lineage, the extended kin ('your parents and grandparents and the rest of your kin), coupled with the formal prohibition against speaking to them, can illustrate and signify a situation of profound ambivalence to tradition and the cultural inheritance; a situation that moreover evolved towards the disavowal of ancestrality and the denial of the customary transmission of knowledge that the initiation of the future healer reserved to those close to him. One can also decipher, which is not at all contradictory, distances taken from the extended family, under the influence of the patterns of Christian conjugal life. It is moreover a similar attitude that would be made manifest in the condemnation, indeed the satanization of *pulque*, by brutally confirming the rejection of a weakened cultural complex, still rooted in the land, as we know through Ruiz de Alarcón. By placing emphasis on the nefarious aspect of drink, the episode would be the equivalent of becoming conscious of the ravages of drunkenness, a process that has been observed in the denunciations recorded by the *Relaciones geográficas*. Thus nothing rules out Domingo's reactions having a personal origin as well as a collective background, disturbed by the tensions of a group confronted with breakdown, disavowal, disorientation: stress attributable to the disruptive effects of the Spanish domination, insecurity accountable to exploitation, mortality, the shipwreck of memories, alcoholism aggravated by the colonial system and sickness. These deductions and even more this sequence of hypotheses lead us to posit the impact of a basic, implicit and unconscious substratum that eluded verbalization, but that would evolve at the pace of its psychological and sociocultural components. To take up the expression of Edward Sapir,[2] by the *patterning* it exercised and to which it was identical this substratum would decisively orient the conduct and acculturation of the subject, the choice of his borrowings as well as the meaning of his resistances.

Before coming back to this point, let us look more closely at the extensions of the initiatory vision in order to grasp its true impact. From the admission of Domingo itself, it was first the source of two therapeutic practices: the incantatory formulae, that is, the *conjuros*, and the insertion of needles into the patient's stomach. It goes without saying that the hallucinatory experience could not refer to healing rituals except in a condensed and allusive way, leaving to a later process the secondary elaboration (Devereux, 1972, pp. 233–48), the task of developing acts and words and relating dreamlike reminiscences to invocations learned elsewhere. That was quite obviously the case of formulae whose dense and complex contents could in no way have been memorized in the course of visions, even repeated ones. As to the rest, Domingo ended up later admitting that 'he had learned them from another Indian, also a healer'. But the initiatory vision acquired its true prominence only when, ceasing to consider it as an isolated phenomenon, we return it to Domingo's overall practice. Everything leads us to believe, in fact, that the healer voluntarily recounted his visions in the context of his cures and even outside them, in the presence of the Spanish. In a way he mixed up the exercise of his art with the tale of the origin of his gifts, and it is highly probable that the repetition of his story – a guarantee of effectiveness and a remarkable consecration of his power – supplanted in his mind the old Nahua formulae repeated by his colleagues. This reorientation could not but draw attention to the personal contribution of the *curandero* – the Christianized initiation – at the expense of more traditional and more stereotyped elements. Broadly disseminated, associated with critical moments of everyone's existence – the confrontation with evil and misfortune – the narration of visions surrounded Domingo with a repertory of composite images. In that way it contributed to familiarizing his clientele and his hearers with a dream universe both remote and extraordinarily close. We believe that we are touching here on one of the surest and most subtle routes to the acculturation of the indigenous *imaginaire*, since it developed apart from any Spanish or ecclesiastical interference. But it was also one of the sources of cultural innovation to the extent that the personal organization experienced and made public by Domingo did not correspond literally as a whole to any premise, any pre-existing reference, Christian or prehispanic.

At first sight the organization is eclectic. We find mixed together formulae, a conception of the body and of sickness, having to do with what we have designated by the term idolatry; the vision of a Christian afterlife, hell and heaven but without purgatory; a strange concept of the relation to the dead; distortions of the Christian tradition that made St Veronica fan the sick person with the veil that wiped the Holy Face. Nor should we forget these two conceptions of the person 'set end to end': one, indigenous, focused on submission to the ambivalent forces of the divine, the other, Christian, based on the free will of the believer. It was certainly a 'fiction', not in the denigrating sense given to it by Ruiz de Alarcón, but rather in the sense of a montage, which would associate scraps, genuine or truncated segments of the organization or assembly. The principal phases can easily be restored. One can distinguish the period of perception and inculcation of Christian symbolism, then the stage of the vision (dream or hallucinatory episode) which transformed the daily residue at the end of a subjective experience; then the stage of secondary elaboration, which tended to make the dream conform to pre-existing references; finally, that of the narrative disseminated and repeated in different contexts.

But this says nothing about how the psychological and sociological matrices of the substratum intervene and evolve or, if we prefer, how the 'patterning' works and is modified. This action is not arbitrary, since it obeys cultural and psychological variables. But we should be wary of exaggerating its organizing property, inertia or immutability. If, as we have seen, the vision is far from the model of idolatry, it is because the 'patterning' is probably more flexible than the terms like 'code', 'logic' and 'programme' that we tend to associate with it suggest. Still this malleability must be defined, and to that end it must be admitted that the distinction of two levels of content and expression is quite inadequate. Frequently, as we shall see, the alteration of content (or expression) was only partial. To take account of this difficulty a closer examination of these visions suggests considering, following other researchers, that expression in itself is the conjunction of two elements: a *substance of expression* that corresponds to the support, the optical, physical, biochemical materiality of the phenomenon; and a *form of expression* which is the sequence, the succession and articulation of the perceived images. In the same way we shall distinguish a *substance of content*, for example, the conceptual and affective repertory used by the vision, and a *form of content* which would relate to the fashion of organizing (intellectual and psychological) concepts and affects.[3] In the case of Domingo's visions, for example, the *content* associated an initiation and a personal disorder which conditioned the *substance* (an apprehension of the body, a means of access of knowledge, an oral dominance) and *form* (the cultural succession and the psychic progression of the sequences). The borrowings from Christianity, on the other hand, seem to have been concentrated on the level of the *form of expression* without having a real echo in the *content*: as is the case with the veil of St Veronica or the Marian apparition. It is also true of the Christian themes of two roads and the punishment of drunkards, which correspond to a still traditional *content* – in the event the *form of the content* – as it related to the schema of the shaman's route, the progress of an initiatory trip riddled with ambushes. But it cannot be ruled out that these features could in the long term introduce troubling elements within the *content* itself, capable of altering its *form* (through the Christian logic of sin) and/or the *substance* (through the individual experience of salvation). To say it another way, the underlying articulation of Christian borrowing with indigenous elements would then cease to be based on a partial analogy (in both cases trials to be overcome), to modify the equilibrium of the whole. We understand then that Christian features, depending on the interpretation that is emphasized, whether emphasis is put on the Christian or the Indian side, can reinforce the shamanic model (of which they would be only supplementary variants) as well as graft on a Christian European conception of the person and sin able to be substituted for the traditional content. It seems that this material, which can be read two ways, and the margin of indeterminacy that it entails, much more than sudden breaks, might account for the alteration and evolution of the 'patterning'. From *form of expression* these alien features appear to have become *form* and/or *substance of the content*.

The origin of the change, the motive for this shift from one level to the other, remain to be determined. Everything suggests that breaches were opened in the substratum by the conjunction of a personal disorder and an unavailability and a collapse of traditional remedies. We might imagine that by inducing him to retain and interiorize new defence elements, the (probable) 'addiction' of Domingo led him to assimilate exotic forms that in the long run could challenge the basis, the form and the substance of idolatry.

In any case the transition from one life experience to another did not constitute a mere symbolic transformation of the person. One might expect that it would also have influence on the psychic registers to which the subject could have recourse. The emphasis on the self put forward by Christianity, the introspection that it advocates, the importance that it accords to the autonomy of the subject, seem to me diametrically opposed to the concept of someone enmeshed and diluted in networks of multiple dependencies. From the second half of the sixteenth century, the demands of Christian preachers and confessors, the spread of a logic of sin and redemption, coupled with the most devastating effects of deculturation, anomy and social ruptures could have contributed among the Indian population to a subject's release, the emergence of an ego closer to the Freudian ego and thus to our own. In these circumstances a reorientation would have taken place, an interiorization of relations to the self which, as well as a modification of symbolic combinations, would have intervened in the evolution of the 'patterning' effected by the substratum. Once again, it is obvious that one cannot dissociate psychological patterns from cultural ones since scrutiny of the self is a probable effect of the Europeanization of the person as much as a different access to the mechanisms of the psyche. But it is probably not without utility to suppose that psychic matrices themselves also evolve together with cultures and societies.

Nevertheless, for the historian the essence of the question does not reside there. It remains for him to attempt to understand the effect of Domingo's tale on the Indians of the region: 'He moved and filled with wonder all those to whom he told this story'. If this unique experience took on a social significance, a cultural dimension that went beyond it, this was so because it could easily be shared by the Indians. As their reactions of *wonder* suggest to us, it was probably assimilated to a *tetzahuitl*, that is, to the emergence into social life of an astonishing divine force, of a phenomenon that imposed itself so irresistibly that neither the engagement of the individual nor the collective adherence of belief was required – which explains why we have no doubts about Domingo's tale. But why understand it in terms of a *tetzahuitl*? Here we must assume that the Indians shared the same substratum with Domingo, where idolatry and an indigenous perception of the divine (the *tetzahuitl*) still predominated, but also and above all that they were sensitive to the shifts, breaks, associations and distortions that the *curandero* imposed consciously and unconsciously on the materials that he used. There were several reasons for this. First, we note that these operations and reorganizations were explicitly integrated into a therapeutic *practice*: that was the case, for example, with Veronica's veil, re-used to this end. Thus the *curandero* did not leave the role imparted to him. Then we discover that these traits belonged to the still present and operational *grid* of indigenous shamanism, and finally that certain sequences referred clearly to generalized *disorders* in the group as a whole (Indian drunkenness). Thus in the midst of the Indian population there existed a cluster of elements of a psychic and existential nature that facilitated the reception of Domingo's experience. To this should be added an additional fact that explains even more about the success of unprecedented features. These are the personal touches or idiosyncrasies that the *curandero* conferred on his experience, which are the basis of his originality, without ever precipitating him into the incommunicable strangeness of a private delirium. The insistence with which the *curandero* played on the uniqueness of his experience, whose detailed account he was pleased to propagate was, of course, a way of countering the influence of other shamans, a way of marking himself off and of drawing to himself a broader clientele by playing on the *form of expression*. Still this personal imprint, which validated an approach without taking away anything of its accessibility, was both the vector of new cultural characteristics and in part the driving force of this 'bewitchment that had so mastered this region'.

In other words, the shamanic complex would behave differently from idolatry. Like idolatry, it would be capable of absorbing exogenous traits by reinserting them into the whole and the various systems informing it. But in addition shamanism had a strong subjective aspect which, by exposing the individual to repeated hallucinatory experiences, exacerbated personal tensions in him or latent tensions in others. This terrain, charged with subjectivity, seems to have favoured an original and *systematic* manipulation of cultural traits which, in the context of an ebbing idolatry and an expanding Christianization, could have stimulated a process of acculturation. This was the case at the end of the sixteenth and the beginning of the seventeenth century.

It would be necessary to make numerous case studies to suggest the diversity of the behaviour of these *curanderos* in the first half of the seventeenth century. For Francisca de Tenancingo (1626), the shamanic experience took the quite traditional form of an underwater initiation. The Indian woman mentioned some 20 other cases, which corroborates the frequency of the phenomenon in the *pueblo*, but above all she cited Christianized visions as if at the same period and in a comparable context different symbolic configurations could coexist without worrying those concerned.[4] The visions of Juan de la Cruz in the mines of Zacualpan (*c*.1631–6) had the mark of a brutal and chaotic acculturation.[5] If the overall content remained that of an initiatory experience of native origins, the borrowings from Christianity were more numerous than in the visions of Domingo. The initiators were explicitly identified (the archangels Michael and Gabriel), God himself was at the origins of the initiation, the Virgin served as mediatrix between the Indian and the Lord who demanded his services. The succession of episodes also suggests a complex psychological itinerary, tricky to restore, marked out by the recurrence in the visions of maternal and feminine images in turn protective and aggressive: the mother of Juan, the Virgin with Child, the Indian Woman who personifies sickness. It is simpler to follow the cultural progress of Juan. His submission to the archangels, the Virgin and God expresses an unquestionable degree of Christianization but it in no way constitutes an irreversible evolution since the *curandero* to his loss fell back into the practice of witchcraft. It is this form of cultural quest, groping and fragile though it may be, that seems to us most deserving of attention.

This experience developed between an idolatrous pole and a Christianized pole. The first was not only manifest in the shamanic grid, but also in the course of a murderous bewitchment triggered by the arrest of the character. The second pole focused on a new organization of the vision inspired by Christian hierophanies. They were already present for Domingo, but in a more superficial way. The initiators remained anonymous white figures and the Virgin had no direct relations with Christ. With Juan, on the other hand, similar elements were taken in a more Christianized sense. Or more precisely from simple *form of expression*, from a collection of images, they became *substance* (Christian style relations to the divine) and *form* (the Marian schema) of the *contents* of the vision. Here we see the example of a shift induced by the very nature of the adopted materials. It was within the Mariophany that the most notorious reorientation came to the surface. The Virgin of Juan was no longer a simple form, a vague silhouette. It seems that she was Our Lady *de los Remedios*, and thus one of the most lively manifestations of Marian devotion in New Spain in the first decades of the seventeenth century. Better yet: the relations between the divine figures were rather faithfully transferred from Christianity. The Virgin was present with her Child, she intervened in the name of her Son and against sickness. Finally, the relation of the sick person to God was assimilated to a personal movement and not to the simple carrying out of a ritual. There we find a redefinition of divine beings and of relations to these powers which does not belong to the ancient world of idolatry and alters in its form and substance the traditional content of the initiatory vision. It seems in the case of Juan that the Christian hierophany was already in the process of substituting itself for the shamanic model. The deep, implicit and unconscious substratum that we mentioned in Domingo's case seems here to operate a twofold 'patterning', or more precisely to evolve towards a different organization from that of idolatry. It took the form of an alteration of the native scenario (the *form* of the *content*), but also of a modification of the conception of the person and the gods (the *substance* of the same *content*). Not only did indigenous reality appropriate Christian elements, but it gave an account of new meanings by increasing its scope and pushing back the limits of plausibility and probability. We can no doubt compare this movement to the beginning of the reorganization of traditional graphic space and the appearance of a European rendering of the human figure following the slow assimilation of exogenous traits, even if these processes, limited to defined group – painters and their public – occurred far earlier. The visions of Juan were more acculturated than those of Domingo. Moreover they were later and emerged from an environment more sensitive to change: from the silver mines where mobile and mixed populations mingled.

However, we could not deduce that the colonization of the indigenous *imaginaire* would take the quiet course of a linear and uniform evolution, even in the heart of the same region. It is rather the diversity and multiplicity of experiences that should be emphasized. For an Indian woman from Iguala, from before 1617, initiatory torments were inspired by the crucifixion as if the sectors that demanded a major affective investment (suffering in initiation) showed themselves to be the most permeable to variation and Christianization.[6] With other *curanderos*, we observe the combination of an old discourse and a new set of acts, a new look, inspired by the devotions (the rosary) and the *venerables* that the baroque Church valued so highly.[7] Variations could slip into the tales that these Indians told of their initiation without that worrying the *curandero* or his audience. This malleability of the tale, and thus of expression, did not disrupt its internal organization, but makes it possible to define anew the way the transition or opening of a traditional organization – the shamanic experience – could take place in different dispositions. This polysemy of expression authorizes successive or simultaneous reinterpretations susceptible of lending a Christian content to personal experience, which was not originally its own, but which agrees without difficulty with the role taken on by these figures. It appears that we are once more approaching processes that ensure the shift from a native reality (idolatry) to acculturation (of expression and content) and thus to cultural creation. The choice of material lending itself to multiple interpretations, forgetting the respective origins of manipulated traits, or simply familiarization with a Christian expression embedded enough in the seventeenth century no longer to be perceived as exogenous, were elements that could progressively influence the content and initiate a remodelling of the substratum, or perhaps in the worst case precipitate its dismantling.

The initiatory experience occupies a far from negligible place in the influence of the *curanderos*. For this reason the *imaginaire* that it conveys seems to us to have had a noteworthy effect on populations where they practised. The valorization and credibility of the vision, thus of a personal and subjective trajectory, are probably to be related to the social position of the *curanderos* in the early seventeenth century. If in their *conjuros* they continued to claim the title of *tlamacazque*, it is true that very little linked them to these figures with institutionalized functions, complex and prestigious knowledge. What they lost in authority, they gained in personal autonomy, acquiring a freedom of movement which led them to seek a divine guarantee in the new forces introduced by the Spanish.

Thus the initiatory experience as basis of knowledge and powers seems to have had a greater impact if it took place within the indigenous community and directly involved sick people constrained to share the belief of their *curandero* in order to get well. Thus began and proliferated an interiorization in a series of images, situations and scenarios, called to mind by the vision of the healer. In this sense this figure seems to have played a key role in the introduction and adaptation of the Christian supernatural (at the level of expression as well as at the level of content). 'Seems to have played', for depending on the dates, places, and even more the personalities, the approaches took on very different and contrasting forms.

The intervention of the *curandero* was obviously not limited to the reflection of an exotic *imaginaire*. Within his means, he was engaged in reinforcing a position, if not of monopoly, at least of the enforced intermediary faced with alien elements that were penetrating indigenous cultures. Thus through the visions that they peddled, the *curanderos* appeared as the favoured interlocutors of saints: 'If it is a question of facing the anger of Our Lord, of the most holy Virgin or of any other saint, [the Indians] believed them to be capable of soothing or appeasing them'.[8] By their intervention, Christian entities crept into the indigenous system of interpretation of sickness and became powers as effective as fire, sun or water. By the same means the Christian after-life was introduced, as we have seen in Domingo's vision. But these *curanderos* were careful always to master the process so as to remain indispensable resources when faced with the proliferation of new features. Some, for example, took on interpreting Christian purgatory and hell, by combining the fire cult with the distressing Christian image of flames beyond the tomb. They even promised those about to expire that 'before dying they would come to an agreement with fire and offer it a sacrifice so that, wherever he found himself after his death, he had it with him so that fire would not torment him as it would have done if he had not made a sacrifice'.[9] These *curanderos* admitted that after death souls might experience the temporary fire of purgatory or in case of mortal sin the eternal fire of hell. The notions of soul, sin, grace, eternity, posthumous punishment and sacraments of the Church progressively invaded the Indian world, without the *curandero* losing his place as a result. Quite the contrary, since he was charged with producing a readjustment of the form of expression (Christian images) and of proposing a modification of content in substance and form (individual salvation / strategies for the afterlife).

The trajectories of some *curanderos* illustrate to what point at the height of the demographic crisis 'popular' indigenous cultures remained astonishingly living groups, capable of reacting to change, much more than inert repositories of idolatry. It is not always easy to understand the protagonists of this creativity, even though it remained without a future. Some were *curanderos*. They enable us to understand almost *in vivo* the hesitant quest for new modes of expression and accommodation with colonial reality and dominant cultures. A course which is not to be confused either with that of the Indian town clerks and notables who left us the Primordial Titles, and still less with that of the nobles of the sixteenth and early seventeenth century. The confluence of the shamanic tradition and a personal disorder thus seems to have favoured the birth of unforeseen features and to have stimulated the emergence of new arrangements. The question of the 'normality' of the shaman has been the subject of numerous controversies into which we do not claim to penetrate.[10] We cannot deny his unique character, his particular sensitivity, his peripheral situation, the precariousness of his position, his aptitude to express more intensely than others the tensions that rippled through the community. But also, unlike other Indians, the shaman was in a context of crisis a person who retained direct access to traditional content, or at least to what remained of it. As he had to provide his patients with culturally effective answers, he had to divert new, exotic materials, which were familiar enough to be integrated (on the level of expression and often of content) into what survived of the indigenous patrimony. Assimilated to different moments of the shamanic initiation, profiting from the permeability of idolatry, these new traits remained susceptible of new interpretations in turn evocative of new contents, which emerged progressively and distanced themselves ever further from idolatry. This polysemy of divine entities and situations unquestionably ensured the impact of the *curandero* on circles whose degree of acculturation could be highly variable. But it was the hallucinatory experience that really tamed the Christian supernatural and gave it indigenous roots, conferring on it a reality, an obviousness, comparable to that of idolatry. This experience corresponds to the 'substance of expression', in other words, to its material quality or support. As it remains essentially native and as it is the indispensable condition of expression, we shall not be surprised that the hallucination offers the last refuge of tradition, even if the form of expression and the entire content were altered and Christianized.

The shamanic initiation and ecstasy often appeared tied to the consumption of hallucinogenic substances. Beyond a doubt this was an ancient custom spread throughout the American continent. In the prehispanic period, hallucinogens had their place in the great rituals: the 'Feast of Revelations' (among the Mexica), princely banquets, sacrifices, divination, curing. Their consumption was a highly valued activity, carefully codified, circumscribed by rules whose observation was imperative and whose infraction was punished. As in many other cultures, drugs acted as biochemical releases which induced passing states, whose content, far from being arbitrary, corresponded to images or sensations that tradition associated with this type of intoxication. In this respect hallucination was a kind of 'conditioned cultural reflex', which took part in the same way as teaching in the interiorization of essential sectors of native cultures. Drugs thus played the role of gearing down the real, and their institutionalized consumption contributed to pushing back the limits of 'ordinary' perception, while conforming to sensations experienced in cultural schemata that were in the event those of idolatry. Drugs served to communicate with the gods, for they set off a double process: they introduced into the body of the consumer the power that they harboured and propelled his *tonalli* towards the divine world. Projected outside human time, or penetrated by divinity, the Indian acquired knowledge of things to come. The plant showed itself to be an omniscient interlocutor, the retainer of the secret sought, the power that resolved a situation that was distressing and uncertain since ordinary recourses had been exhausted. When consumption took a collective form, the consumers exchanged the information thus gathered, and the future hallucinated and glimpsed by each ceased to be a subjective experience to become known to all.[11]

There are indications suggesting that the consumption of drugs, like that of the flesh of the sacrificed or polygamy, was ordinarily reserved for the nobility. The Church had thus by the same expedient abolished these three privileges. As much as ritual cannibalism or human sacrifice, recourse to hallucinogens provoked the repulsion and terror of the evangelizers. When they did not censure the information that related to it, they were busy giving in words and images a demoniacal interpretation of the visions arising from absorption of these plants. They accused the hallucinogens of being the instrument of Satan but also of leading to unreason, temporary or permanent madness, the equivalent of alcoholic drunkenness and even lust.[12]

Despite the hostility of the Church, despite the imposed clandestinity, the consumption of hallucinogens continued to be an extremely common phenomenon at the beginning of the seventeenth century. The resistance of the complex that, in a more general way, was also that of idolatry reveals the limits of Christianization. This consumption was always accompanied by precise rules and certain precautions. The healer who was consulted fixed the day and hour of consumption as a function of the ritual calendar. The room where the experience was to take place was carefully swept and censed; the most total silence had to prevail. The smallest incident – the entrance of another person, a dog passing by or barking – was enough to disturb a consultation that lasted as long as the state induced by the drug. The consultation could take place under the direction of a specialist who took or had the plant taken. But it sometimes happened that an Indian got hold of hallucinogens himself in some market and went ahead by himself. In the after all rather circumscribed sphere of initiatory visions, provoked hallucination could thus have attained considerable currency among the indigenous populations.

In October 1624 an Indian at Chiautla took *peyotl* to find the traces of his wife, who had run away: 'In his drunkenness, he saw an old man who told him where his wife was . . . His wife was in the *pueblo* of Izucar, another Indian had taken her there. He should go to such and such a place. He would find her and bring her back'. The sources offer a number of similar accounts. In the hot lands south of the archbishopric of Mexico and west of the diocese of Puebla, the consumption of the drug retained its traditional forms. It is significant, for example, that it was a 'venerable old man' who showed himself and 'personified' the *ololiuhqui*. This anthropomorphic figure was probably an *imago*, a function more than a person, a bearer of tradition and authority. Moreover, we know that the indigenous *curandero* presented himself to his disciple under the features of Oxomoco the Old, He who knows fates. In other visions of the same years, the consumer put more emphasis on possession: 'His heart did not speak well to him, that is why he did not know what to say'. As used to happen, the heart of the subject opened its receptacle to the divine force that emanated from the plant that had been absorbed. Nevertheless, like that of idolatry, the empire of hallucinogens had singularly diminished with the end of the great rituals, the banquets where they had been consumed, and the practice was no longer subject to the control of a clergy or authority of any kind. On the other hand, colonial domination unquestionably favoured 'wild' consumption.[13]

In an unforeseen way that reveals the complexity of any process of acculturation, the images hallucinated by the Indians invaded the *imaginaire* of the *mestizos*, the blacks, the mulattos and even certain Spaniards. The phenomenon helps to explain the persistence of a practice as well as the images that it aroused and the representation that the Indians made of it. It can be dated from the beginning of the seventeenth century. It seems that the use of hallucinogens had then become common for broad sectors of colonial society. Attracted by this divinatory technique, blacks, mulattos, *mestizos* and Spaniards of modest rank (the '*gente de servicio*', the '*gente vil*') began by engaging the services of an Indian *curandero*, then got the plants for themselves and learned to take them and above all *to see what the Indians saw*. Double revenge of the Indians on the Church: it won followers for a practice without a real equivalent on the European side of the Atlantic, and it evidently made them share the native perception of the real and the numinous. There again, sources abound. We are thinking in particular of the role played by those persons of mixed blood disowned by a Spanish father, separated from a black or mulatto mother, and who lived within indigenous communities, immersed in these cultures and quickly absorbed by them. Spanish sources tirelessly denounce their perturbing presence, although they hardly permit us to approach them, for the *mestizos* are so easily confused with the Indians. But there were other roads and more partial acculturations: first that represented by desperate recourse to an exotic technique – still an indirect consultation, through the medium of an Indian, but which already implied recognition of the efficacity of the practice. It was a single step from indirect consultation to suggestion and personal experience at the beginning of the seventeenth century, a step taken by more and more. We understand that the Indians could teach *mestizos* or mulattos the invocations, ritual songs and gestures that surrounded the consultation and that thus a conditioning had begun that favoured the dissemination of the indigenous vision. It is more astonishing that, carried away by their delirium, consumers who did not know Nahuatl or spoke it brokenly began suddenly to master it easily or to dream in Nahuatl. Images, words, gestures thus won 'people with little, who have close dealings with the Indians and who, in view of their origin, are corrupted in contact with their customs and superstitions'.[14]

If these cases have the merit of drawing attention to the complexity and twists and turnings of certain processes of acculturation, they rule out imagining that some of the new populations would suddenly accede to the universe of idolatry. The apprenticeship of rituals, words and gestures, the assimilation of images, cannot be confused with inte-riorizing another apprehension of the real, any more than it is possible to ignore the resistances that arise or to forget the secondary effects of the colonization of the *imaginaire*.

The repression of the Church, the pursuit of *curanderos* by the ecclesiastical judges, the interventions of the Inquisition against their *mestizo*, black, mulatto and Spanish clients, seem not to have influenced the attraction that drugs exercised in the early seventeenth century. Other obstacles hindered the consultation of hallucinogens. They came from the Indians themselves, who feared the wrath of the power enclosed in the plant. The anger of the hallucinogen was murderous. It could be exercised against whoever did not observe the rules and rituals; or against those who explained forbidden customs to the enemy, the ecclesiastical judge. To such a point that those who had *peyotl* and *ololiuhqui* often preferred to expose themselves to the proceedings of the Church rather than to provoke a reaction that would not only put them in danger but would strike even the Catholic priest who meddled in these things. This explains the reticence, the procrastination, a certain unease among those Indians who agreed to put their art at the service of a mixed group of clients. Visions once again expressed these impasses in their way. Refusal, silence or the anger of the power consulted convey the contradictions of a *curandero* split between concern with satisfying a Spanish clientele, taking some profit from it, and the quite logical necessity of avoiding contacts with a group whose authorities proscribed the use of *peyotl*.[15]

But it seems in a general way that this attitude did not prevail, on the one hand, because from the second half of the sixteenth century idolatry was no longer the subject of systematic and organized repression; on the other hand, because the Spaniards, *mestizos* and mulattos with whom the Indians could have dealings were less the bearers of ecclesiastical prohibitions than avid seekers without embarrassment at having recourse to illicit practices: the ineffable desire to know that animated these lovers of horoscopes, of cut-out paper dolls, the bait of gain among often poor Indians overturned indigenous reticence and the barriers relentlessly raised by the Inquisition. It is even permissible to ask oneself if the complexity of the Church's position did not add to the confusion and even favour dissemination. One must recall that the extirpators accorded an element of truth to indigenous visions, even if it was the devil who had slipped in, while the Holy Office made a distinction between a licit, medicinal use of these plants and a proscribed and divinatory use. These apparently clear distinctions lent themselves to tendentious interpretations: one could, one continually did, under the pretext of medicinal use, seek this truth in the drug that the Church did not systematically deny to it.

But the 'devil' of acculturation played everyone an unforeseen trick by introducing Christian images in place of indigenous perceptions. The process is parallel to Jesuit preaching, or the Christianization of shamanic initiations. But this time we hesitate over its ethnic origins. We know that probably from the end of the sixteenth century Indians under the sway of hallucinogens saw figures borrowed from Christianity, Christ and angels. The diffusion of the cult of saints in indigenous circles, its insertion in the pantheon of local forces, could thus explain their appearance in the delirium of hallucination; moreover, as in the initiatory vision, the preservation of the complex was compatible at the beginning of the seventeenth century with a Christianization of ritual and image. Acculturation of the *form of expression* could quite well accommodate itself to a *content* that remained unchanged.[16]

The Christianization of the indigenous delirium was thus accompanied by a similar phenomenon in other groups of colonial society. It seems that it first affected observance. Prayers, references to the eucharist, the use of holy water and the adoration of holy pictures surrounded consumption in the two first decades of the seventeenth century. It was later, perhaps after 1625, that the subject matter of hallucinations evolved and the delirium progressively opened itself to the Christian pantheon. As a byproduct of those denunciations sent to the Inquisition that have survived, this chronology has just a relative value. It suggests that the Christianization of images occurred later in *mestizo* and black circles than in the indigenous environment, as if (but indications are scarce) the Indians were at the origin of the process. Should we see here the impact of these *curanderos*, some of whose visions have been described? Or the initiative of indigenous soothsayers, concerned to promote sales of their divinatory practices by Christianizing them? Or should we assume a group of parallel or intersecting evolutions that would explain this extraordinary flow of exchanges, secret cross-checks between the *imaginaires* of one another, starting from as specifically indigenous a practice as the ritual consumption of *peyotl*, mushrooms or *ololiuhqui*?[17]

However, we should avoid seeing hallucinogens as an indigenous revenge. For the Spanish, for numerous *mestizos* and mulattos, the assimilation of the complex remained partial, and generally came down to borrowing a divinatory technique and, more or less temporarily, certain indigenous images. For the Indians, the Christianization of images and rituals that governed consumption seems on the contrary to have corresponded to the preservation of a traditional content. It is not easy, it is true, to make out under appearances and forms the exact depths touched by acculturation. The complex evolved differently in the various groups where it took root. Among the blacks and the mulattos, for example, the original form of divination was transformed, taking on the tortured appearance of an epileptic crisis or a spectacular possession. But it was on another level, already noted, that the alteration of the indigenous basis was probably most marked and most systematic. Indian divination became a lucrative business, confined to strictly material ends, cut off from any reference to the group of representations made up by idolatry. It was part of a commercialization that also took over all the domains of idolatry. Idols became good luck charms offered to creditors as pledges, while the Indian sacrificers who hired out their services imposed traditional fasts but also required the *mestizo* client to sign a pact with the devil in his blood. In the course of the seventeenth century the old idolatry ceaselessly and increasingly ran the risk of letting itself be drawn in by colonial magic and the *curandero tlamacazqui* of being no more than one soothsayer among others, a treasure hunter, a sorcerer of rain whom one would not hesitate to denounce when the results let down the expectations of the *mestizo* or Spanish client. The success of indigenous hallucinogens could thus have concealed disintegrative effects to the extent that it participated in a banalization of practice that escaped the Indian people. However that may be, in this field as in that of initiatory visions or miracles a certain form of Christianity found its feet. The divine forces that it concentrated were integrated into Indian daily life and thanks to drugs became familiar and easy of access. More than the local miracle or the ecstasy of the shaman, *peyotl*, a small quantity of *ololiuhqui*, a handful of mushrooms made it possible to join the saints, the Virgin, to obtain what one wanted without having to go through the Church and its Spanish priests.[18]

These scattered elements, which we have reviewed briefly, are only the premonitory signs of a still deeper appropriation of the Christianity of the invaders. It took place in the second half of the seventeenth century, against the background of the drafting of those Christianized memoirs that we saw crystallizing in the Titles. It goes without saying that there is no question of dating to this period a general, simultaneous and irreversible evolution of the mass of indigenous cultures, but rather of picking out new phenomena, revealing new potential that took form here and there depending on the context, the period and the group.

The Christian supernatural served as support for the power of the *curanderos* from the beginning of the seventeenth century. A little later, it inspired miraculous tales that sealed the union of the *pueblo* with a Christian saint, tales that, while inscribed in the prehispanic tradition of the protective *calpulteotl*, set up a direct relationship, anchored in the land, with the new divine forces that had arisen after the arrival of the Spanish. But there was more. It was at this period too that the Indian notables did not hesitate to claim the prestige of a personal communication with the saints, to reinforce their ascendancy over the community. A sign of power in all its forms, the mastery of this supernatural became in the middle of the seventeenth century a stake that the Indians prepared themselves to claim and to fight the Spanish for. The process of appropriation did not appear in the beginning to rest on the degree of credibility and probability to be accorded or denied to the syncretic experience – at least so long as it limited itself to plastering over ancient content a veneer of Christian expressions and representations. On the other hand, as these traditional matrices were erased in favour of more heterogeneous collections, the question of the admissibility of the proposed features acquired a relevance that it had never had until then. It was resolved by taking inspiration from a Christian logic, that of belief and faith. Here are some examples. Around 1665, groups of Indians who worried the Church covered the fertile and temperate plains of the Bajío, which extend from Querétaro to the highlands of Jalisco. Itinerant healers drank a herb, *pipiltzintzintli*, with their patients to work out the origin of the ills with which they were stricken; 'they saw heaven, hell and other things'. They announced to the patient the contents of the images that were supposed to unroll before his eyes: 'Here, with complete faith drink this herb which is St Rose, and in drinking it you will see the Virgin, St Rita, or the guardian angel'. Although these accounts belonged to the realm of hallucinations and Christianized visions, an additional element still distinguishes them from the experiences of the first half of the seventeenth century. The success of the consultation depended less on the strict observance of a ritual than on an act of faith, a belief, since 'those who did not believe, did not see'. In the traditional vision, it was unthinkable that the subject could doubt the occurrence of his vision. If the conditions were respected, clairvoyance should have been produced inevitably, even if it did not provide the hoped-for answers or was not actually received. This ineluctability characterized the content, and more precisely the form of the content, of the traditional vision. This time, even if it reproduced the usual persecution pattern (the visionary tries to identify the perpetrator of the injury) the Christianized vision introduced and demanded a personal adherence, an individual engagement. It swung from the world of fact and idolatry to that of belief and faith, from the true and authentic to that of 'holy and true' visions. The personalization and individualization of the approach (one deserves to see the Virgin) restored a tension that the commercialization of divination tended to blur and even to eliminate. In other words, some *curanderos* of the Bajío connected the consumption of hallucinogens to their perception and interpretation of the Christian supernatural, in somewhat the same way as the traditional healers had integrated (or continued to integrate) this experience in the context of idolatry. All of them took on the role of intermediaries and auxiliaries, but those of the Bajío entered bag and baggage into another universe occupied by hell and paradise, the Virgin and saints of Christianity. Not only was the expression of the visions that they propagated Christianized, but their content belonged in form (indispensable adherence) and substance (redefinition of relations to the divine) much more to Christianity than to idolatry.[19]

At the same period, after 1665, and in the same country, near Celaya and Salvatierra, Indians had themselves called on St Alphonse, St Christopher and the guardian angel. One of them even claimed that he 'was becoming St Paul or St John'. The affair conveys an additional step in capturing the Christian supernatural. It was no longer a question of believing in new forces, but of incarnating them; which led to a still more decisive break with the Church and a radical turn in relations, since the Indians left the fringes of paganism to settle, without knowing it, in those of heresy.[20] Some years earlier an Indian of Tepotzotlán announced that 'he had spoken with Our Lord, who had told him that the glorious St Matthew had complained that he did not sweep and sprinkle the church . . . He had died, descended into hell and had revived once again. He had been with God and spoken with him. He had said that if he was burned, it was not he who burned but Our Lord'.[21] The Indian Miguel Ximénez preached with a crucifix in his hand. He announced the end of the world, the punishment of drunkards, death and damnation for unbelievers: 'If you do not believe what I say, when you leave the church, you will fall dead'. One finds again in Miguel some features of Domingo Hernández, the *curandero* of Tlaltizapan. His experience, as he described it, had also some of the look of shamanic initiation: death, return to life, the trip into the beyond, the dialogue with God, the claim to immortality? The schema is more or less identical. The end, however, is diametrically different since it was not to receive therapeutic powers that Miguel invested the Christian supernatural, but the better to usurp the function and authority of the Catholic priesthood, from which Miguel, like the overwhelming majority of Indians, was excluded. In observing and distorting the feasts and liturgies of the Church, in brandishing the threat of hell, in calling for penance, he evolved far from the paths of traditional idolatry. It is probable that in this case, as in the preceding, ancient complexes prepared and ensured the shift from idolatry towards another approach to reality and divinity. From the end of the sixteenth century, the shamanic itinerary and the consumption of hallucinogens permitted the integration with idolatry of segments of the Christian supernatural, even if by changing their nature and distorting them. They were imperceptibly absorbed into an apparently immutable Indian reality. But when these segments, at first sparse, proliferated, to make up articulated and autonomous groups combining collective concerns, new spaces and rituals, they progressively escaped from a saturated idolatry, which could no longer master them, and the question then arose of their verisimilitude. From the moment when the domain of what was probable stopped being a question of immediate, automatic appropriateness to indigenous matrices to depend only on personal adherence, the deviation of resorting to belief and doubt became inevitable.

The Indians of Celaya identified themselves with the saints. The only thing missing was for others to proclaim themselves God, as did Gregorio Juan in 1559 in the Sierra de Puebla. A word about this case, to which I have devoted a study (Gruzinski, 1989a, pp. 63–88). In the fashion of the visionaries of Celaya or the improvised priest of Tepotzotlán, Gregorio followed a native model, that of the man-god.

Since the end of the classical period, Mesoamerican societies had venerated charismatic leaders who possessed divine energy in their hearts. These men had become *ixiptla*, that is, the 'skin' of the god; they were (as much as the shaman or the consumer of hallucinogens) the privileged holders of access to the world of the gods, but also bearers on the terrestrial surface of absolute power, actors in a minutely detailed liturgy, which ended only with their departure or disappearance. Man-gods appeared in the sixteenth and seventeenth centuries, faithful to this relationship to divinity and this representation of power. The case of Gregorio Juan is different in that the model knew a double orientation, first because externally he borrowed many elements from Christianity, but above all because the Christian conception of incarnation was already acting on the traditional organization of the traits of the man-god. Gregorio Juan claimed to be at the same time 'God the creator of Heaven and Earth' and the 'Son of God'. He was thus, in accordance with prehispanic thought, but also to a certain extent with Christian teachings of the incarnation, the divinity and the human, terrestrial manifestation of the god. With Gregorio Juan, the indigenous inter-pretation of the Incarnation began to cover that of the *ixiptla*, just as with Juan de la Cruz (about 1636) the Mariophany began to modify the shamanic model: still with this insistence on the absolute need for belief. This belief with its limits – the doubt and incredulity that opposed part of the community – as well as the hostility that drove the natives to denounce him to the *fiscal* of the church of Huauchinango, sketched a changing universe where things had ceased to possess the compelling obviousness of idolatry.

Let us not conclude that Indians generally became saints, that they identified with God and conversed daily with the Virgin and saints. The few examples adduced impart another lesson. They reveal that from Morelos to the rocky paths of the Bajío and the hazy solitudes of the Sierra de Pueblo on the edges of the capital (Tepotzotlán), conditions were favourable for the Christian supernatural in its most extreme forms to take on an existence not only credible but above all familiar to Nahua or Otomí Indians. In the form of a changed relationship to the divinity, of a paradisiacal or infernal representation of the afterlife, of a group of forces sufficiently individualized and personalized in which one was expected to believe, with the addition of faith, Christianity became wholeheartedly an element of indigenous culture. The Christian miracle was a given integrated into daily life as it was into the land-scape, space and time of the *pueblo*. It was an indisputable collective and individual experience, whose potential was such that it managed to take on the exaggerated aspects of sanctification or deification. The disparity of the groups studied, the contemporaneity, the analogies that the processes present suggest that our analysis is valid for many regions. After 1650 one can no longer speak of an uncontested ascendancy of idolatry in central Mexico. On the contrary, one must look to indigenous Christianity for original attitudes, creative impulses. Is there a need to underline that the visions of the *curanderos* of the Bajío were also contemporary with the composition of the Otomí 'Conquest of Querétaro', the preachings of Miguel Ximénez, and the production of the *Codex Techialoyan*? Let us not forget the gestation of these new collective memories in the background of these individual experiences. Finally, it is not accidental if all these manifestations correspond to the timid beginning of a demographic revival. Between 1644 and 1688 the number of Indians at Querétaro grew from 600 to 2000; at Celaya it increased from 2184 to 6419 in the second half of the century. The region of Tepotzotlán experienced a progressive revival as did the *alcaldía mayor* of Huauchinango in the Sierra de Puebla. As a general rule the Indian population in central Mexico doubled between 1630 and 1670–80.[22]

A more faithful rendering of the whole of the panorama that we are discovering would require taking into account very numerous variables. The weight of the Indian population in relation to the Spanish, *mestizo*, black and mulatto populations, but also the nature and intensity of the connections maintained by all these groups had a major effect. In some regions the indigenous mass tended to absorb *mestizos*, blacks and mulattos. In others, it was drawn into incessant cross-breeding. Urban areas, mines that attracted a mixed workforce, *haciendas* and sugar mills, where workers detached from their original community lived, favoured exchanges that remained much more sporadic in a traditional rural context, which was never for all that completely inert. The quality and density of Indian memories and of the ecclesiastical context, the policies followed locally by Indian clerks or notables, were added to the preceding variables and explain the disparity of answers to acculturation. The regions of Morelos and Guerrero represented zones of average or weak acculturation. Average in Morelos because of the physical, economic and social presence of whites and even more of blacks and mulattos. Weak in Guerrero for the opposite reasons. The Bajío, that land of new colonization, would perhaps have been close to Morelos if its indigenous populations had not been largely transplanted populations, introduced by the Spanish and thus without regional roots. The Sierra de Puebla, on the other hand, would call to mind in many respects the Guerrero covered by Ruiz de Alarcón, if these mountains had not even better protected the idolatry of certain Otomí populations. In this respect one should compare them with large sectors of the bishopric of Oaxaca, which maintained the observance of collective rituals of prehispanic origin. At the other extreme stood Mexico City, Puebla, their immediate surroundings (Cholula, Tepotzotlán) and, but to a lesser extent, the provincial capitals, Valladolid, Oaxaca, the *pueblos* located on the large commercial routes and in mining zones. It was of course in these urban areas that Spanish influence was greatest and the effects of Christianity and Europe made themselves most felt every day. The geographical and ethnic diversity cannot lead us to neglect a social diversity that we have successively described. Nobles of old, newly arrived notables or *macehuales* did not share the same attitudes, the same apprehension of colonial domination, or the same rhythms of assimilation. Their stakes, their calculations, were different and sometimes contradictory. As the idolatry of the rural inhabitants of Guerrero and Morelos in the seventeenth century seems to plunge us back into prehispanic tradition, so the curiosity and inventiveness of the nobles of the preceding century are surprising in their modernity. This does not mean that impenetrable barriers separated these groups; that would happen only in the eighteenth century.

The seventeenth century was thus a singularly complex age, for which the term syncretism is not in itself adequate. We have the impression in surveying it that a matrix in withdrawal, partly decontextualized — idolatry — continued to influence sparse, more or less altered features, often separated from their original contexts, producing extremely disparate organizations. The fragility and multiplicity of the compromises that were then at work proceeded sometimes from the incompatibility felt with existing systems, but still more frequently from the truncated or compartmentalized character of the features that one tried to join and assemble. Awareness of incompatibility could emerge as failed clairvoyance, a personal delirium or even suicide, like that committed by the Otomí of the region of Tlaxcala who defended a native cult without being able to refrain from drawing on Catholicism, and who hired out his services as a treasure hunter to the Spanish against the advice of the god he revered. In many situations transitory systems emerged that revealed the shifting and diffuse presence of an indeterminate symbolic and conceptual zone, where attempts at *overinterpretation* (the fire of hell and purgatory was also the god Old Fire) rubbed shoulders with *decodification*: hell was no longer the prehispanic Mictlan but not yet the Christian hell; the initiators of Domingo were partly anonymous, unidentified entities; the *conjuros* became a hermetic language without Christianity having been assimilated, and without an overall view of reality, a unified content, having emerged either. In their contradictions, oscillations, and impasses, this is how some of the tendencies sweeping the indigenous cultural field in the mid-seventeenth century appear to us. As there were often only personal, furtive and clandestine syntheses, this explains the precariousness of these productions, their improvised, groping character, the facility with which, denied or admitted, they came undone and crumbled. Their coherence derived from a personal experience, a unique and subjective experience, rather than from a systematic and collective construction. These fleeting undertakings nevertheless remained part of the culture, and the Mexican *curanderos* did not limit themselves 'to representing unrealizable compromises on the collective level, to feigning imaginary transitions, to incarnating incompatible syntheses'.[23] Their productions awoke the adherence of the people and took their place within a process of massive appropriation of the Christian supernatural, of this invisible reality preached by the evangelizers. What image can better illustrate this indigenous seizure than that of the governor of the *pueblo* of Tlapacoya, a tropical village overhanging the plain of Veracruz, who claimed in 1661 to have the Holy Ghost under lock and key in seven caskets nestled one inside the other?[24]

But can we really speak of capture, of diversion? It is not in doubt that the phenomenon took place outside the Church and most often against it. Does that mean that it reflects the autonomy of a cultural creativity or the more subtle games of a muffled alienation that would take indigenous cultures from the rear, by way of the forbidden and the clandestine? We have seen that the *curanderos* were far from being the guardians of an intangible tradition, reduced to silence and radically opposed to Christianity. We have discovered that, rather than being the champions of a counter-culture impenetrable from the outside, they were much more likely to take on numerous traits of the Christian supernatural and to integrate them into their patrimony. And we shall see in their approach a practice of change, an attempt to master intellectually and materially the colonial disorder when it took the form of misfortune, sickness and death. So was syncretism an undertaking of cultural piracy in the badly surveyed waters of the Tridentine Church? That might be the case on the individual level, but did the collective outcome correspond to the sum of these initiatives? In fact, by bringing out a cultural dynamism that has often escaped the historian and even more the anthropologist, we might well over-estimate it, forgetting the limits and constraints that mark out the field. In the long term it seems that the efforts of the *curanderos* and, in a general way, the appropriation of foreign forms ended essentially by weaving indissoluble links between indigenous colonial cultures and imported cultures. Among the latter only the Christianity of the Church could claim, in the last resort, to exercise an overall ascendancy. It alone disposed of institutional structures, men, political, economic and social weight and the internal coherence and persuasive force that enabled it not only to maintain an orthodoxy but also to condition the experiences that voluntarily or not were removed from it, as appears from the indigenous denunciations and repressions exercised against the *alumbrados* of the Bajío or the 'Son of God' of the Sierra de Puebla. Faced with an idolatry losing momentum and with Iberian or African magic, which were only compartmentalized knowledge, Christianity offered from its position of hegemony the timelessness of a presence, a reference, that could not be eluded. With its *venerables*, its miracles and its Mariophanies, it continually penetrated the indigenous worlds, to the point of fascinating the *curanderos*, who wanted to discover the secrets of heaven and the saints, or to take inspiration from that other healer with a hallucinated visit to Rome and the 'most famous cities of Europe':

> When he entered into the chest, it seemed to him that he was embarking on a ship, that he was sailing on the seas for days . . . that he was going by way of Rome, that he saw there the sovereign pontiff, cardinals, sanctuaries, palaces and gardens of lords and that in the end, tired of seeing the grandeurs of the world, he got back on the boat.[25]

A quest endlessly frustrated for a world that a century earlier was half-open to Latinist nobles.

7

A Last Reprieve for Composite
Native Cultures

The analysis of colonial idolatry has led us into the midst of semi-
tropical hills, into canefields, to the shores of the quiet cool rivers
of Morelos. What would a cleric of the calibre of our extirpators
have found there a century later, about 1740? First, apart from more
numerous Indians, the quite remarkable number of *mestizos* and
mulattos. Two data are on the whole rather representative of the demographic evolution of the Indians of New Spain in the eighteenth
century: a revival, more or less pronounced, depending on the region, of
the Indian population, and above all a breakthrough of the *castas*, that
is to say, all the mixed-blood, mulattos and *mestizos*. From fewer than
a million in about 1650 the number of Indians in central Mexico grew
to more than 1.5 million by about 1742 before reaching nearly 2.5
million on the eve of Independence. But at that time the indigenous
people made up only 60 per cent of the total population of the country.[1]

In this region of Morelos in mid-century, recourse to a healer or
soothsayer remained common practice and explanations for difficulties
continued to implicate a third party, another *curandero* or a supernatural power: 'bad air', 'watering places', springs. Like their predecessors, Church Indians and even cantors consulted 'papers of error
and superstition'. Practices of ancient origins were still encountered,
sacrifices offered at night by Indians and their governor in a cave 'where
there was an idol', to whom newborn children were dedicated before
their baptism. But it seems that this collective idolatry had become a
minority, peripheral practice, and that it was losing ground faced with a
'witchcraft' whose scenarios were replayed a thousand times. The least
unforeseen event and the smallest crisis were systematically attributed
to a nefarious aggression. Rivalries in love, arguments of drunkards,

family quarrels, fits of madness or explosions of anger, sudden deaths, accidents, all were brought to the common denominator of witchcraft, of a witchcraft frequently reduced to the expression of a persecution of human origin, quite removed from the network of representations made up by idolatry to constitute a specific space. Now commonplace, witchcraft could be, as in the past, a social regulator that struck anyone who put the community and its goods in danger, but it also became the terrorizing and narcissistic affirmation of an irresistible power, indeed the preferred instrument of grim struggles waged by relatives, neighbours, or spouses. But above all indigenous sorcery overflowed ethnic confines, even when it was exercised apart from Spanish agglomerations. *Mestizos*, mulattos, Spaniards, *mayordomos* and workers in the sugar *trapiches*, slaves, all spied on the activities of the Indians and their associates, peddled rumours and added weight to the tales of witchcraft that were circulating. At one time or another everyone consulted *curanderos*, was bewitched and sometimes in turn did the bewitching.

This ethnic heterogeneity was linked to a diversification of levels of belief and a disintegration of traditional consensuses. Many things were the object of puzzled questions, fearful perplexity, lies, uncertainties, rumours taken up complacently or energetically denied. Personal strategies, the interpretations of each, occupied a place that had little in common with the attitudes described by the extirpators of the seventeenth century, while new practices came to complicate the cultural scene. At Coatlán Indians gathered at night in the church or around the stations of the cross. They were seen whipping and slapping the statues of Christ so as to 'rehearse the whole Passion of Christ'. The blasphemous aggression was mixed with obscene gestures ('they showed their rear to the images, and pulled their pants down'), which made up the clandestine rituals. These Indians flew in the muggy night air, changed into donkeys and balls of fire. A miraculous brightness lit up the church when they gathered for their nocturnal meetings. They did not hesitate to violate tombs and to defy the Almighty to cure the victims of their bewitchings. When these Indians of Coatlán seized upon Christianity, its sacred places, its images, its feast days, its vestments, it was to make use of them in a deliberately sacrilegious and blasphemous way. The Indians' determination, their affective investment, the objectives they established, the acts that they carried out and valued, all reveal that the landmarks, the representations that they made use of, were for the most part drawn from Christianity – but from an indigenous Christianity that they endeavoured to surpass, to master by reversing it. And this iconoclastic and blasphemous reversal was the basis of their power, when they exerted it. This has been a summary sketch of some of the byways offered by this *revisited* Morelos, to go by the account of the Franciscan Antonio de La Rosa y Figueroa, a man as passionate and as frustrated in his efforts as an extirpator as Ruiz de Alarcón or Jacinto de La Serna.[2]

Composite cultures

What became of idolatry in the eighteenth century? Did it founder, carried away by the debacle of memories and the proliferation of syncretisms? Did it still manage to account for reality and to govern observance, while large sectors of indigenous life escaped it? Even in perceptibly acculturated regions, for example Morelos, if idolatry survived as a way of structuring reality, it occupied no more than the fringes and the outskirts. It fell back on practically impregnable positions, the peripheral space that delimited the *pueblo*, mountains, caves, streams, winds, sky, clouds. Peripheral space does not mean distant space. The sierras overhanging the valley of Mexico were in this respect remarkable conservatories. Towards the west, in the heart of the mountains of Santa Fé, in the vicinity of the road that leads to Toluca, were hidden rude sanctuaries, decorated with censers and candles, covered with small terracotta statues – this at the very end of the seventeenth century and no doubt still later. In 1681 towards Tlalnepantla northwest of the capital, singing Indians with *ocote* torches in their hands went to the caves, where they left flowers, oranges, cups of chocolate, earthenware figurines, ploughing instruments and miniature harps. In the eighteenth century, the mountains of the west and the south continued to shelter activities as intense as they were clandestine. To the north of the valley, in the environs of Tizayuca, around 1730, the Otomí adored the mountain deities that governed rain and protected the crops, offered them in other caves 'roast chickens, *tortillas*, cotton dyed with cochineal, needles and earrings'. For many Indians the mountains retained their image and their age-old presence almost intact. They remained the receptacles of irresistible, hostile or beneficent forces. They sheltered the 'masters of storm clouds', as the Otomí of the region of Actopan, to the north of the valley of Mexico, explained. There is thus nothing astonishing in finding that the cloud conjurors have not disappeared. Sometimes enjoying a great notoriety, these Indians continued to go from village to village to offer their services to the peasants. The communities paid them by demanding from each family a modest contribution that the governor and the local authorities made up by adding *tamales*, *pulque* and food.[3] Had nothing changed? A new feature seems, however, to emerge from sources of the period. The conjurors of the valley of Mexico or the mountains of Actopan were no longer all Indians. *Mestizos* and mulattos have joined their ranks. This did not take place without a transformation of observances and beliefs: conjurors relinquished celibacy to which indigenous custom constrained them, mulattos explained the 'idols', claiming to adore beings 'changed into stone'.

If the mountains and caves retained much of what they had signified before the conquest, it was the same for a multitude of places assumed to be dangerous: springs, bridges, canals, thickly wooded and dark willow groves. They were believed to attract 'bad air' and to make those who passed near them fall ill. Before the conquest these areas were believed to be points of passage leading to the world of the gods, to that of divine time. They were the receptacle of threatening, invisible forces, which attacked the *tonalli* of the passerby. To protect oneself from them, it was necessary, as the Otomí of Tenango de Doria related about 1770, 'to pay', 'to pay the *monte*, the earth, the air, the water, what are owed to them so that they will not injure people'. It seems that this interpretation, coming from the remote mountains of the Otomí sierra, can be compared with activities endlessly repeated around the city of Mexico. The prehispanic notion of *nextlahualiztli*, generally and wrongly rendered by the term sacrifice, seems to have weighed on all these offerings. It was in fact, as the name indicates, an *act of payment*.[4] The divine forces needed humans as much as humans needed gods for the world to continue to exist. They perpetually risked being in a state of want and launched their nefarious attacks to provide themselves with energy on earth. To obtain the means of existence from them, to foresee or thwart their attacks, one had to 'pay dues', 'to pay the anger of the *monte*', to avoid the ravages of rain or hail; it was necessary to offer food, objects, to divert their desires, their unappeased covetousness.

In other words, idolatry in the eighteenth century remained something quite different from a 'survival', and it did not cease to organize some of the relations of men to the divine, by relying on the permanence of an environment, a landscape still inhabited by 'masters of the mountains, caves and heavens'. Similarly, a traditional apprehension of divinity persisted, which had little to do with the personalized entities offered by Christianity. This was true for the Otomí of the Sierra de Puebla, the Indians of Oaxaca, but also for the villages of the heights of the valley of Mexico, however exposed to the influence of a *mestizo* and Spanish capital. At the very gates of México-Tenochtitlán, at Churubusco, right into the eighteenth century, old men and women still watched jealously over the ruins of their pagan temple, as they were still supposed to harbour the force of the *pueblo*; while in 1756, at Coatepec in the valley of Toluca, the Indians continued to keep a snake that incarnated the guardian of the community and received offerings of wine and brandy. Proof that the old *calpulteotl*, the tutelary protector, was not yet dead. It was only after the Second World War, with the uprooting and emigration to the wretched conditions of the teeming cities that the tie with the natural environment began to dissolve.

To whom did idolatry still make sense? Among them we find with no difficulty figures by now familiar: the Indian governor anxious to maintain tradition the better to establish his authority; the still anonymous old people of the *pueblo*, present everywhere even up to the outskirts of Mexico and probably in the city itself; *curanderos*; parish officials; *fiscales*; groups of *voladores* who circled in the winds on feast days, throwing themselves into the void from the height of a tall pole (Plate 16);[5] conjurors of hail and clouds, etc. By no means all were Indians. They were not isolated and marginal souls: the Indians who visited the mountains of the valley of Mexico sometimes lived in the city and maintained business relations with the Spanish authorities and merchants. What was the attitude of the colonial administration? The bands of *voladores* who criss-crossed the region of Mexico benefited from the tolerance of the *alcaldes mayores*, whom they had to pay to be allowed to perform. What about the Church? Many parish priests closed their eyes to have peace, 'to avoid lawsuits' and the manoeuvres of their flocks, inclined to drag them before the tribunals at the least pretext. Is the conclusion that the 'idolators' took the forefront by means of threats and corruption? The search for secret places in the mountains protected by inaccessible precipices, clandestinity, silence and discretion remained an unwritten rule for all; and above all the need to mistrust the part of the *pueblo* that disowned these practices. A breach opened from the sixteenth century and the beginnings of the evangelization, the break in consensus continued to reflect religious choices as much as local strategies, apart from the fact that once more it is often difficult and questionable to set orthodox Indians against 'idolatrous' Indians, because the divisions generally depended on contexts more than on individuals.

However, there existed idolatrous nuclei who placed themselves deliberately on the fringes of and even outside colonial society. For example the 'masters of idolatry' who still travelled through the sierras of Puebla and Oaxaca and when they could managed 'houses of idolatry', which their followers called 'good houses'. Once again distance, isolation, the inaccessibility of the land could not account for the phenomenon. In the mountain *pueblos* of the perimeter of the city of Mexico, in the middle of the eighteenth century, Indians maintained by the communities condemned contacts with the Spanish, fought against the parish school, discouraged taking the sacraments and advocated a morality other than that of the Church. The existence of this apparently irreducible fringe helps us to understand better why idolatry did not dissolve, how it preserved in peripheral places the capacity to respond to collective or individual needs for survival, which had not changed since prehispanic times.

Pregnancy, childbirth, marriage, death and desire continued to be held in an entanglement of practices and interpretations as developed as in the seventeenth century, but deprived of the unity and homogeneity that, under the veil of syncretisms, made it possible to locate the old strands of idolatry with no difficulty. It is true that numerous features still call to mind native foundations. Many continued to tremble at the sinister cry of the *tecolote*, the owl, harbinger of death, and to fear eclipses of the sun and the moon. The *tonalli* complex, the group of interpretations that tied life to the circulation and dissemination of divine energy, showed through here and there, but without being systematically extended, as in the seventeenth century, to rituals, invocations, calendars. Elements remained, while the whole was blurred or partly dislocated before the invasion of borrowings of European and African origin, which conferred on whole bands of indigenous culture the appearance of a badly defined medley. See, for example, the different observances and beliefs surrounding death. On the one hand, the precolumbian customs persisted of offerings of food on the tombs, laying the instruments of work or toys in the sepulchre of the dead. On the other hand, Indians spontaneously admitted believing in the fire of purgatory and in the resurrection of the body. The totemism – or better, Indian beliefs related to totemism and Nahualism – that once linked each being to a particular animal distantly inspired histories of metamorphoses ('they usually believe that their dead are changed into cattle'), while Christian rituals taken out of context, transformed in nature and associated among themselves made up the strange practices that broke with idolatry as well as Christianity. The dead could, depending on the case, burn in purgatory, work in the beyond or say Mass there, reappear on earth as cattle or ghosts.[6] It will be claimed that these variations correspond to the various fates awaiting the dead in prehispanic times. This would mean emphasizing survivals, once a common obsession among anthropologists, and refusing to see the irregular assemblage that was progressively undermining indigenous cultures. Not that they were threatened with disappearance at this period or everywhere. The evolution differed considerably with environments and tribes. In this regard the bishopric of Oaxaca once more figures as conservative, and twentieth-century anthropologists will profit from it (as do tourists). On the other hand, the deterioration of idolatry is fully perceptible in the regions most open to acculturation, the valleys of Mexico, Puebla and Cuernavaca, and the Bajío.[7] There idolatry in the eighteenth century had definitely lost the capacity to serve as a grid for reality as a whole. Dispossessed of its monopoly from the previous century, it still operated in circumscribed contexts (mountains, elements, sickness), where it no doubt continued to sketch partial syntheses. But we would have great difficulty reconstituting for the eighteenth century a picture analogous to that of the first half of the seventeenth century (Plate 16).

Faced with idolatry, an interiorized and obviously reinterpreted indigenous Christianity progressively took on an efficacy and immediacy that permitted it to cover and deal with broad sectors of Indian reality. In the eighteenth century it took root and in a way 'crystallized' the potential of rites, beliefs and gestures accumulated for two centuries – first by assuming an air of antiquity. If at the end of the seventeenth century the memories of *pueblos* relinquished the distant times before the conquest to concentrate on Christian and colonial origins, individual memory circumvented the pagan past all the more readily. Without acts, landmarks, accounts from distant generations, it accorded recent institutions, in fact already two centuries old, the prestige of being immemorial. The origin of a feast day, a cult, a brotherhood and often a *pueblo* was lost in obscure times or rather belonged to an omnipresent time, without beginning and end, in that respect like the divine time of the old societies, age old. What means moreover had the overwhelming majority of the population to preserve consciousness of a distant past? In fact very little. The Indians in the cities and big towns could sometimes take part in baroque feast days organized by the Spanish authorities where sumptuously clothed figures represented the sovereigns of old, Xolotl, Quinatzin, Tezozómoc. But what could they understand of these spectacular festivities, conceived by creole erudites in search of exoticism? The dances organized by the *pueblos* at the end of the seventeenth century had quite a different significance but referred in a general way to the conquest and the arrival of the friars. Paradoxically enough, it seems that instead of maintaining the memory of the Spanish irruption and the societies that underwent it, the dances of the conquest in fact contributed to making the conquest an immemorial event. Spread by the Spanish and the friars, they were the local adaptation of an Iberian archetype (the combats of Moors and Christians), which came into the indigenous world in the course of the seventeenth century. As they spread into the cities and countryside, the regulated combats that set Christian Indians against the 'Chichimec' and were organized as part of the cult of Santiago lost any historical connotation to become no more than the periodic celebration, the ritual of a situation become age old. In fact only Indians who still had access to annals, e.g. the notables, or to familial archives, e.g. the nobles, could form a more or less clear idea of historical distance, the old world and even of the century of the conquest.[8]

However, there was a past different from the songs that were heard without much understanding, or from the tale of the true or fictional history of the *pueblo* to which one belonged: that recorded by the wills, of course only when they existed and had been preserved. These documents, which appeared from the second half of the sixteenth century, could offer a material strand of contact with preceding generations. This written memory obviously affected only part of the indigenous population: the *caciques* and notables, it goes without saying, whose prolix wills filled several dozen pages. But for 'estates' of less than 30 pesos, there was also the formula of the 'testamentary memory' where the testator dictated the essence of his dispositions to be recorded on a single sheet. These were, unlike the interminable rhetoric of the *caciques* and nobles, memories that were laconic in every sense of the term. But they were also memories clearly less stereotyped, less flowing from the stylistic effects of a Spanish or Indian notary. The testator only exceptionally held the pen but the diversity, the incomplete not to say botched aspect, the often highly personal tone of these texts make them invaluable testimony to what these sectors of the indigenous population transmitted to their children and posterity. Who were they? Indians who possessed a minimum of goods, that is to say, a roof, a *milpa* (field of maize), however exiguous, sometimes hardly the means to pay the costs of burial. Also Indians who paid tribute and thus belonged to the mass of *macehuales*, stripped of the privileges preserved by the nobles or acquired by those who passed for nobles. With no statistical pretensions whatsoever, the observations that follow offer the interest of drawing attention to the existence and generalization of new attitudes among the Nahua of the valleys of Mexico and Toluca.

One recommended his soul to God, abandoned his body to the earth, implored Marian intervention. The poverty of the testator – 'I have nothing before God' – denied him any pious legacy that would ensure the repose of his soul. It was up to others, to close relatives, to see to it: 'It is my brother Nicolás Salvador who ought to get himself money for my burial . . . I beg my uncle and my brother not to forget me and to have some Masses said for my soul . . . One of my daughters, called María Juana, is here; it is she who ought to give three pesos for a Mass to help my soul'. All in all we find a little capital of formulae and pious intentions, mixing in the desires of the testator and the interventions of the *fiscales*, *topiles*, *alguaciles* or even those old people who helped to draw up the document. It was a capital that lived again each time an heir deciphered or more often had read to him these little texts that made up the Christian memory of families and preserved the memory of descendants and relatives. Personal devotion, belief in purgatory, Marian piety, invocation of the celestial court, ritual obligations made up this profoundly Christianized link, where almost all ancestral sense took refuge from then on. Written in Nahuatl, much more rarely in Spanish, translated to be produced before the tribunals, these wills reveal to what extent Christianity had become an integral part of the community's patrimony in the eighteenth century and often enough, it appears, of the familial and individual inheritance.[9]

Firmly fixed in memories, even the most humble, indigenous Christianity depended also on a territory. This time the phenomenon is older. The destruction of the pagan temples in the sixteenth century, the construction of the church, chapels, crosses planted on peaks, were more or less well received impositions at first. The Primordial Titles show to what extent, from the end of the seventeenth century, the association of the *pueblo* with a patron saint and the possession of a church were experienced as elements as inseparable from as they were essential to community life. In the eighteenth century, taking possession commonly became possessiveness. When the Indians of Santa María Chicmecatitlán, some 150 kilometres south of Puebla, held in respect of their church and its square that 'everything is ours and no one is giving orders', they were expressing a burning sentiment that the other *pueblos* shared. In 1771 the governors and *alcaldes* of Tlatelolco claimed just as energetically the property of the parish church 'which had been built thanks to the money and work of our relatives, our grandfathers and the ancients whose rights we have inherited . . . These friars [the Franciscans] do not have the right to despoil what is ours'. At San Miguel Totolapan, in the hot outskirts of Michoacán, in 1795: 'It was our ancestors who gave the lands and it was we who preserved them. The institution of feast days, the dedication to saints, it was they who did them and it is we who continued. We Indians, we are the ones who did that, we Indians, we are the ones who always saw to it'. But the sanctuary was also the place of the dead, the throng of dead whose return was announced by certain Titles. The wills relate with what intensity the notables asked to be buried near the altar of their favourite saint. But if *caciques* and notables, as in old Europe, had a priority that no one questioned, other more obscure Indians expressed a similar wish. The indigenous domain was, however, not limited to the parish church, to its bells, its square, which was also the community cemetery and where the mysteries of the Passion were staged. It held sway still more freely over a quantity of chapels, hermitages and oratories that the parish priests visited only very sporadically. This proliferation was very old. It went back at least to the second half of the sixteenth century, for from 1585 the Third Mexican Council, denouncing their too great number, had demanded close supervision of these foundations. At the time of the 'congregations' of the end of the sixteenth century, the Indians took very hard the enforced destruction of their chapels and their 'houses of prayer', as well as the abandonment of the tombs of their near ones, to which they came back secretly to pray and leave candles. Let us recall that the *pueblo* of Xochimilco, on the outskirts of Mexico, had a sanctuary for 125 Indians at the end of the seventeenth century, while at the same period at Tlalnepantla, northwest of the capital, there was one church for every 15 indigenous inhabitants. It goes without saying that the chapels of the hamlets with no priest were practically abandoned to the hands of the Indians, who took care of their maintenance, the cult of images, the preservation of the baptismal fonts that no community, however small, would have agreed to give up for anything in the world.[10] But to understand Christianity as the cult of the parish church or that of the chapels is still to neglect the way that it invested the daily existence of the indigenous people from then on. It is true that the domestic sanctuaries that took over from the prehispanic oratories appeared from the second half of the sixteenth century, but these *santocalli*, still subject to the ascendancy of idolatry, as is revealed by the investigations of the extirpators, retained an ambiguous status in the seventeenth century. As we shall see, that is far less true in the following century.

From the end of the sixteenth century and still more in the seventeenth century, all these places were literally saturated with images. Even in the most modest *pueblos* church inventories enumerate dozens of pictures and statues. At Patambán, a Franciscan parish of 2000 faithful located northwest of Michoacán, a count of canvases or statues in the church revealed five St Francises, one St Peter and one St Paul, one St Peter of Alcántara, five St Anthonys, two St Bonaventures, one St Diego of Alcala, two St Johns, one St Christopher, one St Dominic, one St Michael, one St Veronica, one Our Lady of the Assumption, another of the Seven Sorrows, one St Claire, several effigies of Christ ... Let us add some paintings, an Adoration of the Magi, a Nativity of the Infant Jesus, the Stigmata of St Francis. There or elsewhere the accumulation discourages description, which summarily expedites these 'altarpieces made up of paintings by Indians which cannot receive the name of altars' and these 'small, diverse images, made and ruined by the hand of Indians [which] are placed without order and without distinguishable invocations'.[11]

This proliferation suggests forests of images that are lost in an outpouring of forms and colours often designated by the vague term 'indigenous baroque'. The most famous examples come from sanctuaries in the outskirts of the city of Puebla, first among which was the minute church of Tonantzintla, whose exuberant interior is peopled with a myriad of native angels who induce a sense of vertigo in visitors, as they are quickly swept away in the multicoloured and gilt whirl that climbs right up to the bright lantern of the cupola. One has the feeling of being in the presence of an indigenous copy of the famous chapel of the Rosary of the convent of St Dominic of Puebla (1690), but a copy that reduced the mastered virtuosity of the Spanish artists by accentuating to an infinite degree the burgeoning of motifs. One could cite other examples of this flourishing of lines and images in which the indigenous capture of the baroque took shape. In the cities, it was already giving ground, faced with the nascent neoclassicism of the last decades of the eighteenth century.[12] The sanctuaries sagged under the polychrome stuccoes, the famous images under gold, silver and diamonds. But it suffices to penetrate into the dwellings of the principal notables of the *pueblos* to rediscover the echo of the profusion of the sanctuaries and to follow the trembling glimmer of candles reflected in the gold of the statues and the mirrors of the frames. At home, don Miguel Roldán (in 1743 the indigenous governor of Cholula) had an Our Lady *de la Soledad* framed in black wood flecked with gold, surmounted by a gilt wooden baldachin on a crimson ground, an Our Lady of Guadalupe, two Baptisms of St John, three St Michaels, one Flight into Egypt, one Jesus of the Fall, two Our Ladys *de los Dolores*, three St Jameses, one St Nicolas, one Our Lady of Carmel, one Our Lady *de los Remedios*, an Ecce Homo, a St Gaétan, an old engraving of the Last Judgement, a portrait of the king, etc., without counting 40 little pictures and a collection of ornaments of every kind including two wooden stars decorated with images of St Augustine and St Martial. Among the statues there was a Jesus with his clothes (a Cambrai shirt, a Brittany shirt and two tunics) set behind a frame of sculpted wood, itself crowned with a gold eagle carrying a little mirror. Another crystal mirror served as dais for the image. Elsewhere, in other rooms, came a Baby Jesus, a St Joseph, an Our Lady of the Rosary with her ornaments, a St Anthony, a St John the Baptist, a St Michael, a St Peter, two angels . . . More modest was the home of a *principal* of Chalco in the southeast of the valley of Mexico: don Francisco Ximenes, who did not speak Spanish, had shortly before his death a crucifix, four statues and as many paintings. The governor of Xocotitlán among the Mazahua to the north of the valley of Toluca was the proprietor of some 30 paintings, a dozen engravings, a crucifix and two statues. Dozens of other cases bear witness to the existence among all the notables of an often striking collection of images. It is obvious that only a systematic inquiry based on the wills could make it possible to pick out regional variations and increase our knowledge of the main features and the evolution of this iconography. We are aware that these notables were the great providers for the churches and chapels of their *pueblo*, that they more than any other had the means to buy statues in the city, to order them from artists, to have a painting or a sculpture restored.

But what about more modest people? It appears that they too possessed certain images, even if their quantity and the quality of their workmanship were far from attaining that of the preceding examples. It suffices to come back to the subject of wills, which we have left partly open. Frequently the testators leave their oratories, indeed one or two images of saints duly identified or still more often anonymously designated by the term of *los santos*: 'To my son Antonio Nicolás I leave the house with all the saints'; 'To my son Miguel Gaspar, I leave the house and the oratory'. There again we could adduce numerous examples. By their profusion, Christian images became entrenched in the *pueblos*, implanting visible landmarks which, together with the sanctuaries and the chapels, served as medium of indigenous Christianity.[13] In this respect, by revealing a state of congestion that in many places seems sometimes to verge on saturation, church inventories and Indian wills reveal the ubiquitousness of the Christian image. But the physical dissemination of the object was only a secondary aspect of the phenomenon we are considering here.

These images were not objects. They existed only through the collective and individual devotion and attachment to which they gave rise and which were confused with the cult of the saints. The evangelizers baptized *pueblos*, *barrios*, churches, chapels and people by drawing from the repertory of saints' names. Lives of saints were painted, told in sermons, and spread in the indigenous world. The cult of the Virgin enjoyed a parallel expansion from the second half of the sixteenth century. An important stage was the local adoption of a patron saint. In the sixteenth century it was not rare for the Indians to try to accumulate comparisons between local divinities and what was just a name and a sometimes barely decipherable image. In the course of the seventeenth century, on the other hand, patron saints were perceived as an essential aspect of the *pueblo*'s identity, of its reality as of its supernatural. Finally the brotherhood, imported from Spain, from the outset played a major role in the dissemination of the cult of saints. But the written traces left by the brotherhoods (constitutions, account books, licences) show only the visible, sometimes artificial, face of the institution, the one supposed to conform to the ecclesiastical norm and faithfully to reproduce the model offered. As for the other face, apart from scandals or exceptional affairs, it escapes us almost completely. This elusiveness, due to the discretion of the sources, was not characteristic of the brotherhood alone, but it was perhaps more formidable there than elsewhere. From the beginning of their apostolate the mendicant orders had founded brotherhoods or hospitals (with which brotherhoods were associated). These institutions were conceived as the surest means of deepening the Christianization of the faithful (what the texts called the 'Christian governance') and of familiarizing them with the obligations, rituals and devotions of Catholicism. They were governed by written constitutions, dictated by the friars or by the ordinary clergy. A brotherhood like that of Our Lady of the Conception at Coatlán had in 1577 to elect two *mayordomos*, two deputies and a writer. It was supposed to celebrate the feasts of Our Lady. The constitutions also stipulated that on each feast day a Mass would be sung by all the brethren, who would attend with lit candles decorated with three crowns. Three or four brethren were to take care of helping the dying 'to die well', and all undertook to attend the funeral of a deceased brother. Bad conduct, drunkenness or concubinage were punishable by expulsion and the funds of the brotherhood were to be exclusively dedicated to the needs of the cult. An instrument of dissemination of the Marian cult and the 'Christian death', but also a material response to the epidemics that raged, the brotherhood of Coatlán was entirely in the hands of the secular priest, who closely monitored its workings.

Brotherhoods were already numerous in the city of Mexico at the end of the sixteenth century. But it was necessary to await the seventeenth century for them to proliferate throughout New Spain in relatively varied forms, often at the instigation of local notables. Several hundred could quickly be counted in the valley of Mexico alone and indications suggest that in some *pueblos* all or almost all the Indians belonged to a brotherhood. The same situation prevailed in Michoacán, where a number of hospitals established in the sixteenth century and placed under the rule of Indian *priostes* survived for a long time. If some brotherhoods were just a means in the hands of the regular clergy of financing some of the Masses that they celebrated, others progressively acquired relative autonomy as indigenous society seized upon an institution where it perceived a factor of stability, duration, cohesion and collective identity. This did not happen without pro-voking clashes with the ecclesiastical authority. This collective identity was constructed against the Spanish, the *mestizos*, the blacks and the mulattos, who could not become members of the brotherhood let alone have access of the functions of *mayordomos* or *oficiales*. The security of the brotherhood was based on the properties amassed by the institution, which were considered to belong to the saint. The brotherhood was all this. But let us not forget the social role of the institution. It was, of course and above all, an instrument of social and economic domination in the hands of the notables, the governors, the *fiscales*, the *alguaciles*, who collected the product of the sale of harvests or livestock, levied assessments, demolished and reconstructed chapels, bought images and ornaments, advanced the sums necessary for the festivities without submitting accounts to 'ordinary people' or to the priest. The 'classic' brotherhood was thus a weighty enough institution when it followed the usual rules. According to the rules of the Church, it was supposed to preserve its archives, keep its account books, draw up its membership list. So much for the façade and the view it was appropriate to present to the ecclesiastical authorities. But that was just the visible face of a far more diverse institution.[14]

From the end of the sixteenth century, the city of Mexico found itself invaded with pious associations multiplied by the Indians outside Church control. The Third Mexican Council counted 300 by about 1585. In the course of the seventeenth century the phenomenon that was until then, or so it appears, essentially urban, grew and reached the countryside. Ever more numerous Indians took the initiative of creating pious foundations without going through the ecclesiastical court, that is to say the *provisorato de los naturales*. They spared themselves laborious, costly procedures, whose meaning and necessity often escaped them. They evaded the usual written formalities that preceded the setting up of a brotherhood and set the conditions of membership and its functions. Foundations were born that took the most diverse forms. Often they began with a simple act: the pious legacy of a *cacique*, a notable, or a simple tributary Indian dedicating a patch of land to one or several saints. The leasing and working of this land extracted the necessary resources for the upkeep of the image and the celebration of the annual feast of the celestial addressee. The parish priest could designate a *mayordomo* charged with administering the gift, but most often the heirs of the legator kept and controlled what was called the *mayordomía*, and had charge of fulfilling the obligations attached to it. It happened that some families died out or for one reason or another lost the *mayordomía*, which then changed hands. It also happened that Indians installed more or less surreptitiously on the 'saint's lands' dedicated themselves spontaneously to maintaining the cult – so much and so well that the *mayordomo* and the deputies charged with administering the revenues of the land ended up being selected from among them. That was what happened with the 'brotherhood' of Our Lady *de la Soledad* of Acambay, north of the valley of Toluca. On the lands given by a *principal* of the *pueblo*, 'lived from 15 to 16 families of Indians among whom each year a *mayordomo* and a deputy were designated', who were charged with paying for the Masses due to the Virgin. But there were still more rudimentary forms. It was enough for four or five Indians to gather and decide to have a feast day for their favourite saint every year. Elected *mayordomo* by his companions, one of the Indians then got busy gathering funds, asking the parish priest for authorization. What in the eyes of the Church appeared as a simple collection undertaken voluntarily by some individuals took on an entirely different dimension for those involved: 'The Indians called Masses of the brotherhood Masses that were celebrated [thus] each month'. In fact, when the *mayordomía* brought together a larger number of Indians, it became an *hermandad*, a confraternity. The next step was official recognition and the setting-up of a brotherhood (*cofradía*). But the Indians rarely took it, limiting themselves most of the time to taking the name.

The Indians who participated in these foundations, *mayordomías* or *hermandades* received no licence, paid no duty, had no Mass celebrated for the dead; it was enough for them to live in the *barrio* or *pueblo* to consider themselves 'brothers' and to contribute to the saint's feast. As for the image, rather than being kept in the parish church, it was most often preserved in a little chapel, sometimes even in a simple oratory, on a domestic altar. For the Church it was just a 'pious devotion', barely tolerated. Finally, a last illustration, it was equally possible for the private cult of a miraculous image to be at the origin of the foundation. In 1698 the son of the *cacique* of Ocotitlán agreed to place in the church an Ecce Homo which became covered with a miraculous sweat and which he especially venerated. His descendants offered an altarpiece to the image, as well as fields of maize and agaves, and above all they succeeded in keeping the responsibility of the *mayordomía* up to the beginning of the nineteenth century. More modestly, tributary Indians acquired images to which it could happen that the neighbourhood attributed virtues. The house of the owner then became the centre of a more or less ephemeral devotion, the faithful brought him candles and flowers and left their coin. It is nevertheless singularly difficult to study these forms that belong in the margin of official institutions and written documents. At most we observe that they were extremely numerous and they expressed indigenous piety as much if not more than recognized confraternities. Tepotzotlán, an Otomí *pueblo* located 30 kilometres north of the city of Mexico, maintained just three brotherhoods, two Spanish and only one of Indians, but welcomed six *hermandades*. This disproportion, which one finds in all *pueblos* without exception, reveals the considerable expansion of these associations in indigenous daily life. They offered a flexible and relatively autonomous framework, since some Indians did not hesitate to claim that *hermandades* escaped the jurisdiction of the ordinary clergy.[15]

With or without fixed resources, the brotherhoods, *hermandades* and *mayordomías* frequently had recourse to collections to finance Masses, sermons, lighting, feasts, banquets and fireworks, or to reconstruct and restore a sanctuary. Already attested in the seventeenth century, these collections could take place in the confines of the *pueblo*, but sometimes the went far beyond its borders. In the name of a confraternity, an *hermandad* or simply an image, Indians criss-crossed the routes of central New Spain, going from village to village. Surrounded by a few musicians, the collectors carried the image in a kind of shrine, crowds welcomed them as they passed, dances were organized around the image, which was installed on the altar of a private individual at each stage. The collectors sold pious engravings, rosaries, little silver replicas of the image. Each time the sales and alms swelled the slowly amassed savings. In theory, the Indians were supposed to ask for a 'licence' from the *provisor de los naturales* and to submit themselves in all things to the priests and ecclesiastical judges of the lands they went through. In fact, free in their itineraries, often uncontrollable and uncontrolled, anxious to gather tidy sums that nothing would keep them from drawing on at will to cover claimed costs, skilled in negotiating the price of their passage with the priest, the collectors wonderfully incarnated the dynamism, mobility and expansion of Indian Christianity outside the accustomed limits of the *barrio* or *pueblo*. Contacts made here and there, the hospitality encountered in the *pueblos* passed through, the gatherings and rejoicing that marked their passage made up networks complementary to those of the pilgrimages, also more flexible, apparently spontaneous and improvised, still less subject to the vigilance of Church and State.[16]

It is much more arduous to probe the inner spirit of the devotions whose multiple aspects we have seen. Consonant or not with the norms imposed by the Church, they all crystallized about an image and more exactly a singular relationship to this image. This point seems essential, as it illuminates in what way indigenous Christianity found it to be the expression of a physical presence, material for reflection, and support for a massive personal investment and local solidarity.

'I am now leaving a son of mine called Balthasar Antonio, I leave him a "my father holy Christ" so that he will serve him, buy him candles, copal and flowers'. In 1705 near Tenango del Valle, Nicolasa Anna expresses herself in almost the same terms: 'To my son Antonio Nicolás I leave the house with all the saints and Our Lady the Virgin. Let my son Antonio Nicolás venerate and serve them.' The legacy can consist of images. It can consist of lands dedicated to the service of images in the manner of the foundations that we have just described. A father leaves one or several fields, asking his children to serve 'the Most Holy Trinity, Jesus of Nazareth, St Peter, the Virgin of Guadalupe, St Anthony, the Virgin *de los Remedios*, the Most Holy Redeemer of the

Column, the Christ of the Entombment'.[17] Sometimes, in the absence of land, instruments, tools, a carpenter's axe, a team of oxen were left, their work being dedicated to the saints who must be left wanting for nothing. Even in the most modest levels of the Indian population we can thus surmise the inextricable association of material goods and service of the instrument and the image to the saints. Among the most impoverished, the ritual obligation seems even to have prevailed over the transmission of goods. This attitude is broadly attested among the Nahua at the end of the seventeenth century and in the eighteenth century. We cannot fail to compare it with the behaviour denounced by the extirpators of idolatry in the first half of the seventeenth century. At that time, in the oratories of the Indians of Morelos, of the valley of Toluca and Guerrero, sacred objects, linked to the lineage that inhabited or had inhabited the settlement, were often hidden. Saints and 'little idols' coexisted on the domestic altar, without necessarily being treated with the same respect. The Indians showed so passionate an attachment to these objects that their confiscation was generally the scene of particularly dramatic episodes. Chosen by an ancestor, these figurines, terracotta vases and dried plants were supposed to harbour a force on which the prosperity of the home depended. The physical coexistence of these works and Christian images was the product of a choice and an imposition. The Indians were at the same time eager to harness the influence of supplementary powers and to put off the track the priests or Church Indians who visited their homes. With time, the movements of population, demographic slaughter, the collapse of memories and the decline of idolatry, we can imagine that the saints were physically and symbolically substituted for the old sacred things, by an imperceptible transition, quite different from the imposition of the patron saint in place of the god whose temples and effigies were destroyed. From tactical juxtaposition to accepted coexistence, from propinquity to substitution, the Christian image succeeded to the altar of the idol in fragments. Not without certain changes in the nature and transmission of objects, not also without certain 'permanences' (Gruzinski, 1990, pp. 285, 294).

Under the heading of these 'permanences', or more precisely these inertias, for nothing stands up to time, we cannot fail to point to the strong and exclusive attachment to these images that the Indians testified to, wherever they came from. The attachment was conveyed by an often disproportionate material investment in relation to the meagre resources at their disposal. They did not hesitate to dedicate a good part of their wherewithal to the restoration of the image, the decoration of the oratory, the purchase of vestments, without counting the usual offerings or the richer ones on feast days. Likewise, they accepted only with great difficulty giving them up in favour of a chapel or a church. Within a family the images could become the objective of thefts, violent conflicts settled more than once with knives, and negatively convey the extreme price accorded to them. In fact the intensity of the tie with the image served as of old as the basis of the solidarity as well as the continuity of the group. It animated a sequence of obligations, of *cargos* that the descendants were charged with assuming: 'my Lord of Chalma is there so that all the brothers, cousins and nephews serve him together'; '[I am making this legacy] so that my nephew serves my saints as I came to serve for some days, here on this earth.' The same constant prevailed on the level of the association of the saint first to the oratory, then to the house and sometimes to the instrument of work. 'My house and my saint': the formula often recurs in wills. Are not the saints the 'masters of my house'?

But just as the 'paintings' or the shamanic initiations integrated new features that ended by profoundly modifying the contents, the cult of saints was far more than a Christianization of the sacred objects of the home. While the domestic idols followed the lines of filiation and did not leave the house, the saints were often dispersed among children and could be transmitted to the spouse. The new importance of the couple, of the conjugal tie, of the indissolubility of marriage, the inheritance customs tied to the practice of wills and their rules could not fail to weigh on the circulation of holy images. This evolution was perceptible in the very nature of the relationship that joined the owner to the image. It was a familial relationship, drawn after the model of the Christian family; more precisely, a filial relationship that made the images the fathers and mothers of the Indian: '[my heirs] should serve my dear mother Lady St Anne... my dear mother of Guadalupe and my dear father St Anthony Padua'. The possessiveness practised in respect of these images ('*my* saints', '*my* Lady of the Conception', '*my* Lady of Guadalupe') was apparently very close to that which characterized the ownership of 'little idols'. But the tone is different. Now it mixed a personal tie and a sense of proprietorship which was experienced first as that of an individual before being that of the group, in the same way, moreover, as the remainder of the goods left. There we apparently see the imprint of a Spanish juridical conception of ownership, practised in tandem with the influence of the Christian family model.[18]

This evolution of the relationship to the divinity was indissociable from another conception of divine power. The saint was not a name given to a force, it was no longer, like the *sacra* of the beginning of the seventeenth century, a collection of often inchoate objects, some anthropomorphic and others not. The saint was a person individualized enough so that one could maintain familial relations with it, and patrons could be designated for it. Conversely, but I am not sure that this is without a prehispanic precedent, the ineffective image was treated as a person to be punished; a Baby Jesus was buried with his feet and head run through with wooden pegs. Here we are far from those Indians who in 1582 still called a statue of the Virgin *dios*, that is to say *teotl*, as if it was an ambivalent, faceless force.

We could extend almost the same considerations to the relationship that the *pueblo* or the *barrio* maintained with its images. The patron saint, as we saw in the Titles, was the master of lands, the father of the community. But other images crystallized links just as intense, sometimes still more powerful, when, for example, they radiated a force that the Christian miracle made manifest. The act of raising a chapel, of organizing a feast in honour of the image, then became an affirmation of identity and power faced with the neighbouring, less favoured *pueblos*. There again a prehispanic legacy dissolved in a Christianization of the hieropany. Saints were persons. Images moved, walked, sweated, bled, cried like people as only people can. That happened at Ayotzingo, Tultitlán, Tlatelolco, Tulantongo, San José in the valley of Mexico, but also Tlalpujahua or Tepetlazingo, etc. The possessiveness, the attachments to saints sometimes took violent forms that call to mind on quite a different scale the domestic and family conflicts that the ownership of images could trigger. In 1621, with hue and cry, armed with bows and arrows, the Otomí of Ixmiquilpan tore from the hands of the *alcalde mayor* the miraculous Christ demanded by the authorities of México-Tenochtitlán. Much later, in 1786, the Indians of Cuautitlán, under the direction of all their governors, hauled their parish priest before the tribunals because he wanted to take an image of the Immaculate Conception from the parish. An immemorial quality, subjection to the image, pious foundation, official recognition, miracles, burial of brothers in the chapel of the Virgin, all expressed the deep internalization of relations to the saint that in fact masked a specific relationship to time, death, the supernatural and society. The assimilation was expressed in the peremptory formula: 'This image belongs to no Spaniard, it belongs rightfully to the natives'.

However, there is no reason to set two parallel spheres against each other, one corresponding to the domestic group and the other to the community. Often an individual devotion, supported by even a modest miracle, became the cult of a *barrio*, a *pueblo*, indeed a whole region. The process begun at the end of the sixteenth century was pursued throughout the eighteenth century, gaining ground. In the same way it is sometimes difficult to distinguish the part of the group and that of the individual in the struggles that surrounded possession of images. The image was a source of power and prestige for its owner as well as for the faction that had possession of it. The happy owner, if he had the means, could be tempted to impose his saint in place of the community's patron, even if it entailed strong resistance. More modestly, to possess an image that one lent to the church for Lent or a feast day was not a privilege to be disdained.

For images were also the object of a collective investment, demonstrated with verve on the occasion of a feast day: 'Every *pueblo* has its different *barrios*, each *barrio* has its titular saint and each saint its annual feast day. The Indians of the *barrio* alone financed it according to their taste, in their way, in accordance with their devotion and to observe the institution of their ancestors'.[19] The feast conveyed a periodic intensification of all relations constructed around the image, of all the appropriations to which the Indians had succumbed. In this form the phenomenon went back also to the seventeenth century. But it was only in the eighteenth century that it became generalized, profiting from the concurrence of a weakening ecclesiastical establishment (to which we shall return below), the demographic revival and progress in Christianizing the Indians. The same scenarios were repeated everywhere: the parish priest was set apart, confined to his functions of celebrant, unless he was passed over completely by the Indians' singing solemn vespers or celebrating Holy Week alone. The faithful invaded the church despite the protests of the priest, while church squares and cemeteries swarmed night and day with natives drinking and eating happily amidst musicians, crackers, fireworks, casks of *pulque* and brandy. The consumption of food and alcoholic intoxication were then the opportunity for a reaffirmation of the collective identity at the level of the *pueblo* or simply of the *barrio*. This debauchery of food, alcohol, music and noise was close to what we know of the rural festivals of the Ancien Régime in Europe, partly because of our observers, who projected a Spanish vision of things, partly because it consisted of similar elements. But by raising a screen, a barrier, between the indigenous world which communicated in *pulque* and the others – the intruders, the priest who denounced immorality and drunkenness – did intoxication not continue to constitute the specifically indigenous instrument of making a reality of the divine, of collective access to another reality that the Indians in large part constructed around their saints? Already consumed during the great festivities before the conquest, from the end of the sixteenth century *pulque* was offered to the saint before being distributed to the congregation. We also know that the images possessed agave plants, that the brotherhoods were large producers of *pulque* and that some of the drink that they produced flowed during the ceremonies and festivities that they organized. In other words, *pulque*, image and confraternity formed a triptych that probably constituted one of the keys to indigenous sociability in the colony and independent Mexico.[20]

Occupying a major place that it had probably not yet acquired in the time of Ruiz de Alarcón and Jacinto de La Serna, the Christian image served as a link between the members of the domestic group, between the group and the community, between the house and the lands, between the past and the future. A package of multiple connections emerged from the image, in turn increased tenfold by the number of images preserved by individuals, the domestic group or the community. These material and social bonds, which followed and paralleled the circuits of marriage and filiation, were made, unmade and redistributed in the course of generations. They wove a continuous canvas, a coherent reality, in which a large part of Indian existence could find a meaning and a reason for being. The credibility and efficacity of this reality depended not only on its coherence or its texture. It flowed rather from the nature of the object that for the sake of convenience we call the image, but which the Indians designated by the name of saint, *el santo*, *los santos*. In fact, the *santo* was never presented as an object, a statue or a painting; it was never posited as the effigy of something else, and thus was never a representation in the sense that we understand it. The Indians never distinguished between the saint and its representations, as if this type of relationship had no relevance in their eyes. The image was the saint, or rather, the saint was the saint. To treat the saint as an object whose prophylactic or therapeutic function one attempted to define, or which harboured a force, a divine power: in these conditions, was that an entirely satisfactory approach?

It seems that rather than having a meaning to decipher, a 'reading' to offer or a function to which they would be reduced, images of saints were 'instruments of evocation',[21] 'anchoring points' of a reconstructed reality, ordered by the Indians themselves. Such supports, which proliferated, substituted the evidence and immediacy of a divine presence for the uncertainty of belief experienced as subjective initiative. In other words, belief ceased to be a subjective attitude, to become the expression of the state of things. No preliminary adherence, no doubt or questioning: the image was the saint. It brought an unimpeachable presence to the very heart of the dwelling, as the patron saint imposed himself on the *pueblo*. Obtained by merging the signifier (the object) and the signified (the divine entity), this immediacy probably constituted one of the driving elements that made the whole colonial environment plausible and gave a coherence, a unity, to data as disparate as Spanish priests, places of cult, liturgies and the Christian calendar, the territory, the house, death, etc. It appears that, in order to be diffused, repeated and reproduced, and to focus the indigenous perception of the world,

Indian Christianity used the image of the saint, which operated as an omnipresent support able to concentrate and grasp (in the full meaning of the term) the Christian divine. It was indeed an Indian Christianity, in which the saint made possible a personalized relationship (or a 'family' tie, if I dare to put it this way) to divine power (in accordance with the Christian tradition), while the matrix – or, if one prefers, the *form of the content* – remained indigenous and close to what we know of prehispanic cults. The absence of distance between the signifier and the signified, the telescoping of sign and meaning, send us back to processes characteristic of the treatment that pre-conquest societies seem systematically to have reserved to their 'sacred'. The bundle-reliquaries were gods. The victim of the sacrifice was the god, he did not represent the god, nor limit himself to demonstrating his presence; the priest who took on the cut-away skin of the 'god' so sacrificed was confused with him; the man-god was at the same time the divine force and its skin, the deity and his shell; the 'paintings' did not represent the gods, they were identified with them.

The specificity of the relationship of identity between the effigy and the divine in the Christian icon was perhaps a matter of the double priority accorded to the Word and to Writing. The Word was opposed to Matter in a duality that prehispanic cultures did not know. Writing enabled one better to conceive, express and analyse the different relations possible between the perceptible 'matter' of the image and the 'thing represented', to take up the terms of a sixteenth-century Franciscan. The idol, on the other hand, was a presence to show or to hide. It did not have to be made explicit and referred back only to itself, like a closed unit, and not to an ultimate, distant, inaccessible, absolute signified, that would be the divine in the Christian and European meaning of this term. The *tonalli* enclosed in the image was a force based on it. It was by no means what would have called to mind, designated or recalled the image. The prehispanic idol in its finiteness did not seek to demonstrate or to show something else, whence the often formless aspect, non-anthropomorphic, concealed, secret (they were hidden from the eyes of the Indians), of the bundle-reliquaries before the conquest and in the seventeenth century. The *santo*, on the other hand, gave itself over to being seen. But it offered only itself to be seen. In this way it remained, partially, an idol. The *santo* was continually alluded to (by the Indians as by the priests), omnipresent, and yet no one, whether Spaniard or Indian, sought to articulate the nature of the image or of the relationship of the faithful to it. This explains the extreme difficulty of delimiting the *santo* in our sources and of distinguishing it from the popular images of Mediterranean Christianity – but that is another undertaking.

How far can the autonomous space organized by the indigenous communities extend? The seventeenth century gave us the beginning of an answer by offering the spectacle of initiation reduced to individuals or restricted groups. The indigenous Christianity of the eighteenth century was driven by a logic of appropriation still more systematic in that it was based on a collective acquisition, a sedimentation, an interiorization that had little in common with what was observed in the preceding century. Thus the excesses, some widespread, and others more radical but also more atypical, illuminated certain tendencies and modalities of this collective process.

From the earliest period of evangelization, Indians had filled ecclesiastical functions and ensured the celebration of certain Christian rituals. It was entirely acceptable, among relations, for a sacristan or a midwife to administer baptism to a newborn in the absence of the priest. It was more clandestine when, from the sixteenth century no doubt, cantors took it upon themselves to celebrate funerals, with more or less serious infringements of canonical law. The responses were left out, since they were unknown, and as of old 'food for the trip and the instruments of his station so that he could work in the other life' were placed near the dead.[22] The practice is attested among the Nahua, the Otomí and other tribes in the middle of the eighteenth century. Cantors did not hesitate if need be to wear priestly vestments. That is to say death remained in large part an indigenous monopoly, marked not only with traits of prehispanic inspiration but also with beliefs of colonial origin. Moreover, Death, figured by a skull haloed with rays, took his place regularly at the end of the seventeenth century in domestic oratories and offerings of candles and incense were addressed to him, to delay his arrival.

In another field, the Indian population had still more room for manoeuvre: that of the theatre. Religious drama resisted appropriation by the Indians no more than the brotherhood or the cult of saints. We are aware of the role that the missionary theatre played in the evangelization of the Indians in the sixteenth century. Friars introduced the custom of representing scenes of religious history, provided themes, the outline, the production, and they had the Indian people take part in these edifying shows that borrowed the language, certain costumes and some dances from native cultures. This theatre had several objectives. It was meant to present the distant and exotic origins of Christianity, or to transmit a moral message, an 'example' and, beyond that, to set out models of conduct and misconduct in a striking and accessible way to the largest number of people. The experience was a remarkable success in view of its limited means. But with the decline of the mendicant orders, the undertaking progressively ceased to be an instrument placed exclusively at the service of the Church. Besides an exploitation that continued to serve missionary ends (the spread of the cult of the Virgin of Guadalupe is one example) a more specifically indigenous theatrical usage emerged in the seventeenth century. At México-Tenochtitlán and into the most remote countryside, Indians themselves had taken the habit of representing dramas that could last several hours, in church sequares, chapels or cemeteries. Nahua representations were based on more or less detailed written outlines (no doubt inspired by the texts of the first evangelizers) which circulated over vast territories, from Amecameca to Huejotzingo, from the valley of Mexico to that of Puebla, from one side of Popocatepetl to the other. These manuscripts 'from which they drew their roles' were probably not without connections to a pious literature in the indigenous language whose influence and dissemination has generally been underestimated. It is true that only the titles remain: the *Will of Our Lord*, the *Revelations of the Passion*, the *Prayers of St James, St Bartholomew, St Cosmas and St Damien*, etc. These texts, and many others whose traces remain to be rediscovered, probably guided the authors of the plays. We know, moreover, that cantors, catechists and writers took on recopying, compiling and often revising the outline in their care or that they borrowed from a neighbouring *pueblo*. This literary work was also a work of interpretation in the course of which Indians took liberties with the Catholic tradition. But who were they? They probably belonged to the literate class that drafted the Primordial Titles. We know too that in the important *pueblos*, at Huejotzingo, for example, the 'leading roles' – Christ, the Virgin, Mary Magdalen, the Apostles – were monopolized by local *caciques* and their families, who generally learned their lines by heart. Women as well as men were part of the cast, while in the case of Huejotzingo, at least, the *macehuales* contented themselves with performing supporting and character roles. However important the participation of the notables, indigenous theatre was still a collective, not to say mass phenomenon. Preparations took considerable time, almost two months of the year, and a considerable number of Indians, since no fewer than 30 to 40 roles were given out in the Passions. There reigned an effervescence comparable to that surrounding the preparation of traditional festivals. On a set date the Indians thus had the opportunity to produce their own representation of Christianity under the direction of the notables and to interpret it in all senses of the term by improvising part of their lines and making up their own costumes.

For the Indians, the representation was more of a presentation or more precisely a re-presentation. It reproduced identically a character or a ritual that, in the case of the Eucharist, was the exclusive monopoly of the Catholic priest. It even produced relics, since the audience shared the carmine that coloured the wounds of the image, gathering it on pieces of cloth or cotton. Preserved piously, these objects healed the sick who had recourse to them. In 1621 an observer noted: 'The Indians do not know how to make the distinction or tell the difference, or to see that it is only a representation and not a real Mass'. In these circumstances didn't the dramatic representation constitute a supplementary means of access to the divine sphere, a capture in the flesh, as real as the blood that flowed from the wounds of him who, with the features of Christ, was violently whipped, as real as the bread-host that this same Indian had consecrated shortly before? It is quite obviously impossible and unthinkable to establish a *direct* line of descent from prehispanic rituals to the indigenous drama of New Spain. Still we can observe astonishing correspondences. The Indian who for 40 days *was* the god Quetzalcoatl and rehearsed the death of the god under the sacrificial knife, behaved and spoke according to a precise code, he 'spoke his lines', 'he was served and revered like [the god]'. It was the same for the victim who *was* the god Tezcatlipoca, and we could without difficulty accumulate examples of this unusual relation of the 'ritual actor', of the man to the god, whose origins go back to the end of the historical period (López Austin, 1973). The colonial 'actor' prepared for the performance by subjecting himself to Christian penance, he confessed and took communion. As for the bad characters, after the spectacle their interpreters felt the need to request absolution. At Huejotzingo, representations of the Passion were stopped in the middle of the eighteenth century, from the day when an Indian who 'played' Judas died accidentally in an excess of drunkenness. Then no one dared to take the role, so intensely was the connection felt between the figure to be represented and his titulary.

It is not superfluous to dwell upon a process that we experience as confusion but that is, after all, only a different way, just as acceptable, of conceiving the relationship between the signifier and the signified, as a collision, a telescoping, an encounter. The perception of the image of the saint was, moreover, founded on the same principle. We understand that the re-presentation (as much as the *santo* or the vision) can be one of the indigenous paths to evocation (in the strongest sense) of a Christianized reality. Production and *presentation* of their own reality, the indigenous theatre then lent its context and its physical aspect to a collective vision, periodically replayed. It opened a massive and direct access to what the Church claimed to hold the key to.[23]

The logic of appropriation could in certain circumstances emerge as overtaking and challenging Christianity. Our 'heretical' Indians of the seventeenth century went beyond the limits of orthodoxy, without for that reason seeking deliberately to break with the Church or Christianity. The crazes of the eighteenth century indicated that this further step had been taken. We recall the sacrilegious practices of the Indians of Coatlán, in Morelos, the relentlessness shown towards the effigies, treated like people in the nocturnal rituals. We see in these one of the most exacerbated expressions of relations to the image and to the saint. We recognize an extension of scenes of flagellation borrowed from the repertory of the Passions, but also an explosion of aggressiveness entirely conditioned this time by a Christianized reality and probably inspired by *mestizo* or Spanish excesses pursued by the Inquisition. It is revealing that far from hiding the old 'idolatries' as before, going to chapels and diverting Christian rituals conveyed the indigenous seizure of Christianity, the subjection of its symbolic capital. Half a century later, far from there, between Querétaro and San Luis Potosí, in the *pueblo* of San Luis de La Paz, the Church uncovered rather similar conduct. The *hermandades* which met in these chapels now lent their setting to other nocturnal meetings where Indians got drunk on *peyotl*, wore the sacred ornaments, whipped crosses with candles or buried them with dog heads or human bones, when they were not threatening an image of Santa Muerte with a flogging if she did not grant them the miracle they demanded. Currents drifting towards blasphemy but also towards witchcraft, these beliefs and practices have been mentioned less for their frequency or their representative nature than because they illustrate, as at Morelos, the potential attitudes concealed in the relationship to Christian effigies and because they represented a break from and going beyond the norm and tradition that the heretical Indians of the seventeenth century experienced without really conceiving it as such. But it will be observed that this behaviour was produced in isolation, as if the autonomy and omnipotence sought could be exercised only in clandestinity and in strictly limited groups.

The treatment and manipulation of images probably reached their peak in a Messianic movement that I have studied elsewhere (Gruzinski, 1989a, pp. 105–72). Of an exceptional breadth, the phenomenon contributed to filling in the details of our interpretation of the indigenous image and the way it participated in the evocation, the sudden appearance of another reality. The movement culminated in 1761 in the southeast of the valley of Mexico and northeast of Morelos. The leader claimed that the great sanctuaries of the region were devils and had engravings of saints burned, stating that they were damned. This Indian and his numerous followers rediscovered in 1761 the acts and arguments that the evangelizers had had against the indigenous effigies more than two centuries earlier, with all their ambiguity, since these fallen images were considered demons and treated at the same time as vulgar pieces of wood good only for burning, like the 'inventions', the 'constructions of the world' in the sense of objects made by men.

The iconoclasm of these Indians spared the 'good images', those that 'appeared' to them, that 'came from heaven' and that in fact the Indians made with their own hands. Their *santo* was originally conceived as a copy, the 'imitation' of a shapeless effigy; then it received a name, a 'title' before becoming the saint, the divinity. There we have at the same time the recognition of human intervention and the denial of this same intervention, a fine example of denial ('I know very well, but even so . . .') that made it possible to reconcile two antithetical propositions and that we see at work in many other processes of acculturation. Quite exceptionally, the accounts reveal the material modalities of the process:

> 'Antonio had Balthazar open the image of the [Virgin of the] Palm by making a hole in the chest of the statue; into which he put hearts of [corn] stalks, kernels of variegated corn, a piece of an ear [of wheat], and a glass vinegar cruet that contained the blood of a young virgin, taken from the right hand of his daughter María Antonia. He had him make another hole in the head, where he put the heart of a white pigeon, and he asked that the holes be blocked up . . . In the stomach [of the Lord of Purgatory] he had a hole made in which he put a piece of lightning-blue stone, saying that it was a saint's heart.'[24]

Elsewhere I have suggested the relations that existed between this practice and prehispanic customs, even if there could not have been direct transmission. In any case there persists a common relationship to the effigy, not through the object but *in* the object, in the hollow of the matter. This relationship is expressed not by words, speeches, or a theology, nor even exactly in a ritual, but in a material practice, in a hollowing out. I also indicated the possible memory of a prehispanic concept of vital energies, which suggests the relationship introduced between the lightning stone and the heart of the saint. The impregnation of the heart by celestial fire that signifies this lightning stone goes back to the concept of *tonalli* and to the way that prehispanic societies thought of the hemming in of the human being or objects by divine power. Through these exceptional accounts, we can perhaps have a better sense of the saint turning in upon himself, who contains the force and refers back only to himself. These sources attract our attention less for their strangeness than because they articulate a relationship that the Indians did not generally need to spell out. They usually adored, asked, thanked, paid back or threatened the *santo*, they did not speculate about the relationship of the signifier and the signified as the Church or more rarely the historian could. Except, of course, as in this case when the rules of the game were overturned and the official saints dethroned so that others could come to take their place. At the heart of this movement, the practices surrounding it and the representation of the world and the hereafter to which it gave rise, images once again took the role of introducing and evoking a different reality, conceived and experienced by the Indians without any ecclesiastical interference.

Another effect of going beyond the norm and tradition, also exceptional but just as revealing of profound potential, was linked to the capacity that the Indians had for identifying themselves with the divinity. The identification sometimes went beyond the dramatic stage to take unprecedented dimensions. Think of those Christian man-gods, the first of whom we see appearing in the second half of the seventeenth century. Sources reveal their sporadic appearance in the eighteenth century. In 1770 at San Miguel El Grande (today San Miguel Allende), an indigenous *curandero* had himself called God the Father; an Indian woman who lived with him and exercised the same profession, God the Holy Ghost; and a *mestizo* who accompanied them, God the Son. A quarter century later, not far from there, in nocturnal meetings at San Luis de La Paz, the *mayordomo* of the 'Lord Patron St Louis' had himself adored as if he were God, installed on the altar, clothed with priestly ornaments, preaching and promising to grant all that the Indians asked of him. An Indian woman received the same honours. But let us go back to the movement of Popocatepetl (1761). It was exemplary in constituting an outcome, a summing up and a synthesis of all the movements to capture the Christian supernatural that had arisen and multiplied since the beginning of the seventeenth century. About 1757, at the borders of the valley of Mexico and the region of Cuautla, an indigenous shepherd, Antonio Pérez, met a mysterious Dominican who taught him the art of healing. It was the well-worn (because now familiar to us) scenario of the predominantly Christian syncretic initiation where the memory of the *venerables* floats, roams. In the second scenario, following on from the first, Antonio acquired an image, the painting of a Christ, that gave rise to devotion among the Indians. Individual piety and collective piety became entangled in this episode that went wrong, since the Church proscribed the devotion. At this point, faced with the hostility of the clergy, Antonio committed himself to a course that removed him from the Church and even from indigenous Christianity. But this remove had less to do with the form of the process than with the content given to it. It relied on the role that the Indians accorded to images, as we have just seen, but also took up the theme of the Mariophany – the Virgin appeared in a cave of the volcano Popocatepetl – by extending it, although it was still the Marian tradition, by the construction of an image. The list of borrowings did not end with the Mariophany; it included the whole range of Christian rituals and sacraments, and continued by the usurpation of priestly functions; Antonio became priest, archbishop, pontiff and finally God. There the accelerated projection of a history already glimpsed in the seventeenth century in dispersed episodes got carried away. The accession to divinity was only a first step; in Antonio's wake rushed dozens of Indians who became angels, Apostles, the Virgin or rather Virgins, the Three Marys, the Three Kings, the Holy Trinity. Everything took place as if what had a fleeting role on the occasion of a liturgical feast had become daily reality. Taken to extremes, this chain of turning aside and appropriation ended by setting up an apprehension of objective reality supported not only by images created by Indians but also by these dozens of man-gods who realized in their persons the living osmosis of the signified and the sign. At the same time a transmutation of space and the environment revealed the imposition of hell, purgatory and paradise in the volcano Popocatepetl. Meanwhile a similarly transformed approach to time unfurled, in which memories of pagan divine time (to which some of the faithful had privileged access) were combined with human time that now ceased to be cyclical to focus on an end of the world conceived as a Christian Apocalypse.

Built on spatial and temporal structures, human and material supports, written in letters that disseminated the Mariophany of Popocatepetl, this reality was, quite obviously, totally incompatible with the colonial world as the Spaniards, the *mestizos*, the 'men of reason' conceived it. It was an incompatibility that paradoxically flowed from elements all adopted from the colonial Church: the imperative of belief and conversion, religious exclusivity ('the real God was theirs'), the economy of redemption and damnation. These features together imprinted an explosive radicalism on the movement and a universalist consciousness that precipitated it towards a break with, and rejection without appeal of the leadership of the Church and the king: the credibility of the edifice thus constructed demanded the elimination of unbelievers in an Apocalypse that would spare only the Virgin's faithful. The messianic, millenarist and apocalyptic overstatement was the only outlet offered to those Indians who turned against the dominant (Spanish, *mestizos* and acculturated Indians) the treatment that had for a long time been reserved for them. This obvious lack of realism, this fantastic construction, emerged as a lucid consciousness of colonial exploitation, a radical challenge, and a group of proposals for action ('the world is a cake that ought to be shared among all . . . All the riches should go to the natives'), where, moreover, the imprint of Christianity showed through again. It was in fact Christianity that posed individual *belief* as a condition of participation in the movement and that opened a *universal* perspective on New Spain as a whole and the world. It was also Christianity that made it possible to think of indigenous society as no longer a conglomeration of *pueblos* or at best of tribes, but as a group, the 'natives', linked by a common faith in the Virgin of the volcano. The notion was not new; it went back to the first period of Christianization. The important thing is that here it was taken up by the Indians themselves and by Indians belonging for the most part to the world of the *macehuales*, to the rural plebeians ever more numerous and more starved for land. To these Indians without a past was promised a liberated furture, it too inspired by a Christianized interpretation of time.

However exceptional it might be, the movement of Antonio Pérez was not completely isolated. It unearthed tendencies buried in indigenous Christianity and revealed what recapturing total ascendancy over reality signified for the Indians. It would have been worthwhile to broaden the study to other examples less well documented by the sources but revealing about the extent of the phenomenon. I am thinking for example, of a movement that appeared in the steep mountains of the eastern Sierra Madre around Tulancingo, Tututepec, Tenango de Doria and Pahuatlán in 1769. Among these Otomí of the Sierra, religious acculturation was less perceptible, the substratum of idolatry more manifest. Numerous features however bring this movement close to that of Antonio Pérez. The protagonists took on the identity of divine figures, they were God ('Lord of heaven and Earth'), the Virgin of Guadalupe, the saints. One of the leaders, Juan Diego, was supposed to marry his Virgin after their resurrection. Christian images taken from churches were mixed with other images constructed by the Indians. Churches were feverishly built, crosses set up everywhere. Waiting for the end of the world and the descent (or the fall to earth) of God gave an apocalyptic tone to the predictions of these Indians, accompanied by a systematic reversal of spiritual and social roles. What shows through here, as elsewhere among the followers of Antonio Pérez, is the concern to force the Spaniards to recognize indigenous supremacy and to submit to the way these Indians conceived the divinity, social and political relations, space, and the meaning of history.

In the Otomí Sierra of Tututepec, at the foot of Popocatepetl or on the wooded edges of Michoacán, it is clear that the growing population considerably increased tensions and multiplied the conflicts expressed sometimes through the words of the man-gods. We know that between 1760 and 1820 rural emotions exploded in the centre of Mexico and the bishopric of Oaxaca twice as often as in the first half of the century.

It was then that in certain conditions messianic and millenarist answers were outlined, a condemnation of colonial domination based on the systematic appropriation of images and saints, the radicalization of indigenous Christianity and its rejection of official Christianity. It corresponded to the unprecedented will to impose an approach to life that was no longer that of the victors. An ephemeral attempt, a dream of mastery regained from reality, it remained illusory, so deprived were the natives of the social and political means to accomplish it. But it was also an encounter of 'charismatic' personalities, of indigenous Christianity and a native substratum that conferred on this generalized disquiet an ideological expression, a religious projection and a political dimension.[25]

Idolatry in isolated rural areas or service of the saints have in common offering and effecting two potential structurings of objective reality – but two structurings that, as we have seen, confirm each other not at all. While stagnant idolatry established a specific relationship to the natural environment, to mountains, clouds, the air, on which it conferred a meaning and a being, service of the saints developed dynamically as a network of images and oratories that marked out inhabited space, followed the history of families and set up personalized relations with the divine. Colonial idolatry and indigenous Christianity thus corresponded to two registers that in the eighteenth century were perceived as both distinct and equivalent, since as a general rule the same individuals resorted to them at various times depending on the context. If it is true that idolatry had lost its monopoly, its very persistence sufficed to show that Christianity, however revised and corrected by the Indians, could not claim in its turn to govern the whole of relations to reality. There existed between them, or on their fringe, fears, beliefs, acts, practices, that really had nothing to do with the saints or the old gods or a theory of pollution or the *tonalli* – as if there had remained an empty space which had in part taken the form of colonial witchcraft. How can one not wonder about the significance of the omnipresent proliferation of practices and accusations wherever the law (ecclesiastical and, to an increasing extent, civil) consented to take a look at what it too often scorned? When idolatry did not explain the event, when the intervention of the saint did not account for it, witchcraft intervened. This witchcraft was distinguished from prehispanic witchcraft in that it was no longer linked to the matrix of idolatry, which defined the play of forces and the accepted conventions, the more easily since contacts with other groups had intensified. The indigenous witchcraft of the eighteenth century, at least that of the valley of Mexico, Morelos, the region of Tlaxcala, the cities and their surroundings, had neither its own space nor specific objects; it did not presuppose an extensive knowledge; it had ceased to be the monopoly, real or imagined, of evil guilds. It tended to become a conglomeration of beliefs that welcomed African and European borrowings alike. It constituted a flexible and light device, a set of keys whose origins were confused enough for Indians, *mestizos*, mulattos or even the Spaniards to be able to find their match. Moreover, unlike the cult of saints and idolatry, witchcraft often operated on a mode of denial: 'I know very well that I ought not to believe these things but . . .' It was this 'poverty' and this heterogeneity that enabled it to make the connection between idolatry and Indian Christianity. Witchcraft still maintained links with idolatry that showed through in therapeutic rituals and beliefs, while Indian Christianity often inspired its sacrilegious and blasphematory tendencies. It thus offered the possibility of a transition, a coming together based on a grid nebulous enough to be open to several interpretations. Most of the time witchcraft could be reduced to an expression of affective states (fear, anger, desire) that reproduced the same simple pattern that was stereotyped enough to work in different cultures and contexts: the individual had to cope with the aggression he was provoking or experiencing. Finally and above all witchcraft monopolized a domain common to all groups in colonial society, the treatment of sickness and misfortune. From the seventeenth century, around certain constant principles accepted by all ethnic groups – the driving out of evil conceived in the form of a foreign and often foul body, its transfer to an object, an animal or another person – witchcraft ordered a package of beliefs that drew from it meaning, coherence of practical aims and immediate efficacity. It is thanks to these characteristics that witchcraft was in a position to offer a terrain, a language, a common sense, to Indians and others, Spanish, *mestizo* or mulatto, who, ever more numerous, cut across the daily life of the natives. Not only did the Spaniards believe themselves to be the victims of bewitchment and ask the Indians to find the authors, but they themselves made very good sorcerers, according to an Indian from Querétaro. We should not forget that in the eighteenth century there were still clerics who believed in indigenous witchcraft or, inversely, were accused by the Indians of diabolical practices. The relative autonomy of witchcraft in relation to cultural references only reflected a society where biological and cultural inter-breeding occupied an ever increasing place. Thus, when Indians consulted a *tlamatini* or *tepatiani*, it often hardly mattered to them whether he was Indian or *mestizo*, *pardo* or *moreno*.

An accusation of witchcraft could concern undesirable groups, Indians foreign to the *pueblo* or rebelling against payment of tribute, or rival factions who wanted to separate from the community. It made it possible to get rid of all supposed deviants or to silence them at will, and sometimes to do so without the knowledge of the parish priest and the Spanish authorities. Among the Otomí of the region of San Juan del Río, the Nahua of Cuautla or Zacualpan west of Morelos, or the Chinantec of Oaxaca the process was repeated with monotonous regularity in the second half of the eighteenth century. But increasingly eighteenth-century witchcraft followed individual, singular, improvised paths; it flowed into interpersonal strategies, while the service of saints and idolatry ruled the relations of the individual or the group to the divine in institutionalized and pre-established frameworks. The two domains had their own places, their liturgies, their pharmacopoeias, their cult objects. They imposed constraining practices that subordinated the petitioner to the forces that he appealed to. The domain of colonial witchcraft, on the other hand, left freer rein to improvisation, personal initiative. Interpreting the accidental, identifying the responsible person, peddling a strange rumour had long occupied an important place. What seemed to change in the eighteenth century was the occurrence of witchcraft, or more precisely the frequency of the accusation of witchcraft. The attack on witchcraft was no longer fantasized as the monopoly of specialized sorcerers or evil-doing groups whose fearful names were rehearsed in prehispanic societies and were still feared in the seventeenth-century countryside. Probably under the influence of Iberian beliefs, it seems that the accusation of witchcraft became banal in the eighteenth century. Any conflict, every accident or unexplained death was amenable to sorcery and any Indian could become the potential source of an attack. It was thus not exclusively the aggression of a professional sorcerer, socially and culturally marked, that one feared but that of the Other, the neighbour, the *compadre*, a relative, whose true face had to be revealed under its innocent appearance. It is not ruled out that a deterioration of traditional sociability (in which the Christian norms of marriage and the family, the Spanish definition and practice of property, the pressures of colonial domination, as well as the weakening of certain domestic and community constraints were implicated) thus found in colonial witchcraft a field of action, a source and a supplementary outlet. In this respect, the secret or whispered violence of witchcraft seemed often to echo domestic violence. The constant tensions, the violent outbursts that the indigenous couple experienced in certain domains, opposing it to in-laws, setting it against allies, appeared not only to convey the difficult emergence of conjugal unity but also to express in their way a progressive redefinition of the relationship of the individual to the group.

To this accent placed on the individual, often at the expense of community, family or spiritual (or godparent with godchild) solidarity, was added the weakness of touchstones, the superficiality of cultural references that surrounded witchcraft. This conjunction seems to have structured subjective reactions, the fantasy that swelled rumour, accusation and fear. In 1750 some of the Chinantec of Oxitlán, a *pueblo* lost in the wooded mountains northeast of the bishopric of Oaxaca, denounced sorcerers who changed into billy goats, held gatherings and drank the blood of their victims, celebrated black Masses, and sucked the blood of the children that they devoured. An Indian woman was even changed into 'a person in a wheeled carriage, as if she were a queen'. The accusers superimposed on political rivalries, where the priest and the *alcalde mayor* of Teutila were also implicated, internal quarrels, neighbours' disputes and even a suicide attempt (a rare event in indigenous circles), interpretations partly drawn from European demonology. Still the group made up a heterogeneous jumble of beliefs, fears and frenzies arising from the imagination of each, an amalgam that mixed manifestations of Nahualism, the stench of human sacrifices, apparitions of devouring fantasies and of abortionist monsters that consumed the foetus that they tore from the belly of its mother. Panicky fear eradicated the ordinary cultural landmarks and saturated a new space that was close to European witchcraft without being identical to it – for the devil was never mentioned – and distanced itself from an indigenous idolatry that appeared only as a distant shadow. The proliferation of accusations of witchcraft, the multiplication of victims, the disparity of interpretations, the emergence of a fantastic production that favoured individual delirium and of which traces were discovered among the Nahua of Morelos as well as among the Chinantec of Oaxaca, not only convey a greater openness of the indigenous world to colonial society. They reveal in the short term the setting up of a new domain that would take shape in indigenous folklore. Finally and above all, they invite us to follow the development of a cultural framework distinct from the matrices of idolatry and the cult of the saints, fragile, unstable, ephemeral, subject to the hazards of beliefs, deprived of institutional basis, local legitimacy and profound coherence, and which distantly prefigures the universe without roots in which *mestizos* and Indians struggle today.[26]

Enforced interlocutors

If the excesses of Indian Christianity led only to dead ends, if witchcraft hardly worried the colonial authorities, it was because the *macehuales* and petty notables could not by themselves represent the whole of Indian society, and they were far from mastering the elements of which their cultures were composed. While Indian Christianity set up remarkable mechanisms of defence and adaptation, this cannot diminish the weight of other just as essential components of Indian society, even if we sometimes tend, for convenience, to make abstractions of them.

From the sixteenth century, the wills of the Indian nobility never ceased to express an exemplary and generous piety. They reflect lives of ease, led in the shade of vast dwellings decorated with a profusion of paintings and statues of saints. The fervent and ostentatious devotions, the sumptuous donations, can be surmised. The close ties linking these nobles to the confraternities can be reconstituted, and the pre-eminence that is invariably accorded to them in the ceremonies, the rank owed them, the candles presented to them in the great Corpus Christi processions are well known. We can imagine the solemn funerals in the presence of Indian notables with regal arms and shields against the background of a clamour of drums. The generosity of the *caciques*, the prestige and property that they retained, the households that they maintained and the example that they gave constituted an important feature in the life of the *pueblos* or the cities. By their presence and by their intermediation, the *caciques* incarnated in the great feasts (Corpus Christi, Holy Week or the *autos da fé* of Mexico City) the integration of indigenous communities into colonial society.[27] But they sustained even more energetically the field of action of the Church, by two closely associated devices: the priesthood and pious foundations. From the sixteenth century, Indian families, like the rich Spaniards, set about collecting a capital whose revenue was to assure the celebration of Masses in memory of the generous donors. In the seventeenth and eighteenth centuries, foundations increasingly functioned as family strategies intended to protect part of the patrimony and to guarantee the access of members of the family to an ecclesiastical career. In the manner of the modest legacies made to an image, the chaplaincy consecrated and perpetuated the link between a pious donation and an Indian family that in the long term remained the beneficiary. In both cases the act was, or could become, a source of prestige. But a gulf in fact separated the two processes. The *caciques* based the hope of social rise on the capital invested, while the *macehuales*, excluded from the priesthood, invested an object with sacred force. For the former, the investment of financial capital assured a regular revenue to its owner; for the latter, the work of the owner supported the needs of the image. For the former, we see only the faithful assimilation of Spanish models; for the latter the saint, symbolic as well as social capital, was the instrument of a reinterpretation of Christianity and the beginning of a reorganization – a restructuring and redefinition – of indigenous reality. This distance expresses, in fact, that more general distance that opened between the indigenous, acculturated nobility in search of integration, and the remainder of the Indian populations.[28]

We shall perhaps be surprised to discover that for the *caciques* an ecclesiastical career constituted a means of social ascent that they greatly appreciated. It seems that at the end of the seventeenth century Indians began regularly to enter the priesthood. Towards the middle of the eighteenth century, New Spain numbered about 50 indigenous priests, few in relation to the some 400 Jesuit priests that made up the Company, or the 573 parishes in the centre of the country. It is much less modest, if we consider that these Indian priests received indigenous parishes exclusively, where their mastery of the local language could be put to profit. As a general rule only a well-off Indian *cacique*, endowed with a comfortable chaplaincy, seems to have possessed, at least in the bishopric of Puebla, the requirements for obtaining the priesthood.[29] Among them we find heirs of the Indian people who discovered writing and European literature in the sixteenth century, less affluent in goods and power but still outstanding. In the region of Tlaxcala and Puebla, at the end of the seventeenth century and at the beginning of the eighteenth century, Indian priests did not hesitate to take up the pen; they have left behind religious dramas and even that *Manual de confesores* published in 1715. The case is not isolated. The city of Mexico offers other examples of lettered priests linked to the Indian aristocracy of the capital, who fought against the 'ignorance, superstition and idolatry' of their Indian parishioners. Here again there are two quite different processes, two relationships to Christianity without much in common: that of the nobles, based on the Spanish Church, and that of the *macehuales*, whose exclusion could in some cases end in Messianic outbursts unless it came out as sacrilege and blasphemy. The words 'ignorance' and 'superstition' that bloomed from the pens of these priests demonstrate the vast distance between them and the 'popular' and colonial experiences of their ancient cultures. A distance that does not imply a scornful abandon of the indigenous populations but rather a commiseration of these Indians who 'deprived of instruction have only what nature has instilled in them of the rational', as one of the most active spokesmen of this circle put it. In any case, not all the indigenous priests sought, in the footsteps of the Enlightenment, to 'drive away ignorance'.[30] Some priests came from the provinces, belonged to the more obscure nobility, were sons of chapel masters, *fiscales* or governors, or descendants of the *mayordomos* of the confraternities. Others slipped into the priesthood surreptitiously, without having a right to or fulfilling the conditions of the office. The memory of a black great-grandmother, the stigma of a grandmother who had been a mulatto or a witch, parents pursued by the law, a doubtful right of *cacique*, were enough to sweep aside the support given by a *morisco* godfather, lackey of the archbishopric, or by the possession of a chaplaincy. That being so, Indian priests and nuns belonged for the most part to a native ruling class that retained an undeniable symbolic and social influence on indigenous society. Through their piety, the models that they interiorized and the domination that they still exercised, they integrated indigenous groups into the society of New Spain and, a little like witchcraft but on a quite different level, linked together and mixed the two worlds. It is true that the assimilation to which they could lay claim removed them more every day from the mass of indigenous populations and that if their language and ethnic origin still attached them to their fellows, their view can be assimilated to that of the Church and the colonial elite.[31]

The blossoming of indigenous Christianity in the eighteenth century was also the product of the overall evolution of colonial society and, in particular, that of the Church. It seems at first that the religious framework had lightened. New Spain had about 5000 priests by 1650; one and a half centuries later, at the dawn of Independence, with a population that had quadrupled, there were about 6000. These are just approximations and one ought in fact to compare only the data concerning indigenous parishes. Nevertheless, if the Indian population had tripled, or almost, the number of priests is far from having followed the same evolution. Let us note that it was still relatively more numerous in the baroque period than in the period of the Englightenment, to which should be added the repercussions of secularization, that is, the progressive transfer of indigenous parishes from the hands of the regular to those of the secular clergy. The decline of influence of the regular clergy, the strengthening of episcopal power, the strict application of the Tridentine decrees, the desire of the Crown to take over part of the tithes until then wholly collected by the mendicants were at the origin of these measures of 'secularization'. Sporadic from the end of the sixteenth century, the movement continued at an irregular pace in the course of the seventeenth century, to revive even more strongly in 1749, when the Crown decided to provide all the regular parishes vacant on the decease of their titulary with seculars. Three years later the regular clergy administered no more than a quarter of the parishes of the archbishopric of Mexico. From 1757 secularization followed a slower pace, to bounce back in 1770 under the influence of archbishop Lorenzana y Buitrón. In 1813, some years from Independence, of the 715 parishes of the four dioceses of Mexico, Puebla, Oaxaca and Valladolid, there remained only 23 in the hands of the regulars. Secularization had been accomplished.

How did the Indians react to this brutal transfer? It was hard for them to bear the sight of secular priests stripping the confraternities of their ornaments, dismissing some of the Indian personnel who had served the friars, proscribing the customs introduced by the mendicants, forbidding festivals that took place in the *patios* of convents, demolishing churches and chapels. Once the innovation had been undergone, the interruption of immemorial custom, the break with the founders, the loss of credibility of the clergy who displayed its internal quarrels, the freedom of action and boldness that the Indians discovered in themselves precipitated the emergence of Indian Christianity, as well probably as the progressive transformations of religious geography. They began in the last quarter of the seventeenth century and corresponded to the expansion of the *haciendas* and the demographic revival of the same period. It was no longer a time of deserted chapels, churches in ruins in *pueblos* desperately empty of inhabitants. Villages were repopulated, hamlets sprang up that sought to free themselves from the trusteeship of the old *cabecera*. Secessions, requests for separation, proliferated in the course of the eighteenth century. The opening of a place for cult then became a major sign of autonomy and the Indians multiplied the proceedings and lawsuits to obtain recognition. These creations took on all the more importance in that they developed on the fringes of the traditional *pueblos* and, in the case of the *haciendas*, they accustomed the Indians to sharing their material and religious existence with other farm workers, Spanish, *mestizo* or *mulatto*. To these Indians – *gañanes*, *acasillados* or *calpaneros*, that is, permanently settled – was added the support of a fluctuating temporary workforce (Indians in *cuadrillas*), workers of uncertain status, who managed to elude the priest to whom they were subject, without being properly attached to the *hacienda* chapel.

Tradition and custom set up delicate equilibriums between the demands of the Church and the claims of the Indians. It is true that no one really dreamed of challenging the role of the Catholic priest in its sacramental dimension, apart, of course, from the messianic movements that we have glimpsed. But the Indians did not hesitate to criticize the priests' bad administration, their too regular absence or non-residence, the disorder of their registers, their ignorance of indigenous languages, the casualness with which they treated cult objects, their loose morals. Was it the zeal of fervent Indians? Sometimes. But also and more often it was an indirect manoeuvre to intimidate or bring about the transfer of a priest who went beyond the rights prescribed by custom, or interfered too much in what the Indians considered 'their thing'. To wish 'to abolish the very ancient custom' or to introduce 'novelties' was sufficient to set the community against its priest.

Parish dues were in fact a thorny area. In the sixteenth century the friars in their *doctrinas* made use of them as they pleased, without tolerating any intervention by the bishop. The reconquest effected by the secular clergy modified fundamental relations between the Church and the Indian community. Complex tariffs were imposed, which did not cancel the customs practised locally and fed endless controversies, trying the patience of the scholar wishing to know more and to cross this barrier of quibbles, depositions and counter-depositions. Raising dues in kind or the introduction of new charges, the allegedly exorbitant cost of burials and Masses, particularly in times of food shortage and epidemic, the duty to pay first fruits, the compulsory staff services ceaselessly agitated the history of very many *pueblos*. The Indians went on strike against Mass or, not without a sort of Machiavellianism, stopped célebrating their feast days, thus depriving the parish of considerable revenue, while the priest refused to bury the dead as long as the dues were not paid.

The Indians disputed the parish priest's right to choose *fiscales* as they did for their governors. They did not agree to the priest's ignoring the privileges of a *cabecera*. Nor did they tolerate the priest's claim to rule over the brotherhoods, change the patron saints, supervise processions, or tamper with the saints and their images. The Indians demanded the right to administer the confraternities, the *hermandades* as they pleased, without the priest's intervention, without reference to the ecclesiastical judge, from whose jurisdiction were systematically removed the election of the *mayordomo*, the designation of collectors, transactions undertaken and even the celebration of feast days. Silence, indeed clandestinity, was the rule in this domain. The nature, location and value of the goods and revenues that they procured, the books of constitutions, when they existed, were frequently hidden from the priest, who sometimes did not even know of the existence of the *hermandades* in his parish! The accounts were nonexistent, or at best demonstrably rigged, lining up a credit and a debit imperturbably balanced.

If the priest sometimes received the support of some of the notables, he was also subjected to the pressures of unrestrained blackmail, which forced him to submit or withdraw. Still more revealing were the by-passing strategies that undermined the power of the priest. To escape the Sunday obligation, some claimed to attend Mass in a neighbouring parish, whose obliging *fiscales* provided them, against a financial consideration, with the indispensable certificate of attendance and Christian instruction. Others passed themselves off as sick and the same *fiscales* produced other certificates. Marriage was also the subject of frauds and subterfuges. It was easy to track down witnesses ready to swear anything at all for an invitation to the wedding; simple also, with the help of the *fiscal* and the *escribano*, to present falsified data to dissimulate the condition of one of the spouses and above all links of consanguinity, a first marriage or an impediment that rendered the marriage illicit and incestuous; easy also to bring about the 'lodging' of the fiancée before the wedding in the care of the future in-laws and thus to disguise prenuptial cohabitation. For those living as concubines, it was permissible to obtain a false certificate of marriage or to choose to marry in a distant parish before an undemanding or unscrupulous curate. Let us add less subtle and more expeditious practices, like those of avoiding taking communion, confessing, marrying, those of deserting Mass, not requesting baptism for the newborn, hiding the dead to bury them hurriedly. Thus one managed in essence to dodge the payment of parish dues, but it was also the sign of an indifference opposed to a certain Christianity, that of the priest and his curates, while being ready to commit large sums, far greater than the standard *arancel* dues, to honour the saints. Absenteeism made it impossible to take the usual census on Sundays before Mass, and so to know the number of faithful. When tensions ran higher, the same absenteeism became a flight towards more isolated parts, towards another *pueblo* or towards the city. Then one let one's hair grow to lose oneself in the *mestizo* crowds and so to escape the tribute. Indications gathered in the trials, the transformations of the religious map corroborate what the overall evolution of the number of clergy suggests. The expansion of Indian Christianity was probably contemporary with a relaxation of the ecclesiastical ascendancy, as well as the demographic revival. That would explain the vitality, autonomy and combativity that were expressed within the *hermandades*, the brotherhoods, in the cult of saints and the celebration of the Indian feast days.[32]

The first onslaughts of modernity

The agitated *status quo* that governed the relations of the indigenous populations with the clergy was brutally challenged in the second half of the eighteenth century. Christianity as practised and diverted by the Indians made the Church uneasy and came to worry the Crown: a Crown, as we know, committed to the road of enlightened absolutism and desirous of profoundly changing the Empire, the better to subject it to the power of the monarch and the interests of the metropolis. Charles III and his entourage multiplied political, institutional and economic reforms without ever concerning themselves with local realities. They did not fail to attack popular cultures and in particular indigenous cultures, orchestrating a second acculturation with unprecedented stakes. Measures were taken against feast days, dances, 'false miracles' and so-called 'revelations'; against devotions that united a neighbourhood or that drew Indian and *mestizo* crowds, charged with being 'unseemly and pernicious cults that provided libertines with the opportunity to ridicule true miracles'. Pilgrimages and the *romerías* of Chalma and Amecameca gave rise to the same disquiet among the elite; drunkenness and taverns open late at night, promiscuity, obscenity, loose women, and above all the then gathering masses obsessed the ecclesiastical and civil authorities. Indian religious drama endured the same attacks. Not only were the *nescuitiles* (or indigenous Passions) prohibited in 1756 and 1769 but so were the representations of *Pastores y Reyes*, under the pretext of preventing the profanation of cult ornaments by the Indians. In the second half of the eighteenth century, the Indian people came up against priests who closed off access to the church at night, especially during Holy Week, and wanted to regulate the occupation of the cemeteries. There were priests who replaced the 'old and indecent' images, who forced them to dress correctly when they marched in the processions, who wanted to forbid them to hire and wear costumes and arms to represent the centurions of Holy Week. These last measures were among the ones that banished the indigenous theatre. From the 1770s and above all the end of the 1780s, the civil authorities intervened to 'moderate' the excesses of the Holy Week processions, while the bishop of Michoacán forbade them purely and simply in part of his diocese, and the diocese of Oaxaca went to war against all the profane festivities that enlivened the churches and their surroundings. It seems, it is true, that these decisions often remained without effect. Prudence demanded granting a reprieve to measures that might well stir up the Indians and, in fact, their strict application unleashed disorders that it was desirable to check. The prohibition of *armados* (the soldiers of the Passion) around the capital seems to have been more effective. It made the Indians, as the parish priest of Azcapotzalco boasted, into simple spectators, 'they no longer have the role of assistants', while it was the Spanish and the *mestizos* who dressed up as soldiers and centurions. Frustrated, dispossessed, the Indians crowded into the parishes where the practice had managed to be preserved.[33] In any case, many enlightened administrators of the end of the century shared the exasperation of this subdelegate (1794): 'I am scandalized to see that so few tributary Indians spend so much on feast days that result only in weakening their strength, since they are voluntary slaves of the Church, motivated by a badly understood devotion'.[34] Displaced devotions, 'unconsidered' cults, piety led astray. The indigenous societies discovered a new language and a new face of Europe that struck them in the heart of their recovered vitality.

An offensive on quite a different scale had to be taken against the brotherhoods, whose number, expenditures and autonomy became a subject of constant preoccupation. This time too the Indians confronted the interference of the Church before enduring harassment by the State. Archbishop Lorenzana, it appears, was the first to propose systematically to 'extinguish' all the indigenous brotherhoods, proposing to reunite their goods under the trusteeship of a *mayordomo de razón*, in other words a Spaniard. The project implied nothing less than the disappearance of an essential indigenous institution. But it was only in 1794 that the archbishop of Mexico gave an account of his action, announcing to the Crown that, of the 951 brotherhoods in his diocese, he had abolished 500, or more than half. The indigenous confraternities were by far the most affected in the diocese, while those of Oaxaca, on the advice of the intendant who preached prudence, were spared to a greater extent. As we have seen, most brotherhoods had an autonomous existence, functioned outside any control and rule, without account books, without sufficient property or funds. They were unable to produce their constitutions and quite often they had never had them. In the best case they had received only the approval of the ordinary clergy. Now, in order to exist, they had to apply for a *real permiso*, even if their foundation went back to the beginning of the seventeenth century. One hardly dares to imagine the material and administrative difficulties encountered by the *mayordomos* and confraternites that had to comply with the new regulations. In fact, we know little about Indian reactions. The possibility of belonging to confraternities directed by Spaniards that was sometimes offered to the Indians led to uneasiness and discontent. When the Spaniards and the men of reason claimed to take possession of the brotherhoods' images, under the pretext of restoring them and of taking in hand the management of the institutions' goods, unrest fermented or broke out, and the Indians pursued the Spanish intruders, whom they call 'dirty negroes', hurling stones. It is probable too that official extinction resulted in a regrowth of 'wild' forms, flexible solutions that escaped any ecclesiastical and civil hold.[35]

Also at the end of the 1780s and in the 1790s the civil authorities were busy forbidding the collections made in the *pueblos* in the name of a brotherhood or an image. The unhappy collectors were imprisoned by the intendants, subdelegates and *corregidores*, the statues and alms were confiscated, new requests were denied. Like official recognition of the brotherhoods, obtaining the permit required long and complicated procedures. It was necessary to furnish a detailed report on the endowments and income of the image, the designation of the *mayordomo*, the reasons for the collection, often to come up empty-handed in the end, since 'well known abuses behind these requests are sufficient reason to justify their prohibition', and 'if for each image it was necessary to accept a request, in a little while the *pueblos* would begin again to disgorge this kind of vagabond'.[36]

We cannot exaggerate the impact of these measures, which mean more for what they foretell than for their immediate application. But they sketch the new framework in which the indigenous cultures now evolved. Some enlightened prelates, and principally the State of the Enlightenment through its intendants, its subdelegates, its bureaucracy, insisted on reorienting and supervising the existence of the Indians. Under the combined effect of Bourbon despotism and the influence of the Enlightenment, the imperatives of civilization progressively replaced those of Christianization. Public order, material well-being, concern with profit, the 'decency' of individuals, images, gatherings and feast days, the strict separation of the profane and the sacred, were some of the new constraints that the Indians had now to confront. In this regard, the *Regulations so that the natives of these kingdoms are happy in the spiritual realm as in the temporal domain* published by archbishop Lorenzana in 1768 were exemplary. Did they not have greater bearing on the disposition of the dwelling, hygiene, clothing, and marriage, than on spiritual duties proper? After long having attended to the salvation of the Indians, Europe now for the first time meddled in their material well-being.[37]

The assault against indigenous religiosity was not an isolated gesture. It was in fact inseparable from a twofold undertaking that, without being really new, knew an unequalled expansion in the eighteenth century: the alphabetization and Hispanicizing of the Indians. The diffusion of Castilian had always been an objective that possessed the Spanish Crown, which saw it as the means of extending its ascendancy over Indian populations and reaffirming its domination. Measures were conceived and promulgated from the sixteenth century, but without great success. In the course of the seventeenth century, the question came up continually: Philip IV in 1634, Charles II in 1686 promoted a policy of Hispanicizing, but against it the ecclesiastical authorities, not without realism, argued the lack of funds, the dearth of teachers, the resistance of the Indians. At the end of the century, in 1690, the Crown attempted to make a knowledge of Spanish an indispensable condition of accession to office and responsibility in the *pueblos*. Nevertheless, the Church schools vegetated; in the secularized parishes the teaching of catechism was assured only by an old Indian, while reading and writing were often given up. Only in the middle of the eighteenth century did the endeavour experience a sudden revival. In 1754 the archbishopric of Mexico was already the site of 84 schools of Castilian; there were 262 in 1756 in 61 of the 200 parishes that made up the diocese. The archbishop of Mexico, Rubio y Salinas, demonstrated a nice optimism:

> I believe that, thanks to business and the communication that they have with us, they will manage to forget their languages and with the creation

of the schools they will acquire a taste for reading and writing, motivated by the wish to accede to the sciences and liberal arts, to ennoble their spirits and to escape from the poverty, nudity and wretchedness in which they live.

It was a question of nothing less than 'systematically abolishing the use of indigenous languages' to reduce the Indians to 'civic life', to promote 'unity and mixing with the Spanish' and, more concretely, to establish schools where teachers paid from communal goods and the excess left from the payment of tribute would teach catechism, and reading and writing Spanish. In 1768 and 1769 the archbishop Antonio Lorenzana tackled the question still more earnestly, insisting on the need to break the isolation of the Indian populations and to associate them with the economic and social life of the country. The Marquis of Croix, viceroy of Mexico, and Charles III supported this policy, enlightened despotism being unable to tolerate a linguistic pluralism that impeded 'complete subordination to the sovereign'. But they gave it a different spin, making school and Castilian an instrument of strengthening the State to the detriment of the Church and its American subjects. Measures would follow one another in the 1780s and be repeated until the end of the Spanish domination, despite numerous opposition movements. At the beginning of the 1780s for the first time the country was covered with schools, according to the reports of the *alcaldes mayores*: almost all the young natives would learn Castilian under the rod of their masters. Let us not believe that the step of obligatory schooling had been taken all at once. The agricultural crisis and the famine of 1785–6 got the better of most schools opened in those years. Moreover the schools were subject to the agricultural cycle, opening only between 'the sowing and the harvest'. It is still undeniable that at the end of the eighteenth century and in the first years of the nineteenth century we are witness to an unprecedented offensive of school and Castilian, even if the weaknesses and contradictions of the enterprise rule out exaggerating the short-term impact on indigenous cultures.[38]

It is unquestionable that, faced with the measures of the Church and then those of the State, there was a real demand for schooling in certain sectors of indigenous society. It is not necessary to emphasize that there we find the cleavage noted several times between the urban elite and the remainder of the populations. When in 1728 (or some years later) the spokesman of the Indian nobility of Mexico demanded the reopening of the college of Tlatelolco, he expressed (in vain) the desire to confide to Indian hands the education of the native populations. As in the case of the priesthood, these groups understood the considerable significance of the political stakes. In 1754, the Indian priest Julián

Cirilo y Castilla rose up against the obligation imposed on the Indians of learning Castilian, relying on the laws that forbade using the slightest coercion towards them. But he was among those who demanded the benefits of instruction for their fellow men. This preoccupation was conveyed by concrete, meticulous actions undertaken by Indian governors who deplored the lack of schools or the decay of those that existed. Alongside these demands, more isolated initiatives also emerged. They came from Indians who directed or wanted to open public schools. Midway between the literate marginal and the teacher, concerned with instructing the Indians and probably not without ulterior political motives, some of them claimed to be *caciques* and perhaps gained a stronger influence on the *pueblo*. Moreover, these were not the only Indians to interest themselves in the instruction of their fellows. From the sixteenth century *fiscales*, cantors and sacristans had discharged this function by teaching, in principle, catechism to children. It even seems that they sometimes also taught reading and writing. For a long time, finally, Indian *doctrineros* more discreetly followed this career. We know still less about these men charged with all possible defects by both Church and State and who in the eighteenth century went into homes to teach certain rudiments to the children of the Indians who received them. The contents of the teaching dispensed by the *doctrineros* remains enigmatic. Was it just a tissue of 'superstitions and absurdities', as the Church affirmed? Or should we discern the trace of an autonomous literate culture, analogous to that expressed in indigenous dramas or the writings pursued by the *provisor* of the archbishop? We lose ourselves in conjectures before phenomena which once more reveal the many levels of culture within the indigenous societies of the eighteenth century. So much so that it would probably be wrong to identify ruling circles and demand for education. It is permissible to ask if the *escribanos*, the Indian interpreters – the *nahuatlatos* – who held the monopoly of written communication between the Indian world and the Castilian world, did not contribute to restraining a policy that undermined their positions.[39]

However that may be, in the middle of the eighteenth century, outside the cities and their immediate environs, the Indians grumbled or refused to speak Castilian, even when they knew it. For religious matters, to pray and to confess, the overwhelming majority used only their language. Before the notables and the elders of the *pueblo* they never dared to speak Spanish. Elsewhere and in general, they learned only the minimum required by the exercise of the *cargos* of the community or required by commercial contacts made with the Spanish. It is true that the creole priests who spoke their language encouraged them in this negative attitude, since the Hispanicizing of the natives would

open access to indigenous parishes to priests from Spain who were consequently ignorant of local dialects. Opposition to school was thus
general, and sometimes virulent. Parents complained of the violence, the
inadequacy or ignorance of the master imposed on them; they bore
badly having to contribute to the salary of the schoolmaster and still
worse seeing their children wasting their time at school when they could
be subsidizing the needs of the family with their work. For their part,
the indigenous authorities preferred often to divert the funds intended
for the masters to their profit, when they did not oppose the use of
community income to pay their salaries.[40]

The indigenous refusal seems to cover deeper pitfalls and motives. If
the Indians 'like idiots' seemed not to be sensitive to the 'spiritual good
and the culture of their children', if they 'did not embrace a project so
useful for the young', it was because they held to what the authorities
scornfully designated by the name of 'superstition, irreligiosity and
odious and blind barbarism', in other words, all that made up the
essence of indigenous cultures in the eighteenth century. If the presence
of the priest was often the subject of a *status quo*, if it had long been
accepted and assimilated by the community, the master and the school
(as the Church in the eighteenth century, then the enlightened State,
conceived them) introduced a perturbing element that came between the
pueblo, the parents and their children. They imposed a supplementary
charge that put the economy of the community in question to the extent
that, at the beginning of the nineteenth century, the administration
sought by all means to turn aside communal funds from their festive use
to pay the salary of the teacher or the schoolmistress – a salary that
almost everywhere exceeded the annual sum of the expenses officially
engendered by the festivals. The schooling of the Crown threatened the
fragile equilibrium of indigenous cultures, made up of refusal, compromise with and capture of the outside world. In this way, the educational and linguistic offensive joined the measures directed against
Indian Christianity. It put the finishing touches to the policy of secularization that excluded the regular clergy hostile to Hispanicizing. It
signified a much tighter economic control of the communities, by
imposing a necessarily 'transparent' management, constantly in the
sight of the subdelegates. But it also favoured a cultural interventionism
in which we shall see the start of another secularization, this time in the
sense of the laicization of indigenous life: 'The income of the communities of each *pueblo* as a function of their annual product should
first be destined for primary schools before paying for feast days'.
However, ending the festivals meant attacking the brotherhoods and the
cult of saints and, beyond them, overturning the structure of beliefs and
practices, the relatively autonomous space, the existential landmarks

and sociability that the Indians had in successive stages laboriously constructed. Again, was it not the start, often ephemeral and superficial, of a policy that took shape in the course of the nineteenth century under the impulse of the liberals, and then following the Mexican revolution? Too many factors, too much opposition, insufficient material and lack of knowledge of local realities combined so that these measures had real repercussions in the eighteenth century. Carried away in the Napoleonic torment, the Spain of the Bourbons had neither the time nor the means to 'civilize' its Indians.[41]

The first onslaughts of modernity could not conceal the older and more brutal paths of acculturation, those that were linked to the organization of work, production, or urbanization. They presuppose other cultural scenarios that I have neglected to the extent that they long remained, despite everything, in the minority. Their setting was, for example, the mines, those death houses where generations of Indians were consumed. But from the sixteenth century mines also constituted an important place for ethnic groups to meet, blend and integrate themselves into the European economy. They drew a manpower that temporarily or permanently abandoned the indigenous community, to share the existence of the free blacks and slaves, mulattos and *mestizos* in the teams of miners. These Indians discovered new ways of life, often brutally. Though they thus escaped communal obligations, paying tribute and the ascendancy of the *principales*, though they received a salary in money and in kind and even part of the production in exchange for their work, Indian workers were now plunged into the mobile, unstable world of the mines, a distant, foreign universe, if we think of the mining camps in the north of the country, the deserts of Zacatecas where there were already 1500 by 1572. Some accommodated themselves to this complete removal from their accustomed surroundings and learned to go from one mine to another as the lodes of silver were exploited, '*conforme a como andan las minas*' ('depending on how the mines are going'). Others became merchants or peddlers. Indian carpenters and masons quickly learned to charge for their services, or they hired themselves out to several miners at once, spent their pay in a day, and became indebted for life. It is true that the less fortunate, the majority, stagnated in the sodden shadows of airless tunnels, where they drank the brandy sold by the mine boss. But we should not forget that it was often of their free will that these Indians from the valley of Mexico, Michoacán or Tlaxcala reached the mines of the north of Mexico.

The *obraje* represented another place of uprootedness and wretchedness. This workshop-prison was one of the pillars of the colonial economy, since the production of the fabric, clothes, hats, shoes and bread of the viceroyalty depended on the labour concentrated there. The promiscuity of races and sexes, the locking up of voluntary workers and of delinquents working off their sentences, the absence of any religious practice and even sometimes the prohibition of contacts with outside, the terrible treatment, the unlimited indebtedness, alarmed the Third Mexican Council in 1585 and the Crown at the same period. Subjected to an often frenzied exploitation, the Indian there forgot the veneer of Christianity that the Church had been able to inculcate elsewhere. The bosses did not celebrate the religious feast days, they prevented their workers from marrying by forcing them into concubinage or fleeting relationships. At the end of the eighteenth century, the situation seems to have become still worse. Sources depict a universe that prefigured life in a concentration camp; they reveal that traffic of every kind took place, including profits from the sale of the condemned to the highest bidder. The conditions of work and existence there were among the most harsh that the Indians of New Spain had to endure.

There were other places where the supervision of the Church and the indigenous community was blurred: the *trapiches* of hot regions, where Indians and blacks worked the sugar cane, the *haciendas* that drew a temporary or fixed manpower who settled on their lands. However, links with the community of origin were not finally broken, even if the forms of sociability, religiosity and even festivity characteristic of the basic great estate were taking shape. An interested paternalism, moreover, assured the *gañanes* established on the *hacienda* an elementary security that they appreciated when the harvest was bad. But it is necessary to wait for the nineteenth century for the world of the *hacienda* to come to occupy the foreground of the Mexican scene.[42]

By far the best stage for all the cross-fertilization, social, cultural and physical, was the city, that is to say, in the sixteenth century, basically Mexico, before Puebla, Valladolid and Querétaro developed in the seventeenth century. The Indians of the capital lived in principle in two districts or *parcialidades*, San Juan and Santiago. They practised the indigenous forms of Christianity that I have described, more precociously than in the countryside, because they were confronted with a strong ecclesiastical presence from the beginning of the evangelization. Chapels, churches and brotherhoods structured a daily life that attempted to combine the retention of indigenous identities and openness to the outside world. But what was the situation of those who, numerous and more or less surreptitiously, inhabited the Spanish district, collected in the courts of their masters, dressed like the *mestizos* or whites, making a mockery of the Church and its laws that separated populations? Already perceptible after the great inundation of 1629, the mix of races worried the authorities after the uprising of 1692. At that point they attempted in vain to impose on the Indians segregation, a return to the *parcialidades* and the wearing of traditional costume. They did not succeed either in sending the Indian *extravagantes* who loitered in the city back to their *pueblos*. For the relative anonymity that it made possible, the mobility that it favoured and the diversions that it offered, the city exerted an attraction for the entire indigenous population, vagabonds, Indians who sidestepped banishment, fleeing spouses, sons of provincial *caciques* 'who became infatuated with the city and filled with horror at their *pueblos*'. The question of these Indians 'come from elsewhere' grew acute from the beginning of the seventeenth century. A brotherhood (1619), then a parish (1677–8) were successively charged with assembling these immigrant 'Zapotec, Mixtec, Indians of the sierra of Meztitlan . . .' The solution was so feeble and unsatisfactory that in 1753 the viceroy decided to suppress it, explaining that the parish served only to attract to the capital 'vagabond and idle Indians' whose residence was unknown. In 1750 no less than 10,000 Indians made up this population, while some 30 years later it was calculated that 18,000 to 20,000 persons came into and went out of the city every day. From the seventeenth century on, this moving mass juggled ethnic identities, passing for Indians, *mestizos*, and even Spaniards, according to circumstances.

To those who broke communal ties, seeking to melt into *mestizo* society and to slip into the ranks of poor whites in the urban proletariat, to those who learned Castilian and multiplied the ties of comradeship with mulattos or whites, the underworlds of delinquence, prostitution and alcoholism also became accessible. Without a doubt, in the seventeenth century and even at the beginning of the eighteenth century, the preparation of *pulque* (the fermented juice of the agave) was still accompanied by ritual practices and offerings to fire, and the drinking sessions that punctuated the festivals of the brotherhoods, funerals and solemn Christian occasions even in the big cities echoed pre-conquest collective celebrations. None the less, this form of consumption was indissociable from pathological manifestations already present in prehispanic societies and exacerbated by the Spanish colonization. The commercialization of *pulque* in the cities, its sale by certain *mestizos* and Spaniards, its spread into mixed circles, and finally the competition of other drinks fed this progressive loss of meaning that was in fact close to a 'secularization' of alcohol in the seventeenth century and even more in the eighteenth century. The context of the *pulquería*, the colonial tavern, which broke with control by the domestic group or the community, favoured this evolution by broadening the range of drinks consumed and thus manners of drinking. For if the Indians continued to drink *pulque* or *tepache*, they very early acquired a taste for Castilian wine, before discovering distilled alcohols like *mezcal* or poor quality brandy, or even pomegranate, cherry or coconut wines. These forms of alcohol introduced by the conquerors, without ancient connotations and traditional safety nets stimulated an individual and solitary consumption where the quest for intoxication swept away all cultural references. Observers have left black descriptions of the *pulquerías* of the seventeenth and eighteenth centuries: dirty taverns, devoid of exotic qualities, that clogged streets and squares, brawls and murders, husbands squandering the housekeeping money, beaten women, abortions, impossible flights from wretchedness and sickness, 'human beings covered with filth and transformed into living torsos in the middle of the roads', derelict humans who collapsed on to haggard children before fetching up in sordid hospitals to die.[43] It remains unclear if the phenomenon really took the dimensions attributed to it by the clergy and the authorities of the viceroyalty, too inclined to confuse chronic drunkenness and the traditional expression of ritual and festive conduct. Contemporaries unanimously denounced the constant growth in the consumption of *pulque* in the course of the seventeenth century, but we are unable to verify the truth of their statements. We do know that around Mexico, on the lands lying fallow, abandoned by the decimated populations, agave very often replaced maize. In 1692 numerous accounts revealed that the cities of Puebla and Querétaro, the country around Michoacán and even the more isolated lands of the bishopric of Oaxaca were stricken by the same 'epidemic'. If we stick to the capital, the phenomenon is unquestionable and grows in the eighteenth century: by 1784 the city of Mexico numbered 200,000 inhabitants and more than 600 *pulquerías*, which easily accommodated about a hundred drinkers inside and outside.

Let us meanwhile refrain from making the *pulquería* the lowest point of acculturation, a dead end for Indians who had lost all sense of life's landmarks. The *pulquería* was also one of the key elements of a *mestizo* culture, half tolerated, half clandestine, on the fringes of the norms invoked by the Church and the Inquisition: a culture distinct from the façade of laws and constraints surrounding colonial power. Sheltering clandestine love, opening its dark cubbyholes to concubines, prostitutes, transvestites, covering illicit traffic, the *pulquerías* taught the Indians another Europe which was the complement and the exact opposite of that which the Church and the Crown strove to impose on them. Active melting pot of acculturation and interethnic sociability, it served as anchor to a vast register of deviances that vaguely associated blacks, mulattos, *mestizos*, Indians and Spaniards, to the great concern of the Spanish authorities, as if shared drunkenness dissolved barriers and antagonism. If the *pulquerías* led in the end to prisons where other complicities were formed, and from there even to the *obrajes* where alcohol again served as a companion in wretchedness, taverns were also places for living, the only alternatives offered to a home. One ate and slept there, with more than 50 people piled in amidst the cigar smoke, the shouts, in a deafening racket that sometimes overwhelmed the voice of the priest celebrating Mass in a neighbouring church. For the *pulquería* was also a constant hotbed of anticlericalism and, even more lastingly than idolatry, it challenged the spiritual conquest of the Indian people by undertaking a process of acculturation and deculturation over which the Church had no hold.[44]

In other words, if the *pulquería* was the outcome of a profound deculturation, the search for a 'survival mechanism', it also marked the apprenticeship and interiorization of a 'culture of the poor',[45] where unrootedness and cross-breeding prefigured the 'popular' cultures of independent Mexico, cultures based on cross-breeding of bodies, beliefs and practices, but also of ambiguous cultures, of the fringe and aliena- tion. The colonial authorities and creole circles that dominated New Spain were able to appreciate what the chronic drunkenness of the natives and the others could harbour in the way of reassurance for the established order. The sordid webs of corruption and profit clasped the world of the taverns too tightly for it to be able to hope to escape the colonial machine: from the farmer (*asentista*) of *pulque* to the least *corregidor* or the little *alguacil de doctrina*, all knew how to take advantage of Indian drunkenness and of the least deviance, to sell their tolerance and merchandise their laxity. Parallel to the witchcraft that joined worlds, colonial corruption just as clandestinely overturned norms and values, sketching more or less lasting compromises between the forces, appetites and contradictory interests that organized indig- enous, *mestizo* and white life. Like witchcraft, corruption was an exemplary colonial practice in that it was determined to serve a daily life that continually escaped the mechanisms, models and projects of the distant metropolis. While strengthening insidiously or brutally the domination of the Iberian and creole groups over New Spain, it con- strained the native subjected to it (or who benefited from it) to manage on the fringe of the community, the domestic group, the established norms, Indian and Spanish. Through the skill with which the Indians contrived to turn the social and moral ascendancy of the Church or the Crown by buying the complicity of the *fiscales*, the *alguaciles* or the *corregidores*, by inventing more or less clandestine ways of life, was promoted the (progressive or accelerated) acculturation of the person that I have more than once suggested. It would be necessary to come back to the fate of these Indian *naborías*, who learned to survive in a society and an economy in the city or the mines, which forced them to assimilate new codes of behaviour, to combine initiative and mobility, in fact to experience the whole spectrum of acculturation from the sixteenth century and in the space of a few years. This would serve to nuance the general evolution that I have tried to reconstitute. For a minority of Indians who did not belong to the nobility, contact with Europe could take the form of a rapid assimilation of forms of economic behaviour, probably as deep as the spread in other circles of the European aesthetic and alphabet. It was the same for the social practices among those who, from the 1530s, discovered at the same time as they invented it the alternative of bigamy to Christian marriage with what it presupposed of lying about the past and exchanges of identity. Through this process of becoming different, they invented patterns that diverged from both prehispanic values and those promulgated by the Church. But it was also a difference that ended up in anonymity. In the course of the seventeenth century, *ladino* Indians of the capital even became so transparent that apart from their clothes and haircut 'there was no other sign to distinguish very many Indians from the Spaniards'. This invisibility explains why the archives are of little help in sorting out the motives of these men who moved from one end of New Spain to the other, from one ethnic reference to another. During the whole colonial period, the clergy worried about these indigenous *ladinos y españolados* who lived in the cities and big towns. These 'not only rational but also quite skilful' Indians gave rise to mistrust on the part of all the authorities, as if their Hispanicizing progressively removed them from the purview of the Church, as if thanks to the protection of their Spanish *compadres*, their 'fellows of the taverns', they managed to frustrate all definition. The image is exaggerated but it draws attention to the Indians who, throughout the colonial period, individually set aside the signs of their origin (language, clothing), tried out new conduct and improvised behaviour outside the paths prescribed by the community, indigenous custom or the Church. Nowhere better than in the city of Mexico, from the sixteenth century, the Indians were confronted with these networks of multiple relations, obligations, contradictory allegiances, torn between the parish priest, the indigenous authorities of their neighbourhood, the wishes of a Spanish master who welcomed them to his house, and relations with the blacks and *mestizos* who served as godfathers for their children or as witnesses for a wedding. Colonial chaos, immense spaces where mobility was extreme, an awkward or Utopian transposition of European models to American soil, the inability of the authorities to be faithful to these particularly dynamic social realities strongly contributed to favouring the birth of singular attitudes and individual breaks among Indians who escaped the frameworks of their societies without necessarily declining into chaos, or indeed death. For the eradication of native references was not only balanced by the abyss of deculturation and alcoholism; it also prepared the slow emergence of an individual who very quickly learned to orient himself in colonial society. It was as if the loss of ancestral landmarks had forced human beings to individualize themselves in relation to others and to fashion destinies unknown until then. If this fringe of isolated behaviour remained a minority event in indigenous societies, it still prefigured one of the major effects of Europeanization and one of the salient features of the *mestizo* society that prevailed in the eighteenth century, in more or less happy alliance with uprootedness, chaos and adaptation. But, let us not forget, the distancing, the individualization in relation to native or Christian references in fact only marked a first stage and did not lead irreversibly to the ability to assume an individual fate. We are also aware that exchanges of identity, yesterday as today, were too often just a prelude to the loss of all identity. In this respect, the nineteenth and twentieth centuries had a decisive influence on the tendencies that I have summarily sketched.[46]

Conclusion

A quick overview of these three centuries has revealed the nature and breadth of the westernization – that is to say Europeanization – that accompanied the colonial undertaking: Europeanization rather than acculturation, for the acculturation of the indigenous populations of Mexico cannot be dissociated from a protean colonial domination that inexorably dictated the meaning of the changes. This was anything but a rigid process. It continually readjusted its aims to the rhythms of western Europe rather than to local evolution. This accounts for the differences of phase, the perpetual gaps, which meant that no sooner were the Indians won over to baroque Christianity than they were all at once summoned to embrace the 'civilization' of the Enlightenment, before liberalism or Jacobinism proposed other models to them, before a 'made in USA' society of consumption revealed its showcases. Of course the Indians obviously never had the wherewithal to attain the paradises in turn flourished before their eyes. But the Europeanization at work from the sixteenth century did not have the means to realize its ambitions, as it was woven of contradictory interests and objectives that seriously impeded any projects of integration into colonial society. This difference of phase brought about a respite for the indigenous populations, a freedom of action and reaction that they have for the most part lost these days. From it poured a cascade of compromises to repair the 'torn nets', syntheses as variable as the regions, social groups and periods in which they developed. From it too continually emerged individual and collective experiences that mixed interpretation with improvisation and fascinated copying. For if the Indians of New Spain sought to conform to imposed models, it was always by inventing accommodations and 'combinations' (in all senses of the term) that took the most diverse forms. There is no doubt that the narrow course of a linear account that fixes movement and levels differences results in an account which does not do justice to the multiplicity, the irresistibility and the simultaneity of the processes. It is however the task of the historian to restore the confrontation replayed ceaselessly between the indigenous populations and the changing demands, vagaries and fallout of the colonial domination. It was a Europeanization more than Hispanicizing process, for it implied codes, models, techniques and policies that went beyond the borders of the Iberian peninsula, whether it was a question of the eighteenth-century Enlightenment, the Counter-Reformation or the undertakings of Charles V's missionaries. Europeanization cannot be reduced to the accidents of Christianization and the imposition of the colonial system; it gave life to more profound and determining processes: the evolution of the representation of the person and relations between persons, the transformation of figurative and graphic codes, of means of expression and transmission of knowledge, the transformation of temporality and belief, and finally the redefinition of the *imaginaire* and the real in which the Indians were committed to expressing themselves and to surviving, constrained or fascinated. In the margin of brutal or authoritarian manifestations of the colonial domination, and perhaps better than them, fascination with western Europe – with its writing, books, images, techniques, saints and cities – also explains its irresistible ascendancy.

Nor can we forget the crucial fact of demographic death. Collective death had a considerable impact on memories, societies and cultures, by setting up often irreparable interferences and breaks. With less brutality, the demographic revival of the eighteenth century highlighted tensions that newly endangered the equilibrium of the community: too many men for ever less land. The indigenous societies had thus to react to diametrically opposed situations. Never, however, did these reversals manage to destroy the springs of indigenous creativity, even at the demographic low point. But they displaced them. Thus by altering the relations of force and destroying a promising Mexican renaissance, the seventeenth-century crisis left free rein to other layers of the indigenous population who profited from it to produce forms as original and innovative, even if they remained restricted to marginality and clandestinity.

Clear cuts, reversals of tendencies, pressures and constraints of every kind, *laissez-faire* mixed with indifference and impotence conferred on the indigenous cultures of New Spain the appearance of a hybrid and unfinished task. In this respect, is there a more universal and misleading word than tradition (or traditional), which I have misused and which can now be seen to refer to a process of constant reconstitution and loss? Stripped of the prestige of the archaic, deprived of their 'pyramids' and their human sacrifices, the Indians of New Spain, unlike pre-columbian Indians, have apparently largely escaped the grasp of the scholar. They by no means lend themselves to being systematized, although their precolumbian predecessors served more or less happily to illustrate theories inspired by Marxism, cultural materialism and other theories. But they incite one to pursue an anthropology of the temporary, the mixture and the juxtaposition with which, moreover, we are daily confronted, like it or not. The history of the indigenous and *mestizo* cultures of New Spain in many ways prefigures the exchanges and shocks towards which our 'syncretic' European cultures are rushing without in any way being prepared for them. We experience the same crossing of races and codes, overlapping of realities, abrupt setting in contact or harmony of the most exotic elements, profound fusion or superficial bringing together, in the disorientation of a process of becoming uniform or massive deculturation.

This state of unstable equilibrium, of uninterrupted change, demands not only challenging the notion of tradition, but also the coherence that we generally attribute to societies and the cultural structures that we intend to reconstruct. Several times I have had a sense that the indeter-minacy, the coexistence of contradictory traits, the absence of references or their eradication, the decontextualization of features, in a general way the discontinuous were, up to a certain point, favourable to the birth of new cultural organizations. I would have wished to look further along this road and to shake up habits of thought that tend to distinguish or delineate entities as more closed, logical and coherent than they actually were. Moreover, I fell into this intellectual habit every time I forgot that prehispanic societies were certainly less uniform than the writings of the Spanish chroniclers or the accounts of their indigenous informants allow us to understand. This study is an invita-tion to pick out in the cultural configurations and symbolic arrange-ments the fuzzy zones, the uncoded or badly coded sectors that allow an often significant initiative to the individual and the group, when they can stand up to vertigo and the void. It is an invitation also to explore the criteria that made up realities other than our own, and to seek out the factors that support their likelihood, that guarantee the quality of their rendering or alter their credibility, depending on the period, group or culture. It is perhaps by opening up these roads, by measuring the highly relative character of our categories (time, religion, images: Bernand and Gruzinski, 1988), in rendering to other forms of expres-sion the essential role that belongs to them (the visual, the affective), that the historian or the anthropologist will invent other visions rather than just notching up another new territory, field, or monograph.

Notes

Introduction

1   The real (as opposed to reality) is the objective universe as it exists outside us, independently of the way our senses and our intellect perceive it. Reality is the way we perceive and interpret the real. Each group, each culture produces its own reality through contact with the real. If the real remains by definition beyond our reach, realities, on the other hand, which are inevitably multifarious and changing, always proceed from roots in a society, a given environment and a historical period.

2   It is hardly necessary to recall what my study owes to the work of Georges Devereux, Nathan Wachtel, the research of Solange Alberro, Carmen Bernand, Jean-Michel Sallmann, Nancy M. Farriss, Alfredo López Austin and Monique Legros. I should like to thank them here, together with all those in France, Italy, Spain, Mexico (especially the AGN) and the United States who offered generous support and encouragement. This book is an abridged version of a thesis for the Doctorat d'Etat entitled *Le Filet déchirée. Sociétés indigènes, occidentalisation et domination coloniale dans le Mexique central. XVIe–XVIIIe siècle*, defended before the Université de Paris I in January 1986.

3   The works of Aguirre Beltrán, for example.

4   See the bibliography, pages 319–29. We have not been able to draw on the new contributions of research published since the drafting of the thesis on which this work is based (1983–5), such as Louise M. Burkhart's fine book, *The Slippery Earth: Nahua-Christian Moral Dialogue in Sixteenth-Century Mexico*, Tucson, University of Arizona Press, 1989, and Susan D. Gillespie, *The Aztec Kings. The Construction of Rulership in Mexican History*, Tucson, University of Arizona Press, 1989.

5   Motolinía (Toribio de Benavente), *Memoriales o Libro de las cosas de la Nueva España y de los naturales de ella*, Mexico City, UNAM, 1971; Bernardino de Sahagún, *Historia general de las cosas de Nueva España*, Mexico City, Porrúa, 1977, 4 vols; Diego Durán, *Historia de las Indias de Nueva España...*, Mexico City, Porrúa, 1967, 2 vols; Gerónimo de

Mendieta, *Historia eclesiástica indiana*, Mexico City, Chávez Hayhoe, 1945, 4 vols; Juan de Torquemada, *Monarquía indiana*, Mexico City, UNAM, 1975–1983, 7 vols.

Chapter 1 Painting and Writing

1 On this chapter, see Miguel Léon-Portilla, 1983a, p. 68, and 1983b, pp. 13–108; Garibay, 1971, I, *passim*; Karttunen and Lockhart, 1980, pp. 15–64. On prehispanic music, Stevenson, 1976.

2 Motolinía (Toribio de Benavente), *Memoriales o Libro de las cosas de la Nueva España y de los naturales de ella*, Mexico City, UNAM, 1971, p. 5.

3 Juan Bautista Pomar, 'Relación de Texcoco', ed. Joaquín García Icazbalceta, Mexico City, Francisco Díaz de León, 1892, pp. 1–2; Motolinía, *Memoriales*, pp. 34–5, 439; Diego Durán, *Historia de las Indias de Nueva España...*, Mexico City, Porrúa, 1967, I, p. 226; Juan de Torquemada, *Monarquía indiana*, Mexico City, UNAM, 1975–83, I, p. 6, IV, p. 331.

4 *Procesos de Indios idolatras y hechiceros*, Mexico City, AGN, III, 1912, pp. 8, 115 and *passim*; Motolinía, *Memoriales*, pp. 86–7.

5 León-Portilla, 1976, p. 108, conveying an account from Tlatelolco, first edition in Nahuatl and German: 'Unos annales históricos de la nación mexicana', *Baessler Archiv*, Berlin, 1939, XXII, pp. 67–168, XXIII, pp. 115–39.

6 *Proceso inquisitorial del cacique de Tetzcoco*, Mexico City, AGN, 1910, p. 2.

7 *Procesos de Indios*, p. 215; Gerónimo de Mendieta, *Historia eclesiástica indiana*, Mexico City, Chávez Hayhoe, 1945, I, p. 107.

8 Durán, *Historia*, I, pp. 227–8, 235.

9 On these paintings, see Glass and Robertson, 1975, pp. 197–8, 184–5, 241, 219, 195–6, 131.

10 *Procesos de Indios*, p. 181.

11 *Epistolario de Nueva España, 1505–1818*, ed. Francisco del Paso y Troncoso, Mexico City, Antigua Librería Robredo, 1939, IV, p. 166.

12 Bernal Díaz del Castillo, *Historia verdadera de la conquista de la Nueva España*, Mexico City, Porrúa, 1968, I, p. 336; Durán, *Historia*, II, pp. 513–14.

13 Glass and Robertson, 1975, pp. 214–17; let us cite the editions of Alfredo Chavero, *Antigüedades mexicanas publicadas por la Junta Columbina*, Mexico City, Secretaría de Fomento, 1892, and of Josefina García Quintana and Carlos Martínez Marín, *Lienzo de Tlaxcala*, Mexico City, Cartón y Papel de México, 1983.

14 The now lost *Lienzo* of the Tecpan of Mexico, inaugurated in 1556.

15 Robertson, 1959, pp. 163–6; Glass and Robertson, 1975, pp. 212–13. See also the facsimile reproduced in *Anales de Tlatelolco*.

16 *Códice Sierra, Fragmento de una nómina de gastos del pueblo de Santa Catarina Texupan, Mixteca Baja*, ed. Nicolás León, Museo Nacional de Arqueología, Historia y Etnografía, 1933.

17 Spores, 1967, pp. 113, 119–20; *Epistolario*, 1939, IV, p. 165.

18 *Códices indígenas de algunos pueblos del Marquesado del valle de Oaxaca*, Mexico City, AGN, Talleres Gráficos de la Nación, 1933.

19 Tepoztlán: AGN, Ramo *Tierras*, vol. 2719, exp. 8, fo. 20; Cuautitlán:

Joaquín Galarza, *Estudios de escritura indígena tradicional azteca-náhuatl*, Mexico City, AGN, 1979, pp. 133–57; Teteutzinco: AGN, Ramo *Tierras*, vol. 3331, exp. 24, fo. 3.

20 Bartolomé de Las Casas, *Apologética historia sumaria*, ed. Edmundo O'Gorman, Mexico City, UNAM, Instituto de Investigaciones Históricas, 1967, p. 505.

21 Pedro Ponce de León, 'Breve relación de los dioses y ritos de la gentilidad', in Angel María Garibay K., *Teogonía e historia de los mexicanos*, Mexico City, Porrúa, 1973, p. 122.

22 Galarza, *Estudios de escritura indígena*.

23 Dibble, 1971, p. 331; Robert Barlow and Byron MacAfee, *Diccionario de elementos fonéticos en escritura jeroglífica*, Mexico City, UNAM, 1949.

24 Smith, 1973, pp. 89–121, which does not rule out the treatment of western European ornamental motifs as if they were more than decorative features, that is, as if they were glyphs.

25 Our analysis concerns the period 1530–1619, that is 858 maps, of which 39 were earlier than 1570; maps probably of indigenous origins represent a little more than a third of the total production (306). All are recorded in the *Catálogo de ilustraciones* ..., vols 2, 3, 4, 5, Mexico City, AGN, 1979.

26 *Catálogo*, nos 1822, 1088, 1679, 1678, 2133, 2018, 867.

27 Nos 1626, 2131, 2133, 2152, 2177, 1611, 2206, 2015, 1240, 1448, 1449.

28 Nos 1685, 566, 1088, 1540, 1822, 1829, 1705, 1867, 1868, 1882, 2064, 2091.

29 Indigenous and Spanish 'sketch' maps: nos 1692–1, 2126, 2015, 1682, 1758; 'written' maps; nos 2159–1, 2110.

30 Nos 2016, 2019, 2126; compare 589 and 590; 2049. See Gruzinski, 1987.

31 Mendieta, *Historia eclesiástica indiana*, II, p. 62; III, pp. 62–5; IV, p. 53; Motolinía, *Memoriales*, pp. 236, 238; García Icazbalceta, 1947, II, p. 307. On the bibliography, Goméz Canedo, 1982.

32 Kobayashi, 1974, pp. 248, 218–3; Motolinía, *Memoriales*, p. 237.

33 *Historia tolteca-chichimeca*, Mexico, INAH-SEP, 1976 (ed. Paul Kirchhoff, Lina Odena Güemes and Luis Reyes García).

34 On books in New Spain, see Joaquín García Icazbalceta, *Bibliografía mexicana del siglo XVI*, Mexico City, FCE, 1981, Toribio Medina, 1907; Fernández del Castillo, 1982; and on illustrations: Yhmoff Cabrera, 1973.

35 See *Códice Chimalpopoca, Anales de Cuauhtitlán y Leyenda de los Soles*, trans. Primo Feliciano Velázquez, Mexico City, UNAM, Instituto de Historia, 1945.

36 Bernardino de Sahagún, *Códice Florentino*, ed. Giunti Barbéra and AGN, Florence, 1979, Libro décimo, Capitulo VIII, fo. 18v°.

37 See *Códice Chimalpopoca* ...

38 For example Pedro Carrasco Pizana and Jesús Monjarás-Ruiz, *Colección de documentos sobre Coyoacán*, Mexico City, INAH, 1976–8, 2 vols; Hildeberto Martínez, *Colección de documentos coloniales de Tepeaca*, Mexico City, INAH, 1984; Anderson, Berdan and Lockhart, 1976.

39 'Letter to King Carlos V by *encomendero* Jerónimo López, 20 October 1541', Joaquín García Icazbalceta (ed.) *Colección de documentos inéditos para la historia de México*, Mexico City, Porrúa, 1971, II, p. 148.

40 'Letter by don Pedro Motecuhzoma Tlacahuepantzin et al., Tacuba, 11 May 1556', *Epistolario*, 1942, XVI, pp. 64–6.

41 Fernández del Castillo, 1982, p. 36; *Concilios provinciales Primero y Segundo* ..., Mexico City, Superior Gobierno, 1769, pp. 143–4.

42 In Bernardino de Sahagún, *Historia general de las cosas de Nueva España*, Mexico City, Porrúa, 1977, III, pp. 255–63.

43 Bernardino de Sahagún, *Coloquios y Doctrina cristiana*, Mexico City, UNAM and Fundación de Investiaciones Sociales, A.C., 1986.

44 Sahagún, *Historia general*, III, pp. 165–7; Juan Bautista, *Sermonario en lengua mexicana*, Mexico City, López Dávalos, 1606–7 ('Prólogo' in Garibay, 1971, II, pp. 218–56).

45 Garibay, 1971, II, p. 231; *Epistolario*, X, 1940, pp. 89–108.

46 Pizana and Monjarás-Ruiz Carrasco, *Colección de documentos*, II, pp. 15–16, and *passim*; on the duties of the indigenous *escribano*, Alonso de Molina, *Confesionario mayor en lengua mexicana y castellana*, Mexico City, Antonio de Espinosa, 1569, fos 58r°–58v°.

47 *Epistolario*, 1939, IV, pp. 168–9.

48 Torquemada, *Monarquía indiana*, V, p. 172.

49 *Descripción del arzobispado de México hecha en 1570*, Mexico City, J. J. Terrazas (1897), 1976, pp. 53–66; *Códice Franciscano, Siglo XVI*, Mexico City, Chávez Hayhoe, 1941, p. 57.

50 López Sarrelangue, 1965, pp. 95–6; *Epistolario*, 1940, VII, p. 297.

51 Mendieta, *Historia*, III, pp. 223–4.

Chapter 2 Memories to Order

1 On the *Relaciones*, the studies of H. F. Cline and D. Robertson, contained in HMAI, Part I, vol. 12, 1972; Carrera Stampa, 1968. A new edition in Spanish published by the UNAM (Mexico City) was not available when we wrote these pages: *Relaciones geográficas del siglo XVI*, ed. René Acuña, Mexico City, UNAM, 10 vols, 1982–8.

2 *Papeles de Nueva España...*, ed. Francisco del Paso y Troncoso, 2nd series (cited *PNE*), Madrid, 7 vols, 1905–6, VI, p. 13.

3 Juan Bautista Pomar, 'Relación de Texcoco', ed. Joaquín García Icazbalceta, Mexico City, Francisco Díaz de León, 1892; Diego Muñoz Camargo, *Descripción de la ciudad y provincia de Tlaxcala...*, Mexico, UNAM, Instituto de Investigaciones Filológicas, 1981.

4 For example, the conception of climate, the mechanism of winds, the notion of the exceptional and that of a natural wonder.

5 *PNE*, IV, p. 11.

6 Mention of paintings: *PNE*, VI, pp. 41 (Coatepec), 65 (Chimalhuacan), 79 (Chicoloapan); IV, pp. 22 (Ixtepejí), 70 (Tilantongo); V, pp. 70–3 (Petalcingo); Gibson and Glass, 1975, pp. 344, 337, 325–6; Gibson, 1975, p. 314.

7 *PNE*, V, p. 13.

8 *PNE*, VI, pp. 66, 42, 24, 26, 32; V, pp. 131, 139; IV, p. 14.

9 *PNE*, IV, pp. 73, 78.

10 *PNE*, VI, pp. 243, 125, 246, 258–9; IV, p. 240.

11 *PNE*, VI, pp. 67, 46; V, pp. 49, 100; IV, pp. 80, 59; VI, pp. 278, 57, 245, 315.

12 *PNE*, VI, pp. 175, 235, 10, 189, 97; *Relaciones geográficas de la diócesis de Michoacán*, ed. José Corona Nuñez (cited *RGM*), Guadalajara, 1958, I, pp. 12, 33; *PNE*, VI, pp. 150, 33, 147; IV, pp. 19, 106, 75, 208; V, pp. 61, 67.

13 *PNE*, VI, pp. 57, 84, 135, 91, 119, 129, 76; V, p. 171; VI, pp. 224, 229, 217, 244, 91, 102, 111.
14 *PNE*, VI, pp. 84, 57, 227, 244, 259; IV, pp. 117–18.
15 *PNE*, VI, pp. 57, 146–7, 16, 29, 91.
16 *PNE*, IV, pp. 179, 141, 146; *RGM*, II, p. 114.
17 *PNE*, VI, p. 147; *RGM*, II, p. 114; *PNE*, IV, p. 121.
18 *PNE*, VI, pp. 196, 318, 278; V, pp. 32, 145; *RGM*, II, p. 167; *PNE*, VI, p. 286; IV, pp. 200, 63.
19 *PNE*, IV, pp. 236, 140.
20 *PNE*, IV, p. 135.
21 *PNE*, VI, pp. 222, 214–17, 139, 16, 36, 107; IV, pp. 73, 61, 166, 167, 79; VI, p. 74; IV, pp. 34, 101, 61, 48, 74; VI, pp. 244, 242, 90.
22 *PNE*, VI, p. 213; V, p. 66; IV, pp. 48, 73; VI, p. 276.
23 *PNE*, VI, pp. 90, 95, 133, 129; IV, p. 167.
24 Bernardino de Sahagún, *Florentine Codex, General History of the Things of New Spain*, 12 vols, trans. C. E. Dibble and A. J. O. Anderson, Santa Fe, University of Utah, 1950–69, VI, p. 235; López Austin, 1980, I, pp. 71–2.
25 Juan de Torquemada, *Monarquía indiana*, Mexico City, UNAM, III, p. 78; López Austin, 1980, I, p. 74.
26 *PNE*, VI, pp. 239–45.
27 *PNE*, VI, pp. 32, 34, 14, 26, 42, 118, 263, 132, 269, 229; V, p. 152.
28 *PNE*, VI, pp. 45, 222; *RGM*, II, p. 21; *RGM*, I, pp. 11, 25, 33; *PNE*, IV, pp. 198, 184, 84, 79.
29 López Austin, 1973, pp. 86–90; *PNE*, VI, pp. 101, 45, 73; IV, p. 79.
30 *PNE*, VI, pp. 84, 242, 243, 141, 286. On the alimentary changes introduced by the Spanish, Cook and Borah, 1979, III, pp. 129–76.
31 *PNE*, VI, pp. 16, 36, 129, 91, 146, 123, 96.
32 *PNE*, IV, pp. 220, 111, 149, 102, 146.
33 *Cédula real* of May 1582 of Philip II, in Genaro García, ed., *Documentos inéditos o muy raros para la historia de México*, Mexico City, Porrúa, 1974, pp. 498–9.

Chapter 3 The Primordial Titles or the Passion for Writing

1 Without a satisfactory knowledge of the native languages in the colonial period, whose systematic study is just beginning – and also in the absence of adequate working tools – I have depended for the most part on the translations made by the official interpreters, by those interested (or, for some texts, by modern specialists), while referring to the original to try to clear up or establish certain important points. It goes without saying that this analysis can be only an introduction; only a true linguistic and philological study would make possible the use of these documents that they merit.
2 These titles come from among the *Tierras* of the AGN: vol. 2860, exp. 1, fos 59r°–73r° (San Bartolomé Capulhuac); vol. 2998, exp. 3B, fos 1r°–38v° (San Martín Ocoyoacac); vol. 2819, exp. 9, fos 40r°–87v° (San Mathías Cuijingo); vol. 1665, exp. 5, fos 166r°–190v° (San Antonio Zoyatzingo); vol. 2674, exp. 1, fos 6r°–19r° (San Miguel Atlautla); vol. 2548, exp. 11, fos 20r°–28r° (Santiago Sula); vol. 3032, exp. 6,

fos 262r°–286r° (Los Reyes Acatliscoayan); vol. 1671, exp. 10, fos 13r°–24v° (San Nicolás Tetelco); vol. 3032, exp. 3, fos 190r°–218v° (Santa Marta Xocotepetlalpan); San Francisco Cuaucuauzentlalpan (*Tlalocan*, UNAM, IV, 1, 1962, pp. 64–73); San Gregorio Acapulco (*Tlalocan*, III, 2, 1952, pp. 122–41); Santo Tomás Ajusco (*Tlalocan*, VI, 3, 1970, pp. 193–212); Tetcotzinco (*Tlalocan*, II, 2, 1946, pp. 110–27). To these should be added the Titles of San Pedro Tlahuac and Santa Catarina Tlamacaztonco preserved in the National Library of Mexico.

3 Atlautla, fo. 14v°; Ocoyoacac, fo. 35r°.
4 Capulhuac, fo. 59r°; Ocoyoacac, fo. 34v°; Sula, fo. 20r°.
5 Compare Atlautla, fos 7r°–8r°, Santa Marta, fo. 2r°, San Gregorio Acapulco, p. 104.
6 An analogous evolution in the colonial part of the *Codex Telleriano-Remensis* (León Abrams, Jr, 1970–1).
7 Compare Santa Marta, fo. 193r° and Atlautla, fo. 12v°; San Gregorio, p. 126 and Santa Marta, fo. 193r°; Ocoyoacac, fo. 35r° and Atlautla, fo. 14r°.
8 Ocoyoacac in *Catálogo de ilustraciones* . . . , Mexico City, AGN, 1979, vol. 5, nos 2270–7.
9 *Catálogo*, Cuijingo, no. 2234; Zoyatzingo, no. 1178.
10 Zoyatzingo, no. 1177; Cuijingo, no. 2235.
11 Cuijingo, nos 2236 and 2237.
12 Ocoyoacac, no. 2270.
13 Ocoyoacac, no. 2277.
14 Santos Reyes, no. 2304.
15 The Titles of Santa Isabel Tola bring together elements still easily discernible; cf. Glass and Robertson, 1975, pp. 219–20.
16 Sula, fos 23r°–23v°; Cuijingo, fos 83v°–84v°; Milpa Alta, fos 207r°–216r°, 226r°–227r°.
17 Ocoyoacac, fos 37r°, 30r°; Cuijingo, fo. 73r°; Ocoyoacac, fo. 33r°; Zoyatzingo, fo. 186r°.
18 Zoyatzingo, fo. 183v°; Cuijingo, fo. 85r°; Capulhuac, fo. 61v°; Santa Marta, fo. 201r°.
19 Cuijingo, fo. 76r°–76v°.
20 Zoyatzingo, fo. 184v°; Cuijingo, fo. 78v°; San Gregorio Acapulco, pp. 128–9.
21 Cuijingo, fo. 77r°; Ocoyoacac, fo. 29r°; Sula, fo. 22v°.
22 Cuijingo, fos 79v°, 80v°; Ocoyoacac, fos 35r°, 33v°; Atlautla, fos 18r°, 12v°.
23 Atlautla, fo. 12v°; Santa Marta, fo. 193v°; Zoyatzingo, fo. 185v°; Cuijingo, fo. 73v°.
24 Santa Marta, fo. 197v°; San Gregorio Acapulco, p. 124; Capulhuac, fos 60v°–61r°; Cuijingo, fo. 64r°; Sula, fo. 3r°; Santa Marta, fo. 196r°; Atlautla, fo. 15r°.
25 Ocoyoacac, fo. 34r°; Cuijingo, fo. 80r°; Santa Marta, fos 193v°, 198v°; Atlautla, fo. 14v°.
26 Cuijingo, fo. 64v°; Zoyatzingo, fo. 188v°; Ocoyoacac, fos 29r°, 32r°.
27 Cuijingo, fos 69v°–70r°.
28 Chimalpahin, *Octava Relación*, Mexico City, UNAM, 1983, pp. 183–99.
29 This exceptional text is preserved in Italy, in the Archivio Generale Franciscano in Rome (vol. XI/35 of the *Chronache ed altre carte, México, Querétaro y Guadalupe, siglo XVIII*).

30   AGN, Ramo *Tierras*, vol. 335, exp. 5.
31   AGN, *Tierras*, vol. 236, exp. 6 (*pueblos* of Chapultepec and San Martín).
32   Zapotec Titles (San Juan Juquila in AGN; *Tierras*, vol. 335, exp. 5); Mixtec (San Juan Chapultepec, *ibid.*, vol. 236, exp. 6); Otomí ('Relación de la conquista de Querétaro', studied in Gruzinski, 1985b); on the *lienzos* of Guerrero, Galarza, 1972; Gibson and Glass, 1975, pp. 324–6, 379–98.

Chapter 4   Colonial Idolatry

1   B. de Sahagún, *Historia general de las cosas de Nueva España*, Mexico City, Porrúa, 1977, III, p. 354; Diego Durán, *Historia de las Indias de Nueva España...*, Mexico City, Porrúa, 1967, I, pp. 244, 6; Israel, 1975, p. 48.

2   Pedro Ponce de León *Breve relación de los dioses y ritos de la gentilidad*, Mexico City, Imprenta del Museo Nacional, 1892, and in *Tratado de las idolatrías...*, Mexico City, Fuente Cultural, 1953, X, pp. 369–80 and in Angel María Garibay K., *Teogonía e historia de los mexicanos*, Mexico City, Porrúa, 1973 (cited P). English translation, 'Brief Relation of the Gods and Rites of Heathenism', in J. Richard Andrews and Ross Hassig, eds, *Treatise on the Heathen Superstitions that Today Live Among the Indians Native to this New Spain (1629)*, Norman, University of Oklahoma Press, 1984, pp. 211–18. Hernando Ruiz de Alarcón, *Tratado de las superstciones y costumbres gentílicas que hoy viven entre los indios...*, 1629: several editions, in Spanish *Anales del Museo Nacional de México*, Epoca I, 6, 1892 (1900), pp. 123–223; in *Tratado de las idolatrías...*, Mexico City, Fuente Cultural, 1953, XX, pp. 17–180 (our reference for the Spanish text: cited A). Two English editions: Michael D. Coe and Gordon Whittaker, *Aztec Sorcerers in Seventeenth Century Mexico. The Treatise on Superstitions*, Albany, State University of New York, 1982 (cited C & W); and Andrews and Hassig, *Treatise on the Heathen Super-stitions...*, 1984 (cited A & H). On this work one consults Eike Hinz, *Die Magischen Texte im Tratado Ruiz de Alarcóns (1629)*, Hamburg, Hamburgischen Museum für Volkerkunde und Vorgeschichte, 1970, and W. H. Fellowes, 'The Treatises of Hernando Ruiz de Alarcón', *Tlalocan*, 1977, VII, pp. 309–55; see also AGN, Ramo *Inquisición*, vol. 304, fo. 258r°; AGN, Ramo *Bienes nacionales*, vol. 596, 'Los naturales de S. Miguel Totoquitlapilco, 1677' (2 pages attributable to Ruiz de Alarcón). Jacinto de La Serna, *Manual de ministros de indios para el conocimiento de sus idolatrias y extirpacíon de ellas*, editions: *Colección de documentos inéditos para la historia de España*, Madrid, 1892, CIV, pp. 1–72; *Anales del Museo Nacional de México*, pp. 261–480; *Tratado de las idolatrías...*, Mexico City, Fuente Cultural, X, 1953, pp. 41–368 (cited LS). See also AGN, *Inquisición* vol. 369, exp. 24; *Bienes nacionales*, leg. 1061, exp. 6.

3   This was the case with the *Informe contra idolorum cultores* of Pedro Sánchez de Aguilar (Madrid, 1639); the *Relación auténtica de las idolatrías...* of Gonzalo de Balsalobre (Mexico City, 1656); *Luz y método de confesar idólatras y destierro de idolatrías...* (Puebla, 1692) of Diego Jaymes Ricardo Villavicencio.

4   A, p. 30; LS, p. 93.

5   Motolinía, *Memoriales o Libro de las cosas de Nueva España y de los naturales de ella*, Mexico City, UNAM, 1971, p. 35.
6   A, pp. 30–4; LS, pp. 93–5; on *tlapialli* and *ytlapial*, López Austin, 1967a, p. 23, and A & H, p. 314. For LS, '*itlapial . . . quiere decir cosa que se debe guardar como herencia y que nosostros llamamos vinculada*' ('*itlapial . . .* means something that must be guarded as an inheritance and which we call entailed').
7   A, pp. 31–3, 47.
8   A, p. 24; LS, p. 65; A, pp. 140–1; LS, p. 66; López Austin, 1980, I, pp. 223–52, 341; LS, pp. 76–7.
9   A, pp. 76–88 (hunting), 91–7 (fishing), 98–101 (*magueyes*), 101–5 (maize), 66–7 (woodcutting), 70–2 (lime).
10 LS, pp. 77–81.
11 A, pp. 128–32, 141, 137, 142–5, 153, 170, 175.
12 LS, pp. 248–56, 101–3, 241; A, pp. 124, 66, 103.
13 A, pp. 27, 65; López Austin, 1966, and 1967b.
14 A, pp. 125, 69; LS, p. 333.
15 LS, pp. 62, 74–5, 100–1.
16 A, pp. 130–1; LS, pp. 260, 265; C & W, pp. 214–15; A & H, p. 154.
17 A, p. 124.
18 LS, pp. 240–1.
19 A, pp. 128, 145, 104, 60, 63–4, 121.
20 A, p. 67; LS, pp. 240–1; Motolinía, *Memoriales*, pp. 67, 71, 50; Alonso de Molina, *Vocabulario en lengua castellana y mexicana . . .* (1571), Mexico City, Porrúa, 1977, fo. 125; Sahagún, *Historia general*, I, p. 45.
21 LS, pp. 240–1.
22 A, pp. 60–1 and C & W, pp. 105–6; A, p. 78 and C & W, p. 133; A, p. 63 and C & W, p. 110; A, pp. 36, 64, 96–7, 29, 62–6; LS, p. 244.
23 A, p. 163 and C & W, p. 268; A, pp. 176–80, 77.
24 Personal communication by Monique Legros.
25 A, pp. 128, 63 and C & W, p. 110; A, pp. 68, 79, 81, and C & W, p. 135; C & W, pp. 138, 203; López Austin, 1980, I, p. 67.
26 A, pp. 62, 80, 139, 89, 153, 139, 150, 78, 104.
27 On Nahualism, López Austin, 1980, I, pp. 416–30.
28 A, pp. 52, 55.
29 A, pp. 94, 96, 114, 172, 105, 89.
30 A, pp. 83, 86, 77–8, 120, 93–9, 174, 128, 82, 39. Carrasco Pizana, 1966; Gardner, 1982.
31 A, pp. 87, 102, 138, 169, 159, 170, 171, 154, 173, 157.
32 LS, p. 269; A, pp. 90, 95–6, 60, 72, 100, 101, 179, 154, 83; anger, *çumalli*: pp. 79, 93; fury, *tlahuelli*: p. 77; covetousness: p. 68.
33 LS, p. 269.
34 A, p. 122; LS, p. 264.
35 Durán, *Historia*, I, p. 79.
36 A, p. 115.
37 LS, pp. 217–18.
38 LS, p. 141.
39 A, p. 86; LS, pp. 82, 112, 143, 232.
40 Durán, *Historia*, I, p. 237.
41 LS, pp. 337, 78, 338, 345.
42 A, p. 125.

43 A, p. 122.
44 P, p. 122; A, p. 156; AGN, *Inquisición*, vol. 303, fo. 246.
45 LS, p. 79.
46 Durán, *Historia*, I, p. 79; AGN, *Bienes nacionales*, vol. 596, 'Petición de S. Ana Tlaxmalac', 1681; ARSI, *Mex.* 17, 'Relación de la misión de los P. Pérez y Zappa', 1685–7; Agustín Dávila Padilla, *Historia de la fundación... de la provincia de Santiago de México...*, Mexico City, Academia literaria, 1955, p. 618.
47 LS, pp. 78, 289–90, 80–1.
48 Balsalobre, *Relación auténtica de las idolatrías*; AGI, *Audiencia de México*, 357, 879, 882; AGN, *Inquisición*, vol. 615, fo. 64v°; Alcina Franch, 1979.

Chapter 5 The Christianization of the *Imaginaire*

1 Motolinía, *Memoriales ohibro de las cosas de Nueva España y de los naturales de ella*, Mexico City, UNAM, 1971, pp. 32, 89; Bernadino de Sahagún, *Historia general de las cosas de Nueva España*, Mexico City, Porrúa, 1977, II, p. 287; I, pp. 85, 94; Juan de Torquemada, *Monarquía indiana*, Mexico City, UNAM, 1975–83, VI, p. 262.
2 Martín de León, *Camino al cielo en lengua mexicana con todos los requisitos necessarios...*, Mexico City, Diego López Dávalos, 1611, fo. 112v°; Diego de Nágera y Angas, *Doctrina y enseñanza en lengua mazahua...*, Mexico City, Juan Ruyz, 1637, p. 26; Jacinto de La Serna, 'Manual de ministros de indios para el conocimiento de sus idolatrías y extirpación de ellas', *Tratado de las idolatrías...*, Mexico City, Fuente Cultural, X, 1953, pp. 111, 114, 235, 253, 275; Torquemada, *Monarquía indiana*, III, p. 41.
3 Torquemada, *Monarquía indiana*, VI, p. 369; Esteban J. Palomera, *Fray Diego Valadés, OFM, Evangelizador, humanista de la Nueva España. Su obra*, Mexico City, Jus, 1962.
4 AGN, Ramo *Bienes nacionales*, leg. 732, exp. 1; Llaguno, 1963, p. 60; AGN, Ramo *Inquisición*, vol. 312, fo. 97r°; *Estudios acerca del arte novohispano. Homenaje a Elisa Vargas Lugo*, Mexico City, UNAM, 1983, p. 86; Gruzinski, 1990, pp. 263–82.
5 Motolinía, *Memoriales*, pp. 96–7; García Icazbalceta, 1947, II, p. 42; Fernández del Castillo, 1982, pp. 4–37; Torquemada, *Monarquía indiana*, VI, pp. 172, 201, 262; Weckmann, 1984, I, pp. 286–7.
6 Gruzinski, 1976, and, in collaboration with J.-M. Sallmann, 'Une source d'ethnohistoire: les vies de Vénérables dans l'Italie méridionale et le Mexique baroque', *Mélanges de l'Ecole française de Rome*, 88, 1976, 2, pp. 789–822.
7 Motolinía, *Memoriales*, pp. 140–1, 163; Weckmann, 1984, I, pp. 216–19, 286.
8 La Torre Villar and Navarro de Anda, 1982; Sahagún, *Historia general*, III, p. 352; AGI, *Audiencia de México*, 22, exp. 81 *bis*; La Maza, 1981, pp. 30–1, 73–81, 182–6; Jacques Lafaye, *Quetzalcoatl et Guadalupe*, Paris, Gallimard, 1974; Brading, 1973; AGN, *Bienes nacionales*, leg. 1162, exp. 5; AGN, Ramo *Tierras*, vol. 2278, exp. 2 (text of a performance given in 1684); Gruzinski, 1990, pp. 152–61, 180–200.

9 Gerónimo de Mendieta, *Historia eclesiástica indiana*, Mexico City, Chávez Hayhoe, 1945, III, pp. 108–9; IV, p. 49.
10 AGN, *Inquisición*, vol. 133, exp. 23 [1583].
11 Alberro, 1988; Greenleaf, 1969; AGN, *Inquisición*, vol. 335, exp. 12, fo. 127r°; vol. 572, exp. 18, fos 363r°–363v°; vol. 187, exp. 11; vol. 312, exp. 57, fos 300r°–316r°; AGN, Ramo *Indiferente general*, 'Libro de testificaciones del obispo Frai Juan de Zumárraga' (1536).
12 Aguirre Beltrán, 1973, pp. 112, 204, 219, 209; *Concilio III Provincial Mexicano celebrado en México el año de 1585...*, Mexico City, Maillefert y Compañía, 1859, pp. 405, 375, 376; Noemi Quezada Ramírez, 'Oraciones mágicas en la colonia', *Anales de Antropología*, XI, 1974; pp. 141–67, and 1975; Alberro, 1988.
13 AGN, *Inquisición*, vol. 225, fo. 96r°; vol. 312, exp. 55; vol. 369, exp. 24; vol. 605, exp. 10; AGI, *Audiencia de México*, 337, 'Relación de la visita general del arzobispo de México Juan de Mañosca y Zamora' (1646).

Chapter 6 Capturing the Christian Supernatural

1 Hernando Ruiz de Alarcón, 'Tratado de las supersticiones y costumbres gentílicas que hoy viven entre los indios...', 1629, in *Tratado de las idolatrías...*, Mexico City, Fuente Cultural, 1953, XX, pp. 157–8 (cited A).
2 Edward Sapir, *The Unconscious: A Symposium*, New York, Dummen, 1927, and *Selected writings of Edward Sapir in Language, Culture and Personality*, ed. David Mandelbaum, Los Angeles, University of California Press, 1949, pp. 544–59.
3 See the Hjelmslevian theory of the sign in Lindekens, 1976, p. 64.
4 Jacinto de La Serna, 'Manual de ministros de indios para el conocimiento de sus idolatrías y extirpación de ellas', in *Tratado de las idolatrías...*, Mexico City, Fuente Cultural, 1953, X, pp. 98–9 (cited LS).
5 LS, pp. 103–5.
6 A, p. 52.
7 A, pp. 160–1.
8 LS, p. 102.
9 LS, p. 103.
10 On a case of visions that turn into idiosyncratic delirium, AGN, Ramo *Inquisición*, vol. 303, fos 68r°–70r° (1624).
11 Diego Durán, *Historia de las Indias de Nueva España...*, Mexico City, Porrúa, 1967, II, pp. 416, 310, 484; López Austin, 1980, I, p. 411; Diego Muñoz Camargo, *Historia de Tlaxcala*, Mexico City, Ateneo Nacional de Ciencias y Artes de México, 1947, p. 146.
12 Alonso de Molina, *Confesionario mayor en lengua mexicana y castellana*, Mexico City, Autonio de Espinosa, 1569, fo. 82r° Bernardo de Sahagún, *Historia general de las cosas de Nueva España*, Mexico City, Porrúa, 1977, III, pp. 192, 292–3; Motolinía, *Memoriales o Libro de las cosas de Nueva España y de los naturales de ella*, Mexico City, UNAM, 1971, p. 32.
13 A, pp. 43, 51; Pedro Ponce de León, 'Breve relación de los dioses y ritos de la gentilidad', in Angel María Garibay K., *Teogonía e historia de los mexicanos*, Mexico City, Porrúa, 1973 (cited P), p. 132; AGN, *Inquisición*, vol. 304, fo. 62r°; vol. 303, fo. 78r°; vol. 335, exp. 96, fo. 372v°.

14 A, p. 49; LS, p. 239; AGN, *Inquisición*, vol. 312, fo. 270r°; vol. 486, fo. 229r°; vol. 342, exp. 10; vol. 341, fo. 313r°; vol. 304, exp. 26; vol. 340, fo. 362r°; vol. 342, exp. 15, fo. 354r°; vol. 340, exp. 4; vol. 746, fo. 500r°; vol. 317, exp. 21.

15 AGN, *Inquisición*, vol. 478, fo. 273r°; AGN, Ramo *Misiones*, vol. 26, 'Relación de la misión que hicieron . . . los PP. L. López, M. de Urroy y P. de Orga' (1645).

16 P, p. 132; A, p. 52; LS, p. 100; Jean-Michel Sallmann and Serge Gruzinski, *Visions indiennes, visions baroques, les métissages de l'inconscient*, Paris, Presses Universitaires de France, 1991.

17 AGN, *Inquisición*, vol. 317, exp. 21; vol. 342, fo. 273r°; vol. 356, exp. 11; vol. 339, exp. 34, fo. 275r°.

18 Aguirre Beltrán, 1973, p. 113; AGN, *Inquisición*, vol. 668, exp. 5–6; vol. 510, exp. 25, fo. 69r°; vol. 356, fo. 180r°; vol. 674, exp. 27.

19 AGN, *Inquisición*, vol. 507, fos 46r°–46v°.

20 AGI, *Audiencia de México*, 375, 'Carta del cabildo eclesiástico de Valladolid' (1667).

21 AGN, Ramo *Indiferente general*, 'Información contra Miguel Ximénez' (1662).

22 *Historia general de México*, Mexico City, El Colegio de México, 1977, II, p. 100; Brading, 1978, p. 19; Gerhard, 1972, pp. 119, 128.

23 Claude Lévi-Strauss, 'Introduction à l'oeuvre de M. Mauss', in Marcel Mauss, *Sociologie et anthropologie*, Paris, Presses Universitaires de France, 1950, p. xx.

24 AGI, *Audiencia de México*, 78, 'Memorial de F. Bartolomé Velázquez' (1665).

25 AHPM, ms. II, 'Templo místico de la gracia . . .', p. 594 (beginning of the eighteenth century). The episode can be dated to between 1680 and 1692.

Chapter 7 A Last Reprieve for Composite Native Cultures

1 On Morelos, AGN, Ramo *Inquisición*, vol. 1349, exp. 8; on demography, *Historia general de México*, Mexico City, El Colegio de México, 1977, II, pp. 98–105; Brading, 1978, pp. 39–60; Taylor, 1972, pp. 17–34; Gibson, 1964, pp. 140–4.

2 BN, *Fondo franciscano*, caja 106, exp. 1462.

3 Diego Jaymes Ricardo Villavicencio, *Luz y método de confesar idólatras y destierro de idolatrías . . .*, Puebla, Fernández de León, 1692, pp. 48–9; AGI, *Audiencia de México*, 85 (1681) and AGN, Ramo *Civil*, vol. 270, 'Gaspar de Lara, cura de Tlalnepantla al virrey' (1680); AGN, Ramo *Criminal*, vol. 120, exp. 4; AGN, Ramo *Bienes nacionales*, vol. 976, exp. 39; AGN, Ramo *Misiones*, vol. 25, exp. 15; AGN, *Inquisición*, vol. 715, exp. 18; Antonio Joaquín de Rivadeneira y Barrientos, *Disertaciones . . . sobre los puntos que se le consultaron por el Cuarto Concilio Mexicano*, Madrid, 1881, p. 64; AGN, *Inquisición*, vol. 1055, fos 301r°–313v°.

4 AGN, *Inquisición*, vol. 1176, fo. 75r°; López Austin, 1980, I, pp. 291, 369–70, 82; AGN, *Inquisición*, vol. 1149, exp. 24, fo. 83v°.

5 BN, *Fondo franciscano*, caja 102, exp. 1534; Gibson, 1964, pp. 133–4.

6 Rivadeneira y Barrientos, *Disertaciones*, pp. 64–6.

7 AGN, *Bienes nacionales*, vol. 663, exp. 19. On Mexico and Guerrero,

Manuel Pérez, *Farol indiano y guía de curas de indios*..., Mexico City, Francisco de Rivera Calderón, 1713; On Puebla, Andrés Miguel Pérez de Velasco, *El ayudante de cura instruido*..., Puebla, Colegio Real de San Ignacio, 1766.

8 Arturo Warman, 1972; Manuel Romero de Terreros, *Torneos, mascaradas y fiestas reales en Nueva España*, Mexico City, Editorial Cultura, 1918, IX, pp. 42–8; AGI, *Audiencia de México*, 1042, 'Festivo y real aparato [de] Pásquaro' (1701); Agustín de Vetancurt, *Teatro mexicano. Descripción breve de los sucesos exemplares, históricos, políticos, militares y religiosos*..., Part IV, Mexico City, María de Benavides, 1697, p. 58.

9 AGN, Ramo *Tierras*, vol. 2539, exp. 6; vol. 2616, exp. 4; vol. 2554, exp. 10; vol. 2540, exp. 5; vol. 2546, exp. 14; vol. 2535, exp. 14; vol. 2201, exp. 6; AGN, *Bienes nacionales*, leg. 414; Loera y Chávez, 1977, pp. 66–99.

10 AGN, *Criminal*, vol. 334, 'El cura de S. María Chicmecatitlán...' (1811); AGI, *Gobierno México*, 727, 'Carta de los governadores... de Tlatelolco' (1771); AGN, *Criminal*, vol. 326, exp. 2; AGN, Ramo *Indios*, vol. 69, exp. 399, fo. 310v°; AGN, *Tierras*, vol. 2553, exp. 3; AGN, *Bienes nacionales*, leg. 1076, exp. 9; AGI, *Audiencia de México*, 26, exp. 80A; Vetancurt, *Teatro mexicano*, pp. 56–7, 72.

11 AGI, *Audiencia de México*, 2713, Valladolid, 4 May 1754.

12 Toussaint, 1967, pp. 203–5; Pedro Rojas, *Tonantzintla*, Mexico City, UNAM, 1956; Reyes Valerio, 1960.

13 AGN, *Tierras*, vol. 650, exp. 2; vol. 1820, exp. 1; vol. 2169, exp. 1; vol. 1874, exp. 2; vol. 2554, exp. 6; vol. 2450, exp. 5; vol. 2546, exp. 16.

14 Gibson, 1964, pp. 128–35; *Códice Franciscano. Siglo XVI*, Mexico City, Chávez Hayhoe, 1941, pp. 65–9; Muriel, 2 vols, 1956–60; AGN, *Indiferente general* (Coatlán) (1577); Bancroft Library (Berkeley), *MM268*; Vetancurt, *Teatro mexicano*, passim; AGN, Ramo *Clero regular y secular*, vol. 103, exp. 11.

15 AGN, *Tierras*, vol. 1874, exp. 2; AGN, *Indiferente general*, 'Varios oficios del virrey Revillagigedo [1794] con Informes de los curas de Acambay, Atotonilco el Grande, Temascaltepec del Valle, Tepozotlán' (1777); *Tierras*, vol. 2467, exp. 2.

16 AGN, *Bienes nacionales*, leg. 732; AGN, *Clero regular y secular*, vol. 22; AGN, Ramo *Cofradías*, vol. 18, passim.

17 AGN, *Tierras*, vol. 2616, exp. 7; vol. 2540, exp. 5; vol. 2467, exp. 2; vol. 2547, exp. 7.

18 AGN, *Tierras*, vol. 2535, exp. 5; vol. 2547, exp. 7; vol. 2551, exp. 8; vol. 2539, exp. 5; vol. 2539, exp. 4; AGN, *Criminal*, vol. 274, exp. 4; AGN, *Bienes nacionales*, leg. 446, exp. 7; *Tierras*, vol. 2201, exp. 6.

19 AGN, *Tierras*, vol. 1478, exp. 10.

20 Gibson, 1964, p. 133; AGN, *Bienes nacionales*, leg. 420, exp. 19; vol. 1086, exp. 10; AGN, *Clero regular y secular*, vol. 103, exp. 11; BN, *Fondo franciscano*, caja 109, exp. 1494; AGN, *Tierras*, vol. 1478, exp. 10; AGN, Ramo *Historia*, vol. 437; Taylor, 1979, p. 59.

21 Remo Guidieri, 'Statue and mask. Presence and Representation in Belief', *Res*, 5, Spring 1973, Cambridge, Mass., pp. 15–22.

22 AGN, *Bienes nacionales*, leg. 1113, exp. 45.

23 AGN, *Bienes nacionales*, leg. 1113, exp. 45; leg. 1087, exp. 2; Horcasitas, 1974, pp. 25–30, 36, 87–8, 193, 421; AGN, *Inquisición*, vol. 1072, fo.

242r°; vol. 1037, fo. 288r°; *Bienes nacionales*, leg. 90, exp. 10; *Inquisición*, vol. 339, exp. 81, fo. 574r°.

24 AGI (Seville), *Gobierno México*, 1696, 'Extracto testimoniado de la causa de los indios idólatras', Mexico City, 4 December 1761, fo. 19r°.

25 Archivo Casa Morelos (Morelia), *Doc. Inquisición*, leg. 41, 'Contra varios indios de San Luis La Paz' (1797); AGN, *Inquisición*, vol. 1415, fos 85r°–87v°; AGN, *Bienes nacionales*, leg. 663; Gruzinski, 1989a, pp. 105–88; AGN, *Criminal*, vol. 308, exp. 1; Gruzinski, 1990, pp. 301–4.

26 AGN, Ramo *Cédulas reales*, vol. 86, exp. 140, fo. 298r°; Pérez de Velasco, *El ayudante de cura*, pp. 93, 95; AGN, *Criminal*, vol. 147, exp. 19; vol. 255, fo. 11v°; vol. 175, exp. 5; AGN, *Inquisición*, vol. 527, exp. 9; vol. 1284, fo. 208r°; vol. 960, exp. 17; AGN, Ramo *Judicial*, vol. 61, 'Causa contra Antonio Isidro...' (1796); AGN, *Bienes nacionales*, leg. 663, 'Causa contra Ma Paula' (1818).

27 AGN, *Tierras*, vol. 427, exp. 3; vol. 2001, exp. 1; vol. 2555, exp. 3; vol. 1874, exp. 2; AGN, *Clero regular y secular*, vol. 130, exp. 10.

28 AGN, *Bienes nacionales*, leg. 185, exp. 90; leg. 1674, exp. 2; leg. 1540, exp. 1; leg. 62, exp. 1; *Descripción del arzobispado de México hecha en 1570*, Mexico City, J. J. Terrazas (1897), 1976, p. 227.

29 AGI, *Gobierno México*, 1937; AGN, *Bienes nacionales*, leg. 223, exp. 78; legs 373, 569, 576, 584, 581, 464; AGI, *Gobierno México*, 1937; Cuevas, 1946, IV, pp. 181, 108; AGN, *Indios*, vol. 90, exp. 47.

30 AGI, *Gobierno México*, 1937, 'El Consejo de Indias sobre cartas de Juan Cyrilo de Castilla', April 1766.

31 Horcasitas, 1974, p. 516; Nicolás Simeón de Salazar Flores Citlalpopoca, *Directorio de confesores que ofrece a los principiantes y nuevos ministros de el sacramento de la penitencia...*, Puebla, Viuda de Miguel de Ortega, 1715; Zavala, n.d., pp. 77, 73.

32 Cuevas, 1947, V, pp. 36–7; AGI, *Audiencia de México*, 879, 2714, 2712, 2716, 35, exp. 37A/D; AMNAH, *Fondo franciscano*, 183; AGN, *Bienes nacionales*, leg. 450; leg. 1182, exp. 28; leg. 153; on the conflicts between Indians and priests, AGN, *Indios, Indiferente general, Bienes nacionales, Clero regular y secular, Criminal*.

33 Hipólito Fortino Vera, *Colección de documentos eclesiásticos de México...*, Amecameca, Imprenta del Colegio Católico, 1887, II, p. 150 and III, p. 6; Francisco Antonio Lorenzana y Buitrón, *Cartas pastorales y edictos*, Mexico City, Imprenta del Superior Gobierno, 1770; BN, *Fondo franciscano*, caja 109, exp. 1494; AGN, *Bienes nacionales*, leg. 992, exp. 23; AGN, *Clero regular y secular*, vol. 215, 'Carta del obispo de Puebla', 7 April 1810; *Bienes nacionales*, leg. 990, exp. 10; leg. 330, exp. 2; AGN, Ramo *Obispos*, vol. 2, fo. 309r°; *Bienes nacionales*, leg. 1443, exp. 29; AGN, *Historia*, vol. 437; AGN, *Indios*, vol. 70, exp. 7 and vol. 80.

34 AGN, *Indios*, vol. 80, Malinalco, 1794.

35 AGN, *Clero regular y secular*, vol. 84, exp. 5; AGN, *Bienes nacionales*, leg. 944, exp. 3; leg. 230, exp. 5; *AGN, Cofradías*, vol. 18, fos 215r°–231v°; exp. 6 and 7; AGN, *Indiferente general*, 'Cuaderno segundo de varios expedientes... anexos al arreglo de cofradías...' (1788–9) and 'Varios oficios del virrey Conde de Revillagigedo' (1794); *Cofradías*, vol. 19, exp. 8; *Bienes nacionales*, leg. 1059, exp. 4.

36 AGN, *Clero regular y secular*, vol. 22, exp. 14, fo. 246r°.

37 AGN, *Clero regular y secular*, vol. 22, exp. 7; vol. 123; AGN, *Cofradías*,

vol. 18; AGN, *Bienes nacionales*, leg. 112, exp. 4; Francisco Antonio Lorenzana y Buitrón, *Reglas para que los naturales de estos reynos sean felices en lo espiritual y temporal*, in *Cartas Pastorales*.

38 Tanck de Estrada, 1977; BN, *Fondo franciscano*, caja 106, exp. 1462; AGN, *Historia*, vols 493, 494, 495, 496; AGN, *Indios*, vols 76, 77, 78, 79, 80, 81, 84, 85, 86, 87.

39 AGN, *Historia*, vol. 500, fos 295r°, 168r°; vol. 494, fo. 348r°; vol. 501, fo. 120r°; AGN, *Indios*, vol. 55, exp. 5.

40 AGN, *Indios*, vol. 90, 'Alcalde mayor de Tochimilco' (1771); AGN, *Criminal*, vol. 222, exp. 21; *Indios*, vol. 57, exp. 194; AGN, *Historia*, vol. 495, 'Escuelas en Tehuacan' (1786).

41 On the sources concerning this 'second acculturation', see Gruzinski, 1985a; AGN, *Historia*, vol. 500, fo. 304r°; AGN, *Indios*, vol. 79, fo. 49r°; vol. 78, fo. 48v°; vol. 76, fos 97v°–98r°, 50v°.

42 Ignacio del Río, 'Sobre la aparición del trabajo libre asalariado . . .', in Elsa Cecilia Frost, Michael C. Meyer and Josefina Zovaida Vázquez, eds, *El trabajo y los trabajadores en la historia de México*, Mexico City, El Colegio de México, 1979, pp. 92–111; on the mines: *Descripción del arzobispado*, *passim*; Zavala and Castelo, 1980, I and II; AGN, *Civil*, vol. 241, fo. 93r°; on the *obrajes*: Salvucci, 1987; AGI, *Audiencia de México*, 20, 21, 26; Israel, 1975, p. 20; for the *haciendas*: John M. Tutino, 'Provincial Spaniards, Indian Towns, and Haciendas: Interrelated Agrarian Sectors in the Valleys of Mexico and Toluca, 1750–1810', in Altman and Lockhart, 1976, pp. 177–94.

43 AGI, *Audiencia de México*, 1659, 'Ordenanza de la división de la Ciudad de México en quarteles', Mexico City, 1782, and 333, 'Informe de Fray Joseph La Barrera', Santa María la Redonda, Mexico City, 7 July 1692.

44 On the city: Gibson, 1964, p. 391; AGN, *Indios*, vol. 32; AGI, *Audiencia de México*, 2712 (1753), 332 (1670), 333 (1692), 872, 1656 (1746), 75 (1638), 766 (1658); AGN, *Bienes nacionales*, leg. 223, exp. 86; Taylor, 1979, pp. 35–57.

45 We are thinking of the analysis of popular environments by Richard Hoggart, in *The Uses of Literacy*, London, Chatto & Windus, 1957.

46 AGI, *Audiencia de México*, 2329 (1778), 872, 559, 2333; Pérez, *Farol indiano*, *passim*, and Pérez de Velasco, *El ayudante de cura instruido*, pp. 68, 87; Taylor, 1979, p. 154.

Glossary

acasillado (Spanish): Indian worker settled on the land of a *hacienda*:

achcautin, achcauhtli (Nahuatl): elder brother, leader of youths, high priest

agave: plant of the genus *Agave*, such as the American aloe, with rosettes of narrow spiny leaves and tall inflorescences

alcalde mayor (Spanish): official of the Crown charged with civil government in his jurisdiction (*alcaldía mayor*)

alguacil (Spanish): minor agent of Crown justice

alguacil mayor (Spanish): official of Crown justice reporting to an *alcalde mayor*

alguacil de doctrina (Spanish): Indian official in charge of the parish

altepe-amatl (Nahuatl): from *altepetl*, community, and *amatl*, book

altiplano (Spanish): highland

alumbrados (Spanish): the *illuminati*, prosecuted by the Inquisition in seventeenth-century Spain

amate (Spanish): from Nahua *amatl* – species of ficus whose fibre was used in the manufacture of paper

asentista (Spanish): one who received the right to collect a tax in exchange for the payment of a sum of money to the Crown

atl (Nahuatl): water, liquid

atole from *atolli* (Nahuatl): drink made from cornflour

Audiencia (Spanish): court of law and administrative body for New Spain, located in Mexico City

auto sacramental (Spanish): mystery play, religious drama

barrio (Spanish): territorial subdivision of the *pueblo*

beato (Spanish): very devout man

blasón (Spanish): coat of arms; honour, glory

cabecera (Spanish): principal town of a parish

cabildo (Spanish): town council

cacique: word of Caribbean origin used as a title by the indigenous nobles of Spanish America

calmecac (Nahuatl): prehispanic school intended for nobles

calpanero (Spanish from Nahuatl): Indian worker settled on the land of a *hacienda calpulli* (Nahuatl): territorial unit based on kinship reinforced by bonds of reciprocity, solidarity and common economic activities

calpulteotl (Nahua): god of the *calpulli*

camote (Nahuatl): sweet potato

cantor (Spanish): Indian official in charge of liturgy and catechism

cargo (Spanish): responsibility of office; hierarchy of civic and religious offices

carta de concierto (Spanish): contract or agreement concluded between two parties

carta de venta (Spanish): deed of sale

cartouche (French): an oval panel or imitation scroll often containing an inscription

cédula real (Spanish): royal order

coa (Nahuatl?): hoe

cocoliztli (Nahuatl): illness, disease

cofradía (Spanish): parish confraternity dedicated to the cult of one or more saints

compadres (Spanish): persons bound by ritual ties of kinship, e.g. a godparent and the father of his godson

conformidad (Spanish): consent, approval

conjurador de nubes (Spanish): sorcerer acting on clouds and rain

copal (Nahuatl): incense made from a *copalli* tree

corral (Spanish): corral, pen or enclosure for cattle or horses

corregidor (Spanish): official with powers similar to those of the *alcalde mayor*

cuadrilla (Spanish): team, gang

cuicatl (Nahuatl): song

curandero (Spanish): healer

diphrasism: linguistic device in which two complementary nouns, whether synonyms or antonyms, are juxtaposed to express a single concept

doctrina (Spanish): Indian parish administered by regular clergy; also catechism classes

encomendero (Spanish): holder of an Indian *pueblo* or series of *pueblos* (*encomienda*) from which he collects tribute

escribano, escribano de república (Spanish): town clerk or secretary

estancia (Spanish): cattle ranch

falsos cronicones (Spanish): short chronicles written in the seventeenth century, whose contents were false or for the most part invented

fiscal, fiscal mayor (Spanish): Indian charged with monitoring the religious duties of the community

fundadores del pueblo (Spanish): founders of the town

gañan (Spanish): farmhand

gentility: from biblical gentile, heathenism, paganism

guardapapeles (Spanish): keepers of paper

hacendado (Spanish): owner of a *hacienda*

hacienda (Spanish): large landed estate devoted to grain production and ranching

henequén (Maya): fibre used for rope; the plant (a Mexican agave) producing the fibre

hermandad (Spanish): brotherhood

hidalgo (Spanish): noble

hierophany: apparition of a saint or a divine entity

huacal (Nahuatl): wooden crate or hamper

huehuehtlahtolli (Nahuatl): ancient word, speech of an elder, embodying moral teachings

huipil (Nahuatl): long garment shaped like a blouse worn by Indian women

icpalli (Nahuatl): seat, specifically seat for persons of authority; hence, a person of authority

ideolect: network of stable and coherent meanings, capable of organizing and integrating new data

ihíyotl (Nahuatl): breath of life

ilhuicatl (Nahuatl): heaven, sky

imaginaire: not to be confused with the imaginary or with the imagination, the *imaginaire* is the ability to represent the real to oneself, to perceive it intuitively and affectively, and to interpret it intellectually by generating what each culture considers to be 'the' reality, although it is actually only 'its' reality. This faculty, the schemata that organize it and the representations that flow from it make up the *imaginaire*

interrogatorio (Spanish): formal interrogation

ixiptla (Nahuatl): bark, skin, envelope; representative, delegate

ladino (Spanish): Spanish-speaking Indian, accustomed to the lifestyle of Europeans

librillo (Spanish): booklet, small book

lienzo (Spanish): painting, canvas

macehual (Nahuatl): plebeian

maestro de pintores (Spanish): master of the Indian painters in Mexico City

Mariophany: apparition of the Blessed Virgin Mary

matlalçagua or *matlalzahuatl* (Nahuatl): green pox

matlaltotonque (Nahuatl): medicinal plant used against pleurisy

mayordomía (Spanish): informal brotherhood administered by a *mayordomo*

mayordomo (Spanish): custodian, officer of the *cofradía*

memoria probanza (Spanish): report intended as proof of rights before the Spanish authorities

merced (Spanish): royal or viceregal grant

merino (Spanish): town official

mestizo (Spanish): person of mixed European and Indian ancestry

metl (Nahuatl): maguey, a type of agave plant

mezcal (from Nahuatl): mescal, liquor obtained from maguey

Mictlan (Nahuatl): the realm of the dead

milpa (Nahuatl): maize field

monte (Spanish): mountain, woodland, country

moreno (Spanish): a kind of mulatto

morisco (Spanish): In Spain, Moors converted to Christianity. In America, a kind of mulatto

naboría (Caribbean): free Indian bound to sell his labour

Nahualism: body of beliefs according to which Indians, or *Nahuales*, can take various forms to attack their victims

nahuatlato (Nahuatl): interpreter

nescuitil or *neixcuitili* (Nahuatl): example, model, pattern; Indian drama in colonial Mexico

nochtli (Nahuatl): fruit of the prickly pear cactus

obraje (Spanish): workshop

ocote (Nahuatl): resinous pine used for torches

ololiuhqui (Nahuatl): hallucinogen identified with various plants: *Ipomoea sidaefolia, Rivea corymbosa, Datura metaloïdes*

pantli (Nahuatl): flag, banner

parcialidad (Spanish): ward or subdivision of town (*barrio*); also town annexed to another town

pardo (Spanish): kind of mulatto

partido (Spanish): district

patio (Spanish): courtyard of a house or sanctuary

patronato (Spanish): patronage, privilege granted by the Holy See to the king of Spain, giving him direct control of the Church throughout his kingdom and possessions

peyotl or *peyote* (Nahuatl): hallucinogen from the cactus *Lophophora williamsii*

pilli (Nahuatl): member of the nobility

pintura (Spanish): painting

pipil (pl. *pipiltin*) (Nahuatl): noble

pipiltzintzintli (Nahuatl): literally the 'Most Noble Child', an unidentified hallucinogen

poblador (Spanish): colonist, settler

posesión (Spanish): the act of taking possession of something

principal (Spanish): Indian notable

prioste (Spanish): official in charge of a brotherhood or a confraternity

provisor (Spanish): ecclesiastical head of the tribunals of the bishopric or archbishopric

provisorato (Spanish): tribunal of the bishopric or archbishopric

pueblo (Spanish): the village, the community and its territory

pulque (Caribbean): a drink made from the fermented juice of the agave

pulquería (Spanish): a *pulque* bar

quetzal (Nahuatl): bird, a trogon with long green tail feathers, *Pharomachrus mocinno*

Quetzalcoatl: under the name of Topiltzin, priest or king of Tula, at the end of the Toltec era

real (Spanish): monetary unit, one eighth of a *peso*

regalo (Spanish): gift, present; treat

regidor (Spanish): councilman, member of the *cabildo*

regular clergy: made up of religious orders, that is, of communities that observe a rule (Franciscans, Dominicans, Augustinians, etc.)

repartimiento (Spanish): forced sale of foodstuffs to the Indians

república (Spanish): community, autonomous Indian municipality

romería (Spanish): pilgrimage

saludador (Spanish): quack, healer

santiguador (Spanish): healer using the sign of the cross in tending his patients

santo (Spanish): saint

santocalli (Nahuatl): domestic oratory

scotomization: in psychiatry, formation of mental blind spots, partial loss to the subject's consciousness of events actually experienced

secular clergy: made up of priests and parish priests placed under the direct supervision of the bishop

serranía (Spanish): mountain range, mountains

sujeto (Spanish): a subject community

tamal (Spanish): ground meat wrapped in cornmeal dough and roasted in banana leaves or corn husks

tameme from *tlameme* (Nahuatl): porter, bearer

tecolote from *tecolotl* (Nahuatl): owl

tecuhtli or *teuctli* (Nahuatl): lord, member of the high nobility

telpochcalli (Nahuatl): school for young plebeians of the period before the Spanish conquest

Tenan (Nahuatl): possibly a corruption of Tonan, Tonantzin, 'Our Mother', goddess of the earth

teotlahtolli (Nahuatl): divine word, doctrine

tepache (from Nahuatl): Mexican drink made from *pulque*, water, pineapple and cloves

tepatiani or *tepahtiani* (Nahuatl): healer, curer

tequitqui style: term used to designate indigenous art of the sixteenth century influenced by the style of the European Renaissance

Testerian (Spanish): named for the Franciscan friar Jacobo de Testera; designates the pictorial catechisms of colonial Mexico which use images to express the contents of the Christian faith

tetzahuitl (Nahuatl): wonder, miracle

teutl (Nahuatl): god

Tezcatlipoca (Nahuatl): the most important indigenous god; the creator and dispenser of riches and affliction.

ticitl (Nahuatl): healer

tira (Spanish): strip (e.g., of paper or cloth)

títulos primordiales (Spanish): titles to land, supposed to be those upon which the primordial rights of a *pueblo* were based

tlacuilo (Nahuatl): indigenous painter or writer

tlahtolli (Nahuatl): word, speech, statement, language

tlaloque (Nahuatl): rain gods

tlamacazqui (Nahuatl): priest

tlamatini (Nahuatl): wise person, sage, scholar

tlapializtli (Nahuatl): action of preserving and protecting something

tlapialli (Nahuatl): that which is kept, preserved

tlapicatzin (Nahuatl): caretaker, guardian

tlaquetzalli (Nahuatl): legend, tale

tlaquimilolli (Nahuatl): covered, surrounded

tlatocayotl or *tlahtohcayotl* (Nahuatl): kingdom, realm, rulership

Tonacateuctli (Nahuatl): god of subsistence

tonalamatl (Nahuatl): astrological, divinatory guide for the ritual calendar

tonalli (Nahuatl): life force, fate

tonalpohualli (Nahuatl): ritual 360-day calendar (literally 'count of days')

tonalpouhqui (Nahuatl): counter of fates, priest responsible for reading fates

Tonantzin from *Tonan* (Nahuatl): Our Mother

Tonatiuh (Nahuatl): the sun divinity

topil (Nahuatl): minor official in a *pueblo*

tortilla (Spanish): thin, flat maize cake

trapiche (Spanish): sugar mill

traza (Spanish): plan of a town

Triple Alliance: pact uniting the cities of México-Tenochtitlán, Texcoco and Tlacopan from the first half of the fifteenth century

tzitzimime (Nahuatl): dreadful creatures who lived in the air
venerable (Spanish): living friar with a reputation for holiness
viejos, ancianos (Spanish): old men, elders
visita (Spanish): tour of inspection; also subordinate town in a parish
visitador (Spanish): inspector
vista de ojos (Spanish): inspection of boundaries
Xiuhtecutli (Nahuatl): 'Turquoise Lord', the god of fire
zazanilli (Nahuatl): story, legend, tale

Sources

Sources and methodology

To explore the conquest of the Indian mind in Spanish Mexico and to write my doctoral thesis – and consequently to offer to the English reader this abridged version – many archives were visited. As appears below, only the most significant collections and sources have been referred to here, in the first place those of the Archivo General de la Nación of Mexico. The Mexican national archives preserve the documents produced by the principal institutions in New Spain during the colonial period, namely:

the great civil and criminal tribunals of the *Audiencia (Salas de Justicia y del Crimen)*;
the special jurisdiction reserved for the Indians, the *Juzgado General de Indios* (or *de los Naturales*);
the Inquisition;
the archbishopric of Mexico and its tribunal exclusively charged with Indian affairs, the *Provisorato de naturales*, which heard appeals in matters of concubinage, bigamy, superstition, idolatry and witchcraft;
finally, from the eighteenth century, the *Secretaría del Virreinato*, which brought together the services of the viceroy.

Several families of sources turned out to be particularly fruitful:

the proceedings of the ordinary ecclesiastical tribunal (*Provisorato*) scattered in the *Bienes nacionales, Criminal, Indiferente general* and *Clero regular y secular*;
those of the extraordinary ecclesiastical tribunal (*Inquisición*), as long as the Indians were subjected to the monastic, then episcopal Inquisition. The excellent state of preservation of the archives of the Inquisition almost makes one regret that the Indians were exempt from pursuit by the tribunal from 1571 on. There remains the often irreplaceable testimony of the Indians' accomplices or their Spanish, black or

mestizo clients who, less lucky, got into trouble with the tribunal;

cases that were taken to the *Juzgado General de Indios* (*Indios, Clero regular y secular*), which exercised its jurisdiction over the indigenous population in civil and criminal matters;

litigation about real estate (*Tierras*), property deeds, indigenous maps and the sketches that accompanied them;

indigenous wills produced in a number of variegated civil and criminal matters (*Tierras, Civil, Bienes nacionales*);

the major investigations carried out by the administration of the vice-royalty and the regional jurisdictions (*corregidores, alcaldes mayores,* intendants, *subdelegados*) of the confraternities and community properties (*Cofradías, Indios, Clero regular y secular*), etc.

The sources of the archbishopric of Mexico, which came into the AGN in the nineteenth century, are incomplete, scattered and in part still buried in the *Indiferente general*, which I explored for two years (1978–9), not without success from time to time. I was unable to consult the documents held by the archbishopric even now, still less to find and use all the archives of its court, the *provisorato*. They are of capital importance since, as we have just recalled, the Indians escaped the competence of the Inquisition and in matters of faith and marriage were judged by the *provisor de Indios* of the archbishopric (or of other dioceses). Numerous fragments reveal the astonishing richness of a source which, if it were to reappear in its entirety, could be subjected to systematic treatment, like that used on the archives of the Inquisition (Alberro, 1988).

Consolation for this disappearance or this inaccessibility is provided by the archives of two great religious orders, the Franciscans and the Jesuits. The first are divided between the National Library of Mexico and the National Museum of Anthropology and History; the second are preserved in part by the province of Mexico of the Company of Jesus, which was willing to provide access to me, and in part by the AGN in the *Misiones* and *Jesuitas* collections. I have used as a basic source the reports made by Franciscan priests or by Jesuit missionaries on the populations that they were trying to Christianize.

Ideally, one should have explored hundreds of local and parish archives (or the microfilm made by the Mormons and preserved by the AGN) and to examine those of the dioceses of Puebla, Oaxaca and Michoacán. Time was lacking. Nevertheless, the microfilm collections of the Library of the National Museum of Anthropology and History enabled me to familiarize myself with those of Puebla, Tlaxcala, Tehuacan and, for Michoacán, of the Casa de Morelos.

It goes without saying that the Mexican archives, however rich they may be, need to be completed by Spanish collections, in the first place those of Seville. Perhaps one should say substituted rather than completed, since in the course of the uprising of Mexico City of June 1692 the archives in the palace of the viceroy burned and very little remains of the criminal proceedings before the eighteenth century. But above all it is through the Archivo General de Indias that one can comprehensively encompass the history of New Spain, through the correspondence of viceroys, bishops, the *Audiencia de México*, reports (*Informes, Sumarias*) made on important affairs, whether it was a question of alarming troubles (the riots of the city of Mexico in the seventeenth century, those of the Bajío and Guanajuato in the eighteenth century), highly problematic files (the condition of the manpower in the *obrajes*, alcoholism, the secularization of the parishes, etc.) or more or less resounding trials brought before the Crown and its councils. My attention was held especially by the *Justicia, Patronato* and *Audiencia de México*. The Archivo General de Indias also preserves a part of the *Relaciones geográficas*, which I have used a good deal.

The collections of Madrid are less generous, at least from our point of view. One might cite, among other works, the *Relaciones geográficas* of the sixteenth century (Archivo Histórico Nacional), those of the eighteenth century (Biblioteca Nacional) or files on the secularization of the regular parishes (Biblioteca del Palacio Real).

Paradoxically, my research began in Rome. Paradoxically, for the privilege of *patronato* enjoyed by the Spanish Crown, which made the king a patron of the Church (and his Mexican viceroy a vice-patron) set between Rome and the Spanish empire distances that we might believe to be unbridgeable. A fortunate appointment thus let me discover archives often without equivalent in Spain and Mexico: those of the Dominicans and Augustinians, of the ex-Congregation of the *Propaganda Fide*, and the Archivio Segreto Vaticano (ASV). The decisions of the Congregation of the *Propaganda Fide* on the indigenous priesthood, the reports sent by missionaries, starting in 1622, the beatification proceedings of the Congregation of Rites (ASV), the proceedings of the chapters of the Dominican and Augustinian provinces all provided a rich harvest, of which the pages that follow will give only a very selective impression. The Archivum Historicum Societatis Jesu offered very detailed reports on the activity of the Jesuits in the creole and Indian worlds (in the famous Annual Letters or *Cartas Anuas*). Finally, in the Archivio Generale Franciscano were manuscripts of chronicles and indigenous texts of the greatest interest. Nor must one forget numerous works produced or gathered by the Apostolic Colleges of the *Propaganda Fide* (Querétaro, Guatemala, Zacatecas), of which the Franciscans had charge.

If a Roman stay is a bit unusual, the European Americanist knows, in contrast, that trips to the states of Texas and California are a necessity: for the *Relaciones geográficas* of the sixteenth century (Netty Lee Benson Library in Austin, Texas), and for the Mexican Councils (Bancroft Library, Berkeley). Many other North American collections could have and should have completed this study. The means and time once again were not available.

Libraries have marked out this progress. There again dispersal prevails. The study of the printed sources of the Biblioteca Nacional of Mexico, of the Biblioteca de la Ciudad de México, of that of the Museo Nacional de Antropología e Historia, of the Condumex Centre for Historical Studies would be incomplete without consulting the collections of the Bancroft Library in Berkeley and above all the Netty Lee Benson Library in Austin, one of the richer, if not the wealthiest collection in the world dedicated to Latin America. I was particularly concerned to go through and analyse religious works, catechisms, confession manuals, collections of sermons, and treatises intended for priests published in New Spain from the sixteenth to eighteenth centuries.

The limits marked by the sources and the perspectives opened in the introduction explain the abandonment of any serial approach. Counting marriages and baptisms furnishes indices of external conformity to a model, but says nothing about its interiorization. Nor have I used explorations based on very complete, coherent series (brotherhoods and feast days at the end of the eighteenth century), which would take us into a domain (the vision of the

Spanish administration) other than the one chosen. Indeed, I had the feeling that as the percentages accumulated they distanced me from the indigenous reality that I was seeking. Quantitative estimates could also have been based on the archives of the Church tribunals (or *provisoratos*) analogous to those produced on the basis of the archives of the Inquisition (Alberro, 1988). But only ruins have survived, whose treasures would not make up true series. However that may be, I would have come up against the same stumbling block, and been drawn along the trail of the history of the ecclesiastical repression more than that of the Indians. This in no way denies the value of those attempts which, extended to other fields – indigenous wills – and carried out prudently on the considerable sources that have been preserved, should fill out or invalidate some of my hypotheses.

This prudence or these lacunae impose an often impressionistic approach, sowed with accumulations, juxtapositions and cross-checking, which in the last resort rests only on relating data gathered from the most different sources. Thus a gigantic puzzle emerged, where more than once a piece from Seville ended up fitting between Mexican and Roman data, where a prehispanic reference enlightens a piece of colonial information of indigenous and/or Spanish origin, where the text of a chronicler makes clear the confession of an Indian. This was the pleasure of this long *giocho di pazienzia*, in the course of which the discovery of documents and often the accidents of reading played an essential role by the successive orientations and reorientations that they continuously imprinted on the original project. Such was the conjunction in 1974 of Jesuit sources and elements of ethnopsychiatry drawn from the work of Georges Devereux, and later the elucidation of an indigenous literature of unsuspected richness at the moment I was going through the already long published works dedicated by Jack Goody to literacy in traditional societies.

Cut off from quantitative reckoning, the approach led me to pursue case studies with all that this choice implies in the way of risks, but also makes it possible to approach indigenous cultures by way of individuals and not exclusively those vague (and sometimes vaguely mythical) entities: 'groups', communities, 'tribes', Indians. I am convinced that the in-depth study of an individual case, as much as the multiplication of examples, allows us to observe the making and workings of a culture, detecting the modulations that are characteristic of it, provided that one knows and is able to differentiate dialectic from personal idiosyncracies and cultural registers, registers that have been documented by other means and other sources.

Sources: printed and painted

Rather than giving an exhaustive list of sources employed, I have preferred to indicate those that proved to be the most rewarding as well as those that might in many respects extend or adjust this study. In the major works marked with an asterisk possible extensions are to be found.

1 Collections of documents

Acuña, René (ed.), *Relaciones geográficas del siglo XVI*, Mexico City, UNAM, 10 vols, 1982–8.
Actas de Cabildo de la ciudad de México, 54 vols, Mexico City, 1889–1916.

Carrasco Pizana, Pedro and Jesús Monjarás-Ruiz (eds), *Colección de documentos sobre Coyoacán*, Colección Científica, Fuentes (Historia Social): 39 and 65, 2 vols, Mexico City, INAH, 1976–8.

Cartas de Indias . . ., Madrid, Ministerio de Fomento, 1877.

Colección de documentos inéditos relativos al descubrimiento, conquista y organización de las antiguas posesiones españolas de América y Oceanía, 42 vols, Madrid, M. Bernaldo de Quirós, 1864–84.

Colección de documentos para la historia de Oaxaca, Mexico City, AGN, 1933.

Cuevas, Mariano (ed.), *Documentos inéditos del Siglo XVI para la historia de México*, Talleres del Museo Nacional de Arqueología, Historia y Etnología, 1914 (2nd edn Mexico City, Editorial Porrúa, S.A., 1975).

*Epistolario de Nueva España, 1505–1818, ed. Francisco del Paso y Troncoso, 16 vols, Mexico City, Antigua Librería de Robredo de José Porrúa e Hijos, 1939–42.

Florescano, Enrique (ed.), *Fuentes para la historia de la crisis agrícola de 1785–1786*, Documentos para la historia I, 2 vols, Mexico City, AGN, 1981.

García, Genaro (ed.), *Documentos inéditos o muy raros para la historia de México*, Mexico City, Editorial Porrúa, S.A., 1974 (1st edn Mexico City, 1905–11).

García Icazbalceta, Joaquín (ed.), *Colección de documentos inéditos para la historia de México*, 2 vols, Mexico City, Editorial Porrúa, S.A., 1971 (1st edn Mexico City, J. M. Andrade, 1858–66).

——, *Nueva colección de documentos para la historia de México*, Mexico City, Francisco Díaz de León, 1892.

Hanke, Lewis (ed.), *Cuerpo de documentos del siglo XVI*, Mexico City, FCE, 1943 (2nd edn 1977).

Konetzke, Richard (ed.), *Colección de documentos para la historia de la formación social de Hispanoamérica, 1493–1810*, 3 vols, Madrid, Centro Superior de Investigaciones Científicas, 1952–3.

Martínez, Hildeberto (ed.), *Colección de documentos coloniales de Tepeaca*, Colección Científica, Catálogos y Bibliografías: 134, Mexico City, INAH, 1984.

*Papeles de Nueva España publicados de orden y con fondos del gobierno mexicano por Francisco del Paso y Troncoso, 2nd Series, Geografía y Estadística, 7 vols, Madrid, Sucesores de Rivadeneyra, 1905–6. (The *Relaciones geográficas* have been published in a new edition by René Acuña, Mexico City, UNAM, 10 vols, 1982–8.)

*Procesos de Indios idólatras y hechiceros, AGN, Mexico City, Tip. Guerrero Hnos, 1912.

*Proceso inquisitorial del cacique de Tetzcoco, AGN, Mexico City, Eusebio Gómez de La Puente, 1910.

Reyes García, Luis (ed.), *Documentos sobre tierras y señoríos en Cuauhtinchan*, Colección Científica, Fuentes (Historia Social): 57, Mexico City, INAH, 1978.

Velázquez, Primo Feliciano (ed.), *Colección de documentos para la historia de San Luis Potosí*, 4 vols, San Luis Potosí, 1897–9.

*Zavala, Silvio, and María Castelo (eds), Fuentes para la historia del trabajo en Nueva España, 8 vols, Mexico City, FCE, 1939–46 (2nd edn Mexico City, Centro de Estudios Históricos del Movimiento Obrero Mexicano, 1980).

2 Ecclesiastical sources

For works published in New Spain in the sixteenth century, the *Bibliografía mexicana del siglo XVI* (Mexico City, FCE, 1981) of Joaquín García Icazbalceta remains a precious working tool.

Acosta SJ, José de, *Historia natural y moral de las indias*, ed. Edmundo O'Gorman, Mexico City, FCE, 1940.

Aguilar, Francisco de, *Relación breve de la conquista de la Nueva España*, ed. Jorge Gurría Lacroix, Mexico City, UNAM, 1977.

Alegre SJ, Francisco J., *Historia de la Compañía de Jesús en Nueva España*, 3 vols Mexico City, 1941, and Rome, Institutum Historicum SJ, 1956.

Anglería, Pedro Mártir de, *Décadas del Nuevo Mundo*, 2 vols, Mexico City, José Porrúa e Hijos, 1964–5.

*Balsalobre, Gonzalo de, 'Relación auténtica de las idolatrías...' (1656) in *Tratado de las idolatrías, supersticiones, ritos, hechicerías y otras costumbres gentílicas de las razas aborígenes de México*, vol. XX, Mexico City, Ediciones Fuente Cultural, 1953, pp. 339–90.

Basalenque OSA, Diego, *Historia de la provincia de San Nicolás Tolentino de Michoacán de la Orden de N. P. San Agustín*, Mexico City, Barbedillo y Comp., 1886, and Mexico City, Editorial Jus, S.A., 1963.

Bautista, Juan, *Confessionario en lengua mexicana y castellana*, Mexico City, Melchior Ocharte, 1599.

——, *Advertencias para los confesores de los naturales...*, Mexico City, Melchior Ocharte, 1600.

——, *Sermonario en lengua mexicana*, Mexico City, López Dávalos, 1606–7.

Beaumont, Pablo de la Purísima Concepción, *Crónica de Michoacán*, Mexico City, Talleres Gráficos de la Nación, 1932.

*Burgoa, Francisco de, *Geográfica descripción*, 2 vols, Mexico City, AGN, 1934.

——, *Palestra historial*, 2 vols, Mexico City, AGN, 1934.

Cartas de religiosos de Nueva España, cf. above, García Icazbalceta, *Nueva colección...*, and Mexico City, Editorial Salvador Chávez Hayhoe, 1941.

Ciudad Real, Antonio de, *Tratado curioso y docto de las grandezas de la Nueva España*, eds Josefina García Quintana and Victor M. Castillo Ferreras, Serie de historiadores y cronistas de Indias: 6, 2 vols, Mexico City, Instituto de Investigaciones Históricas, 1976.

Clavijero, Francisco Javier, *Historia antigua de México*, Prologue by Mariano Cuevas, Mexico City, Editorial Porrúa, S.A., 1976.

Códice Franciscano. Siglo XVI, cf. above, García Icazbalceta, *Nueva Colección...*, and Mexico City, Editorial Salvador Chávez Hayhoe, 1941.

Concilios provinciales Primero y Segundo..., Mexico City, Superior Gobierno, 1769.

Dávila Padilla, Agustín, *Historia de la fundación y discurso de la provincia de Santiago de México de la Orden de predicadores por las vidas de sus varones insignes y casos notables de Nueva España*, Brussels, 1625 (new edn Mexico City, La Academia literaria, 1955).

Descripción del arzobispado de México hecha en 1570 y otros documentos, ed. Luis García Pimentel, Mexico City, José Joaquín Terrazas, 1897 (new edn Guadalajara, Edmundo Aviña Levy, 1976).

*Durán, Diego, *Historia de las Indias de Nueva España e Islas de la tierra firme*, ed. Angel María Garibay, 2 vols, Mexico City, Editorial Porrúa, S.A., 1967.

Escobar, Fray Matías de, *Americana Thebaida*, Mexico City, Imprenta Victoria, 1924.

Espinosa, Isidro Félix de, *Crónica de los Colegios de Propaganda Fide de la Nueva España*, Mexico City, José Bernardo de Hogal, 1746 (2nd edn Washington, Academy of Franciscan History, 1964).

——, *Crónica de la provincia franciscana de los apóstoles San Pedro y San Pablo de Michoacán*, Mexico City, Editorial Santiago, 1945.

Florencia, Francisco de, *Historia de la provincia de la Compañía de Jesús de Nueva España*, Mexico City, Editorial Academia literaria, 2nd edn, 1955.

Gante, Pedro de, *Doctrina cristiana en lengua mexicana*, facsimile of 1553 edition, Mexico City, Centro de Estudios Históricos Fray Bernardino de Sahagún, 1981.

García Pimentel, Luis (ed.), *Relación de los obispados de Tlaxcala, Michoacán, Oaxaca y otros lugares en el siglo XVI*, Mexico City, Casa del Editor, Paris, A. Donnamette, Madrid, Gabriel Sánchez, 1904.

González Dávila, Gil, *Teatro eclesiástico de la primitiva iglesia de las Indias occidentales, vidas de sus arzobispos, obispos y cosas memorables de sus sedes . . .*, 2 vols, Madrid, 1649–55 (2nd edn Madrid, Porrúa, 1959).

Grijalva, Juan de, *Crónica de la orden de N.P.S. Agustín en las provincias de la Nueva España en quatro edades desde el año de 1533 hasta el de 1592*, Mexico City, 1624 (2nd edn, ed. Nicolás León, Mexico City, 1926).

La Anunciación, Juan de, *Doctrina christiana muy cumplida a donde se contiene la exposición . . .*, Mexico City, Pedro Balli, 1575.

La Cruz y Moya, Juan de, *Historia de la santa y apostólica provincia de Santiago de predicadores de México en la Nueva España*, 2 vols, Mexico City, 1954–5.

*La Peña Montenegro, Alonso de, *Itinerario para párrocos de indios . . .*, Madrid, Pedro Marín, 1771.

La Rea, Alonso de, *Crónica de la orden de N. Seráfico P. S. Francisco . . .*, Mexico City, Viuda de Bernardo Calderón, 1643 (2nd edn J. R. Barbedillo y Cía, 1882).

*La Serna, Jacinto, 'Manual de ministros de indios para el conocimiento de sus idolatrías y extirpación de ellas', in *Tratado de las idolatrías, supersticiones, ritos, hechicerías y otras costumbres gentílicas de las razas aborígenes de México*, vol. X, Mexico City, Ediciones Fuente Cultural, 1953, pp. 41–368.

*Las Casas, Bartolomé de, *Apologética historia sumaria*, ed. Edmundo O'Gorman, Serie de historiadores y cronistas de Indias: 1, 2 vols, Mexico City, UNAM, Instituto de Investigaciones Históricas, 1967.

León, Martín de, *Camino al cielo en lengua mexicana con todos los requisitos necessarios . . .*, Mexico City, Diego López Dávalos, 1611.

Lorra Baquio, Francisco, *Manual mexicano de la administración de los santos sacramentos*, Mexico City, Diego Guttierez, 1634.

Martínez de Araujo, Juan, *Manual de administrar los santos sacramentos en el idioma de Michoacán*, Mexico City, María de Benavides, 1690.

*Mendieta, Gerónimo de, *Historia eclesiástica indiana*, 4 vols, Mexico City, Editorial Salvador Chávez Hayhoe, 1945.

Mijangos, Joan de, *Espejo divino en lengua mexicana en que pueden verse los padres y tomar documento para acertar a doctrinar bien a sus hijos y aficionallos a las virtudes*, Mexico City, Diego López Dávalos, 1607.

Molina, Alonso de, *Confesionario mayor en lengua mexicana y castellana* (1565), Mexico City, Antonio de Espinosa, 1569.

*Motolinía, Toribio de Benavente de, *Memoriales o Libro de las cosas de la

Nueva España y de los naturales de ella, ed. Edmundo O'Gorman, Serie de historiadores y cronistas de Indias: 2, Mexico City, UNAM, Instituto de Investigaciones Históricas, 1971.

Navarro y Noriego, Fernando, *Catálogo de los curatos y misiones que tiene la Nueva España en cada una de sus diócesis o sea la división eclesiástica de este reyna . . .*, Mexico City, 1813.

Palafox y Mendoza, Juan de, *Virtudes del indio*, Madrid, Imprenta de M. de los Ríos, 1893.

*Pérez, Manuel, *Farol indiano y guía de curas de indios . . .*, Mexico City, Francisco de Rivera Calderón, 1713.

*Pérez de Velasco, Andrés Miguel, *El ayudante de cura instruido . . .*, Puebla, Colegio Real do San Ignacio, 1766.

——, *El pretendiente de curato instruido*, Puebla, Colegio Real de San Ignacio, 1768.

*Ponce de León, Pedro, 'Breve relación de los dioses y ritos de la gentilidad . . .' in *Tratado de las idolatrías, supersticiones, ritos, hechicerías y otras costumbres gentílicas de las razas aborígenes de México*, vol. X, Mexico City, Ediciones Fuente Cultural, 1953, pp. 369–80 (English edn: J. Richard Andrews and Ross Hassig, eds, *Treatise on the Heathen Institutions that Today Live Among the Indians Native to this New Spain (1629)*, Norman, University of Oklahoma Press, 1984, pp. 211–18).

Relación de las ceremonias y ritos y población y gobierno de los indios de la provincia de Michoacán (1541), eds José Tudela and José Corona Núñez, Morelia, Blasal Editores, 1977.

Relación de los obispados de Tlaxcala, Michoacán, Oaxaca y otros lugares en el siglo XVI, ed. Luis García Pimentel, Mexico City, Casa del Editor, Paris, A. Donnamette, Madrid, Gabriel Sánchez, 1904.

*Ruiz de Alarcón, Hernando, 'Tratado de las supersticiones y costumbres gentílicas que hoy viven entre los indios . . .' (1629), in *Tratado de las idolatrías, supersticiones, ritos, hechicerías y otras costumbres gentílicas de las razas aborígenes de México*, vol. XX, Mexico City, Ediciones Fuente Cultural, 1953, pp. 17–180 (English edns: Michael D. Coe and Gordon Whittaker, eds, *Aztec Sorcerers in Seventeenth Century Mexico. The Treatise on Superstitions*, Albany, State University of New York, 1982; J. Richard Andrews and Ross Hassig, eds, *Treatise on the Heathen Superstitions that Today Live Among the Indians Native to this New Spain (1629)*, Norman, University of Oklahoma Press, 1984).

Sahagún, Bernardino de, *Coloquios y Doctrina cristiana*, ed. Miguel León-Portilla, Mexico City, UNAM and Fundación de Investigaciones Sociales, A.C., 1986.

*——, *Historia general de las cosas de Nueva España*, ed. Angel María Garibay K., 4 vols, Mexico City, Editorial Porrúa, S.A., 1977 (1st edn Mexico City, 1956).

——, *'Primeros memoriales' de Fray Bernardino de Sahagún*, ed. and trans. by Wigberto Jiménez Moreno, Mexico City, INAH, Colección Científica, 1974.

Serra, Angel, *Manual de administrar los santos sacramentos*, Mexico City, Joseph Bernardo de Hogal, 1697.

*Torquemada, Juan de, *Monarquía indiana*, ed. Miguel León-Portilla, Serie de historiadores y cronistas de Indias: 5, 7 vols, Mexico City, UNAM, Instituto de Investigaciones Históricas, 1975–83.

Vázquez de Espinosa, Fray Antonio, *Descripción de la Nueva España en el siglo*

XVII ... y otros documentos del siglo XVII, Mexico City, Editorial Patria S.A., 1944.

Velázquez de Cárdenas y León, Carlos Celedonio, *Breve práctica y régimen del confessionario de indios ...*, Mexico City, Imprenta de la Biblioteca Mexicana, 1761.

Vetancurt, Agustín de, *Teatro mexicano. Descripción breve de los sucesos exemplares, históricos, políticos, militares y religiosos del nuevo mundo occidental de las Indias*, Mexico City, María de Benavides, 1697.

*Villavicencio, Diego Jaymes Ricardo, *Luz y método de confesar idólatras y destierro de idolatrías ...*, Puebla, Diego Fernández de León, 1692.

Zumárraga, Juan de, *Doctrina breve muy provechosa de las cosas que pertenecen a la fe católica*, Tenochtitlán-México, Juan Cromberger, 1544.

3 Civil sources

The compilation by Beristain y Souza remains a useful introduction, despite its lacunae and errors.

Beristain y Souza, José Mariano, *Biblioteca hispanoamericana septentrional*, Amecameca, Oficina de don Alejandro Valdés, 1883 (3rd edn Mexico City, Ediciones Fuente Cultural, 1947).

Cervantés de Salazar, *Crónica de la Nueva España*, Madrid, Hauser & Menet, 1914, and Mexico City, Editorial Porrúa, S.A., 1985.

*Cortés, Hernán, *Cartas y documentos*, Introduction by Mario Hernández Sánchez-Barba, Mexico City, Editorial Porrúa, S.A., 1963.

*Diaz del Castillo, Bernal, *Historia verdadera de la conquista de Nueva España* (reprint of 1944 edn with introduction and notes by Joaquín Ramírez Cabañas), 2 vols, Mexico City, Editorial Porrúa, S.A., 1968.

Díez de la Calle, Juan, *Memorial y noticias sacras y reales del imperio de las Indias occidentales al muy católico, piadoso y poderoso señor Rey de las Españas y Nuevo Mundo, D. Felipe IV ...*, Madrid, 1646 (Mexico City, 1932).

Dorantes de Carranza, Baltasar, *Sumaria relación de las cosas de la Nueva España con noticia individual de los descendientes legítimos de los conquistadores y primeros pobladores españoles*, Mexico City, Imprenta del Museo Nacional, 1902 (reprint Mexico City, Jesús Medina Editor, 1970).

Gage, Thomas, *The English-American: A New Survey of the West Indies, 1648*, London, A. P. Newton, 1928.

Gómez de Cervantes, Gonzalo, *La vida económica y social de la Nueva España en el siglo XVI*, Biblioteca histórica mexicana de obras inéditas: 19, Mexico City, Editorial Porrúa, S.A., 1944.

Guijo, Gregorio M. de, *Diario 1648–1664*, 2 vols, Mexico City, Editorial Porrúa, S.A., 1953.

Gemelli Careri, Giovanni Francesco, *Viaje a la Nueva España*, Mexico City, UNAM, Instituto de Investigaciones Históricas, 1976.

Herrera, Antonio de, *Historia general de los hechos de los castellanos en las islas y Tierra-Firme de el mar Oceano*, Asunción, Editorial Guaranía, 1945.

Humboldt, Alexandre de, *Ensayo político sobre el reino de la Nueva España*, Mexico City, Editorial Porrúa, S.A., 1966.

El Libro de las tasaciones de pueblos de la Nueva España. Siglo XVI, Prologue by Francisco González de Cossío, Mexico City, AGN, 1952.

López de Velasco, Juan, *Geografía y descripción universal de las Indias recopiladas por el cosmógrafo-cronista Juan López de Velasco desde el año de 1571 al de 1574...*, Madrid, Boletín de la Sociedad de geografía, 1894.

López de Villaseñor, Pedro, *Cartilla vieja de la nobilísima ciudad de Puebla*, Mexico City, Instituto de Investigaciones Estéticas, Imprenta Universitaria, 1961.

Relación de méritos y servicios del conquistador Bernardino Vázquez de Tapia..., Study and notes by Jorge Gurría Lacroix, Mexico City, UNAM, 1972.

Robles, Antonio de, *Diario de sucesos notables (1665–1703)*, 2 vols, Mexico City, Editorial Porrúa, S.A., 1946.

Solís, Antonio, *Historia de la conquista de Méjico*, Buenos Aires, Emecé, 1944.

Villaseñor y Sánchez, José Antonio, *Theatro americano. Descripción general de los reynos y provincias de la Nueva España y sus jurisdicciones...*, 2 vols, Mexico City, Viuda de don José Bernardo de Hogal, 1746–8 and Editorial Nacional, 1952.

——, *Suplemento al Theatro americano (La ciudad de México en 1755)*, Mexico City, UNAM, 1980.

Zorita, Alonso de, *Breve relación de los señores de la Nueva España*, Mexico City, Editorial Salvador Chávez Hayhoe, n.d., and UNAM, 1942.

4 Judicial sources

Aguiar y Acuña, Rodrigo, *Sumario de la recopilación general de las leyes*, Mexico City, 1677.

Alvarez, José María, *Instituciones de derecho real de Castilla y de Indias*, Preliminary study... by Jorge Mario García Laguardia y María del Refugio González, Serie A, Fuentes, 2 vols, Mexico City, UNAM, Instituto de Investigaciones Jurídicas, 1982 (1st edn 1818–20).

Barrio Lorenzot, Francisco del, *Ordenanzas de gremios de la Nueva España*, Mexico City, Secretaría de Gobernación, 1920.

Beleña, Eusebio Bentura, *Recopilación sumaria de todos los autos acordados de la Real Audiencia y Sala del Crimen de esta Nueva España*, 2 vols, Mexico City, Felipe de Zúñiga y Ontiveros, 1787 (1st facsimile edn with prologue by María del Refugio González, Mexico City, UNAM, Instituto de Investigaciones Jurídicas, 1981).

Carreño, Alberto María, *Cedulario de los siglos XVI y XVII...*, Mexico City, Ediciones Victoria, 1947.

Concilio III Provincial Mexicano celebrado en México el año de 1585..., publicado por Mariano Galvan Rivera, Mexico City, Eugenio Maillefert y Compañía, 1859.

Encinas, Diego de, *Cedulario indiano*, Madrid, Cultura Hispánica, 1946.

Ordenanzas de minería y colección de las ordenes y decretos de esta materia, Mexico City, J. de Rosa, 1846.

Palacios, Prudencio Antonio de, *Notas a la recopilación de leyes de Indias*, Study, ed. and indices by Beatriz Bernal de Bugeda, Mexico City, UNAM, 1979.

Puga, Vasco de, *Provisiones, Cédulas, Instrucciones de su Magestad...*, Mexico City, 1563 (Colección de incunables americanos, vol. III, Madrid, Cultura Hispánica, 1945).

Recopilación de leyes de los reynos de las Indias, Madrid, Bartholomé Ulloa, 1774, 1791, and 3 vols, Madrid, 1943.

Rodríguez de San Miguel, Juan N., *Pandectas hispano-americanas*, Introduction by María del Refugio González, Serie A, Fuentes, 3 vols, Mexico City, UNAM, Instituto de Investigaciones Jurídicas, 1980 (1st edn Mexico City, 1839).

Solórzano Pereira, Juan, *Política Indiana*, Antwerp, Henrico & Cornelio Verdussen, 1703 (new edn 2 vols, Mexico City, Secretaría de Programación y Presupuesto, 1979).

Vera, Fortino Hipólito, *Colección de documentos eclesiásticos de México, o sea antigua y moderna legislación de la Iglesia mexicana*, 3 vols, Amecameca, Imprenta del Colegio Católico, 1887.

5 Linguistic sources

A general introduction will be found in:

Handbook of Middle American Indians. Linguistics, vol. 5, General Editor, Norman A. McQuown, Austin, University of Texas Press, 1967.

A still unsurpassed working tool for Nahuatl:

Siméon, Rémi, *Dictionnaire de la langue nahuatl ou mexicaine*, Paris, Imprimerie nationale, 1885 (reprint Graz, 1963).

Also the bibliography drawn up by:

León-Portilla, Ascención H. de 'Bibliografía . . .' in *Estudios de Cultura Náhuatl*, Mexico City, UNAM, X, 1972, pp. 409–41.

Alvarado, Francisco de, *Vocabulario en lengua misteca*, Mexico City, Pedro Balli, 1593.

Arenas, Pedro, *Vocabulario manual de las lenguas castellana y mexicana . . .*, Mexico City, Henrico Martínez, 1611.

Basalenque, Diego, *Arte de la lengua matlaltzinca*, ed. L. Manrique C., Mexico City, Biblioteca Enciclopédica del Estado de México, 1975.

——, *Arte de la lengua tarasca*, Mexico City, Francisco Rivera Calderón, 1714.

Córdova, Juan de, *Arte en lengua zapoteca*, Mexico City (ed. Pedro Ocharte), 1571; (ed. Pedro Balli), 1578 and Morelia, Imprenta del Gobierno, 1886 (Facsimile of latter, Mexico City, INAH, Ediciones Toledo, 1987).

Cortés y Zedeño, Gerónimo Thomás de Aquino, *Arte, vocabulario y confesionario en el idioma mexicano . . .*, Puebla, Colegio Real de San Ignacio, 1765.

Gilberti, Maturino, *Arte de la lengua de Mechoacán*, Mexico City, Juan Pablos, 1558.

——, *Vocabulario en lengua de Mechoacán*, Mexico City, Juan Pablos, 1559.

La Barreda, Nicolás de, *Doctrina christiana en lengua chinanteca*, Mexico City, 1730.

Lagunas, Juan Baptista de, *Arte y diccionario con otras obras en lengua de Mechoacán*, Mexico City, Pedro Balli, 1574.

*Molina, Alonso de, *Vocabulario en lengua mexicana y castellana . . . (1571) Mexico City, Editorial Porrúa, S.A., 1977.

——, *Arte de la lengua mexicana y castellana*, Mexico City, Pedro Ocharte, 1571.

Nágera y Angas, Diego de, *Doctrina y enseñanza de la lengua mazahua...*, Mexico City, Juan Ruyz, 1637.

Olmos, Andrés de, *Arte para aprender la lengua mexicana*, ed. Rémi Siméon, Paris, 1875.

Paredes, Ignacio de, *Compendio del arte de la lengua mexicana...*, Mexico City, Imprenta de la Biblioteca mexicana, 1759.

Quintana, Agustín de, *Arte de la lengua mixe...*, Puebla, 1729.

——, *Confessionario en lengua mixe...*, Puebla, Viuda de Miguel de Ortega, 1733.

Tapia Zenteno, Carlos de, *Noticia de la lengua huasteca...*, Mexico City, Imprenta de la Bioblioteca mexicana, 1767.

Vázquez Gastelu, Antonio, *Arte de la lengua mexicana*, Puebla, Diego Fernández de León, 1689.

Vetancurt, Agustín de, *Arte de la lengua mexicana...*, Mexico City, Francisco Rodríguez Lupercio, 1673.

6 *Indigenous sources and* mestizo *manuscripts*

A general overview of these sources in:
Handbook of Middle American Indians. Guide to Ethnohistorical Sources. Part Four, vol. 15, ed. Howard F. Cline, Austin, University of Texas Press, 1975.

Alva Ixtlilxóchitl, Fernando de, *Obras históricas*, ed. Edmundo O'Gorman, Serie de historiadores y cronistas de Indias: 4, 2 vols. Mexico City, UNAM, Instituto de Investigaciones Históricas, 1977.

Alvarado Tezozómoc, Fernando, *Crónica mexicayotl*, trans. from Nahuatl and introd. by Adrián Léon, Mexico City, UNAM, Instituto de Historia and INAH, 1949.

——, *Crónica mexicana*, Notes by Manuel Orozco y Berra, Mexico City, Editorial Leyenda, 1944 (reprint of 1878 edn).

Anales de Tecamachalco, ed. Antonio Peñafiel, Mexico City, Coleccion de documentos para la Historia publicados por A.P., 1903 (reprint Editorial Innovación, S.A., 1981).

Anales de Tlatelolco. Unos Annales [sic] *históricos de la nación mexicana y Códice de Tlatelolco*, Robert H. Barlow, and Heinrich Berlin ed., Mexico City, Robredo, 1948 (2nd Spanish edn Mexico City, Rafael Porrúa, 1980).

Bautista, Juan, *Diario de Juan Bautista*, manuscript, Archivo Capitular de Guadalupe, Mexico City.

Castillo, Cristóbal del, *Fragmentos de la obra general sobre Historia de los mexicanos escrita en lengua náhuatl...*, ed. Francisco del Paso y Troncoso, Florence, Salvador Landi, 1908 (reprint Mexico City, Editorial Erandi, 1966; new edition, ed. Federico Navarrete Linares, Mexico City, INAH, 1991).

Chimalpahin Cuauhtlehuanitzin, Francisco de San Antón Muñón, *Die Relationen Chimalpahin's zur Geschichte Mexico's*, ed. Günter Zimmermann, Hamburg, Cran de Gruyter, 1963–5.

——, *Relaciones originales de Chalco-Amequamecan*, Paleography, introduction and notes by Silvia Rendón, Mexico City, FCE, 1965.

——, *Octava Relación*, Ed. and Spanish version by José Rubén Romero Galván, Serie de Cultura Náhuatl, Fuentes: 8, Mexico City, UNAM, Instituto de Investigaciones Históricas, 1983.

Códice Aubin. Manuscrito azteca de la Biblioteca de Berlín. Anales en mexicano ..., Mexico, 1902 (facsimile edn Mexico City, Editorial Innovación, S.A., 1980).

Códice Chimalpopoca, Anales de Cuauhtitlán y Leyenda de los Soles, trans. Primo Feliciano Velázquez, Mexico City, UNAM, Instituto de Historia, 1945.

Muñoz Camargo, Diego, *Historia de Tlaxcala*, Mexico City, Ateneo Nacional de Ciencias y Artes de México, 1947.

——, *Descripción de la ciudad y provincia de Tlaxcala de las Indias y del mar Oceana* ..., ed. René Acuña, Mexico City, UNAM, Instituto de Investigaciones Filológicas, 1981.

Pomar, Juan Bautista, 'Relación de Texcoco', ed. Joaquín García Icazbalceta, Mexico City, Francisco Díaz de León, 1892.

Ponce de León, Pedro 'Breve relación de los dioses y ritos de la gentilidad' in Angel María Garibay K., *Teogonía e historia de los mexicanos*, Mexico City, Editorial Porrúa, S.A., 1973.

7 Indigenous painted sources

A recent guide to the paintings and works about them:

Guzmán, Virginia and Yolanda Mercader M., *Bibliografía de códices, mapas y lienzos del México prehispánico y colonial*, 2 vols, Colección Científica, Fuentes para la Historia: 79, Mexico City, INAH, 1979.

A global overview in:

Handbook of Middle American Indians. Guide to Ethnohistorical Sources. Part Three, vol. 14, ed. Howard Cline, Austin, University of Texas Press, 1975.

Working tools:

Barlow, Robert Hayward and Byron MacAfee, *Diccionario de elementos fonéticos en escritura jeroglífica (Códice mendocino)*, Mexico City, UNAM, Instituto de Historia, 1949.

Benson, Elizabeth P. (ed.), *Mesoamerican Writing systems*, Washington, D.C., Dumbarton Oaks Research Library, 1973.

Galarza, Joaquín, *Estudios de escritura indígena tradicional azteca-náhuatl*, Mexico City, AGN, 1979.

Glass, John B., *Catálogo de la colección de códices*, Mexico City, Museo Nacional de Antropología, INAH, 1964.

Matos Higueras, 'Catálogo de los códices indígenas del México antiguo', Mexico City, Suplemento del *Boletín bibliográfico de la Secretaría de Hacienda*, 1957.

An important historical introduction, which is also a reflection on the early colonization:

*Robertson, Donald, *Mexican Manuscript Paintings of the Early Colonial Period, The Metropolitan Schools*, New Haven, Yale University Press, 1959.

Boban, Eugène, *Documents pour servir à l'histoire du Mexique. Catalogue raisonné de la collection de M. E. Eugène Goupil* ..., 2 vols, Paris, E. Leroux, 1891.

Codex Chavero, in Chavero, Alfredo, *Pinturas jeroglíficas. Segunda parte*, Mexico City, Imprenta del Comercio de J. E. Barbero, 1901.

Codex Cuautitlán, in Barlow, Robert H., 'El códice de los alfareros de Cuautitlán', *Revista Mexicana de Estudios Antropológicos*, XII, 1941 (1952), pp. 5–8.

Codex Magliabecchiano, CL. XIII.3 (B.R.232) Biblioteca Nazionale Centrale di Firenze, *Codices Selecti*, XXIII, ed. Ferdinand Anders, Akademische Druck-u Verlagsanstalt, Graz, 1970.

(*Codex Mendoza*) *Codex Mendocino o Colección Mendoza, Antigüedades de México* based on the collection of Lord Kingsborough, vol. I, Mexico City, Secretaría de Hacienda y Crédito Público, 1964, pp. 1–150.

——, ed. James Cooper Clark, 3 vols, London, Waterloo & Sons, 1938.

Codex Mexicanus 23–24, ed. Ernst Mengin, 'Commentaire du Codex Mexicanus de la Bibliothèque Nationale de Paris', *Journal de la Société des Américanistes*, XLI, Paris, 1952, pp. 387–498.

Codex Osuna, Mexico City, Instituto Indigenista Interamericano, 1947.

Codex Ramírez. Relación de los indios que habitan esta Nueva España según sus historias, Study and appendix by Manuel Orozco y Berra, Mexico City, Editorial Leyenda, 1944 (edn Editorial Innovación, 1979) (see above Alvarado Tezozómoc, *Cronica mexicana*).

Codex Telleriano-Remensis, Antigüedades de México, based on the collection of Lord Kingsborough, vol. I, Mexico City, Secretaría de Hacienda y Crédito Público, 1964, pp. 151–338.

Codex de Tlatelolco, in Barlow, Robert H. and Heinrich Berlin, *Anales de Tlatelolco. Unos Annales* [sic] *históricos de la nación mexicana y Códice de Tlatelolco*, Mexico City, Antigua Librería Robredo de José Porrúa e hijos, 1948 (see above, *Anales de Tlatelolco*).

Codex Vaticano Latino 3738 o Codex Vaticano-Ríos o Codex Ríos in *Antigüedades de México* based on the collection of Lord Kingsborough, vol. III, Mexico City, Secretaría de Hacienda y Crédito Público, 1964, pp. 7–314.

Codex Xolotl, ed. C. E. Dibble, Publicaciones del Instituto de Historia, Primera serie: 22, Mexico City, UNAM, 1951.

Códice Florentino, see below, Sahagún.

Códice Sierra, Fragmento de una nómina de gastos del pueblo de Santa Catarina Texupan, Mixteca Baja, ed. Nicolás León, Mexico City, Museo Nacional, 1906, and Mexico City, Museo Nacional de Arqueología, Historia y Etnografía, 1933.

Códices indígenas de algunos pueblos del Marquesado del valle de Oaxaca, Mexico City, AGN, Talleres Gráficos de la Nación, 1933.

Historia tolteca-chichimeca, with studies by Paul Kirchhoff, Lina Odena Güemes and Luis Reyes García, Mexico City, INAH-SEP, 1976.

Lienzo de Tlaxcala (El), Texts by Josefina García Quintana and Carlos Martínez Marín, Mexico City, Cartón y Papel de México, 1983.

Martín de la Cruz, *Libellus de medicinalibus Indorum herbis. Manuscrito azteca de 1552*, Mexico City, Instituto Mexicano del Seguro Social, 1964.

Sahagún, Fray Bernardino de, *Florentine Codex, General History of the Things of New Spain*, 12 vols, trans. from the Aztec into English with notes by Charles E. Dibble and Arthur J. O. Anderson, Monographs of the School of American Research, Santa Fe, University of Utah, 1950–69 (*Códice Florentino*, facsimile edn, ed. Giunti Barbéra and AGN, 3 vols, Florence, 1979).

Bibliography

The historiography of the Indian societies of New Spain is dominated by the works of G. Aguirre Beltrán and Charles Gibson. Closer to us, W. B. Taylor enlarged the field of their research; but it was Nancy M. Farriss who was able to construct a subtle, coherent and original approach to the questions posed by the indigenous societies after the conquest, in:

* Farriss, Nancy M. 1984: *Maya Society Under Colonial Rule. The Collective Enterprise of Survival*, Princeton, Princeton University Press.

The bibliography compiled by John Glass (1975: 'Annotated References' in *Handbook of Middle American Indians*, vol. 15, Austin, University of Texas Press, pp. 537–724) provides an exhaustive survey up to the beginning of the 1970s. In the same volume appears a panorama of indigenous manuscript sources. Vol. 14 of the same collection is to be consulted for the 'paintings'. With rare exceptions, we have taken account of works available when this study was written, in 1984–5.

Aguirre Beltrán, Gonzalo 1953: *Formas de gobierno indígena*, Mexico City, Imprenta Universitaria.
—— 1970: *El proceso de aculturación en México*, Mexico City, Universidad Iberoamericana.
—— 1972: *La población negra de México 1519–1810*, Mexico City, FCE (1st edn 1946).
—— 1973: *Medicina y magia. El proceso de aculturación en la estructura colonial*, Mexico City, SEP/INI.
Alberro, Solange 1988: *Inquisition et société au Mexique, 1571–1700*, Mexico City, Centre d'Etudes Mexicaines et Centraméricaines, vol. XV.
Alcina Franch, José 1979: 'Calendarios y religión entre los zapotecos serranos durante el siglo XVII', *Mesoamérica. Homenaje al Dr Paul Kirchhoff*, Mexico City, SEP/INAH, pp. 212–24.
Alpers, Svetlana 1983: 'L'oeil de l'histoire. L'effet cartographique dans la peinture hollandaise au XVIIe siècle', *Actes de la Recherche en Sciences Sociales*, 49, pp. 71–99.
Altman, Ida and James Lockhart (eds) 1976: *Provinces of Early Mexico. Variants of Spanish American Regional Evolution*, Los Angeles, UCLA.

Anderson, Arthur, Frances Berdan and James Lockhart 1976: *Beyond the Codices. The Nahua View of Colonial Mexico*, Berkeley and Los Angeles, University of California Press.

Arrom, Silvia Marina 1985: *The Women of Mexico City, 1790–1857*, Stanford, Stanford University Press.

Arróniz, Othón 1979: *Teatro de evangélización en Nueva España*, Mexico City, UNAM.

Bakewell, Peter 1971: *Silver Mining and Society in Colonial Mexico, Zacatecas 1546–1700*, Cambridge, Cambridge University Press.

Baudot, Georges 1977: *Utopie et Histoire au Mexique. Les premiers chroniqueurs de la civilisation mexicaine (1520–1569)*, Toulouse, Privat.

Bernand, Carmen and Serge Gruzinski 1988: *De l'idolatrie. Une archéologie des sciences religieuses*, Paris, Seuil.

—— 1991: *Histoire du nouveau monde. De la découverte à la conquête*, Vol. 1, *Une expérience européenne, 1492–1550*, Paris, Fayard.

Bierhost, John 1985: *Cantares mexicanos. Songs of the Aztecs*, Stanford, Stanford University Press.

Bonfil Batalla, Guillermo 1973: *Cholula la ciudad sagrada en la era industrial*, Mexico City, UNAM.

Borah, Woodrow 1943: *New Spain's Century of Depression*, Ibero-Americana, 35, Berkeley and Los Angeles, University of California Press.

—— 1985: *El juzgado general de Indios en la Nueva España*, Mexico City, FCE.

—— and Sherburne F. Cook 1960: *The Indian Population of Central Mexico, 1531–1610*, Berkeley and Los Angeles, University of California Press.

—— 1963: *The Aboriginal Population of Central Mexico on the Eve of the Spanish Conquest*, Ibero-Americana, 45, Berkeley and Los Angeles, University of California Press.

—— 1968: *The Population of the Mixteca Alta, 1520–1960*, Ibero-Americana, 50, Berkeley and Los Angeles, University of California Press.

Bourdieu, Pierre 1980: *Le sens pratique*, Paris, Editions de Minuit.

Braden, Charles S. 1930: *Religious Aspects of the Conquest of Mexico*, Durham, Duke University Press.

Brading, David 1971: *Miners and Merchants in Bourbon Mexico 1763–1810*, Cambridge, Cambridge University Press.

—— 1973: *Los orígenes del nacionalism mexicano*, Mexico City, SepSetentas, 82.

—— 1978: *Haciendas and Ranchos in the Mexican Bajío, León 1700–1860*, Cambridge, Cambridge University Press.

Calnek, Edward E. 1974: 'Conjunto urbano y modelo residencial en Tenochtitlán', *Ensayos sobre el desarrollo urbano de México*, Mexico City, SepSetentas, pp. 11–65.

—— 1982: 'Patterns of Empire Formation in the Valley of Mexico. Late Postclassic Period, 1200–1521', in G. A. Collier, R. I. Rosaldo and J. D. Wirth (eds), *The Inca and Aztec States, 1400–1800. Anthropology and History*, New York, Academic Press, pp. 43–62.

Cardona, Giorgio Raimondo 1981: *Antropologia della scrittura*, Turin, Loescher Editore.

Carrasco Pizana, Pedro 1950: *Los Otomíes, Cultura e historia prehispánicas de los pueblos mesoamericanos de habla otomiana*, Mexico City, UNAM.

—— 1961: 'The Civil-Religious Hierarchy in Mesoamerican Communities: Pre-

Spanish Background and Colonial Development', *American Anthropologist*, LXIII, pp. 483–97.
—— 1964: 'Family Structure of Sixteenth-Century Tepoztlán', in Robert Manners (ed.), *Process and Pattern in Culture: Essays in Honor of Julian H. Steward*, Chicago, University of Chicago Press, pp. 185–210.
—— 1966: 'Sobre algunos términos de parentesco en el náhuatl clásico', *Estudios de Cultura Náhuatl*, VI, pp. 149–66.
—— 1975: 'La transformación de la cultura indigena durante la colonia', *Historia Mexicana*, XXV, pp. 175–202.
—— 1976: 'The Joint Family in Ancient Mexico: The Case of Molotla', in Hugo G. Nutini, Pedro Carrasco and James M. Taggart (eds), *Essays on Mexican Kinship*, Pittsburgh, Pittsburgh University Press, pp. 45–64.
—— Johanna Broda, et al. 1976: *Estratificación social en la Mesoamérica prehispánica*, Mexico City, INAH.
Carrera Stampa, Manuel 1968: 'Relaciones geográficas de Nueva España, siglos XVI y XVIII', *Estudios de Historia Novohispana*, II, pp. 233–61.
Castillo F., Victor M. 1972: *Estructura económica de la sociedad mexica*, Mexico City, UNAM.
Castro Morales, Efraín 1969: 'El mapa de Chalchihuapan', *Estudios y documentos de la región de Puebla-Tlaxcala*, I, Puebla, pp. 5–22.
Chance, John K. 1978: *Race and Class in Colonial Oaxaca*, Stanford, Stanford University Press.
Chevalier, François 1952: *La formation des grands domaines au Mexique. Terre et société aux XVIe–XVIIIe siècles*, Paris, Institut d'Ethnologie.
Christian Jr., William A. 1980: *Local Religion in Sixteenth-Century Spain*, Princeton, Princeton University Press.
Clendinnen, Inga 1987: *Ambivalent Conquests, Maya and Spaniards in Yucatan 1517–1570*, Cambridge, Cambridge University Press.
Cline, Howard F. 1949: 'Civil Congregations of the Indians in New Spain 1598–1606', *The Hispanic American Historical Review*, XXIX, pp. 349–69.
Cook, Sherburne F. and Woodrow Borah 1971–9: *Essays in Population History*, 3 vols, Berkeley, Los Angeles, London, University of California Press.
Cuevas, Mariano 1946–7: *Historia de la Iglesia en México*, 5 vols, Mexico City, Editorial Patria S.A., 5th edition.
Dahlgren de Jordán, Barbro 1954: *La Mixteca. Su cultura e historia prehispánicas*, Mexico City, Imprenta Universitaria.
Davies, Nigel 1968: *Los señorios independientes del imperio mexica*, Mexico City, INAH.
—— 1973a: *Los mexicas: primeros pasos hacia el imperio*, Mexico City, UNAM.
—— 1973b: *The Aztecs: a History*, London, Macmillan.
—— 1980: *The Toltec Heritage: From the Fall of Tula to the Rise of Tenochtitlán*, Norman, University of Oklahoma Press.
Decorme, Gérard 1941: *La obra de los jesuitas mexicanos durante la época colonial, 1572–1767*, Mexico City.
Devereux, Georges 1971: *Essais d'ethnopsychiatrie générale*, Paris, Gallimard.
—— 1972: *Ethnopsychanalyse complémentariste*, Paris, Flammarion.
Dibble, Charles E. 1971: 'Writing in Central Mexico', *Handbook of Middle American Indians*, vol. 10, Austin, University of Texas Press, pp. 322–31.

Duverger, Christian 1978: *L'esprit du jeu chez les Aztèques*, Paris and the Hague, Mouton.

—— 1979: *La fleur létale. Economie du sacrifice aztèque*, Paris, Seuil.

—— 1983: *L'Origine des Aztèques*, Paris, Seuil.

Eco, Umberto 1978: *La estructura ausente*, Barcelona, Lumen.

Everett Boyer, Richard 1975: *La gran inundación. Vida y sociedad en la ciudad de México (1629–1638)*, Mexico City, SepSetentas, 218.

Farriss, Nancy M. 1968: *Crown and Clergy in Colonial Mexico 1759–1821: The Crisis of Ecclesiastical Privilege*, London, The Athlone Press.

Favre, Henri 1971: *Changement et continuité chez les Mayas du Mexique*, Paris, Anthropos.

Fellowes, W. H. 1977: 'The Treatises of Hernando Ruiz de Alarcón', *Tlalocan*, VII, pp. 309–55.

Fernández del Castillo, Francisco 1982: *Libros y libreros en el XVI*, Mexico City, AGN/FCE (first edn 1914).

Fernández de Recas, Guillermo S. 1961: *Cacicazgos y nobiliario indígena de la Nueva España*, Mexico City, Biblioteca Nacional.

Florescano, Enrique 1976: *Origen y desarrollo de los problemas agrarios de México*, Mexico City, Era.

—— and Isabel González Sánchez 1980: *La clase obrera en la historia de México. De la colonia al imperio*, Mexico City, Siglo XXI.

—— and Elsa Malvido 1982: *Ensayos sobre la historia de las epidemias en México*, I, Mexico City, Seguro Social.

Foster, George M. 1960: *Culture and Conquest: America's Spanish Heritage*, New York, Wenner Gren Foundation.

—— 1967a: *Tzintzuntzan. Mexican peasants in a Changing World*, Boston, Little, Brown and Company.

—— 1967b: *Etudes de sociologie de l'Art*, Paris, Denoël-Gonthier.

Frost, Elsa Cecilia, Michael C. Meyer, et al. 1979: *El trabajo y los trabajadores en la historia de México*, Mexico City, El Colegio de México.

Galarza, Joaquín 1972: *Lienzos de Chiepetlan*, Mexico City, Mission Archéologique et Ethnologique française au Mexique.

—— 1980: *Codex de Zempoala, Techialoyan E 705. Manuscrit pictographique de Zempoala, Hidalgo, Mexique*, Mexico City, Mission Archéologique et Ethnologique française au Mexique.

Galinier, Jacques 1979: *N'yuhu. Les Indiens Otomís. Hiérarchie sociale et tradition dans le sud de la Huasteca*, Mexico City, Mission Archéologique et Ethnologique française au Mexique.

Gallini, Clara 1971: *Il consumo del sacro. Feste lunghe di Sardegna*, Bari, Laterza.

García, Esteban 1918: *Crónica de la provincia augustiniana del Santísimo Nombre de Jesús de México*, Madrid, López del Horno.

García Icazbalceta, Joaquín 1947: *Don Fray Juan de Zumárraga, primer obispo y arzobispo de México*, 4 vols, Mexico City, Editorial Porrúa, S.A.

García Martínez, Bernardo 1969: *El Marquesado del Valle. Tres siglos de régimen señorial en Nueva España*, Mexico City, El Colegio de México.

Gardner, Brant 1982: 'A Structural and Semantic Analysis of Classical Nahuatl Kinship Terminology', *Estudios de Cultura Náhuatl*, XV, pp. 89–124.

Garibay, Angel M. 1971: *Historia de la literatura náhuatl*, 2 vols, Mexico City, Editorial Porrúa S.A. (first edn, 1953).

—— 1964–8: *Poesía náhuatl*, 3 vols, Mexico City, UNAM.

Geertz, Clifford 1973: *The Interpretation of Cultures*, New York, Basic Books.

Gerhard, Peter 1972: *A Guide to the Historical Geography of New Spain*, Cambridge, Cambridge University Press.

—— 1977: 'Congregaciones de indios de la Nueva España antes de 1570', *Historia mexicana*, XXVI, pp. 295–347.

Gernet, Jacques 1981: *Chine et christianisme. Action et réaction*, Paris, Gallimard.

Gibson, Charles 1952: *Tlaxcala in the Sixteenth Century*, New Haven, Yale University Press (new edn Stanford, Stanford University Press, 1967).

—— 1960: 'The Aztec Aristocracy in Colonial Mexico', *Comparative Studies in Society and History*, vol. II, 2, The Hague.

—— 1964: *The Aztecs Under Spanish Rule. A History of the Indians of the Valley of Mexico, 1519–1810*, Stanford, Stanford University Press.

—— 1975: 'A Survey of Middle American Prose Manuscripts', *Handbook of Middle American Indians*, vol. 15, Austin, University of Texas Press, pp. 311–321.

—— and John B. Glass 1975: 'A Census of Middle American Prose Manuscripts', *Handbook of Middle American Indians*, vol. 15, Austin, University of Texas Press, pp. 322–400.

Ginzburg, Carlo 1976: *Il formaggio e i vermi*, Turin, Einaudi.

Glass, John B. 1975a: 'A Survey of Native Middle American Pictorial Manuscripts', *Handbook of Middle American Indians*, vol. 14, Austin, University of Texas Press, pp. 3–80.

—— 1975b: 'A Census of Middle American Testerian Manuscripts', *Handbook of Middle American Indians*, vol. 14, Austin, University of Texas Press, pp. 281–96.

—— and D. Robertson 1975: 'A Census of Native Middle American Pictorial Manuscripts', *Handbook of Middle American Indians*, vol. 14, Austin, University of Texas Press, pp. 81–252.

Gómez Canedo, Lino 1977: *Evangelización y conquista. Experiencia franciscana en Hispanoamérica*, Mexico City, Editorial Porrúa, S.A.

—— 1982: *La educación de los marginados durante la época colonial. Escuelas y colegios para indios y mestizos en la Nueva España*, Mexico City, Editorial Porrúa, S.A.

Gómez Orozco, Federico 1983: *El mobiliario y la decoración en la Nueva España en el siglo XVI*, Mexico City, UNAM.

González Obregón, Luis 1952: *Rebeliones indígenas y precursores de la Independencia mexicana en los siglos XVI, XVII y XVIII*, Mexico City, Ediciones Fuente Cultural.

González Sánchez, Isabel 1969: *Haciendas y ranchos de Tlaxcala en 1712*, Mexico City, INAH.

Goody, Jack 1977: *The Domestication of the Savage Mind*, Cambridge, Cambridge University Press.

—— (ed.) 1968: *Literacy in Traditional Societies*, Cambridge, Cambridge University Press.

Greenberg, James B. 1981: *Santiago's Sword. Chatino Peasant Religion and Economics*, Berkeley and Los Angeles, University of California Press.

Greenleaf, Richard E. 1962: *Zumárraga and the Mexican Inquisition, 1536–1543*, Washington, D.C. Academy of American Franciscan History.

—— 1965: 'The Inquisition and the Indians of New Spain: A Study in Jurisdictional Confusion', *The Americas*, XXII, pp. 138–66.

—— 1969: *The Mexican Inquisition of the Sixteenth Century*, Albuquerque, University of New Mexico Press.

—— 1971: 'Religion in the Mexican Renaissance Colony', in *The Roman Catholic Church in Colonial Latin America*, under the direction of R. E. Greenleaf, New York, Alfred Knopf.

—— 1978: 'The Mexican Inquisition and the Indians: Sources for the Ethnohistorians', *The Americas*, XXXIV, pp. 315–44.

Gruzinski, Serge 1974: 'Délires et visions chez les Indiens du Mexique', *Mélanges de l'Ecole Française de Rome*, LXXXVI, 2, pp. 445–80.

—— 1976: 'Le passeur susceptible. Approches ethnohistoriques de la Conquête spirituelle du Mexique', *Mélanges de la Casa de Velázquez*, XII, pp. 195–217.

—— 1979: 'La mère dévorante: alcoolisme, sexualité et déculturation chez les Mexicas (1500–1550)', *Cahiers des Amériques latines*, XX, pp. 5–36.

—— 1982: 'La Conquista de Los Cuerpos. Cristianismo, alianza y sexualidad en el altiplano mexicano: Siglo XVI', *Familia y Sexualidad en Nueva España*, Mexico City, Sept. 80, pp. 177–206.

—— 1985a: 'La segunda aculturación: el estado ilustrado y la religiosidad indígena en Nueva España (1775–1800)', *Estudios de Historia Novohispana*, UNAM, VIII, pp. 175–201.

—— 1985b: 'La memoria mutilada: construcción y mecanismos de la memoria en un grupo otomí de la mitad del siglo XVII', *IIº Simposio de Historia de las Mentalidades: la Memoria y el Olvido*, Mexico City, INAH, pp. 33–46.

—— 1987: 'Colonial Indian Maps in Sixteenth-Century Mexico: An essay in mixed cartography', *Res*, 13, Cambridge, Mass., pp. 46–61.

—— 1988: 'Confesión, alianza y sexualidad entre los indios de Nueva España. Introducción al estudio de los confesionarios en lenguas indígenas', in *El afán de normar y el placer de pecar*, Mexico City, Joaquín Mortiz, pp. 169–215.

—— 1989a: *Man-Gods in the Mexican Highlands, 16th–18th centuries*, Stanford, Stanford University Press (First, French, edition, *Les Hommes-Dieux du Mexique. Pouvoir indigène et société coloniale, XVIe–XVIIIe siècles*, Paris, Archives Contemporaines, 1985).

—— 1989b: *El poder sin límites, cuatro respuestas indígenas a la dominación española*, Mexico City, INAH.

—— 1990: *La Guerre des images de Christophe Colomb à Blade Runner (1492–2019)*, Paris, Fayard.

—— 1991: *L'Amerique de la Conquête peinte par les Indiens du Mexique*. Paris, Flammarion (in English, Flammarion, 1992).

Guidieri, Remo 1984: *L'abondance des pauvres*, Paris, Seuil.

Hanke, Lewis 1976: *El prejuicio racial en el Nuevo Mundo*, Mexico City, SepSetentas, 156.

Heyden, Doris 1983: *Mitología y simbolismo de la flora en el México prehispánica*, Mexico City, UNAM.

Hinz, Eike 1970: *Die Magischen Texte in Tratado Ruiz de Alarcóns (1629)*, Hamburg, Hamburgischen Museum für Volkerkunde und Vorgeschichte.

Historia de la lectura en México, Seminario de historia de la educación en México de El Colegio de México, Mexico City, El Colegio de México–El Ermitaño, 1988.

Hobsbawm, Eric, and Terence Ranger (eds) 1983: *The Invention of Tradition*, Cambridge, Cambridge University Press.

Horcasitas, Fernando 1974: *El teatro náhuatl. Épocas novohispana y moderna, Primera parte*, Mexico City, UNAM.

Huerta Preciado, María Teresa and Patricia Palacios 1976: *Rebeliones indígenas de la época colonial*, Mexico City, INAH.

Ichon, Alain 1969: *La religion des Totonaques de la Sierra*, Paris, Centre National de la Recherche Scientifique.

Israel, J. I. 1975: *Class and Politics in Colonial Mexico, 1610–1670*, London, Oxford Historical Monographs.

Ivins Jr, W. M. 1975: *Imagen impresa y conocimiento. Análisis de la imagen fotográfica*, Barcelona, Gustavo Gili.

Jímenez Moreno, Wigberto 1958: *Estudios de historia colonial*, Mexico City.

Jímenez Rueda, Julio 1946: *Herejías y supersticiones en la Nueva España*, Mexico City, UNAM.

Karttunen, Frances and James Lockhart 1976: *Nahuatl in the Middle Years: Language Contact Phenomena in Texts of the Colonial Period*, Publications in Linguistics: 85, Berkeley, University of California Press.

—— 1980: 'La estructura de la poesía náhuatl vista por sus variantes', *Estudios de Cultura Náhuatl*, XIV, Mexico City.

Katz, Friedrich 1966: *Situación social y económica de los aztecas durante los siglos XV y XVI*, Mexico City, UNAM.

Keen, Benjamin 1971: *The Aztec Image in Western Thought*, New Brunswick, Rutgers University Press.

Klor de Alva, J. Jorge 1982: 'Spiritual Conflict and Accommodation in New Spain: Toward a Typology of Aztec Responses to Christianity', in *The Inca and Aztec States 1400–1800. History and Anthropology*, New York and London, Academic Press, pp. 345–66.

Kobayashi, José María 1974: *La educación como conquista. Empresa franciscana en México*, Mexico City, El Colegio de México.

Kubler, George 1948: *Mexican Architecture of the Sixteenth Century*, 2 vols, New Haven, Yale University Press.

La Fuente, Julio de 1977: *Yalalag. Una villa zapoteca serrana*, Mexico City, Instituto Nacional Indigenista.

La Maza, Francisco de 1981: *El guadelupanismo en México*, Mexico City, FCE (first edn, 1953).

Lanternari, Vittorio 1974: *Movimenti religiosi di libertà e di salvezza dei popoli oppressi*, Milan, Feltrinelli.

La Peña, José F. de 1983: *Oligarquía y propiedad en Nueva España 1550–1624*, Mexico City, FCE.

La Torre Villar, Ernesto de and Ramiro Navarro de Anda 1982: *Testimonios históricos guadalupanos*, Mexico City, FCE.

Lavrín, Asunción (ed.) 1989: *Sexuality and Marriage in Colonial Latin America*, Lincoln and London, University of Nebraska Press.

León Abrams Jr, H. 1970–1: 'Comentario sobre la sección colonial del Códice Telleriano-Remensis', *Anales del INAH*, Época 7a, III, pp. 139–76.

León-Portilla, Miguel 1959: *La filosofía náhuatl estudiada en sus fuentes*, Mexico City, UNAM (English trans., *Aztec Thought and Culture: A Study of the Ancient Nahuatl Mind*, trans. Jack Emory Davis, Norman, University of Oklahoma Press, 1963).

—— 1976: *Culturas en peligro*, Mexico City, Alianza Editorial.

—— (ed.) 1979: *Un catecismo náhuatl en imágenes*, Mexico City, Cartón y Papel de Mexico.

—— 1980: *Toltecayotl. Aspectos de la cultura náhuatl*, Mexico City, FCE.

—— 1983a: *Los antiguos mexicanos a través de sus crónicas y cantares*, Mexico City, FCE/SEP.

—— 1983b: 'Cuicatl y tlahtolli. Las formas de expresión en náhuatl', *Estudios de Cultura Náhuatl*, XVI, Mexico City, pp. 13–108.

Leonard, Irving 1959: *Baroque Times in Old Mexico*, Ann Arbor, University of Michigan Press.

Liehr, Reinhard 1976: *Ayuntamiento y oligarquía en Puebla 1787–1810*, 2 vols, Mexico City, SepSetentas, 242–3.

Lindekens, René 1976: *Essai de sémiotique visuelle*, Paris, Klincksieck.

Llaguno, José A. 1963: *La personalidad jurídica del indio y el III° Concilio Provincial Mexicano (1585)*, Mexico City, Editorial Porrúa, S.A.

Lockhart, James 1982: 'Views of Corporate Self and History in some Valley of Mexico Towns: Late Seventeenth and Eighteenth Centuries', in G. A. Collier, R. I. Rosaldo and J. D. Wirth (eds) *The Inca and Aztec States, 1400–1800. Anthropology and History*, New York, Academic Press, pp. 367–93.

Loera y Chávez, Margarita 1977: *Calimaya y Tepemaxalco. Tenencia y trasmisión hereditaria de la tierra en dos comunidades indígenas. Epoca colonial*, Mexico City, INAH.

López Austin, Alfredo 1966: 'Los temacpalitotique: brujos, profanadores, ladrones y violadores', *Estudios de Cultura Náhuatl*, VI, pp. 97–117.

—— 1967a: 'Terminos de nahuallatolli', *Historia Mexicana*, XVII, I.

—— 1967b: 'Cuarenta clases de magos del mundo náhuatl', *Estudios de Cultura Náhuatl*, VII, pp. 87–118.

—— 1973: *Hombre-Dios. Religión y política en el mundo náhuatl*, Mexico City, UNAM.

—— 1975: *Textos de medicina náhuatl*, Mexico City, UNAM.

—— 1980: *Cuerpo humano e ideología. Las concepciones de los antiguos nahuas*, 2 vols, Mexico City, UNAM.

López Sarrelangue, Delfina Esmeralda 1965: *La nobleza indígena de Pátzcuaro en la época virreinal*, Mexico City, UNAM, Instituto de Investigaciones Históricas.

MacAndrew, John 1965: *The Open Air Churches of Sixteenth-Century Mexico. Atrios, Posas, Open Chapels and Other Studies*, Cambridge, Cambridge University Press.

Madsen, William 1951: *The Virgin's Children. Life in an Aztec Village Today*, Urbana.

—— 1960: 'Christo-paganism, a Study in Mexican Religious Syncretism', in *Nativism and Syncretism*, New Orleans, Tulane University Press, pp. 105–79.

Martin, Norman F. 1957: *Los vagabundos en la Nueva España*, Mexico City, Editorial Jus.

Martino, Ernesto de 1972: *Sud e magia*, Milan, Feltrinelli.

Mathes, Miguel 1982: *Santa Cruz de Tlatelolco. La primera biblioteca académica de las Américas*, Mexico City, Secretaría de Relaciones Exteriores.

Medina Rubio, Arístides 1983: *La Iglesia y la producción agrícola en Puebla 1540–1795*, Mexico City, El Colegio de México.

Mignolo, Walter 1989: 'Literacy and Colonization – The New World Experience', in *1492–1992: Re/Discovering Colonial Writing*, The Prismo Institute, pp. 53–96.

Miranda, José 1965: *La función económica del encomendero en los albores del régimen colonial (Nueva España 1525–1531)*, Mexico City, UNAM.

—— 1980: *El tributo indígena en la Nueva España durante el siglo XVI*, Mexico City, El Colegio de México (1st edn 1952).

Monjarás-Ruiz, Jesús 1980: *La nobleza mexica*, Mexico City, Edicol.

Moreno, Manuel M. 1971: *La organización política y social de los Aztecas*, Mexico City, INAH.

Moreno Toscano, Alejandra (under the direction of) 1978: *Ciudad de México. Ensayo de construcción de una historia*, Mexico City, INAH.

Morin, Claude 1973: *Santa Inés Zacatelco (1646–1812). Contribución a la demografía histórica colonial*, Mexico City, INAH.

—— 1979: *Michoacán en la Nueva España del siglo XVIII*, Mexico City, FCE.

Muriel, Josefina 1956–60: *Hospitales de la Nueva España*, 2 vols, Mexico City, UNAM and Jus.

—— 1963: *Las indias caciques de Corpus Christi*, Mexico City, UNAM.

—— 1974: *Las recogimientos de mujeres*, Mexico City, UNAM.

—— 1982: *Cultura femenina novohispana*, Mexico City, UNAM.

Nutini, Hugo 1968: *San Bernardino Contla. Marriage and Family Structure in a Tlaxcalan Municipio*, Pittsburgh, Pittsburgh University Press.

—— 1980–4: *Ritual Kinship. The Structure and Historical Development of the Compadrazgo System in Rural Tlaxcala*, 2 vols, Princeton, Princeton University Press.

Nutini, Hugo, and Barry L. Isaac 1974: *Los pueblos de habla náhuatl de la región de Tlaxcala y Puebla*, Mexico City, SEP/Instituto Nacional Indigenista.

Olivera, Mercedes 1978: *Pillis y macehuales. Las formaciones sociales y los modos de producción de Tecali del siglo XII al siglo XVI*, Mexico City, Casa Chata, Centro de Investigaciones Superiores, INAH.

Padden, R. C. 1970: *The Hummingbird and the Hawk. Conquest and Sovereignty in the Valley of Mexico 1503–1541*, New York, Harper Torchbooks.

Parsons, Elsie Clews 1936: *Mitla, Town of the Souls and Other Zapoteco-speaking Pueblos of Oaxaca, Mexico*, Chicago, University of Chicago Press.

Pastor, Rodolfo, Lief Adleson et al. 1979: *Fluctuaciones económicas en Oaxaca durante el siglo XVIII*, Mexico City, El Colegio de México.

Paz, Octavio 1982: *Sor Juana Inés de la Cruz, Las trampas de la fe*, Mexico City, FCE.

Pérez Rocha, Emma 1982: *La tierra y el hombre en la villa de Tacuba durante la época colonial*, Mexico City, INAH.

Phelan, John Leddy 1956: *The Millenial Kingdom of the Franciscans in the New World*, Berkeley, University of California Press.

Piho, Virve 1981: *La secularización de las parroquías en la Nueva España y su repercusión en San Andrés Calpan*, Mexico City, INAH.

Powell, Philip Wayne 1952: *Soldiers, Indians and Silver. The Northward Advance of New Spain, 1550–1600*, Berkeley and Los Angeles, University of California Press.

Prem, Hans J. 1978: *Milpa y hacienda: tenencia de la tierra indígena y española en la cuenca del alto Atoyac, Puebla, Mexico, 1520–1650*, Wiesbaden, Franz Steiner Verlag.

Quezada Ramírez, Noemí 1972: *Los Matlatzincas. Epoca prehispánica y época colonial hasta 1650*, Mexico City, INAH.

—— 1975: *Amor y magia amorosa entre los aztecas*, Mexico City, UNAM.

Reyes Valerio, Constantino 1960: *Tepalcingo*, Mexico City, INAH.

—— 1978: *Arte Indocristiano. Escultura del siglo XVI en México*, Mexico City, INAH.

Ricard, Robert 1933: *La 'Conquête spirituelle' du Mexique. Essai sur l'apostolat et les méthodes missionnaires des ordres mendiants en Nouvelle-Espagne de 1523/24 à 1572*, Paris, Institut d'Ethnologie.

Robertson, Donald 1959: *Mexican Manuscript Paintings of the Early Colonial Period, The Metropolitan Schools*, New Haven, Yale University Press.

—— 1975: 'Techialoyan Manuscripts and Paintings with a Catalog', *Handbook of Middle American Indians*, vol. 14, Austin, University of Texas Press, pp. 253–80.

Rojas, Basilio 1964: *La rebelión de Tehuantepec*, Mexico City, Sociedad Mexicana de Geografía y Estadística.

Salvucci, Richard J. 1987: *Textiles and Capitalism in Mexico. An economic history of the obrajes, 1539–1840*, Princeton, Princeton University Press.

Signorini, Italo 1981: *Padrini e compadri, un analisi antropologica della parentela spirituale*, Turin, Loescher Editore.

Simpson, Leslie B. 1934: *Studies in the Administration of the Indians in New Spain*, Ibero-Americana No. 7, Berkeley, University of California Press.

Smith, Mary Elizabeth 1973: *Picture Writing from Ancient Southern Mexico*, Norman, University of Oklahoma Press.

Soberanes, Fernández, José Luis 1980: *Los tribunales de Nueva España. Antología*, Mexico City, UNAM.

Soustelle, Jacques 1937: *La famille otomi-pame du Mexique central*, Paris, Institut d'Ethnologie.

—— 1979: *L'Univers des Aztèques*, Paris, Herman.

Spores, Ronald 1967: *The Mixtec Kings and their People*, Norman, University of Oklahoma Press.

Steck, Francis Borgia 1944: *El primer colegio de América, Santa Cruz de Tlatelolco*, Mexico City, Centre de estudios franciscanos.

Stevenson, Robert 1976: *Music in Aztec and Inca Territory*, Berkeley, University of California Press.

Super, John C. 1983: *La vida de Querétaro durante la colonia 1531–1810*, Mexico City, FCE.

Tanck de Estrada, Dorothy 1977: *La educación ilustrada: 1786–1836. Educación primaria en la ciudad de México*, Mexico City, El Colegio de México.

Taylor, William B. 1972: *Landlord and Peasant in Colonial Oaxaca*, Stanford, Stanford University Press.

—— 1979: *Drinking, Homicide and Rebellion in Colonial Mexican Villages*, Stanford, Stanford University Press.

Toribio Medina, José 1907: *La imprenta en México, 1539–1821*, vol. I, Santiago de Chile.

Toussaint, Manuel 1965: *Pintura colonial en México*, Mexico City, UNAM.

—— 1967: *Colonial Art in Mexico*, Texas Pan American Series, Austin, University of Texas Press. (1st, Spanish, edn, Mexico City, UNAM, 1948).

Tranfo, Luigi 1974: *Vida y magia en un pueblo otomí del mezquital*, Mexico City, SEP/Instituto Nacional Indigenista.

Tutino, John M. 1976a: *Creole Mexico. Spanish Elites, Haciendas and Indian Towns 1750–1810*, University of Texas (typescript).

Ulloa, Daniel 1977: *Los predicadores dividos. Los dominicos en Nueva España, Siglo XVI*, Mexico City, El Colegio de México.

Vargas Lugo, Elisa 1969: *Las portadas religiosas de México*, Mexico City, UNAM.

Warman, Arturo 1972: *La danza de moros y cristianos*, Mexico City, SepSetentas, 46.

Warren, J. Benedict 1977a: *La conquista de Michoacán 1521–1530*, Morelia, Fimax Publicistas.

—— 1977b: *Vasco de Quiroga and his Pueblo-Hospitals of Santa Fe*, Washington D.C., Academy of American Franciscan History.

Weckmann, Luis 1984: *La herencia medieval de México*, 2 vols, Mexico City, El Colegio de México.

Whitecotton, Joseph W. 1977: *The Zapotecs: Princes, Priests and Peasants*, Norman, University of Oklahoma Press.

Yhmoff Cabrera, Jesús 1973: 'Los capitulares y los grabados en los impresos de Antonio de Espinosa', *Boletín del Instituto de Investigaciones Bibliográficas*, Mexico City, UNAM, 10, pp. 17–111.

Yoneda, Keiko 1981: *Los mapas de Cuauhtinchan y la historia cartográfica prehispánica*, Mexico City, AGN.

Zantwijk, Rudolf A. M. van 1974: *Los servidores de los santos. La identidad social y cultural de una comunidad tarasca en México*, Mexico City, SEP/ Instituto Nacional Indigenista.

Zavala, Silvio 1973: *La encomienda indiana*, Mexico City, Editorial Porrúa, S.A.

—— n.d.: *¿El castellano, lengua obligatoria?*, Mexico City, SEP.

—— and María Castelo 1980: *Fuentes para la historia del trabajo en la Nueva España*, 8 vols, Mexico City, Centro de Estudios Históricos del Movimiento Obrero Mexicano.

Index